COMMAND PERFORM

C0-EFK-073

COMMAND PERFORMANCE

LOTUS® 1-2-3®

EDDIE ADAMIS

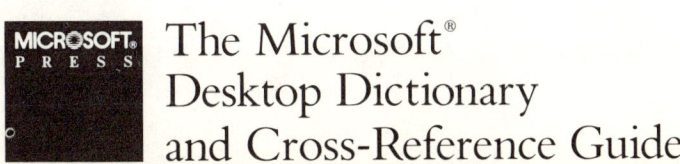

The Microsoft® Desktop Dictionary and Cross-Reference Guide

PUBLISHED BY
Microsoft Press
A Division of Microsoft Corporation
10700 Northup Way, Box 97200, Bellevue, Washington 98009

Copyright © 1986 by Eddie Adamis
All rights reserved. No part of the contents of this book may
be reproduced or transmitted in any form or by any means without
the written permission of the publisher.

Library of Congress Cataloging in Publication Data
Adamis, Eddie, 1921–
  Command performance—Lotus 1-2-3
  (Command performance)
  Includes index.
  1. Lotus 1-2-3 (Computer program)
  2. Business—Data processing
I. Title. II. Series.
HF5548.4.L67A33 1986 650'.028'5369 8529811
ISBN 0-914845-64-0

Printed and bound in the United States of America.

1 2 3 4 5 6 7 8 9 RRDRRD 8 9 0 9 8 7 6

Distributed to the book trade in the
United States by Harper and Row.

Distributed to the book trade in
Canada by General Publishing Company, Ltd.

Distributed to the book trade outside the
United States and Canada by Penguin Books Ltd.

Penguin Books Ltd., Harmondsworth, Middlesex, England
Penguin Books Australia Ltd., Ringwood, Victoria, Australia
Penguin Books N.Z. Ltd., 182-190 Wairau Road, Auckland 10, New Zealand

British Cataloging in Publication Data available

dBASE II® and dBASE III® are registered trademarks of Ashton-Tate.
Epson® is a registered trademark of Epson America, Incorporated.
HP® is a registered trademark of Hewlett-Packard.
IBM® is a registered trademark of International Business Machines Corporation.
Lotus® and 1-2-3® are registered trademarks and Jazz™ and
Symphony™ are trademarks of Lotus Development Corporation.
Microsoft® and MS-DOS® are registered trademarks of Microsoft Corporation.
VisiCalc® is a registered trademark and DIF™ is a trademark of Software Arts, Incorporated.

Acknowledgments

It has often been said that the writer's work is lonely work. But writing is only the first step in the process by which a book is created. Rounds of review and rewriting refine the original manuscript until the final product emerges. For the development and production of this book, I owe much to the outstanding professional team at Microsoft Press, most notably to JoAnne Woodcock and Jeff Hinsch, who spent long hours ensuring that this book will be as useful for users of the new version of Lotus 1-2-3 as it will be for users of the original version. Their efforts and mine also benefited greatly from the technical expertise of Jabe Blumenthal.

Introduction

This dictionary of Lotus 1-2-3 for IBM and compatible personal computers is a reference book for you to keep close at hand while using 1-2-3. The information in these pages is based on Release 2 of 1-2-3, which was issued in the fall of 1985, but the book is appropriate for earlier versions as well. Release 2 expands the capabilities of 1-2-3, but it is not a completely different product. Thus, while some commands and functions described in this book may not be available in earlier versions of 1-2-3, effort has been made to point out these differences and to distinguish features that apply only to Release 2.

Overall, this book is designed so that, whenever you have a question about a command, function, or operation, you can find the answer quickly, without wasting time searching through pages of unrelated information.

This dictionary contains entries on all of 1-2-3's commands and functions. Each command entry offers a complete explanation of a particular 1-2-3 feature. Each function entry includes examples of how you might use the function. Each entry provides a simple, clear explanation of what you really need to know to use that particular feature.

In addition, this book contains a number of extended, conceptual entries on subjects of broader scope. These entries, on such topics as cells, ranges, macros, iteration, data tables, and so on, seek to explain the concept, as well as its use in 1-2-3. It is hoped that these entries will serve you well during those times you feel like "just browsing" to discover capabilities and applications you may not yet have used.

As you refer to entries in this book, you may notice that some information is repeated in several places. This repetition is intentional. Since this is a reference book, and reference books are not meant to be read straight through, cover to cover, you are not expected to have read anything presented earlier, nor are you expected to remember everything you've previously read. Instead, each entry is, itself, as complete as possible.

If you want to learn more about a concept mentioned in the entry you're reading, you can do that by using the cross references included in the text.

Command Performance: Lotus 1-2-3

This cross-referencing (which I call a logical moving index) will lead you to the pages where you will find additional information about a particular 1-2-3 feature. Three cross-referencing marks are used.

A page number followed by a star refers you to the page where you'll find a complete dictionary entry covering the feature referenced. One of these cross-referencing marks might look like this:

   the /Data Table 1 **87**★ command

which means you can find an entry entirely devoted to the /Data Table 1 command on page 87.

A page number followed by a diamond refers you to the page where you will find a definition of the feature referenced; the definition itself will be marked simply by a diamond to help you locate it on the page. For example, the first of these two cross-referencing marks might look like this:

   specify a criterion range **47**♦ before

which means you can find a definition of a criterion range on page 47. On page 47, you will find a mark like this:

   the criterion range ♦ is

to help you zone in on the passage where a criterion range is defined.

Another way to find information is to use the index. In my view, the index is one of the most important parts of a reference book. I often base my decision on whether to buy a book on the quality of the index, and I have compiled the index for this book assuming that you are like me. You can turn to the index to locate the subject you are interested in, or to a particular entry, knowing you can use the cross-referencing marks for additional information.

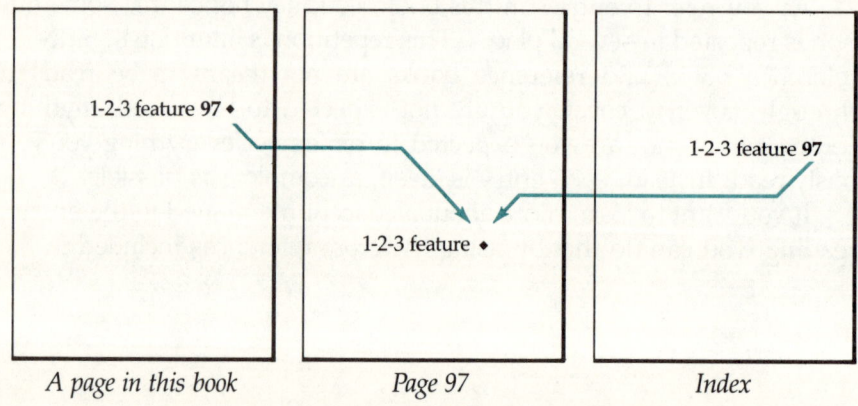

A page in this book   *Page 97*   *Index*

Finally, one word of guidance: I learn new skills by doing, because I feel it helps me learn more thoroughly. I hope you will use the examples and ideas in this book, incorporating them into your own worksheets, and that *Command Performance: Lotus 1-2-3* will help you master this powerful program.

@@()

@@() A Release 2 special function

■ **Format**

@@(cell address)

■ **Description**

@@ works as a pointer into your worksheet by returning the value of the cell referred to by the cell address. In this function, the cell address can be either the name or the address (such as A1) of a single cell. The contents of this cell, however, must be one of the following string types:

☐ A label prefix followed by a cell address, such as 'B1.

☐ A single-cell range name, such as BAL_FWD.

☐ A string formula that results in a cell address, such as +"B"&"1".

Essentially, the @@ function points to a cell that contains a label or a string that, in turn, points to *another* cell whose value is then returned by the function. The steps in this procedure are shown in the following diagram and illustration:

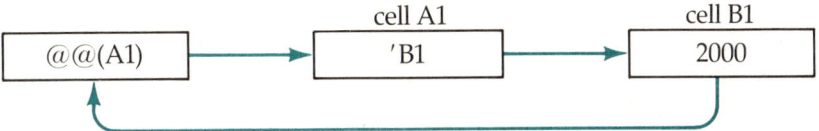

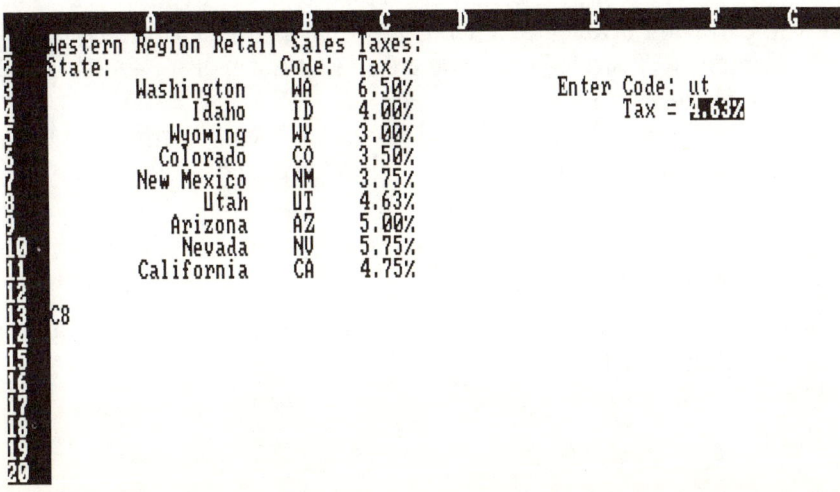

1

The formula in cell A13 uses nested @IF statements to return the cell location containing the tax percentage for the code entered in cell F3. The @@ function in cell F4 reads the string returned by the @IF function and fetches the number from the cell the string points to. The formula in A13 is:

@IF(F3="WA","C3",@IF(F3="ID","C4",@IF(F3="WY","C5",
@IF(F3="CO","C6",@IF(F3="NM","C7",@IF(F3="UT","C8",
@IF(F3="AZ","C9",@IF(F3="NV","C10",@IF(F3="CA","C11",
@IF(F3="MT",@NA,@IF("F3=OR",@NA,"Incorrect Code")))))))))))

@ABS()

- **Format**
@ABS(argument)

- **Description**
@ABS is a function 145★ that returns the absolute value of the number specified by *argument*. The absolute value of a number is its magnitude, and is always either positive or zero. Thus, @ABS converts negative values to positive values of the same magnitude—in other words, it strips away the − sign.

The argument can be a number, a cell name or address, another function, or a formula, so these are all valid forms of the @ABS function: @ABS(−12); @ABS(A1); @ABS(@AVG(VALUES)); @ABS(SALES); and @ABS(A1∗A2/A3).

Because @ABS returns the absolute value of a *single* number, multiple-cell ranges or range names are not allowed unless they are part of functions or formulas that calculate a single value. In other words, you cannot enter *@ABS(C1..C10)* because the argument refers to values in a range 291★ of cells. But you can enter *@ABS(@SUM(C1..C10))* because the @SUM 335★ function in the argument will produce a single calculated number for which @ABS can return an absolute value.

The @ABS function can be used to ensure the correct input of numbers or, perhaps, to strip away the negative sign for printing purposes. For example, the formula:

@IF(balance<0,"You are overdrawn by "&@STRING(@ABS(balance),2),"Thank you for your business")

returns the phrase *You are overdrawn by* and the negative balance, but without a minus sign in front of it.

Access System

The 1-2-3 Access System is a program that presents a menu of 1-2-3's various other programs. From this menu, you can choose and run the 1-2-3 worksheet or one of the utility programs, such as PrintGraph.

The Access menu presents you with six choices; five are programs, and the last is the *Exit* option. To make a choice, move the highlight to the menu selection you want and press Return or, alternatively, just press the key corresponding to the first letter of your choice.

```
1-2-3  PrintGraph  Translate  Install  View  Exit
Enter 1-2-3 -- Lotus Worksheet/Graphics/Database program

                    1-2-3 Access System
                 Lotus Development Corporation
                        Copyright 1985
                       All Rights Reserved
                           Release 2

The Access system lets you choose 1-2-3, PrintGraph, the Translate utility,
the Install program, and View of 1-2-3 from the menu at the top of this
screen.  If you're using a diskette system, the Access system may prompt
you to change disks.  Follow the instructions below to start a program

o  Use [RIGHT] or [LEFT] to move the menu pointer (the highlight bar at
   the top of the screen) to the program you want to use.

o  Press [RETURN] to start the program.

You can also start a program by typing the first letter of the menu
choice.  Press [HELP] for more information.
```

1-2-3's Access System is merely a convenience and is not necessary to run any of the other 1-2-3 programs. The Access System also uses a portion of your computer's memory, so you may not want to use Access, in order to conserve that memory for use by the worksheet.

Access System · @ACOS()

- **Starting from DOS**

  You can start 1-2-3 or any of its companion programs directly from the operating system simply by typing the name of the program you want to use. At the system prompt (for example, A> or C>) type one of the names in the following table to start the corresponding program. If you're using a floppy-disk system (no hard disk), you can use the table to determine which 1-2-3 program disk needs to be in the primary drive (A). If you run 1-2-3 from a hard disk, the 1-2-3 System Disk must be in drive A in order for you to start the worksheet program, unless you've used the Release 2 Install program, as described in your documentation.

Program:	Drive A:	Type:
1-2-3	1-2-3 System Disk	123
PrintGraph	PrintGraph Disk	PGRAPH
View of 1-2-3	View of 1-2-3 Disk	VIEW
Install	Utility Disk	INSTALL
Translate	Utility Disk	TRANS

@ACOS()

- **Format**

  @ACOS(x)

- **Description**

  @ACOS is a trigonometric function that returns the arccosine (the inverse cosine) of x, the angle (in radians) whose cosine is x. The range of x must be between −1 and +1; if the argument falls outside these bounds, the function returns the value ERR. For arguments within the acceptable limits, @ACOS returns values in the range 0 to PI—for example:

  @ACOS(−1)

  returns the value 3.1416 (PI).

■ **Example**

Suppose you have to cross a river and wish to land on the opposite shore without drifting downstream. You know the current is three miles per hour, and that your boat travels five miles per hour in still water. At what angle will you need to travel against the current?

The formula:

@ACOS(3/5)

returns the radian value of the angle formed by the necessary direction of travel and the opposite bank. (The angle of travel relative to the near bank is given by @ASIN(3/5).) To convert radians to degrees, you would multiply the result by 180 and divide by PI:

@ACOS(3/5)*180/@PI

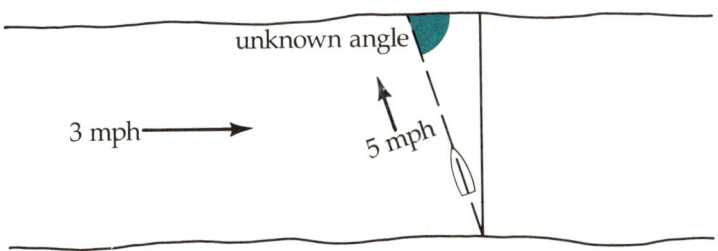

ASCII

ASCII is an acronym for American Standard Code for Information Interchange. It is a standardized code that represents letters, numbers, punctuation marks, and control functions with numbers ranging from 0 through 127.

In a standard ASCII file (often called an ASCII text file), a capital letter A always has the code number 65, a capital letter B always has the number 66, and so on. In addition, the file contains no special characters that might make perfect sense to one computer or application, but not to another. Thus, an ASCII file is readable by any machine or program designed to use this system. 1-2-3, for example, can read an ASCII file stored by any worksheet program, database, or word processor that can save a file in ASCII format.

Since the benefit of being able to move data files back and forth between different types of computers and between different application programs is so considerable, ASCII is nearly universal in the microcomputer world.

- **Extended ASCII**

In addition to the standard ASCII codes, there is an additional set of 128 possible values that can be used for various nonstandard representations. These are included in the extended ASCII set of code numbers 128 through 255.

In Release 2 of 1-2-3, the extended ASCII code numbers 128 through 255 are used to represent accented and other special characters.

Altogether, the standard and extended ASCII codes make up the Lotus International Character Set (LICS), which 1-2-3 uses whenever it transfers character data to a device (monitor, printer, or disk). A complete list of special LICS characters is included in the entry LICS 203★.

@ASIN()

- **Format**

    @ASIN(x)

- **Description**

    @ASIN is a trigonometric function that returns the arcsine (inverse sine) of x, the angle (in radians) whose sine is x. The range of x must be between −1 and +1; if the argument falls outside these bounds, the function returns the value ERR. For arguments within the acceptable limits, @ASIN returns values in the range −PI/2 to PI/2. For example:

    @ASIN(−1)

returns the value −1.5708 (−PI/2 radians)

    @ASIN(@SIN((1))

returns the value 1, as does:

    @ASIN(@SIN(1+2*@PI))

Example

Suppose you are planning to hike uphill and wish to know the angle of the slope you will be climbing. The guidebook tells you that the distance from Elkhorn Point to Sunset Ridge is one mile. You note that the difference in elevation is 400 feet. With this information, you can construct a right triangle whose height is 400 feet and whose hypotenuse is 5280 feet (one mile). If you then use the formula:

@ASIN(400/5280)

you find the angle of the slope in radians (0.075). To convert this measure to degrees, you can multiply the result by 180 and divide by PI:

@ASIN(400/5280)*180/@PI

@ATAN()

Format

@ATAN(x)

Description

@ATAN is a trigonometric function that returns the arctangent (inverse tangent) of x, the angle (in radians) whose tangent is x. The value returned by the function varies in the range −PI/2 to PI/2. For example:

@ATAN(1)

returns the value 0.785 (PI/4 radians)

@ATAN(−1E+05)

returns the value 1.571 (PI/2 radians)

@ATAN(@SQRT(3))

returns the value 1.0472 (PI/3 radians).

Example

Suppose you want to determine the pitch of a roof. To do so, you would build a right triangle. The first step would be to measure the roof's width from its edge to its center. Then, you would measure the perpendicular height of the roof. Then, you would use the formula:

@ATAN(height/width)

to return the pitch of the roof in radians. To convert radians to degrees, you would multiply by 180 and divide the result by PI:

@ATAN(height/width)*180/@PI

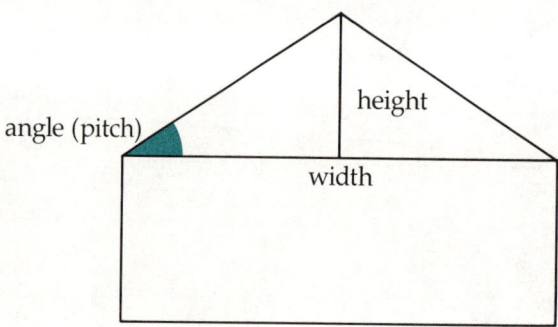

@ATAN2()

Format
@ATAN2(x,y)

Description
@ATAN2 is a trigonometric function that returns the four-quadrant tangent (inverse tangent) of y/x, the angle (in radians) whose tangent is y/x. @ATAN2 supplements @ATAN 7★ by differentiating between angles that lie in the first and third quadrants and between angles that lie in the second and fourth quadrants. Both arguments (x and y) must be numeric and not both equal to zero. If both x and y are equal to zero, the function returns the value ERR.

When both arguments are valid, @ATAN2 returns values in the range −PI/2 to PI/2, as follows:

x	y	Value returned:
+	+	0 to PI/2
−	+	PI/2 to PI
−	−	−PI to −PI/2
+	−	−PI/2 to 0

For example:

@ATAN2(1.732,1)

returns 0.5236 (PI/6 radians)

@ATAN(−1.732,−1)

returns −2.6180 (−5∗PI/6 radians)

@ATAN2(−1,0)

returns 3.1416 (PI radians).

@AVG()

■ **Format**

@AVG(list)

■ **Description**

@AVG is a statistical function 145★ that finds the average (mean) of the values contained in a list. A list is one or more arguments separated by commas. Each argument can be a numeric value, a single cell address, a range of cells, a range name, a formula, or a mixture of these. For example, all of the following lists include valid arguments: @AVG)A10,B23,C9,D14); @AVG(A15..G15); @AVG(Grades); and @AVG(A1..D1,Sales,A2,4+5).

If the list contains no numeric values, the @AVG function returns the value ERR.

@AVG()

The @AVG function ignores all blank cells within a range. It does not, however, ignore label cells; instead, it treats them as equal to 0. These points can affect your calculations in either of two ways: Blank cells (for example, cells in a range that you decide to leave empty, rather than fill with zeros) will not be included in the count of cells, even though you may have meant them to be. Conversely, label cells you inadvertently include in an argument *will* be used in calculating the average and can thus also produce inaccurate results.

For example, if you want to average all six cells in a range containing one blank and the five numbers 20, 25, 30, 50, and 55, the @AVG function will return the value 36, even though the average you want is 30. Likewise, if you specify a six-cell range, but it includes one label and the same five numbers, the @AVG function will return the value 30, instead of 36.

You must also be careful in using the @COUNT 42★ function as part of an @AVG calculation. @COUNT also ignores blank cells, and considers label cells equal to 0. It can thus produce the same types of inaccuracies.

■ **Example**

The following example shows the @AVG function used to average daily expenses for a five-day period. Column B shows the correct average. Column C shows the result of including a label cell, and column D shows the result of including a blank cell within the range.

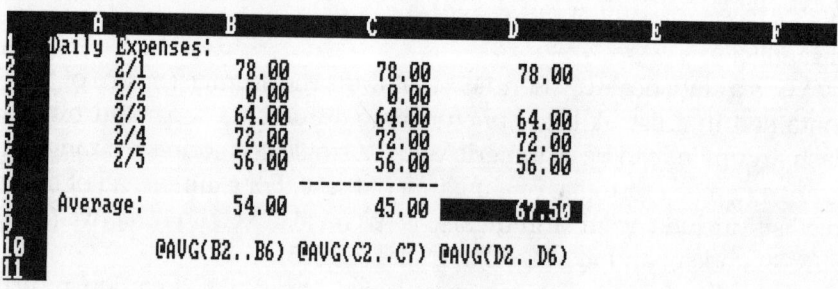

Backup

One of the first instructions new computer users hear is probably, "Make a backup copy." No matter how often it is repeated, this advice remains one of the most important elements in managing and protecting your information from possible loss.

- **The 1-2-3 System Disk**

    You received six disks in the 1-2-3 package (five, if you are using Release 1a). Among these disks is a backup copy of the 1-2-3 System Disk. The Lotus Development Corporation provides this backup disk for you because the System Disk contains information that cannot be copied by the user, but that is essential for the 1-2-3 program to run. The Backup System Disk in the package contains the same information, and thus can function in place of the System Disk if the original is damaged or becomes unusable.

- **Data disks**

    Especially with the large, complex worksheets you are able to create with 1-2-3, backup copies of your data files are well worth the few minutes it takes to create them.

    There are several different ways you can create backups, depending on your computer system, the version of DOS you use, and the version of 1-2-3 you use. The following list describes some of the options available to you:

    ☐ From DOS, use the Diskcopy command to make an exact duplicate of your data disk.

    ☐ From DOS, use the Copy command with the wildcard characters * and ? to copy selected files to another disk. (The command *copy* *.* copies all files to another disk, though not necessarily to the same locations they occupy on the original. For the most part, the difference between this command and Diskcopy is minor and will not affect your everyday use of 1-2-3 files.)

    ☐ From DOS (version 2.0 and above on IBM personal computers), you may use the Backup and Restore commands. These are especially useful with hard disk drives.

    ☐ With Release 2 of 1-2-3, you can use the /System 337★ command to suspend 1-2-3 temporarily and use DOS commands.

    ☐ With Release 1a of 1-2-3, you can use the File Manager, available from the Access System, to manage your disks and files.

Bin

The word *bin* is a term used with the /Data Distribution 52★ command to describe a series of intervals to which you assign different values for use in generating a frequency distribution table. Each bin is part of a bin range which is, in turn, a column of cells on your worksheet. The column to the right of the bin range is used by 1-2-3 for the results of the frequency distribution. The following illustrations show a simple bin range, and the results of performing a frequency distribution on the daily temperatures in cells B3 through E17.

Note that the values in the bin range are in ascending order (as they must always be) and that the results column, which 1-2-3 always places immediately to the right of the bin range, extends one cell below the bin range to hold the count of values greater than the highest specified bin interval.

```
G17: [W4] 78                                                          POINT
Enter Values range: B3..E17        Enter Bin range: G3..G17
         A        B        C        D         E     F    G      H
   1  Temp.    Albany  Buffalo  New York  Syracuse  ||  Bin  Frequency Dist.
   2  ================================================================
   3  01-Oct      51      54       59        53     ||   36
   4  02-Oct      52      52       57        53     ||   39
   5  03-Oct      68      69       72        73     ||   42
   6  04-Oct      49      52       55        50     ||   45
   7  05-Oct      54      54       58        54     ||   48
   8  06-Oct      62      62       66        65     ||   51
   9  07-Oct      58      62       68        62     ||   54
  10  08-Oct      54      56       59        55     ||   57
  11  09-Oct      39      43       46        45     ||   60
  12  10-Oct      48      52       53        51     ||   63
  13  11-Oct      46      49       52        48     ||   66
  14  12-Oct      50      53       54        54     ||   69
  15  13-Oct      51      52       55        55     ||   72
  16  14-Oct      48      49       53        50     ||   75
  17  15-Oct      47      50       52        47     ||   78
  18
  19
  20
```

```
H3: [W12] 0                                                              READY

       A        B       C        D         E      F    G        H
    ┌──────────────────────────────────────────────────────────────────────
  1 │ Temp.   Albany  Buffalo  New York  Syracuse  ││  Bin   Frequency Dist.
  2 │ ═══════════════════════════════════════════════════════════════════
  3 │ 01-Oct   51      54       59        53       ││  36       0
  4 │ 02-Oct   52      52       57        53       ││  39       1
  5 │ 03-Oct   68      69       72        73       ││  42       0
  6 │ 04-Oct   49      52       55        50       ││  45       2
  7 │ 05-Oct   54      54       58        54       ││  48       6
  8 │ 06-Oct   62      62       66        65       ││  51      11
  9 │ 07-Oct   58      62       68        62       ││  54      16
 10 │ 08-Oct   54      56       59        55       ││  57       9
 11 │ 09-Oct   39      43       46        45       ││  60       4
 12 │ 10-Oct   48      52       53        51       ││  63       4
 13 │ 11-Oct   46      49       52        48       ││  66       2
 14 │ 12-Oct   50      53       54        54       ││  69       3
 15 │ 13-Oct   51      52       55        55       ││  72       1
 16 │ 14-Oct   48      49       53        50       ││  75       1
 17 │ 15-Oct   47      50       52        47       ││  78       0
 18 │                                                            0
 19 │
 20 │
```

Cell

A cell is the location on a worksheet at which a column and a row intersect. Each cell is associated with a unique address that gives the coordinates of its location. In the address, the letter of the column (A through IV) precedes the number of the row (1 through 8192 in Release 2, 1 through 2048 in Release 1a). The cell in column D, row 24, thus has the address D24; the "highest" address on a 1-2-3 worksheet is IV8192 (the 2,097,152nd cell in Release 2), or IV2048 (the 524,288th cell in Release 1a).

The default, or beginning width, of a cell is 9 characters. The maximum width you can assign a cell is 240 characters (72 characters in Release 1a).

Cell

1-2-3 offers you enormous flexibility in referring to cells and their contents. You can refer to one cell or to many; you can refer to them by address, or you can give them descriptive names. You can point to them with the cell pointer, or you can type their addresses. And you can combine these techniques as you create worksheet formats, formulas, databases, and graphs. (Since the ways and means of using these references can vary, details are included in such entries as Formulas and Formula Calculation **136★**, Range **291★**, /Copy **31★**, and /Move **250★**.)

- **Cell entries**

Within a cell, you can store any of three kinds of information: numbers, labels (text), or formulas (including functions). The cell you are working with, called the *current cell*, is highlighted by the rectangular *cell pointer*, which you move with the *pointer-movement* keys (see Keyboard **194★**). The content of the current cell—number, text, or formula—is displayed at the top of the screen, at the top of the three-line Control Panel **29★**.

Typically, the value contained in each cell is also displayed in the worksheet, whether or not the cell itself is highlighted. The displayed value in the worksheet may be text, a number you typed in, or the calculated result of a formula in the cell.

- **Entering cell contents**

The basic procedure for entering cell contents is simple: Move the cell pointer to the desired cell, type the entry (which appears, character for character, in the second line of the Control Panel), and either press Return or one of the pointer-movement keys.

If you press Return, 1-2-3 displays the entry both in the cell and in the top line of the Control Panel, leaves the cell pointer where it is, and waits for either a command or another entry.

If you press one of the pointer-movement keys, 1-2-3 displays the entry in the cell, moves the cell pointer in the direction indicated, and waits for you to type another entry or command.

With either the Return or the pointer-movement keys, 1-2-3 will generate a beep if the entry contains any unintelligible or unacceptable keystrokes. It also recalculates the entire worksheet after each entry, unless you have turned on manual recalculation with the /Worksheet Global Recalculation **371★** command.

■ Editing cell contents

If you are typing a new entry and discover an error before you press Return or a pointer-movement key, backspace to erase the old characters and retype the entry, or press either Esc or the Ctrl-Break key combination to cancel the entry and return to READY mode 249♦.

If you discover a mistake *after* you have pressed Return or a pointer-movement key, you can replace the old contents of a cell by highlighting it with the cell pointer and typing the new entry. Alternatively, after pressing Return, you can erase one or more cells completely with the /Range Erase 299★ command.

The EDIT mode: 1-2-3 automatically beeps, puts you into EDIT mode 249♦, and waits for a correction if you make a mistake in entering a formula. You can also request the EDIT mode and change all or part of a highlighted cell's contents by pressing the F2 [Edit] 144♦ key.

Once in EDIT mode, you can edit the entry with the following keys:

Key:	Action:
Right arrow	Move one character right.
Left arrow	Move one character left.
Tab or Ctrl-right arrow	Move five characters right.
Backtab (Shift-Tab) or Ctrl-left arrow	Move five characters left.
Home	Move to beginning of line.
End	Move to end of line.
Del	Delete one character to the right.
Backspace	Delete one character to the left.

You can also insert characters by moving the cursor to the appropriate place and typing the additional characters.

Commands and cell attributes

Cells and their contents have many attributes, such as text and numeric format or cell protection, which are manipulated with 1-2-3's extensive set of commands. Each command is covered elsewhere in this book. However, by way of example, you can:

- Display formulas, rather than their calculated values with the *Text* option of either the /Worksheet Global Format 366★ or the /Range Format 300★ command.
- Format displayed numbers with the *Format* option of the /Worksheet Global Format command or the /Range Format command.
- Align labels 199★ left, right, or center, with either the /Worksheet Global Label-Prefix 368★ command or with the /Range Label 308★ command.
- Assign names to single cells or cell ranges 291★, delete those names, or reset them with the /Range Name 310★ command.
- Copy or move cells with the /Copy and /Move commands.
- Protect and unprotect cells from change with the /Range Protect 314★ and /Range Unprotect 317★ commands.
- Hide certain cells from view with the *Hide* option of the /Worksheet Column 355★ command, or the *Hidden* option of the /Range Format command.

Cell ranges

Often, several or many cells in a worksheet have some feature in common, such as similar data, the same formatting, or formulas that are identical except for their cell references. Then, too, you may want to affect many cells at once with a single command. In the instances in which these cells occupy adjacent locations in a rectangular section of the worksheet, you can refer to cell ranges, rather than individual cells. Ranges are discussed in detail in the entry Range, but briefly:

- A range is a square or rectangular block of contiguous cells.

cell ranges

- Each range is defined by a beginning corner and a diagonally opposite ending corner; which corners you refer to are immaterial. For example, the beginning and ending corners of a range can be: top left-bottom right, bottom left-top right, top right-bottom left, or bottom right-top left. To refer to these cells, you can:

1. Type the addresses of the cells in two diagonally opposite corners, separating them with one or more periods; for example, A1..B20 (1-2-3 adds the second period, but you can type it if you wish).
2. Name the range with the /Range Name command.
3. Expand the cell pointer to cover all the cells in the range. If the command you are using "expects" to affect a range of cells, 1-2-3 automatically *anchors* the currently highlighted cell (anchor cell♦) so you can use the arrow keys to expand the pointer vertically or horizontally. If, as when entering a formula, you must tell 1-2-3 that you wish to refer to a range of cells, you anchor the current cell by typing a period (.) before expanding the cell pointer. The cell diagonally opposite the anchor cell is the free cell♦—the one you "drag" to a new location.

■ **Cell References**

1-2-3 allows you to refer to cell addresses as relative, absolute, or mixed. Once you have defined a cell in one of these ways, 1-2-3 takes care of most of your housekeeping automatically. You do, however, need to understand how these types of references differ before you can use the /Copy or /Move command with assurance (see those entries for more details). Briefly:

- A relative♦ cell reference, shown as simply the column letter and row number (A1, C135, AB3, and so on), is equivalent to telling 1-2-3, "Use the value in the cell so many columns and rows away from this cell." If you use a relative cell reference in a formula, you can move or copy the formula anywhere on the worksheet, and 1-2-3 will still refer to "the cell x rows and y columns away." Relative cell references are useful when you wish to make use of the *relationships* between or among cells.
- In contrast, an absolute♦ cell reference, in which the column letter and the row number are each preceded by a dollar sign ($A$1, $C$135, $AB$3 and so on), tells 1-2-3, "No matter where I copy this formula on my worksheet, *always* fetch information from this particular cell."

☐ A mixed♦ address is one in which relative and absolute references are combined, so that the column is relative and the row is absolute, or vice versa. Examples of mixed addresses include $A1, A$1, $C135, C$135, $AB3, AB$3, and so on. Like absolute cell references, mixed addresses can refer to cell ranges, as well as single cells.

@CELL()   A Release 2 special function

- **Format**

@CELL(attribute,range)

- **Description**

The @CELL function is used to return information on any cell in the worksheet. The attribute is a preset, one-word argument that represents any of nine different types of information that this function can return. The range specifies the cell whose attribute you want returned. 1-2-3 does not automatically update an @CELL function. If you change the attribute of the cell referenced by @CELL, recalculate by pressing the F9 [Calc] 144♦ function key.

- **Attribute**

When entering the @CELL function, you must enclose the attribute keyword in quotation marks. The nine possible keywords are: *address, row, col, contents, type, prefix, protect, width,* and *format*.

You can enter one of the keywords directly, as in @CELL("type",A1..A1), or you can use a cell reference, as long as the cell you refer to contains a label that matches the keyword you wish to specify. Thus, if cell B1 contains the label *type*, then @CELL(B1,A1..A1) is exactly equivalent to the preceding example. (In this and all uses of attribute keywords in the @CELL function, upper- and lowercase do not matter—1-2-3 accepts either, or a combination of capital and lowercase letters.)

- **Range**

  The range portion of the argument points to an *individual* cell, even though it must be specified as a range. You can enter the range as: A1..A1, !A1, or as a single-cell range name. You can also specify a multiple-cell range, either with addresses or a range name, but 1-2-3 will return information only on the upper-left cell of the range.

  Note: Using a single cell address, such as A1, in the range argument will result in the ERR message being displayed in the formula cell.

- **Examples**

  The following examples show the results of using each attribute keyword; for simplicity, the range is specified as A1..A1 in all examples:

  @CELL("address",A1..A1) returns the value $A$1.

  @CELL("col",A1..A1) returns the value 1, because column A is the first column of the worksheet. Since the worksheet has 256 columns, the value returned by *col* can be any number from 1 to 256.

  @CELL("contents",A1..A1) returns the label, number, or formula that is contained in cell A1. Thus, the value returned by this function would be FORECAST if cell A1 contained the label FORECAST.

  @CELL("format",A1..A1) returns the current format of the referenced cell. The values returned by this keyword are one-, two-, or three-character labels that describe the type of format found. For numeric formats, 1-2-3 returns:

  - F and a number between 0 and 15, representing Fixed format and the number of decimal places.
  - S and a number between 0 and 15, representing Scientific format and the number of decimal places.
  - C and a number between 0 and 15, representing Currency format and the number of decimal places.
  - G, representing General format.
  - P and a number between 0 and 15, representing Percent format and the number of decimal places.

@CELL()

- D and a number between 1 and 5, representing date formats♦, or D and a number between 6 and 9, representing time formats♦. The formats are as shown in the following table:

Function value:	Date or time format:	Example:
D1	DD-MMM-YY	14-Aug-86
D2	DD-MMM	14-Aug
D3	MMM-YY	Aug-86
D4	MM/DD/YY	08/14/86
	DD/MM/YY	14/08/86
	DD.MM.YY	14.08.86
	YY-MM-DD	86-08-14
D5	MM/DD	08/14
	DD/MM	14/08
	DD.MM	14.08
	MM-DD	08-14
D6	HH:MM:SS (a.m. or p.m.)	12:11:20 AM
D7	HH:MM (a.m. or p.m.)	12:11 AM
D8	HH:MM:SS (24-hour clock)	00:11:20
	HH.MM.SS (24-hour clock)	00.11.20
	HH,MM,SS (24-hour clock)	00,11,20
	HHhMMmSSs	00h11m20s
D9	HH:MM (24-hour clock)	00:11
	HH.MM (24-hour clock)	00.11
	HH,MM	00,11
	HHhMMm	00h11m

- T, representing Text format—the cell is formatted to display a formula, rather than its calculated value.
- H, representing Hidden format.
- , (a comma), representing the comma separator in numbers of 1,000 and above, plus the number of decimals (for example ,2 indicates the comma separator and two decimals).
- + or –, representing the bar-graph format.

@CELL("prefix",A1..A1) returns the label prefix (', ", or ^) of the referenced cell. If the cell is empty or it contains a number or formula, a blank is returned. The function would return ^ if cell A1 contained the label prefix ^.

@CELL("row",A1..A1) returns the value 1, because row 1 is the first row of the worksheet. Since the worksheet has 8192 rows, the value returned by *row* can be any number from 1 to 8192.

@CELL("type",A1..A1) returns b, v, or l. If the referenced cell is blank, the function returns b. If the cell contains a number or formula, the function returns v. If the referenced cell contains either a label or a string-valued formula, the function returns l.

@CELL("width",A1..A1) returns the width of the referenced cell. Since the width of a cell can be any number from 1 to 240 characters, this value will vary in the same range.

@CELLPOINTER() A Release 2 special function

■ **Format**
@CELLPOINTER(attribute)

■ **Description**
@CELLPOINTER is nearly identical to the @CELL **18★** function but does not require a range argument, because @CELLPOINTER tests whichever cell is currently highlighted by the cell pointer. Attribute is the same argument as specified for @CELL, and the results are the same as well. For a list of attributes and their meanings, refer to the @CELL entry.

Warning: When @CELLPOINTER is used in a macro, it may return information that is not current, because the worksheet is not necessarily updated during macro execution. To guard against this possibility, use the {Calc} or {RECALC} options described in the entries Macro **211★** and Macro Commands **238◆** to ensure that the cell's attribute and value are up-to-date when requested.

@CHAR()   A Release 2 string function

■ **Format**
@CHAR(number)

■ **Description**
The @CHAR function returns the character corresponding to the ASCII/LICS (see ASCII 5★, LICS 203★) number specified in the argument of the function. @CHAR is useful for converting an ASCII/LICS code number to a displayed character; the related function @CODE performs the reverse operation, converting a character to its corresponding ASCII/LICS code number.

The number specified in the argument can only be between 1 and 255, because those are the beginning and ending numbers of the ASCII/LICS character set. If you specify a negative number or a value greater than 255, 1-2-3 returns ERR. If you specify a fraction, 1-2-3 uses the integer portion of the number and returns the corresponding character.

Since numbers greater than 127 represent accent marks, foreign-language characters and currency symbols, and other special graphic elements, some computer monitors cannot display certain characters accurately or at all. In these cases, 1-2-3 uses either a substitute character or a blank.

The code numbers from 1 to 31, all of which are the nonprinting characters, such as Esc and the Ctrl-letter key combinations are returned as blanks.

In this function, as in any dealing with the ASCII/LICS character set, remember that there is a difference in the values for uppercase and lowercase characters. For example, an uppercase L has the code number 76. A lowercase l, however, has the code number 108.

This function and the related function, @CODE, are the means by which macros can create and interpret Compose characters. Both have their greatest application within macros.

@CHOOSE()

■ **Format**

@CHOOSE(x,v0,v1,v2,v3,...vn)

■ **Description**

@CHOOSE is a special function that returns a single alternative from a list (v0...vn). The alternative returned by the function is the value whose position in the list corresponds to the value of x. Note that the first alternative in the list is 0, not 1; thus, you would specify x as 0 to retrieve the first alternative, 1 to retrieve the second, 2 to retrieve the third, and so on, to n, the last item in the list.

When you use this function, x must be a numeric value or a blank cell. Thus, x can be:

- A number.
- The name or address of a cell containing a number.
- A blank cell—in which case, 1-2-3 returns the value of v0.

x must also be less than or equal to the number of items in the list; if x is greater than the number of items, 1-2-3 returns the value ERR. If you specify a cell containing a decimal fraction, 1-2-3 uses the integer portion of the value and returns the corresponding alternative. It does not round the number up beforehand.

The function can be up to 240 characters long. The list itself can contain numeric values, character strings, cell names or addresses, formulas, or a combination of all these.

Any of the following would be a legitimate form of @CHOOSE:

- @CHOOSE(0,0,1,2,3,4,5,6). This would return 0.
- @CHOOSE(1,A1,A2,A3,A4,A5). This would return the value in cell A2.
- @CHOOSE(2,A1/2,A2∗2,A3+A1,A4−A1,A5^2,−A6). This would return the value of A3+A1.
- @CHOOSE(3,0,A1,A1/2,"String",NAME). This would return the value in fourth position: String.

@CHOOSE()

■ **Example**

The following example shows the @CHOOSE function used to calculate markup amounts on a group of items, using the codes and percentages displayed at the top of the screen. The calculated amounts in column D are then added to the initial cost of each item to produce the selling price in column E. The worksheet is shown in the first illustration, the @CHOOSE functions themselves in the second.

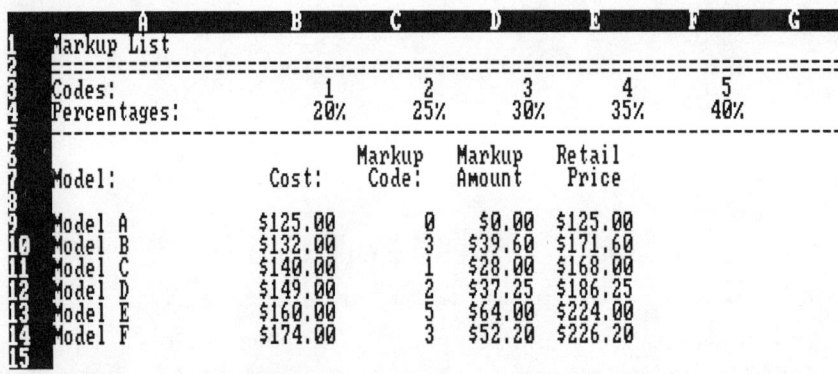

@CODE() A Release 2 string function

■ **Format**

@CODE(string)

■ **Description**

The @CODE function returns the ASCII/LICS (see ASCII **5★**, LICS **203★**) number of the first character in the string specified in the function argument. The value returned by @CODE can only be a number between 1 and 255, because those are the beginning and ending numbers of the ASCII/LICS character set. @CODE is useful for converting a displayed character to its ASCII/LICS code; the related function @CHAR performs the reverse, converting an ASCII/LICS code to the corresponding character.

The argument in the @CODE function can either be entered directly, as a string **332★** enclosed in quotation marks, or it can be entered as an indirect reference (as a cell address or cell name) to a string contained in a cell. In either case, *string* simply means one or more characters entered as *text*. Thus, 123 can as easily be a string as ABC.

For example, if you enter the function @CODE("LOTUS"), 1-2-3 will return the value 76, because the ASCII/LICS number for L, the first character in the string LOTUS, is 76. If the argument is a reference to a string *contained* within a cell—for example, @CODE(A1)—and cell A1 contains the label LOTUS, 1-2-3 will again return the value 76, but this time because L is the first character in the string contained in cell A1. And, similarly, if you enter the function as @CODE(NAME), where the cell named NAME contains the label LOTUS, the result will be the same as in the preceding two examples: 76, for the first character in the string you refer to.

In this function, as in any dealing with the ASCII/LICS character set, remember that there is a difference in the values returned for uppercase and lowercase characters. For example, an uppercase L, as shown in the preceding examples, has the code number 76. A lowercase l, however, has the code number 108.

This function and the related function, @CHAR, are the only way for macros to interpret or create Compose characters (ASCII numbers greater than 127). Both have their greatest application within macros.

@COLS() A Release 2 special function

- **Format**

  @COLS(range)

- **Description**

  The @COLS function returns the number of columns included in a range. Range 291★ can be specified either with cell references or by name, so both @COLS(A1..M17) and @COLS(SALES_FIGS) are valid arguments. You cannot specify a single cell as a range; if you do, the function returns the value ERR.

  @COLS and the related function, @ROWS 324★, are particularly useful in determining the sizes of named ranges. They are valuable when used within macros 211★ and enhance 1-2-3's ability to automate tasks. For example, a fully automatic print macro would take a list of range names and print them with correct margins and page breaks by first determining the size of each range with @ROW and @COL, then determining cell widths with @CELL or @CELLPOINTER.

Column

1-2-3's worksheet is a grid of cells 13★, each of which is located at the intersection of a row 323★ and a column. All rows are horizontal, all columns are vertical. The worksheet contains 256 columns, labeled A through IV. The way in which they are labeled is: A, B...Z, AA, AB...AZ, BA, BB...IV.

- **Changing column width**

  When you first start 1-2-3, each column on the worksheet is nine characters wide. You can change the width of any or all columns, however, narrowing them to as little as 1 character or widening them to as many as 240 characters.

  The entire worksheet: To change column widths on the entire worksheet, you use the /Worksheet Global Column-Width 359★ command, and specify a new width, in characters or with the left/right pointer-movement keys. The new setting affects all columns except those whose widths have been set individually, as described in the following section.

  To check the global column width, you use the /Worksheet Status 374★ command.

Individual columns: You can change the width of an individual column with the *Set-Width* option of the /Worksheet Column 355★ command. (This is equivalent to the *Set* option of the /Worksheet Column-Width command in Release 1a.)

As already described, you specify the new column width in number of characters or by pointing when 1-2-3 prompts for the information. You can change the width of only one column at a time, and must highlight any cell in the column *before* choosing the /Worksheet Column command. The new width is displayed in the Control Panel 29★ whenever a cell in that column is selected.

To return the width of a column to the current global setting, highlight the column and choose the *Reset-Width* option of the /Worksheet Column command. (This is equivalent to the *Reset* option of the /Worksheet Column-Width command in Release 1a.)

Split screens: If you have two windows on-screen, you can specify different column widths in each. The procedure is the same as already described; the column-width command that you choose affects only the window in which the pointer is currently located.

- **Inserting columns**

You can insert one or more blank columns in a worksheet with the /Worksheet Insert 373★ command. Whether you insert one column or several, they appear to the left of the column where the pointer is currently located, and all columns to the right are moved farther in that direction.

You specify the number of columns you wish to insert by either typing a range 291★ or by highlighting the desired number of columns with the right arrow key.

Any inserted columns are automatically given the current global formatting and column width.

Adjustments to cell references: When you insert columns, 1-2-3 automatically adjusts existing references in formulas and defined ranges, increasing the size of any ranges in which the new column or columns appear.

■ Deleting columns

You can remove unwanted columns from the worksheet with the /Worksheet Delete 357★ command. To do this, move the pointer to the column you want to delete, then select and execute the command. To eliminate more than the current column, either specify a range or highlight the appropriate columns.

■ Changes in cell references

Whenever you insert or delete columns, 1-2-3 automatically adjusts cell references in formulas to reflect the change. However:

- ☐ If the deleted column takes with it the endpoint of a range, the range becomes invalid, and any formulas that refer to the range will contain the value ERR.
- ☐ If the deleted column contains a cell referred to in a formula, the formula will contain the value ERR.

■ Comments

In addition to the basic commands discussed here (and in their own entries), 1-2-3 also allows you to manipulate columns with the following commands and command options:

To:	Use:
Hide columns or make them nonprinting	/Worksheet Column Hide (see /Worksheet Column) (Release 2 only)
Display or print hidden columns	/Worksheet Column Display (see /Worksheet Column) (Release 2 only)
Transpose rows and columns in a range	/Range Transpose 316★ (Release 2 only)
Make long labels (to 240 characters) look like text paragraphs	/Range Justify 306★

Configuration file

1-2-3 uses a special file, named 123.CNF, to store information about your computer system, your printer, and the global default settings currently in effect. The configuration file resides on the 1-2-3 program disk. If you change printers or want to make a permanent change to the global default settings on the worksheet, you can update 123.CNF with the various options of the /Worksheet Global Default 360★ command. You should not tamper with this file otherwise.

The types of information stored in 123.CNF include:

- Printer type, connection used (serial or parallel), and default page formatting.
- Default file directory.
- Default date and time formats (Release 2 only).
- Display or non-display of time and date on-screen (Release 2 only).
- Default international formats—punctuation, currency symbols, date, and time (Release 2 only).
- Default (yes or no) for display of zeros (Release 2 only).

Details on each of these defaults and the commands used to check or change them are in the entries on the /Worksheet Global Default command sequences.

Control Panel

The Control Panel is the three-line area at the top of the screen, where 1-2-3 displays a continually updated status report telling you about itself and your work. Each of the three lines contains different and specific information that varies as you interact with 1-2-3.

```
A1: (F2) [W9] 45.67                                                    MENU
Worksheet Range Copy Move File Print Graph Data System Quit
Global, Insert, Delete, Column, Erase, Titles, Window, Status, Page
      A        B        C        D        E        F        G        H
1   45.67    93.20   140.73   188.26   235.79   283.32   330.85   378.38
2   69.44   116.97   164.50   212.03   259.56   307.09   354.62   402.15
3
```

Control Panel

- **First line**

The left side of the first line of the Control Panel tells you about the current cell: location, formatting, width, and contents. The Control Panel displays numbers with up to 9 decimal places; although this is less than the 15 places 1-2-3 is capable of storing, the full value is always used in calculations.

The right side of the first line contains a highlighted rectangle in which 1-2-3 displays the mode currently in effect. For example, if you are indicating a range, it displays POINT, because 1-2-3 is in POINT mode. A list of modes and what they mean is included in the entry Mode Indicators 248★.

- **Second line**

The second line of the Control Panel displays one of three things, depending on what is happening:

□ The current entry, if you are entering or editing cell contents.

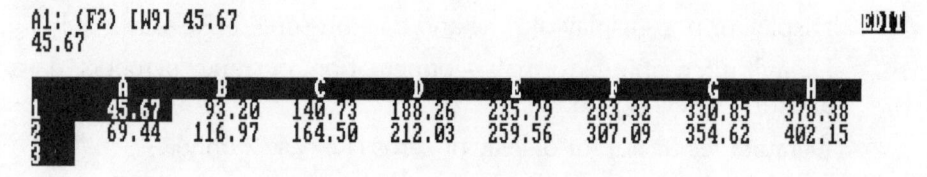

```
A1: (F2) [W9] 45.67                                            EDIT
45.67
```

	A	B	C	D	E	F	G	H
1	45.67	93.20	140.73	188.26	235.79	283.32	330.85	378.38
2	69.44	116.97	164.50	212.03	259.56	307.09	354.62	402.15
3								

□ The Main Menu, as shown earlier, if you indicate that you wish access to a command by pressing / in READY mode.

□ A command prompt, if you are using a command and 1-2-3 needs information from you.

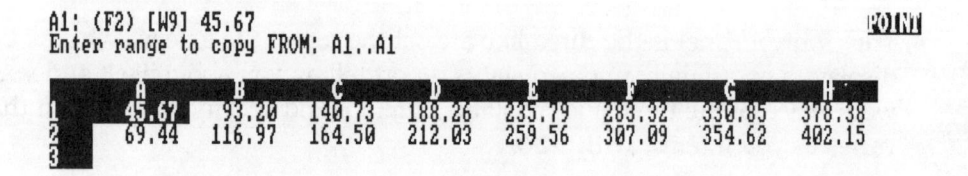

```
A1: (F2) [W9] 45.67                                           POINT
Enter range to copy FROM: A1..A1
```

	A	B	C	D	E	F	G	H
1	45.67	93.20	140.73	188.26	235.79	283.32	330.85	378.38
2	69.44	116.97	164.50	212.03	259.56	307.09	354.62	402.15
3								

Control Panel · /Copy

- **Third line**

  The third line of the Control Panel shows:

  □ A menu of choices, if you are using a command with a group of subcommands from which you must choose.

  ```
  A1: (F2) [W9] 45.67                                               MENU
  Worksheet Range Copy Move File Print Graph Data System Quit
  Format, Label, Erase, Name, Justify, Protect, Unprotect, Input, Value, Transpose
        A        B        C        D        E        F        G        H
   1  45.67    93.20   140.73   188.26   235.79   283.32   330.85   378.38
   2  69.44   116.97   164.50   212.03   259.56   307.09   354.62   402.15
   3
  ```

  □ A brief command description, if you have highlighted a choice in a command menu.

- **Comment**

  If you use Release 2 of 1-2-3 and you are creating macros that include menu commands and options, you may want to turn off continual updating of the Control Panel during macro execution by including the {PANELOFF} macro command 237★ in your routine. You can use {PANELON} to resume normal display of the Control Panel.

/Copy

Worksheet Range **Copy** Move File Print Graph Data System Quit

- **Description**

  The /Copy command enables you to copy one cell 13★ or a range 291★ of cells from one part of the current worksheet to another. Copying is one of the most useful operations available to you when entering information or editing a worksheet, because it enables you to replicate cell contents—values, labels, formats, and formulas—wherever you wish, without retyping. Whenever you perform a copy operation, any cells you copy from are called the *source* cells; any cells you copy to are called the *destination* cells.

/Copy

- **Procedure**

Depending on whether you are copying one cell or many, and whether they are named or have relative, absolute, or mixed addresses, you have several methods of specifying the cells to copy from. The following sections discuss various options. However, the basic procedure for copying cells is as follows:

1. Place the cell pointer on the first cell you wish to copy from.
2. Type a slash (/) to display the Slash commands main menu.
3. Highlight the word *Copy* and press Return, or type the letter C. 1-2-3 displays the *Enter range to copy FROM:* prompt, including the address of the current cell.
4. Leave the pointer where it is to accept the current cell, or expand the highlight to specify a range of cells. Alternatively, you can type a cell address or the name or addresses of a range. Press Return.

    1-2-3 then displays the *Enter range to copy TO:* prompt, including the address(es) of the current cell or cell range.
5. Move the cell pointer or type the address(es) of the cell or cells you are copying to and press Return.
6. The contents of the source cells are copied to the new location and the cell pointer returns to its original position.

Warning: Be very cautious in specifying the cell or cells you are copying *to*. 1-2-3 overwrites any existing contents of destination cells. Formulas or data can thus be irretrievably lost.

Overwritten cells on which other formulas depend will be adjusted to the new values, and as long as those values are acceptable formula entries, they will be used in all subsequent calculations—in other words, 1-2-3 does not know whether you meant cell X100 to contain the value 1 or 100; either will be used with equanimity in a formula such as +X100+X110. Also, be careful about overlapping FROM and TO ranges; the /Copy command copies one cell at a time and could end up copying a cell more than once.

Copying one cell: If you want to copy one cell to another single-cell location, all you need to do is follow the basic procedure. When 1-2-3 prompts for the range to copy to, simply move the pointer to the destination (or, if it is named, type the single-cell range name), and press Return.

Suppose, however, you want to copy a single cell to a range of cells. When 1-2-3 prompts for the range to copy to, move the cell pointer to the beginning cell of the destination range, anchor the pointer by typing a period, and use the arrow keys to highlight the appropriate destination cells. The contents of the source cell, including formatting, will be duplicated in the entire range of destination cells:

```
         A              B           C            D
1  Job #726352   Billing Worksheet
2  ==========================================================
3               Date          Fee    Cumulative
4            01-Jun-86      102.25      102.25
5                                       102.25
6                                       102.25
7                                       102.25
8                                       102.25
9                                       102.25
10
```

- **Copying many cells**

When you copy a range of cells to a new location, your source cells may be:

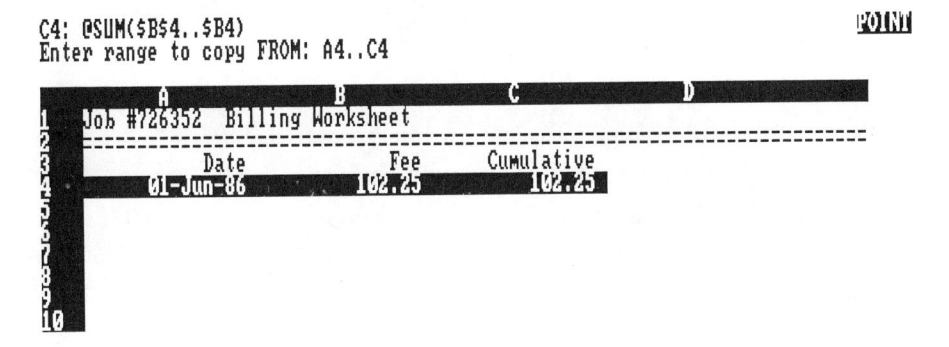

□   A section of a row (for example, A4..C4 in the following illustration).

```
C4: @SUM($B$4..$B4)                                    POINT
Enter range to copy FROM: A4..C4
         A              B           C            D
1  Job #726352   Billing Worksheet
2  ==========================================================
3               Date          Fee    Cumulative
4            01-Jun-86      102.25      102.25
5
6
7
8
9
10
```

/Copy

- A column segment (for example, A4..A6 in the following illustration).

```
A6: (D1) @DATE(86,@MOD((@MONTH(A5)+1),12),1)
Enter range to copy FROM: A4..A6
```
POINT

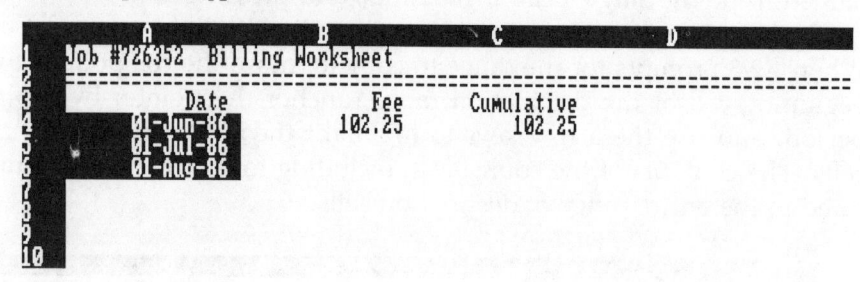

```
     A              B            C            D
1  Job #726352   Billing Worksheet
2  ================================================
3         Date         Fee      Cumulative
4     01-Jun-86      102.25      102.25
5     01-Jul-86
6     01-Aug-86
7
8
9
10
```

- A rectangular portion of the worksheet containing segments of both rows and columns (for example, A5..C7 in the following illustration).

```
C7: (F2) @SUM($B$4..$B7)
Enter range to copy FROM: A5..C7
```
POINT

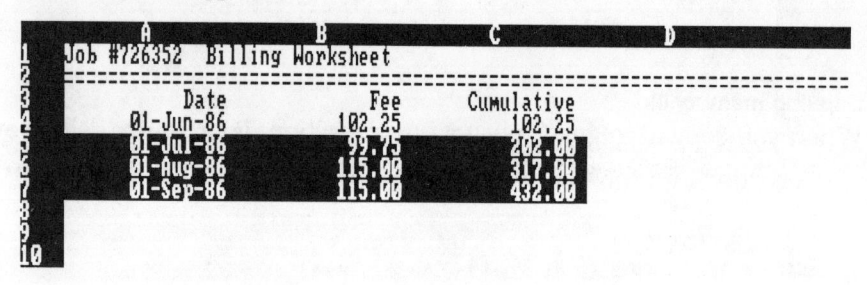

```
     A              B            C            D
1  Job #726352   Billing Worksheet
2  ================================================
3         Date         Fee      Cumulative
4     01-Jun-86      102.25      102.25
5     01-Jul-86       99.75      202.00
6     01-Aug-86      115.00      317.00
7     01-Sep-86      115.00      432.00
8
9
10
```

In all of these instances, when 1-2-3 prompts for the range to copy from, do one of the following:

- Highlight the source cell range with the arrow keys.
- If the range has a name, type the range name or use the F3 function key to bring up a menu of existing range names you can select from. (Ranges and range names are covered in the entry Range 291★; the F3 key is discussed in the entry Keyboard 194★.)

Your destination cells, in turn, may:

☐ Match the size and layout of the source range exactly.

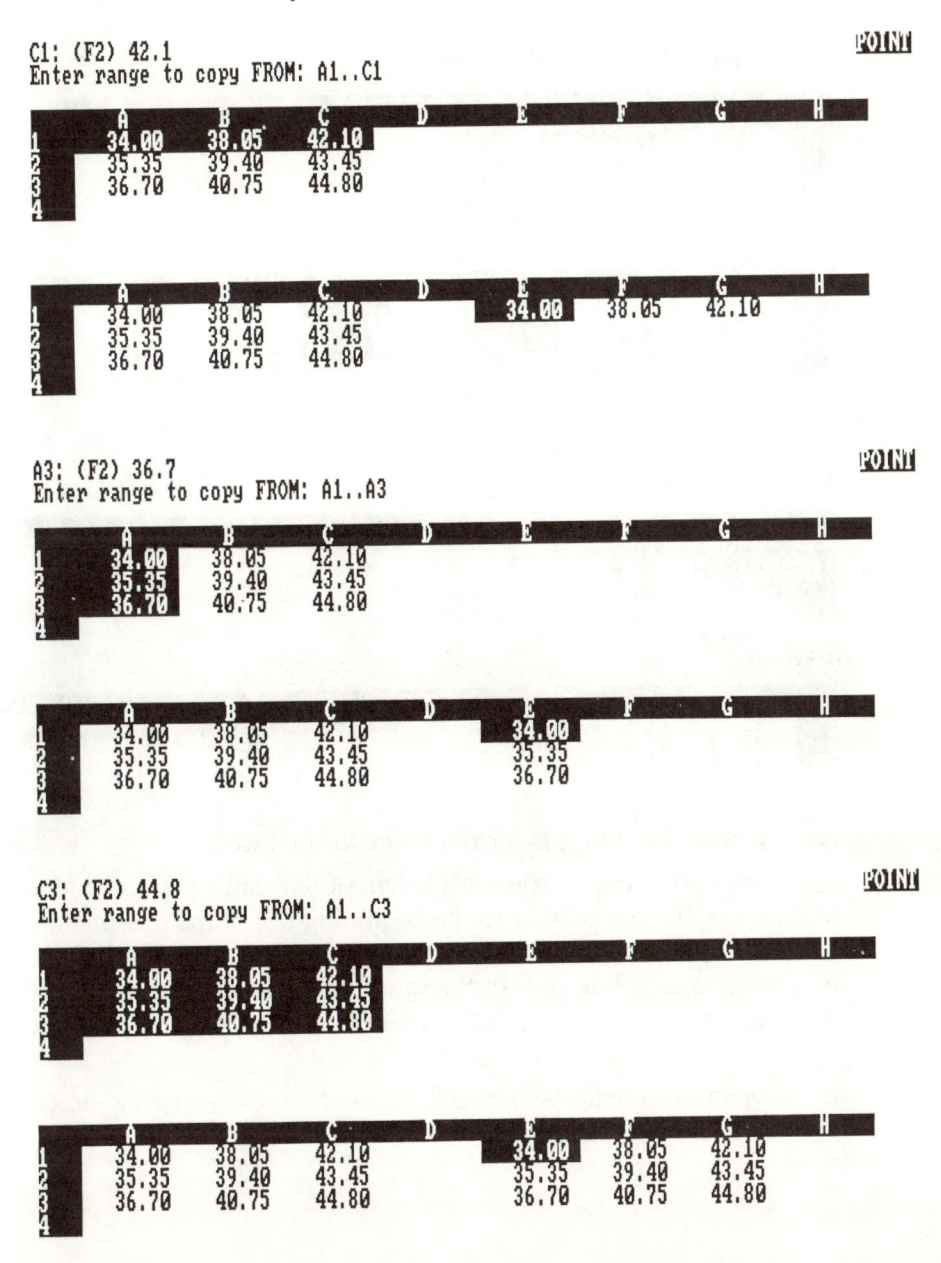

```
C1: (F2) 42.1                                                    POINT
Enter range to copy FROM: A1..C1
      A       B       C       D       E       F       G       H
1   34.00   38.05   42.10
2   35.35   39.40   43.45
3   36.70   40.75   44.80
4
```

```
      A       B       C       D       E       F       G       H
1   34.00   38.05   42.10          34.00   38.05   42.10
2   35.35   39.40   43.45
3   36.70   40.75   44.80
4
```

```
A3: (F2) 36.7                                                    POINT
Enter range to copy FROM: A1..A3
      A       B       C       D       E       F       G       H
1   34.00   38.05   42.10
2   35.35   39.40   43.45
3   36.70   40.75   44.80
4
```

```
      A       B       C       D       E       F       G       H
1   34.00   38.05   42.10          34.00
2   35.35   39.40   43.45          35.35
3   36.70   40.75   44.80          36.70
4
```

```
C3: (F2) 44.8                                                    POINT
Enter range to copy FROM: A1..C3
      A       B       C       D       E       F       G       H
1   34.00   38.05   42.10
2   35.35   39.40   43.45
3   36.70   40.75   44.80
4
```

```
      A       B       C       D       E       F       G       H
1   34.00   38.05   42.10          34.00   38.05   42.10
2   35.35   39.40   43.45          35.35   39.40   43.45
3   36.70   40.75   44.80          36.70   40.75   44.80
4
```

/Copy

- Or, you may want to duplicate the source cells several times in the destination range.

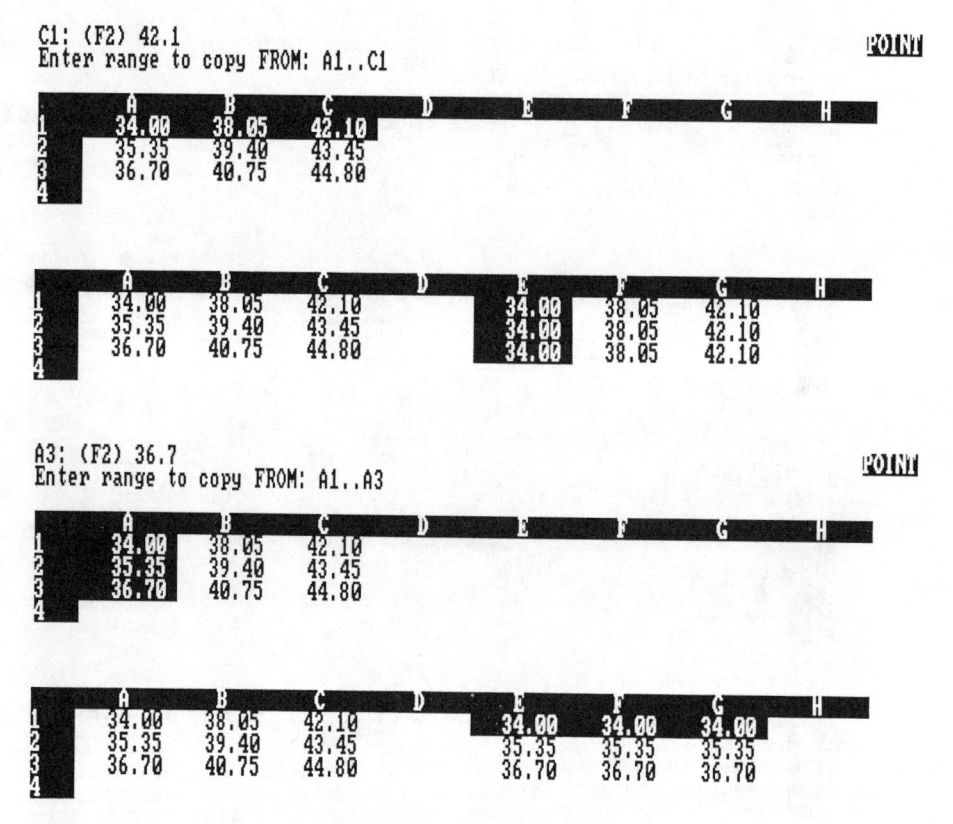

```
C1: (F2) 42.1                                                    POINT
Enter range to copy FROM: A1..C1
    A      B      C      D      E      F      G      H
1  34.00  38.05  42.10
2  35.35  39.40  43.45
3  36.70  40.75  44.80
4
```

```
    A      B      C      D      E      F      G      H
1  34.00  38.05  42.10         34.00  38.05  42.10
2  35.35  39.40  43.45         34.00  38.05  42.10
3  36.70  40.75  44.80         34.00  38.05  42.10
4
```

```
A3: (F2) 36.7                                                    POINT
Enter range to copy FROM: A1..A3
    A      B      C      D      E      F      G      H
1  34.00  38.05  42.10
2  35.35  39.40  43.45
3  36.70  40.75  44.80
4
```

```
    A      B      C      D      E      F      G      H
1  34.00  38.05  42.10         34.00  34.00  34.00
2  35.35  39.40  43.45         35.35  35.35  35.35
3  36.70  40.75  44.80         36.70  36.70  36.70
4
```

Now, when 1-2-3 prompts for the range to copy to:

- If you wish to duplicate the exact layout of the range you are copying from, move the cell pointer to the beginning cell of the destination range and press Return. It is not necessary to specify both the beginning and ending cells of the range you are copying to; 1-2-3 uses the specified cell as the top-left corner of the new range and duplicates the layout of the source cells exactly.
- If you wish to copy the source cells more than once, specify more than one cell to copy to before you press Return.

Copying formulas

1-2-3 has three types of cell references. Two, relative and absolute, are distinct; the third, mixed, is a combination of the other two.

In copying formulas, you must think ahead and decide whether the cell references in the formulas must be relative, absolute, or mixed. If you make a mistake in choosing the form of cell address you use, your worksheet will be inaccurate at best and may present you with a confusing array of error messages you must track down and correct. The only reasons these different methods exist at all are the /Copy command and the /Move **250★** command. Thus, in order to understand the process of copying (or moving) formulas and functions, it is necessary to understand the differences among the three methods of cell referencing.

Relative, absolute, and mixed cell references are discussed in the entries Cell **13★** and Range **291★**. They are treated very differently by 1-2-3 when they occur in formulas or functions that you copy:

- Relative references, which are entered simply as normal cell references, such as A1, always maintain a *positional* relationship between cells. For example, if you enter the formula +A1+B1 in cell C1, it means, "add the contents of the cell two columns to the left (A1) to the contents of the cell one column to the left (B1) and put the result here, in cell C1."

  In terms of the /Copy command: If you copy the formula to cell C2, 1-2-3 will adjust the cell references to maintain their "relativeness" to the formula cell. The formula will become +A2+B2, so that it will still mean, "add the contents of the cell two columns to the left...."

- Absolute references, which are preceded by a $ sign (for example, $A$1), always refer to a particular cell, no matter where they are copied on a worksheet. For example, if you enter the formula in the preceding example as +$A$1+$B$1, the formula will always add the contents of cell A1 to the contents of cell B1, regardless of whether the formula is in cell C1 or D100.

  In terms of the /Copy command: An absolute cell reference remains unchanged, no matter where it is copied, to preserve its "absoluteness."

□ Mixed references, which take the form $A1, A$1, and so on, are a combination of relative and absolute: Whichever coordinate is preceded by the $ sign is treated as an absolute reference, while the other coordinate is treated as a relative reference. For example, if you enter the formula +$A1+B$1 in cell C2, then copy the formula to cell F100, the formula will become +$A99+E$1, because you have told 1-2-3, "add the contents of column A, but one row above the formula row, to the contents of the cell in row 1, but one column to the left."

In terms of the /Copy command: A mixed reference has its relative coordinate adjusted, just as in the case of a relative reference, while the absolute coordinate remains unchanged.

Copying a range of cells containing formulas with relative, absolute, and mixed cell addresses is no more complex than copying formulas with addresses for single cells. A range reference consists of two single-cell references. Thus, when 1-2-3 adjusts a range during a copy procedure, it adjusts the two single-cell references exactly as described in the preceding list.

When copying a formula that contains a range name, make the range name absolute by pressing the F2 [Edit] **144♦** key to move into EDIT **249♦** mode, then type a dollar sign before the name or place the cursor on any character in the name and press the F4 [Abs] **144♦** key. If you do not make the range name absolute, 1-2-3 will treat it as a relative reference when the formula is moved.

Example: The following example shows a practical use of mixed addresses in a Trade Discount worksheet that allows us to calculate different discounts, given various amounts and percentages.

C7: +$A7*C$4   READY

	A	B	C	D	E	F	G	H
1								
2	Trade Discounts							
3								
4	Discounts:		10%	11%	12%	13%	14%	15%
5								
6	Amounts:							
7	10000		1000	1100	1200	1300	1400	1500
8	10500		1050	1155	1260	1365	1470	1575
9	11000		1100	1210	1320	1430	1540	1650
10	11500		1150	1265	1380	1495	1610	1725
11	12000		1200	1320	1440	1560	1680	1800

/Copy

The formula entered in C7 contains two references with a mixed address format. The first address designates a value always located in column A, but in a changing relative row (row 7). When copied, the relative part of this address is adjusted to reflect each row into which the formula is copied. We thus see the successive addresses: $A7, $A8, $A9, $A10, and $A11.

```
C7: (T) [W10] +$A7*C$4                                              READY

         A         B         C         D         E         F         G         H
   1  ═══════════════════════════════════════════════════════════════════════════
   2  Trade Discounts
   3  ═══════════════════════════════════════════════════════════════════════════
   4  Discounts:         10%       11%       12%       13%       14%       15%
   5  ───────────────────────────────────────────────────────────────────────────
   6  Amounts:
   7     10000    |+$A7*C$4  +$A7*D$4  +$A7*E$4  +$A7*F$4  +$A7*G$4  +$A7*H$4
   8     10500    |+$A8*C$4  +$A8*D$4  +$A8*E$4  +$A8*F$4  +$A8*G$4  +$A8*H$4
   9     11000    |+$A9*C$4  +$A9*D$4  +$A9*E$4  +$A9*F$4  +$A9*G$4  +$A9*H$4
  10     11500    |+$A10*C$4 +$A10*D$4 +$A10*E$4 +$A10*F$4 +$A10*G$4 +$A10*H$4
  11     12000    |+$A11*C$4 +$A11*D$4 +$A11*E$4 +$A11*F$4 +$A11*G$4 +$A11*H$4
  12
  13
```

Similarly, the relative part of the formula's second address is adjusted to reflect each column into which the formula is copied. Thus, C$4 becomes D$4, E$4, F$4, and so on.

To copy the formula, the cell pointer was placed on C5. The /Copy command was issued, and the range C7..H11 was designated (by expanding the cell pointer) as the range to copy to (formulas were formatted to display as text with the /Range Format 300* command to show address adjustments):

```
C7: (T) [W10] +$A7*C$4                                              POINT
Enter range to copy FROM: C7..C7

         A         B         C         D         E         F         G         H
   1  ═══════════════════════════════════════════════════════════════════════════
   2  Trade Discounts
   3  ═══════════════════════════════════════════════════════════════════════════
   4  Discounts:         10%       11%       12%       13%       14%       15%
   5  ───────────────────────────────────────────────────────────────────────────
   6  Amounts:
   7     10000    |+$A7*C$4
   8     10500    |
   9     11000    |
  10     11500    |
  11     12000    |
  12
  13
```

```
H11: (T) [W10]                                                    POINT
Enter range to copy TO: C7..H11

    A    B    C           D           E           F           G           H
1  =========================================================================
2  Trade Discounts
3  =========================================================================
4  Discounts:           10%         11%         12%         13%         14%         15%
5  -------------------------------------------------------------------------
6  Amounts:  |
7      10000 |+$A7*C$4
8      10500 |
9      11000 |
10     11500 |
11     12000 |
12
13
```

```
C7: (T) [W10] +$A7*C$4                                            READY

    A    B    C           D           E           F           G           H
1  =========================================================================
2  Trade Discounts
3  =========================================================================
4  Discounts:           10%         11%         12%         13%         14%         15%
5  -------------------------------------------------------------------------
6  Amounts:  |
7      10000 |+$A7*C$4   +$A7*D$4    +$A7*E$4    +$A7*F$4    +$A7*G$4    +$A7*H$4
8      10500 |+$A8*C$4   +$A8*D$4    +$A8*E$4    +$A8*F$4    +$A8*G$4    +$A8*H$4
9      11000 |+$A9*C$4   +$A9*D$4    +$A9*E$4    +$A9*F$4    +$A9*G$4    +$A9*H$4
10     11500 |+$A10*C$4  +$A10*D$4   +$A10*E$4   +$A10*F$4   +$A10*G$4   +$A10*H$4
11     12000 |+$A11*C$4  +$A11*D$4   +$A11*E$4   +$A11*F$4   +$A11*G$4   +$A11*H$4
12
13
```

@COS()

- **Format**

  @COS(x)

- **Description**

  @COS is a trigonometric function that returns the cosine of *x*, an acute angle expressed in radians. Within a right triangle, the cosine of an acute angle is the length of the adjacent side of the angle divided by the length of the triangle's hypotenuse.

@COS()

The value returned by @COS varies in the range −1 to +1. For example:

@COS(@PI)

returns the value −1.

@COS(@PI/2)

returns the value 3.406E−19 (a very small number approximately equal to 0).

@COS(2*@PI)

returns the value 1.

- **Example**

Trigonometric functions are generally used for scientific and engineering purposes. For example, suppose a five-pound weight is suspended by two wires attached to opposing walls. If the wires make an angle of 30 degrees with the walls:

5/(2*@COS(30*2*@PI/360))

determines the tension, 2.89 pounds, in the wires.

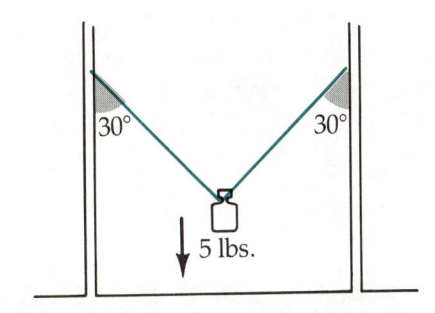

@COUNT()

@COUNT()

■ **Format**

@COUNT(list)

■ **Description**

@COUNT is a statistical function 145★ that counts the number of non-blank cells in a list of arguments. Each argument can be a cell range, or it can be a range name.

The @COUNT function ignores blank cells within a range. It does not, however, ignore text or error values; in other words, this function counts *all* non-blank cells specified in the arguments, whether or not they contain data you want included in the count.

You can, if you wish, include single values or cell addresses as arguments in an @COUNT list. It is important to note, however, that the function always returns a value of 1 for a single cell reference, even when the reference is to a blank cell. In contrast, if a range of cells is empty, 1-2-3 returns a value of 0.

■ **Example**

This example shows the @COUNT function used to count the cells in the range A1..E2. Note that the actual value of the cell contents does not matter; @COUNT simply returns a count of the cells containing either alphabetic or numeric entries. Note also that the cells containing a label and an error value are counted, while the blank cell (E2) is not.

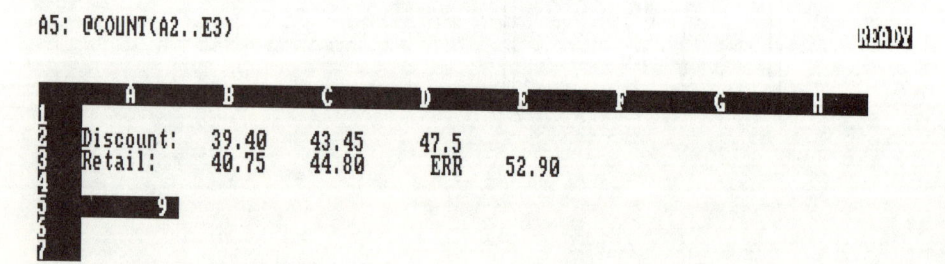

```
A5: @COUNT(A2..E3)                                          READY

        A         B         C         D         E    F    G    H
1
2  Discount:    39.40     43.45     47.5
3  Retail:      40.75     44.80     ERR       52.90
4
5          9
6
7
```

■ **Comment**

The database statistical function @DCOUNT 99★ is the function you would use to count records in a database according to specified criteria.

42

@CTERM()   A Release 2 financial function

■ **Format**

@CTERM(interest rate,future value,present value)

■ **Description**

The @CTERM function computes the number of compounding periods required to achieve a specified *future value*, given an investment's *present value* and a fixed *interest rate* per compounding period.

As when entering other 1-2-3 financial functions, you can type the interest rate either as a percent, such as 10.5%, or as the decimal equivalent (.105). Since the function calculates the number of compounding periods, you may need to divide the interest rate by the frequency at which the investment is compounded. For example, if the interest rate is 10.5 percent per year, compounded monthly, you would enter the interest rate as 10.5%/12. Similarly, to find out the number of years required for the investment to reach the specified future value, you would divide the calculated number of compounding periods by 12.

1-2-3 uses the following formula in its calculation:

$$\ln(fv/pv)/\ln(1+int)$$

where: ln is the natural logarithm; fv is the future value; pv is the present value; and int is the interest rate.

Database

Database

Traditionally, a database is defined as a collection of records grouped into categories containing similar types of information. A telephone book is often presented as an example. Other databases might contain product lists, patient records, stock transactions, or student grades. All, however, consist of individual entries (records) that are divided into fields, each of which gives one item of information about the record.

A 1-2-3 database contains records and fields, just like any other, but in 1-2-3 a database is also simply a *range of cells* in which each *row* is a record and each *column* is a field. The distinction may seem subtle, but its effects are not: Since a 1-2-3 database exists in a range of cells on a worksheet, you can add to, subtract from, reorganize, format, or calculate its contents, just as you would with any other values, labels, or formulas on the worksheet. In this respect, a 1-2-3 database is enormously flexible. It differs from a standard 1-2-3 worksheet in only one respect, but an important one to remember:

The top row of a database always *contains the names of the fields in the database; it should not be separated from the data by a blank row or by a row of dashes or other characters inserted for cosmetic or other reasons. Field names can be text, values, or formulas.*

For example, this is a correctly entered database:

```
E20: [W12]                                                          READY

         A           B           C           D                  E
   ================================================================
 1
 2  Employee Database
 3 ================================================================
 4  Dept.     Last Name   First Name  Address                 Phone
 5  ADV       Williams    Chris       10849 NW 189th          224-6293
 6  MKT       Tramiel     Jan         317 Woodlawn Rd.        771-1503
 7  SALES     Dallas      Dave        211 Garfield St.        783-8547
 8  SHIP      Baier       Maureen     333 Atlantic Ave. S     962-2569
 9  MKT       Fraser      Michel      771 Malden              372-8764
10  PRSNL     Mayes       Lorraine    12561 Eastlake Blvd.    284-1894
11  ADV       Watson      Bill        10245 E. Shelby         882-9716
12  SALES     Jones       Terry       432 Laurelhurst Dr. NW  754-7164
13  SALES     Trescott    Ed          418 SW 186th            522-8000
14  ADV       Jaworski    Steve       4025 54th NW            367-1280
15  WHSE      Anderson    Hans        12222 Henderson N       392-8956
16  MKT       Selle       Ellen       1209 Sand Pt. Way       762-3184
17  PRSNL     Boyer       Connie      25541 Sunnyside Ave.    347-9065
18  SHIP      Woppel      Pascal      4112 NE Maple Pl.       245-9876
19  MKT       Smith       Lee         1705 Howell N           994-4215
20
```

Database

These are incorrect:

E20: [W12] '994-4215   READY

```
     A         B          C          D                    E
1  ============================================================
2  Employee Database
3  ============================================================
4  Dept.     Last Name  First Name  Address               Phone
   -------------------------------------------------------------
5  ADV       Williams   Chris       10849 NW 189th        224-6293
6  MKT       Tramiel    Jan         317 Woodlawn Rd.      771-1503
7  SALES     Dallas     Dave        211 Garfield St.      783-8547
8  SHIP      Baier      Maureen     333 Atlantic Ave. S   962-2569
9  MKT       Fraser     Michel      771 Malden            372-8764
10 PRSNL     Mayes      Lorraine    12561 Eastlake Blvd.  284-1894
11 ADV       Watson     Bill        10245 E. Shelby       882-9716
12 SALES     Jones      Terry       432 Laurelhurst Dr. NW 754-7164
13 SALES     Trescott   Ed          418 SW 186th          522-8000
14 ADV       Jaworski   Steve       4025 54th NW          367-1280
15 WHSE      Anderson   Hans        12222 Henderson N     392-8956
16 MKT       Selle      Ellen       1209 Sand Pt. Way     762-3184
17 PRSNL     Boyer      Connie      25541 Sunnyside Ave.  347-9065
18 SHIP      Woppel     Pascal      4112 NE Maple Pl.     245-9876
```

E20: [W12] '994-4215   READY

```
     A         B          C          D                    E
1  ============================================================
2  Employee Database
3  ============================================================
4  Dept.     Last Name  First Name  Address               Phone
5  ADV       Williams   Chris       10849 NW 189th        224-6293
6  MKT       Tramiel    Jan         317 Woodlawn Rd.      771-1503
7  SALES     Dallas     Dave        211 Garfield St.      783-8547
8  SHIP      Baier      Maureen     333 Atlantic Ave. S   962-2569
9  MKT       Fraser     Michel      771 Malden            372-8764
10 PRSNL     Mayes      Lorraine    12561 Eastlake Blvd.  284-1894
11 ADV       Watson     Bill        10245 E. Shelby       882-9716
12 SALES     Jones      Terry       432 Laurelhurst Dr. NW 754-7164
13 SALES     Trescott   Ed          418 SW 186th          522-8000
14 ADV       Jaworski   Steve       4025 54th NW          367-1280
15 WHSE      Anderson   Hans        12222 Henderson N     392-8956
16 MKT       Selle      Ellen       1209 Sand Pt. Way     762-3184
17 PRSNL     Boyer      Connie      25541 Sunnyside Ave.  347-9065
18 SHIP      Woppel     Pascal      4112 NE Maple Pl.     245-9876
```

■ Using a database

1-2-3 has a group of /Data Query 65★ commands that let you select and manipulate records in the database. With these commands, you can find, copy, modify, and delete certain records by telling 1-2-3 what criteria to use in choosing them. Similarly, you can perform calculations using specific fields of specific records with the database statistical functions 146◆.

When using any of the database-specific commands or functions, you tell 1-2-3 where to look, what to find, and where to put it by specifying an input range, a criterion range, and (if required) an output range.

Input range: The input range ◆ is simply the database itself, including the field names in the first row.

Each record in the input range can contain up to 256 fields. The data in those records can be in the form of blanks, labels, numbers, or formulas, and the formulas can refer to any cells on the worksheet, within the database, or outside of it. It is important, however, that each field be distinct: a label, number, or formula.

In creating or modifying the input range, you can use the /Worksheet 353★, /Range 291★, /Copy 31★, and /Move 250★ commands. You can also use /Print 269★ and /Graph 148★ with database information.

Here is an example of an input range:

```
E19: [W12] '994-4215                                          POINT
Enter Input range: A4..E19
         A         B           C           D                E
    1  ================================================================
    2  Employee Database
    3  ================================================================
    4  Dept.     Last Name   First Name  Address             Phone
    5  ADV       Williams    Chris       10849 NW 189th      224-6293
    6  MKT       Tramiel     Jan         317 Woodlawn Rd.    771-1503
    7  SALES     Dallas      Dave        211 Garfield St.    783-8547
    8  SHIP      Baier       Maureen     333 Atlantic Ave. S 962-2569
    9  MKT       Fraser      Michel      771 Malden          372-8764
   10  PRSNL     Mayes       Lorraine    12561 Eastlake Blvd.284-1894
   11  ADV       Watson      Bill        10245 E. Shelby     882-9716
   12  SALES     Jones       Terry       432 Laurelhurst Dr. NW 754-7164
   13  SALES     Trescott    Ed          418 SW 186th        522-8000
   14  ADV       Jaworski    Steve       4025 54th NW        367-1280
   15  WHSE      Anderson    Hans        12222 Henderson N   392-8956
   16  MKT       Selle       Ellen       1209 Sand Pt. Way   762-3184
   17  PRSNL     Boyer       Connie      25541 Sunnyside Ave.347-9065
   18  SHIP      Woppel      Pascal      4112 NE Maple Pl.   245-9876
   19  MKT       Smith       Lee         1705 Howell N       994-4215
   20
```

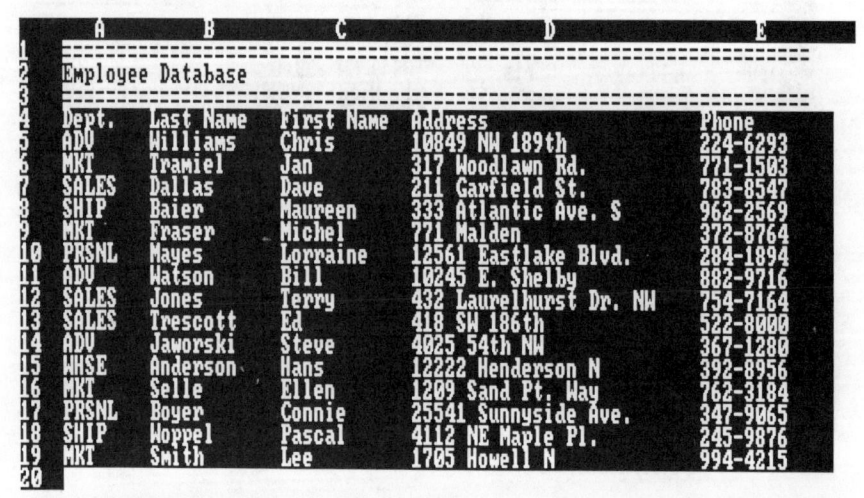

Criterion range: The criterion range ♦ contains criteria that specify which records the database commands and functions will act upon. You create the criterion range in a separate part of the worksheet.

Like the input range, the top row of the criterion range must contain field names from the database. You can include up to 32 field names in the criterion range. The names must be entered exactly as they are in the input range—including spelling, punctuation, capitalization, and any blank spaces that precede, follow, or occur within them.

The second and subsequent rows of the criterion range contain the criteria, the conditions a record must satisfy in order to be evaluated by the command or function you are using.

There are four types of criteria: blank, label, number, and formula.

Blank: A blank is simply an empty criterion cell. It is the equivalent of specifying all records.

Label: A label tells 1-2-3 to examine the specified field of every record in the input range, searching for exact duplicates of the label in the criterion cell. The match must be absolute in all but the following three instances:

- If you include a question mark (?), 1-2-3 will substitute any character for the ?, but will match all others, letter for letter. Example: *p?rt* will cause 1-2-3 to select *part, pert,* and *port.*

- If you include an asterisk (*) at the end of a label, 1-2-3 will substitute any number of characters for the *, but will match all characters at the beginning of the label exactly. Example: *star** will cause 1-2-3 to select *startle, stare,* and *starfish.*

Note: Use of the * character in 1-2-3 is not exactly the same as, for example, its use in DOS. Here, the * can only appear at the end of a label, not in the middle. Thus, you cannot specify *m*n* to select *man, moon, moan,* and *mountain.*

- If you precede the label with a tilde (~), 1-2-3 will match all labels *except* the one following the tilde. Example: *~Friday* will cause 1-2-3 to select all labels in the specified field other than *Friday.*

Database

Number: A number tells 1-2-3 to search for all numbers in the specified field whose stored values are equal to the criterion. The value in the field may be a matching number, or it may be the numeric result of a formula calculation; either will be selected, as long as its value is equal to the number in the criterion cell.

Also, bear in mind that 1-2-3 compares the criterion against the *stored*, not the formatted value of a displayed number. Thus, if you specify 4.56 as the criterion, but have formatted the numbers in the comparison field to two decimals, 1-2-3 will not select 4.562, even though the displayed value is an exact match.

Formula: A criterion cell can contain a formula that includes one of the following logical operators 263★: >, <, =, >=, <=, or <>. The formula is evaluated once for each record in the database, and results in a value of 1 (true) or 0 (false). If the value is 1, the record is selected, because it meets the criterion; if the value is 0, the record is not selected, because it does not meet the criterion.

A formula in a criterion cell can contain one or more cell addresses, the logical operator, and any arithmetic operators or constant values you need to include. A cell address must be relative 17♦ if it refers to a cell within the database. It must be absolute 17♦ if it refers to a cell outside of the database.

Even though you use a relative reference to refer to the first record in the database, 1-2-3 will evaluate all cells below that field. Thus, in the following example, the criterion C5−B5>30 will cause 1-2-3 to calculate the difference between all pairs of cells in columns B and C, and select only those in which the difference is greater than 30.

```
C13: (T) [W10] +C5-B5>30                                        READY
```

```
        A           B          C          D        E         F          G
   ================================================================
 1
 2    Markup List                              Output Range:
 3  ================================================================
 4    Model:      Cost:      Retail:          Model:    Cost:      Retail:
 5    Model A    $125.00    $138.00           Model C   $140.00    $177.00
 6    Model B    $132.00    $160.00           Model D   $149.00    $196.00
 7    Model C    $140.00    $177.00           Model F   $185.00    $230.00
 8    Model D    $149.00    $196.00
 9    Model E    $177.00    $205.00
10    Model F    $185.00    $230.00
11
12    Criteria:              Retail:
13                           +C5-B5>30
14
```

As with any other formulas, you will find formulas in criterion ranges much easier to understand and follow if you use names, rather than cell references (HIGH−LOW>10, for example). You can use the /Range Name Labels Down **312**◆ command to name the cells in a given field of the database.

Arranging criteria: If you are testing more than one criterion, you can enter the criteria *across* one row of the criterion range to tell 1-2-3 to test for "this AND this AND this." Alternatively, you can enter the criteria *down* two or more rows to tell 1-2-3 to test for "this OR this OR this." The first of these two illustrations shows an example of the row-wise "and...and...and" format; the second shows the column-wise "or...or...or" format.

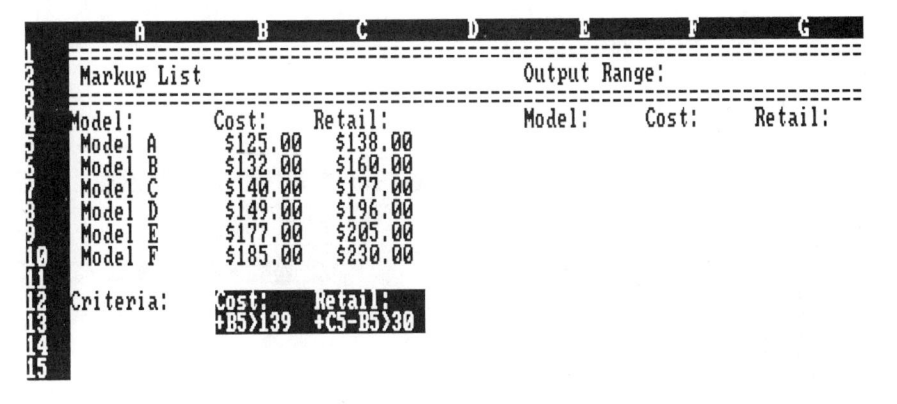

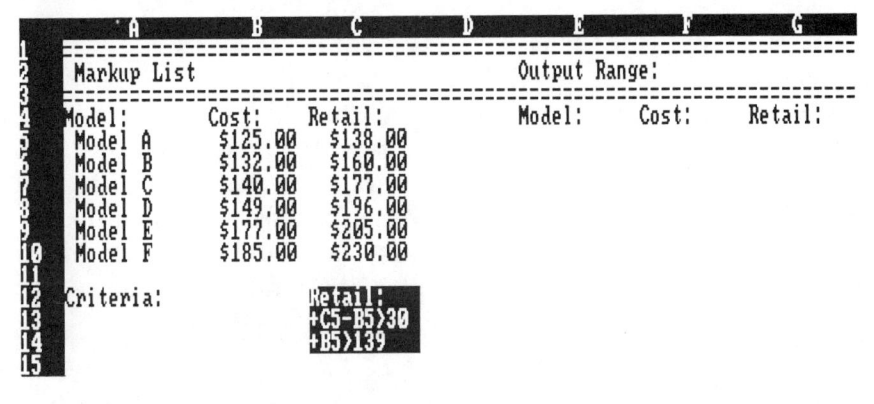

```
C13: (T) [W10] +C5-B5>30                                          POINT
Enter Criterion range: B12..C13
        A         B         C         D         E         F         G
   1  ================================================================
   2    Markup List                        Output Range:
   3  ================================================================
   4    Model:    Cost:     Retail:        Model:    Cost:     Retail:
   5    Model A   $125.00   $138.00
   6    Model B   $132.00   $160.00
   7    Model C   $140.00   $177.00
   8    Model D   $149.00   $196.00
   9    Model E   $177.00   $205.00
  10    Model F   $185.00   $230.00
  11
  12    Criteria: Cost:     Retail:
  13              +B5>139   +C5-B5>30
  14
  15
```

```
C12: [W10] 'Retail:                                               POINT
Enter Criterion range: C14..C12
        A         B         C         D         E         F         G
   1  ================================================================
   2    Markup List                        Output Range:
   3  ================================================================
   4    Model:    Cost:     Retail:        Model:    Cost:     Retail:
   5    Model A   $125.00   $138.00
   6    Model B   $132.00   $160.00
   7    Model C   $140.00   $177.00
   8    Model D   $149.00   $196.00
   9    Model E   $177.00   $205.00
  10    Model F   $185.00   $230.00
  11
  12    Criteria:           Retail:
  13                        +C5-B5>30
  14                        +B5>139
  15
```

Output range: An output range ♦ is the area of your worksheet to which you tell 1-2-3 to copy the results of a database search. Like a criterion range, an output range must include a top row that contains exact duplicates of the database field names. The output range must include each of the fields specified as criteria, but these fields need not be entered in the order in which they appear in the database. Again, as with a criterion range, 1-2-3 allows up to 32 fields.

You can specify an output range that includes only the row of field names, or you can specify a range that includes more than one row. However, if you use either the /Data Query Extract or the /Data Query Unique command and specify only the row of field names, 1-2-3 will erase the portion of the worksheet below (all the way to the bottom of the worksheet) and will then place records in the rows below the row you specified.

The following illustration shows an output range that specifies selected fields of the sample database:

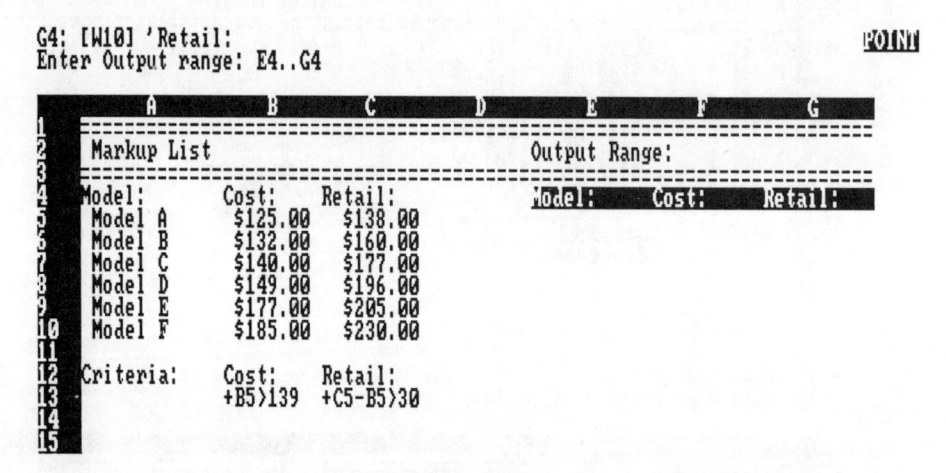

```
G4: [W10] 'Retail:                                          POINT
Enter Output range: E4..G4

        A           B           C           D       E       F       G
    ========================================================================
 1
 2  Markup List                                     Output Range:
 3  ====================================================================
 4  Model:      Cost:       Retail:                 Model:  Cost:   Retail:
 5    Model A   $125.00     $138.00
 6    Model B   $132.00     $160.00
 7    Model C   $140.00     $177.00
 8    Model D   $149.00     $196.00
 9    Model E   $177.00     $205.00
10    Model F   $185.00     $230.00
11
12  Criteria:   Cost:       Retail:
13              +B5>139     +C5-B5>30
14
15
```

■ **Comments**

It is important to remember that input, criterion, and output ranges are affected by the same commands that affect other ranges, and in the same ways. For example, if you use the /Move or /Copy command, 1-2-3 will automatically adjust relative cell references in formulas, just as it does for any other ranges. If you specify an input range in a /Data Query command, then insert or delete columns or rows within the range, 1-2-3 will redefine the range accordingly.

Even though you can specify only a single input, criterion, or output range at any one time, there is no reason why you cannot create as many as you wish and choose among them. For example, if you are an automobile dealer, you might maintain one database for both Renaults and Hondas. One criterion range might specify model, color, and number in stock, while another might specify price, salesperson, and date sold. You could then mix and match input and criterion ranges to suit your immediate needs.

Finally, you can define any of these ranges either before or after you finalize the field names and entries in them. 1-2-3 evaluates their contents on a case-by-case basis, so you can add to, update, or edit them freely, just as long as you take care to specify the correct range when you invoke a database command.

/Data commands

The /Data commands are a group of information-management commands that enable you to list, sort, process, and tabulate your data. Some are relatively simple to understand and use—/Data Fill, for example, fills a specified range with a sequence of numbers. Others are quite complex—/Data Matrix and /Data Regression, for example, perform more sophisticated mathematical calculations.

The following entries discuss the /Data commands: /Data Fill 56★; /Data Table 1 87★; /Data Table 2 89★; /Data Sort 76★ (a database-only command); /Data Query 65★ (a database-only command); /Data Distribution 52★; /Data Matrix 59★ (a Release 2 command); /Data Parse 61★ (a Release 2 command); and /Data Regression 74★ (a Release 2 command).

The entry Database 44★ discusses 1-2-3 databases in general; the entry Data Table 79★ tells about automating your "what if" calculations with 1-2-3's two /Data Table commands.

/Data Distribution

/Data Distribution   /DD

```
Worksheet Range Copy Move File Print Graph DATA System Quit
Fill Table Sort Query Distribution Matrix Regression Parse
```

- **Description**

    With 1-2-3's /Data Distribution command, you can create a table, called a frequency distribution, that allows you to condense large sets of data values by grouping them into numeric categories you specify. A frequency distribution will thus describe statistical data and help you analyze that information by presenting it in a compact form, in which you can more easily see the overall picture.

    When you use the /Data Distribution command, the resulting frequency distribution table tells you how many entries fall into each one of a set of bins (intervals) whose values you specify in the command. This command is particularly useful for condensing large sets of data for use by 1-2-3's graphing facility—presenting the information in a bar or line graph, perhaps.

- **Procedure**

Since the /Data Distribution command requires a pre-existing set of data values (called the *values range*), you must begin with a worksheet that:

☐   Contains the values you want distributed.

☐   Has the values compactly organized in a group of cells you can specify as a range.

Although both of these requirements may seem self-evident, consider the layout of your worksheet before you create a frequency distribution table. For example, suppose your worksheet is organized like the one in the following illustration.

/Data Distribution

```
F20:                                                              READY

         A           B           C           D            E        F
1                Production    Admin.    Shipping
2      01-Jan       $2,362     $1,567      $6,789
3      08-Jan       $3,676     $1,543      $4,888
4      15-Jan       $5,467     $3,414      $4,689
5      22-Jan       $7,856     $1,512     $12,555
6      Totals      $19,361     $8,036     $28,921
7
8      01-Feb       $9,042     $2,155      $7,729
9      08-Feb       $3,577     $3,245     $12,563
10     15-Feb       $7,845     $3,221     $11,222
11     22-Feb       $2,356     $2,441      $8,743
12     Totals      $22,820    $11,062     $40,257
13
14     01-Mar       $6,574     $2,345      $7,547
15     08-Mar       $4,356     $2,345     $11,002
16     15-Mar       $3,788     $2,523      $5,464
17     22-Mar       $3,479     $1,455      $6,774
18     Totals      $18,197     $8,668     $30,787
19
20  1st Quarter    $60,378    $27,766     $99,965
```

If you specify the range B2..D20, the results of your frequency distribution will include counts of *both* monthly and quarterly totals.

Similarly, if the values you want distributed are interspersed with blanks, labels, or the values NA or ERR, your frequency distribution will be inaccurate because:

☐ Blanks and labels are treated as 0.

☐ NA is counted in the first interval, because 1-2-3 considers its value to be less than all numbers.

☐ ERR is counted in the last interval, because 1-2-3 considers its value to be greater than all numbers.

Given these caveats, however, the steps in creating a frequency distribution table are as follows.

Creating a bin range: To tell 1-2-3 the intervals in which you want your data values grouped, you create a bin range in a blank area of the worksheet. The bin range must be a single column of cells immediately to the left of another blank column, the output range, in which 1-2-3 will place the counts of the values in the values range.

/Data Distribution

When creating the bin range, allow for one *extra* cell at the bottom of the output range; 1-2-3 will use this cell to display the count of all values greater than the highest specified bin interval.

In the bin range itself, you enter a series of ascending values. Each value defines the upper limit of the bin to which it is assigned. For example, in the following illustration:

```
G17: [W4] 78                                                    POINT
Enter Values range: B3..E17        Enter Bin range: G3..G17

        A       B       C       D       E    F    G       H
     1 Temp.  Albany  Buffalo New York Syracuse || Bin  Frequency Dist.
     2 ====================================================================
     3  01-Oct   51      54      59      53   ||  36
     4  02-Oct   52      52      57      53   ||  39
     5  03-Oct   68      69      72      73   ||  42
     6  04-Oct   49      52      55      50   ||  45
     7  05-Oct   54      54      58      54   ||  48
     8  06-Oct   62      62      66      65   ||  51
     9  07-Oct   58      62      68      62   ||  54
    10  08-Oct   54      56      59      55   ||  57
    11  09-Oct   39      43      46      45   ||  60
    12  10-Oct   48      52      53      51   ||  63
    13  11-Oct   46      49      52      48   ||  66
    14  12-Oct   50      53      54      54   ||  69
    15  13-Oct   51      52      55      55   ||  72
    16  14-Oct   48      49      53      50   ||  75
    17  15-Oct   47      50      52      47   ||  78
    18
    19
    20
```

the bin range contains the values 36, 39, 42, and so on. These values are conceptually equivalent to the statements: "less than 36," "from 36 to 38," and "from 39 to 41." The last value, 78, is equivalent to "78 or greater."

When you are entering values in a bin range, you can save time and keystrokes by using the /Data Fill **56★** command and letting 1-2-3 fill in the numbers for you.

Specifying the command: Once you have created the bin range, select the /Data Distribution command. 1-2-3 will prompt *Enter Values range:*. If you have used the /Data Distribution command already with the current worksheet, 1-2-3 will prompt you with the range you previously specified. Press Return to accept the proposed range, or specify a new range either by address or by name.

1-2-3 then prompts *Enter Bin range:*. Specify the bin range only—not the column to its right. For example, if the bin range occupies cells D3..D8, and the output range is cells E3..E9, you would enter *D3..D8* in response to this prompt.

Once you have entered the bin range and pressed Return, 1-2-3 immediately carries out the /Data Distribution command, counting the number of values that fall into each bin interval and displaying the result in the output cell to the right of the corresponding bin number.

■ **Example**

The following example assumes you have a set of 60 data values. You know, from examining them, that most are somewhere in the range 45 to 60, but you want to know more precisely how these values are distributed: Are most of them at the high end of the range? the low end? in the middle? To find out, you perform a frequency distribution, as shown in this illustration:

```
H3: [W12] 0                                                          READY

         A        B         C         D          E     F    G            H
    1  Temp.    Albany   Buffalo   New York   Syracuse  ::  Bin     Frequency Dist.
    2  ================================================================
    3  01-Oct     51        54         59        53     ::   36           0
    4  02-Oct     52        52         57        53     ::   39           1
    5  03-Oct     68        69         72        73     ::   42           0
    6  04-Oct     49        52         55        50     ::   45           2
    7  05-Oct     54        54         58        54     ::   48           6
    8  06-Oct     62        62         66        65     ::   51          11
    9  07-Oct     58        62         68        62     ::   54          16
   10  08-Oct     54        56         59        55     ::   57           9
   11  09-Oct     39        43         46        45     ::   60           4
   12  10-Oct     48        52         53        51     ::   63           4
   13  11-Oct     46        49         52        48     ::   66           2
   14  12-Oct     50        53         54        54     ::   69           3
   15  13-Oct     51        52         55        55     ::   72           1
   16  14-Oct     48        49         53        50     ::   75           1
   17  15-Oct     47        50         52        47     ::   78           0
   18                                                                    0
   19
   20
```

/Data Fill

/Data Fill /DF

```
Worksheet  Range  Copy  Move  File  Print  Graph  Data  System  Quit
   Fill  Table  Sort  Query  Distribution  Matrix  Regression  Parse
```

■ **Description**

The /Data Fill command enables you to fill a range of cells with a sequence of numbers. You can specify the beginning and ending numbers, as well as the amount by which each successive number is increased or decreased.

The /Data Fill command is useful in any situation in which you need to enter a regular sequence of numbers in a continuous range of cells. For example, you can use it in creating a numbered list, or for creating a bin range to be used in generating a frequency distribution table with the /Data Distribution 52★ command. You can also use the /Data Fill command with date-related analyses 93★ to automatically generate ranges of dates at specified intervals. Or, as the 1-2-3 manual points out, you can use /Data Fill to create an "index" column before sorting a group of database records; later, you can use the index to restore the original order.

■ **Procedure**

When you choose the /Data Fill command, 1-2-3 first prompts *Enter fill range:*. It is important to remember that 1-2-3 will fill the range downward and, if you specify more than one column, down the columns, stepping from left to right. Determine the area you wish to fill, then:

☐ If you have not previously used the /Data Fill command, specify the range.

☐ If you have previously used the /Data Fill command, 1-2-3 will propose the last range you filled. Press Return to accept the proposed range; use the arrow keys to modify the range; or press Esc and then use the arrow keys to specify a new range.

/Data Fill

1-2-3 then prompts *Start: 0*. Press Return to accept the proposed starting number (0), or enter another number of your choice.

The next prompt is *Step: 1*. Press Return to accept increments of 1, or enter a different interval. The number can be either positive, for an ascending series of numbers, or negative, for a descending series.

Finally, 1-2-3 prompts *Stop: 8191* (2047 in Release 1a). Again, press Return to accept the proposed value, or enter a number.

It is not always necessary to specify a stop value because, when it carries out the command, 1-2-3 will fill cells only until the specified range is filled or until it reaches a stop value. Thus, a stop value is not important unless the range is larger than the number of values you wish to have included in it, and you want 1-2-3 to halt before it fills the entire range.

■ **Examples**

The following examples show the /Data Fill command used in different ways.

First, it is used to number a range of columns:

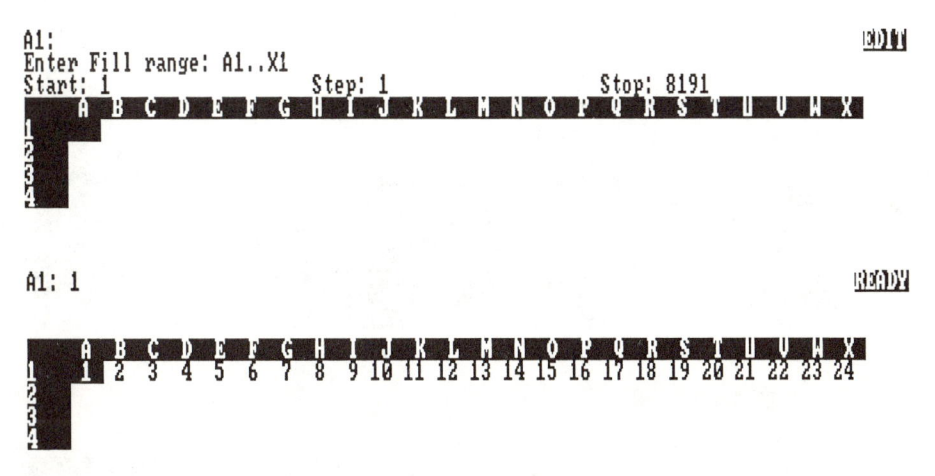

```
A1:                                                                    EDIT
Enter Fill range: A1..X1
Start: 1                    Step: 1                    Stop: 8191
      A   B   C   D   E   F   G   H   I   J   K   L   M   N   O   P   Q   R   S   T   U   V   W   X
   1
   2
   3
   4
```

```
A1: 1                                                                  READY

      A   B   C   D   E   F   G   H   I   J   K   L   M   N   O   P   Q   R   S   T   U   V   W   X
   1  1   2   3   4   5   6   7   8   9  10  11  12  13  14  15  16  17  18  19  20  21  22  23  24
   2
   3
   4
```

Since the start number, stop value, and intervals can be whatever you choose, this is a fast, easy way to create a list of check numbers, invoices, student IDs...any regularly spaced set of numbers.

/Data Fill

Here, for example, it is used with the /Range Format Date 302♦ command to generate a calendar. (The five-digit numbers in the second and third illustrations are date serial numbers, as described for Date-related Analyses.)

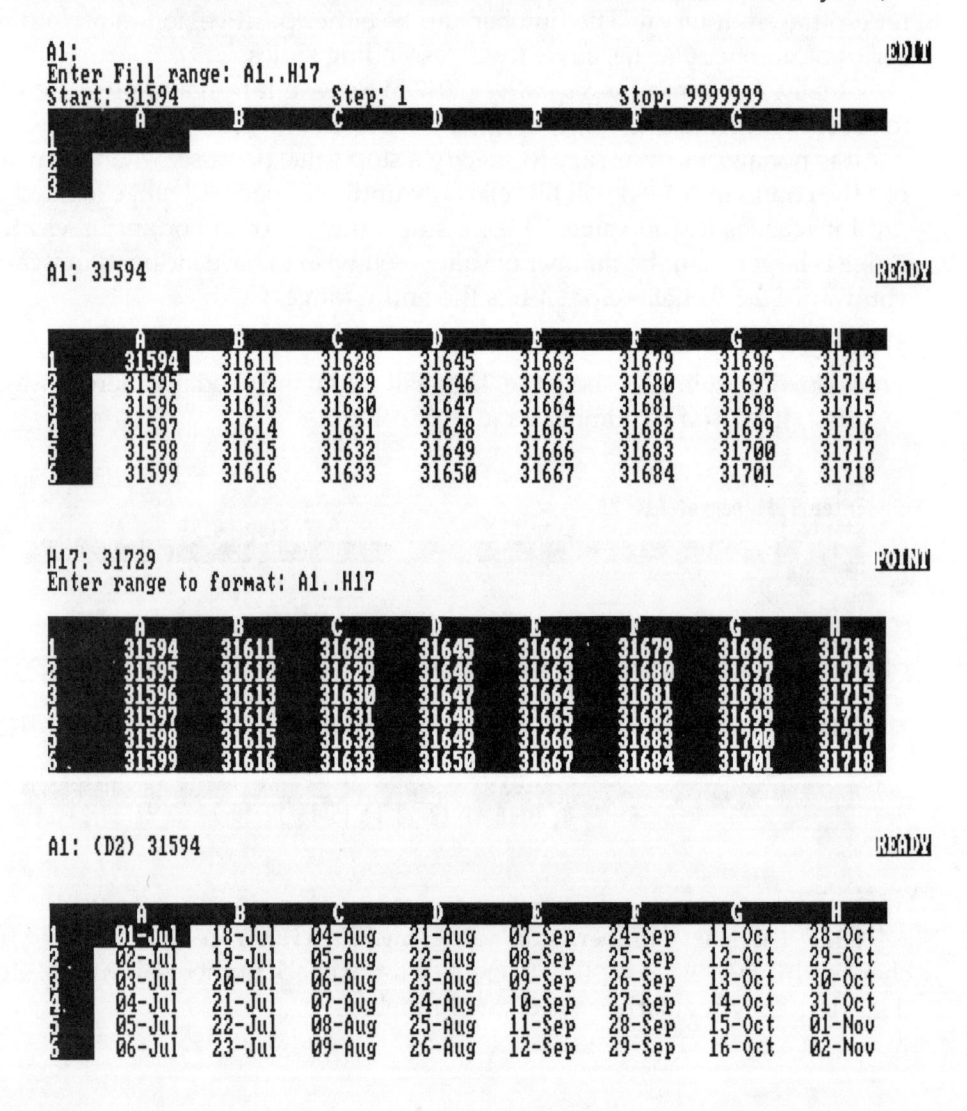

```
A1:                                                                    EDIT
Enter Fill range: A1..H17
Start: 31594            Step: 1                Stop: 9999999
         A          B          C          D          E          F          G          H
    1
    2
    3
```

```
A1: 31594                                                              READY

         A          B          C          D          E          F          G          H
    1  31594      31611      31628      31645      31662      31679      31696      31713
    2  31595      31612      31629      31646      31663      31680      31697      31714
    3  31596      31613      31630      31647      31664      31681      31698      31715
    4  31597      31614      31631      31648      31665      31682      31699      31716
    5  31598      31615      31632      31649      31666      31683      31700      31717
    6  31599      31616      31633      31650      31667      31684      31701      31718
```

```
H17: 31729                                                             POINT
Enter range to format: A1..H17
         A          B          C          D          E          F          G          H
    1  31594      31611      31628      31645      31662      31679      31696      31713
    2  31595      31612      31629      31646      31663      31680      31697      31714
    3  31596      31613      31630      31647      31664      31681      31698      31715
    4  31597      31614      31631      31648      31665      31682      31699      31716
    5  31598      31615      31632      31649      31666      31683      31700      31717
    6  31599      31616      31633      31650      31667      31684      31701      31718
```

```
A1: (D2) 31594                                                         READY

         A          B          C          D          E          F          G          H
    1  01-Jul     18-Jul     04-Aug     21-Aug     07-Sep     24-Sep     11-Oct     28-Oct
    2  02-Jul     19-Jul     05-Aug     22-Aug     08-Sep     25-Sep     12-Oct     29-Oct
    3  03-Jul     20-Jul     06-Aug     23-Aug     09-Sep     26-Sep     13-Oct     30-Oct
    4  04-Jul     21-Jul     07-Aug     24-Aug     10-Sep     27-Sep     14-Oct     31-Oct
    5  05-Jul     22-Jul     08-Aug     25-Aug     11-Sep     28-Sep     15-Oct     01-Nov
    6  06-Jul     23-Jul     09-Aug     26-Aug     12-Sep     29-Sep     16-Oct     02-Nov
```

/Data Matrix

```
Worksheet  Range  Copy  Move  File  Print  Graph  Data  System  Quit
Fill  Table  Sort  Query  Distribution  Matrix  Regression  Parse
Invert  Multiply
```

■ Description

The /Data Matrix command is in Release 2 of 1-2-3 only; there is no equivalent in Release 1a. With the /Data Matrix, you can invert or multiply matrices of cells up to 90 rows deep by 90 columns wide.

Matrices provide a natural way to organize data, and they are commonly used in fields ranging from management to the natural and social sciences, for solving problems ranging from inventory control to population studies and economic modeling.

Regardless of what information it represents, however, a matrix is always a rectangular array of numbers. Each number occupies one cell, and the matrix itself is classified by its dimension, or order—the number of rows and columns it contains. For example, a matrix three rows deep by four columns wide is of the dimension, or order, 3×4. A matrix with the same number of rows and columns is a square matrix. Two matrices of the same order are equal if their contents, cell by cell, are equal.

■ Procedure

When you choose the /Data Matrix command, 1-2-3 offers two options, *Invert* and *Multiply:*

- ☐ You can invert a matrix only if it is a square matrix.
- ☐ You can multiply matrices only if the number of columns in one matrix is equal to the number of rows in the second matrix.

/Data Matrix

To invert a matrix, as shown in the following example:

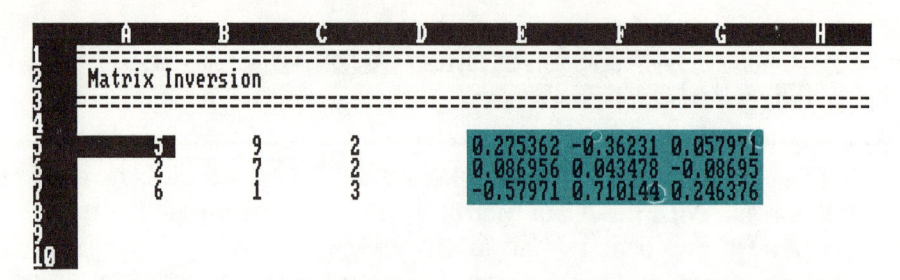

```
       A     B     C     D     E        F        G        H
 1  ===========================================================
 2  Matrix Inversion
 3  ===========================================================
 4
 5        5     9     2        0.275362 -0.36231  0.057971
 6        2     7     2        0.086956  0.043478 -0.08695
 7        6     1     3       -0.57971   0.710144  0.246376
 8
 9
10
```

select the *Invert* option, and 1-2-3 will prompt *Enter Range to invert:*. Enter the range of a square matrix, either by name, pointing, or address, and press Return. 1-2-3 will then prompt *Enter Output range:*. Here, you can either specify an entire output range or only the address of the cell you want to become the top left-hand corner of the range to be occupied by the inverted matrix. In either case, be certain the output range does not contain information you want to keep, because it will be overwritten by the incoming data.

To multiply two matrices, as shown in the following example:

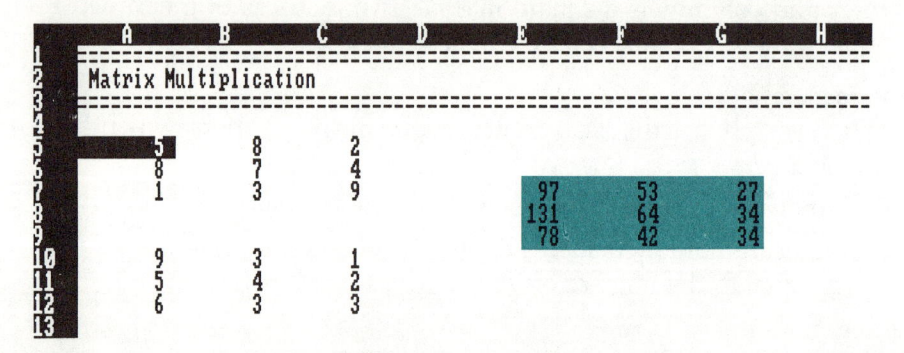

```
       A     B     C     D     E     F     G     H
 1  =====================================================
 2  Matrix Multiplication
 3  =====================================================
 4
 5        5     8     2
 6        8     7     4
 7        1     3     9           97    53    27
 8                                131    64    34
 9                                 78    42    34
10
11        9     3     1
12        5     4     2
13        6     3     3
```

select *Multiply*. 1-2-3 will prompt, in succession, for the first range to multiply, the second range to multiply, and the output range where you want the product of the first two ranges to appear. As for the *Invert* option, you can specify the matrices to be multiplied either by name or by address, and you can, if you wish, specify only the top left corner of the output range. Be certain, however, that the number of columns in the first range is the same as the number of rows in the second range, and that the output range is large enough to contain the product of the two matrices.

/Data Matrix · /Data Parse

■ **Example**

You can also add or subtract matrices by using the /File Xtract 133★ command to save a matrix to a separate file, then using the *Add* or *Subtract* option of the /File Combine 121★ command to overlay a matrix of the same dimensions with the extracted data, as shown in the following two illustrations.

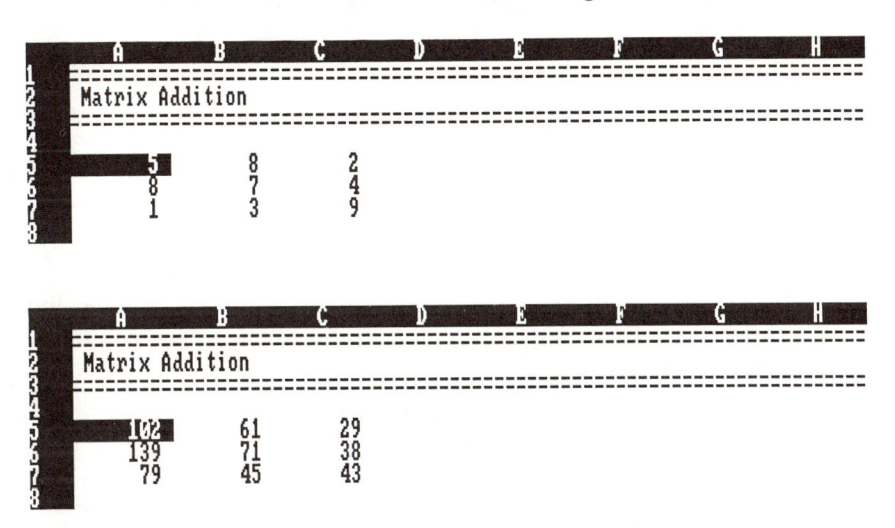

```
         A        B        C        D    E    F    G    H
1 =====================================================
2  Matrix Addition
3 =====================================================
4
5       5        8        2
6       8        7        4
7       1        3        9
8
```

```
         A        B        C        D    E    F    G    H
1 =====================================================
2  Matrix Addition
3 =====================================================
4
5     102       61       29
6     139       71       38
7      79       45       43
8
```

/Data Parse   /DP

```
Worksheet  Range  Copy  Move  File  Print  Graph  Data  System  Quit
Fill  Table  Sort  Query  Distribution  Matrix  Regression  Parse
Format-Line  Input-Column  Output-Range  Reset  Go  Quit
Create  Edit
```

■ **Description**

The /Data Parse command is in Release 2 only. It enables you to convert standard ASCII 5★ files imported from other programs into a row-and-column format you can use with 1-2-3. You use /Data Parse after bringing the other program's file into 1-2-3 with the /File Import Text 127◆ command.

/Data Parse

For the most part, you will probably use the /Data Parse command to convert word-processed tables or ASCII files transmitted via modem, because 1-2-3's Translate Utility **342★** enables you to import the following types of files directly, via the Access System **3★**:

- Files created with other releases of 1-2-3.
- dBASE II and III files.
- DIF files.
- Jazz files.
- Symphony files.
- VisiCalc files.

■ **A note about ASCII files**

ASCII is a convention supported by a great number of software developers to enable users of their own and other application programs to exchange files relatively freely. When a file is saved in ASCII format, the text (including numbers) and certain special characters, such as Return, are given standard ASCII code numbers, which all compatible programs can understand. In the translation to ASCII, however, a file generated by one program must first be stripped of all coding that has no meaning to another program. The result is a very basic text file with little of its original formatting, but with the decided advantage of being highly transportable.

In terms of 1-2-3, all of this means that an ASCII file will be accepted by the program, but you must take a hand in reshaping it into the rows and columns (or database fields and records) that can then be manipulated by 1-2-3.

■ **Procedure**

When you import an ASCII file into a 1-2-3 worksheet or database, the lines of the file are placed in single cells of successive rows, beginning with the cell the pointer was on when you imported the file. Each line is given the ' label prefix. Thus, your data is simply a column of long, left-aligned labels (not values) one cell wide. You can see and print these lines, but cannot use any of the information in tables or formulas, nor can you create graphs with it.

To convert these labels into appropriate cell contents—to tell 1-2-3, "this is text, this is a number; this belongs in one cell, this belongs in another," you use the /Data Parse command.

/Data Parse

First, place the cell pointer on the top label in the column. Then choose the /Data Parse command; 1-2-3 will present the list of options shown at the beginning of this entry. The first, *Format-Line*, is highlighted as 1-2-3's proposed response. Press Return to select this option. 1-2-3 then offers two more choices: *Create* and *Edit*.

Creating a format line: With a newly imported file, choose to *Create* a format line. When you do, a format line—a special label preceded by the character |, and composed of asterisks (*), arrowheads (>), and letters—will appear in the row above the label, highlighted by the cell pointer, as shown in the following illustration:

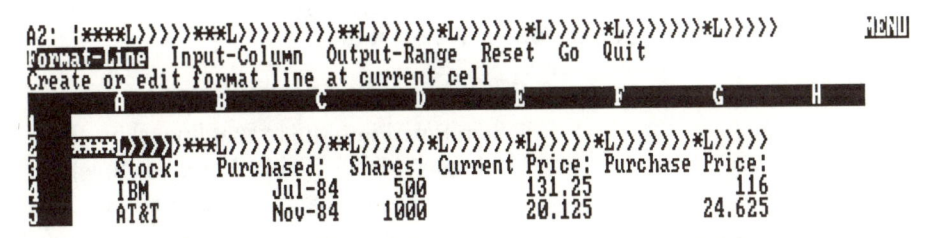

```
A2: |****L)))))***L))))))))**L))))))*L))))))*L)))))*L))))))*L)))))                    MENU
Format-Line  Input-Column  Output-Range  Reset  Go  Quit
Create or edit format line at current cell
        A           B          C         D          E           F           G         H
1
2    ****L))))))***L)))))))))**L))))))*L))))))*L)))))*L))))))))*L)))))
3      Stock:    Purchased:   Shares: Current Price: Purchase Price:
4      IBM         Jul-84       500       131.25           116
5      AT&T        Nov-84      1000        20.125           24.625
```

1-2-3 creates this line after examining the contents of the cell you highlighted. It considers each group of characters that are separated by blank spaces to be a block of data, and offers its guess as to what these characters are by placing one of the following indicators in the format line above the first character of the data block: *V*, for a numeric value; *L*, for a label; *D*, for a date; or *T*, for a time.

The following illustration shows these features. Note that the arrowhead above each character of the data block and the asterisk above each blank space correspond to the first, not subsequent rows.

```
A4: |****L))***********D)))))*****U))*********U)))))*************U))                   MENU
Format-Line  Input-Column  Output-Range  Reset  Go  Quit
Create or edit format line at current cell
        A           B          C         D          E           F           G         H
1
2    ****L))))))***L)))))))))**L))))))*L))))))*L)))))*L))))))))*L)))))
3      Stock:    Purchased:   Shares: Current Price: Purchase Price:
4    ****L))**********D)))))*****U))*********U)))))*************U))
5      IBM         Jul-84       500       131.25           116
6      AT&T        Nov-84      1000        20.125           24.625
7      USSTEEL     Nov-84       500        33               25.625
8      GM          May-83       500        70.5             64.25
9      XEROX       Jun-82       800        49.625           37.25
```

63

/Data Parse

You can create more than one format line to tell 1-2-3 to parse sections of a file in different ways. To do so, select *Quit* to return to READY mode, position the cell pointer above the appropriate label, as before, and again select /Data Parse and *Create*. The previous illustration shows a file with two different format lines.

Editing a format line: If 1-2-3's proposed format line does not match corresponding data blocks in all successive rows of related data, you can edit the format line.

To do this, place the cell pointer on the format line, reselect *Format-Line*, then choose *Edit*.

Now, you can use any of the following keys to edit the format line and check the results against your rows of data:

Key:	Action:
S	When typed into the format line, skips the character below (a blank, for example) when /Data Parse is later carried out.
Right arrow	Moves one character to the right.
Left arrow	Moves one character to the left.
Delete	Deletes the current character.
Backspace	Deletes the character to the left.
Insert	Toggles between inserting and overwriting existing text.
Tab (big right)	Moves right five characters.
Backtab (big left)	Moves left five characters.
End	Moves to last character.
Esc	Deletes format line.
Down	Scrolls down one line.
Up	Scrolls up one line.
Pg Dn	Scrolls down one screen.
Pg Up	Scrolls up one screen.
Home	Returns you to the first character in the format line and the first label in the file.

Press Break to cancel the edit, or press Return when the edit is complete.

/Data Parse · /Data Query

Carrying out the command: To tell 1-2-3 to break the original long labels into the columns of data you have specified in the format line(s), choose *Input-Column*. Specify the input range—the single column containing the format line and all rows of data you want to include.

Next, select *Output-Range*. This time, specify the top left corner cell of the range in which you want the data entered. You should bear in mind that the parsed data will overwrite any existing cell contents, so choose a blank area of your worksheet large enough to hold all the rows and columns you specified in the format line.

Finally, select *Go* to carry out the command.

/Data Query   /DQ

```
Worksheet  Range  Copy  Move  File  Print  Graph  Data  System  Quit
Fill  Table  Sort  Query  Distribution  Matrix  Regression  Parse
Input  Criterion  Output  Find  Extract  Unique  Delete  Reset  Quit
```

■ **Description**

The /Data Query commands are used to search for and manipulate records in a 1-2-3 database. Depending on the option you choose, you can use the /Data Query commands to:

☐ Locate one or more records (/Data Query Find).

☐ Copy records to another part of the worksheet (/Data Query Extract).

☐ Copy records to another part of the worksheet and, at the same time, avoid making duplications (/Data Query Unique).

☐ Delete selected records (/Data Query Delete).

The /Data Query commands are for use with databases only. They are not used with worksheets.

■ **Procedure**

When you choose the /Data Query command, 1-2-3 displays a menu of options. The first three, *Input*, *Criterion*, and *Output*, are used to specify cell ranges that are required by one or another of the /Data Query commands themselves. Without such parameters, the commands cannot operate. For example, /Data Query Find cannot find anything if you do not tell it where to look (input) and what to look for (criterion).

The following sections discuss each of the /Data Query menu choices. For additional information, refer to the entry Database 44★.

65

/Data Query

Input: When you choose *Input* (the proposed response when you first select the /Data Query command), 1-2-3 prompts *Enter Input range:*. The input range is always all or part of the database itself, including the field names in the top row. The following illustration shows an input range:

```
E19: [W12] '994-4215                                            POINT
Enter Input range: A4..E19
     A         B          C          D                   E
 1  ================================================================
 2  Employee Database
 3  ================================================================
 4  Dept.     Last Name  First Name Address              Phone
 5  ADV       Williams   Chris      10849 NW 189th       224-6293
 6  MKT       Tramiel    Jan        317 Woodlawn Rd.     771-1503
 7  SALES     Dallas     Dave       211 Garfield St.     783-8547
 8  SHIP      Baier      Maureen    333 Atlantic Ave. S  962-2569
 9  MKT       Fraser     Michel     771 Malden           372-8764
10  PRSNL     Mayes      Lorraine   12561 Eastlake Blvd. 284-1894
11  ADV       Watson     Bill       10245 E. Shelby      882-9716
12  SALES     Jones      Terry      432 Laurelhurst Dr. NW 754-7164
13  SALES     Trescott   Ed         418 SW 186th         522-8000
14  ADV       Jaworski   Steve      4025 54th NW         367-1280
15  WHSE      Anderson   Hans       12222 Henderson N    392-8956
16  MKT       Selle      Ellen      1209 Sand Pt. Way    762-3184
17  PRSNL     Boyer      Connie     25541 Sunnyside Ave. 347-9065
18  SHIP      Woppel     Pascal     4112 NE Maple Pl.    245-9876
19  MKT       Smith      Lee        1705 Howell N        994-4215
20
```

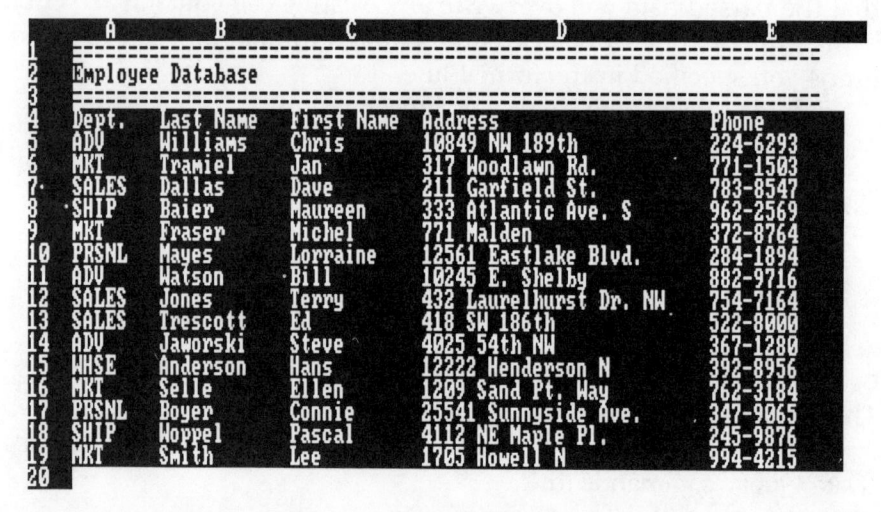

Criterion: The criterion range is a range of cells that contain the selection criteria you want 1-2-3 to use in separating those records you want to evaluate from those you do not. Details and examples are also given in the Database entry.

In setting up a criterion range, choose a blank area of your worksheet at least two rows deep. The top row of the criterion range must contain some or all of the field names in the top row of the database.

You can include up to 32 field names in the criterion range. You are not limited to those you intend to specify in a command, so a simple way to construct this part of the range—especially since the field names must match the database exactly—is to use the /Copy 31★ command to duplicate the database field names in the area you have selected for the criterion range.

In the second and (optionally) the following rows of the criterion range, you enter the criteria 1-2-3 must use in testing database records.

/Data Query

As a simple example, suppose you have entered the criterion Last Name and want 1-2-3 to search for people named Smith, Jones, and Watson. You would enter these names in consecutive rows beneath Last Name, as shown in the following illustration:

```
F7: [W12] 'Watson                                                    POINT
Enter Criterion range: F4..F7
         B            C            D                      E           F
  1 ============================================================Criterion
  2   Database                                                       Range:
  3 ====================================================================
  4   Last Name    First Name   Address                  Phone       Last Name
  5   Williams     Chris        10849 NW 189th           224-6293    Smith
  6   Tramiel      Jan          317 Woodlawn Rd.         771-1503    Jones
  7   Dallas       Dave         211 Garfield St.         783-8547    Watson
  8   Baier        Maureen      333 Atlantic Ave. S      962-2569
  9   Fraser       Michel       771 Malden               372-8764
 10   Mayes        Lorraine     12561 Eastlake Blvd.     284-1894
 11   Watson       Bill         10245 E. Shelby          882-9716
 12   Jones        Terry        432 Laurelhurst Dr. NW   754-7164
 13   Trescott     Ed           418 SW 186th             522-8000
```

Criteria can be blanks, labels or values (entered exactly as in the database), or formulas (which 1-2-3 will evaluate for each record). 1-2-3 allows you considerable flexibility in specifying entries to search for. Depending on your needs, you can:

□ Specify exact matches by using their values or labels.

□ Use the characters ? and * to specify labels that match except for single characters, represented by ?, or that match except for more than one character, represented by * at the end of the label.

□ Precede a label with a tilde (~) to specify all labels except that one.

□ Set conditions by entering formulas that use logical operators 263★. These operators are:

    <   less than
    >   greater than
    <=   less than or equal to
    >=   greater than or equal to
    <>   less than or greater than

67

/Data Query

If you enter a formula in the criterion range, you would include one or more cell addresses, the operator, and any arithmetic operators and values you want to include. For example, if column C contains the current prices of stocks in a portfolio, and column D contains their purchase prices, you could specify all stocks that have risen more than $5 with the formula C2−D2>5.

When you enter a formula in the criterion range, the cell address must be relative if it refers to a cell within the database, and absolute if it refers to a cell outside of the database.

Even though you use a relative reference to refer to a single database cell, 1-2-3 will evaluate all cells in that field. For each cell, if the test is true, 1-2-3 will display a *1* in the criterion range; if the test is false, 1-2-3 will display a *0*. The use of logical operators in a criterion range is shown in the following illustration:

```
B11: (T) [W13] +C2-D2>5                                              MENU
Input  Criterion  Output  Find  Extract  Unique  Delete  Reset  Quit
Copy all records that match criteria to Output range
             A              B              C              D
 1    Stock:          Shares:       Current Price:  Purchase Price:
 2    IBM                500            131.25              116
 3    AT&T              1000             20.125           24.625
 4    USSTEEL            500                 33           25.625
 5    GM                 500               70.5            64.25
 6    XEROX              800             49.625            37.25
 7    DIGITAL           1000            112.875            95.25
 8    PRIMEC             500             20.375             17.5
 9
10    Criterion:      Current Price:
11                    +C2-D2>5
12
13    Output Range:
14    Stock:          Shares:       Current Price:  Purchase Price:
15    IBM                500            131.25              116
16    USSTEEL            500                 33           25.625
17    GM                 500               70.5            64.25
18    XEROX              800             49.625            37.25
19    DIGITAL           1000            112.875            95.25
20
```

Finally, if you are testing more than one criterion, you can enter the criteria *across* one row of the criterion range to tell 1-2-3 to test for "this AND this AND this." Alternatively, you can enter the criteria *down* two or more rows to tell 1-2-3 to test for "this OR this OR this." The first of the following two illustrations shows an example of the row-wise "and...and...and" format; the second shows the column-wise "or...or...or" format.

/Data Query

```
C11: (T) [W19] +C2-D2>5                                    POINT
Enter Criterion range: B10..C11
```

	A	B	C	D
1	Stock:	Shares:	Current Price:	Purchase Price:
2	IBM	500	131.25	116
3	AT&T	1000	20.125	24.625
4	USSTEEL	500	33	25.625
5	GM	500	70.5	64.25
6	XEROX	800	49.625	37.25
7	DIGITAL	1000	112.875	95.25
8	PRIMEC	500	20.375	17.5
9				
10	Criteria:	Shares:	Current Price:	
11		+B2>500	+C2-D2>5	
12				
13	Output Range:			
14	Stock:	Shares:	Current Price:	Purchase Price:
15	XEROX	800	49.625	37.25
16	DIGITAL	1000	112.875	95.25

```
B12: (T) [W13] +C2-D2>5                                    POINT
Enter Criterion range: B10..B12
```

	A	B	C	D
1	Stock:	Shares:	Current Price:	Purchase Price:
2	IBM	500	131.25	116
3	AT&T	1000	20.125	24.625
4	USSTEEL	500	33	25.625
5	GM	500	70.5	64.25
6	XEROX	800	49.625	37.25
7	DIGITAL	1000	112.875	95.25
8	PRIMEC	500	20.375	17.5
9				
10	Criteria:	Shares:		
11		+B2>500		
12		+C2-D2>5		
13	Output Range:			
14	Stock:	Shares:	Current Price:	Purchase Price:
15	IBM	500	131.25	116
16	AT&T	1000	20.125	24.625
17	USSTEEL	500	33	25.625
18	GM	500	70.5	64.25
19	XEROX	800	49.625	37.25
20	DIGITAL	1000	112.875	95.25

/Data Query

Output: An output range is the area of your worksheet in which 1-2-3 places the results of a database search. Like a criterion range, an output range must include a top row that contains exact duplicates of the database field names. The output range must include each of the fields specified as criteria, but these fields need not be entered in the order in which they appear in the database. As with a criterion range, 1-2-3 allows up to 32 fields.

You can specify an output range that includes only the row of field names, or you can specify the range of cells for the output of your /Data Query command. However, if you use either the /Data Query Extract or the /Data Query Unique command and you specify only the row of field names, 1-2-3 will place records in the rows below the row you specify and will erase any existing data, to the bottom of the worksheet.

/Data Query Find◆: The /Data Query Find command tells 1-2-3 to search the database for records that match your criteria. The input range and criterion range must already exist when you choose this command.

To use /Data Query Find, first you select the /Data Query command. Then select *Input*, and specify an input range (all or part of the database, as described in the preceding section, "Input"). Next, select *Criterion* and, when 1-2-3 prompts, enter the criterion range. Last, select *Find* and press Return.

1-2-3 will search the database, from the top down, and highlight the first record that matches the criterion or criteria you have specified, as shown in the following illustration (note the FIND mode indicator in the upper right corner):

```
A11: [W8] 'ADV                                                          FIND

        A        B           C          D                      E
  1    ================================================================
  2    Employee Database
  3    ================================================================
  4    Dept.    Last Name   First Name  Address                Phone
  5    ADV      Williams    Chris       10849 NW 189th         224-6293
  6    MKT      Tramiel     Jan         317 Woodlawn Rd.       771-1503
  7    SALES    Dallas      Dave        211 Garfield St.       783-8547
  8    SHIP     Baier       Maureen     333 Atlantic Ave. S    962-2569
  9    MKT      Fraser      Michel      771 Malden             372-8764
 10    PRSNL    Mayes       Lorraine    12561 Eastlake Blvd.   284-1894
 11    ADV      Watson      Bill        10245 E. Shelby        882-9716
 12    SALES    Jones       Terry       432 Laurelhurst Dr. NW 754-7164
 13    SALES    Trescott    Ed          418 SW 186th           522-8000
 14    ADV      Jaworski    Steve       4025 54th NW           367-1280
```

/Data Query

If there is no match, the computer will beep and you will be returned to the /Data Query menu.

During a /Data Query Find operation, you can use the following pointer-movement keys:

Key:	Action:
Up arrow	Move to previous matching record
Down arrow	Move to next matching record
Right arrow	Move right one field
Left arrow	Move left one field
Home	Move to first record in database
End	Move to last record in database

In addition, you can use Esc or Return to exit the /Data Query Find command; you can use the F2 [Edit] 144♦ key to change or correct an entry in a field; and (provided you are in READY 249♦ mode) you also can use the F7 [Query] 144♦ key to repeat the last /Data Query operation.

/Data Query Extract: The /Data Query Extract command tells 1-2-3 to copy records that match your criterion or criteria from the database to the output range you specify. Depending on your needs, you can copy all, or selected fields, of each record to the output range.

Before you select the /Data Query Extract command, you must already have set up the input, criterion, and output ranges, as described in the preceding sections.

To use the /Data Query Extract command, first select /Data Query. Then, in order, select *Input*, *Criterion*, and *Output*, entering the appropriate ranges for each. Then, select *Extract*.

1-2-3 will carry out the command, copying all specified fields from all matching records to the output range you specified, as shown in the two illustrations on the next page.

/Data Query

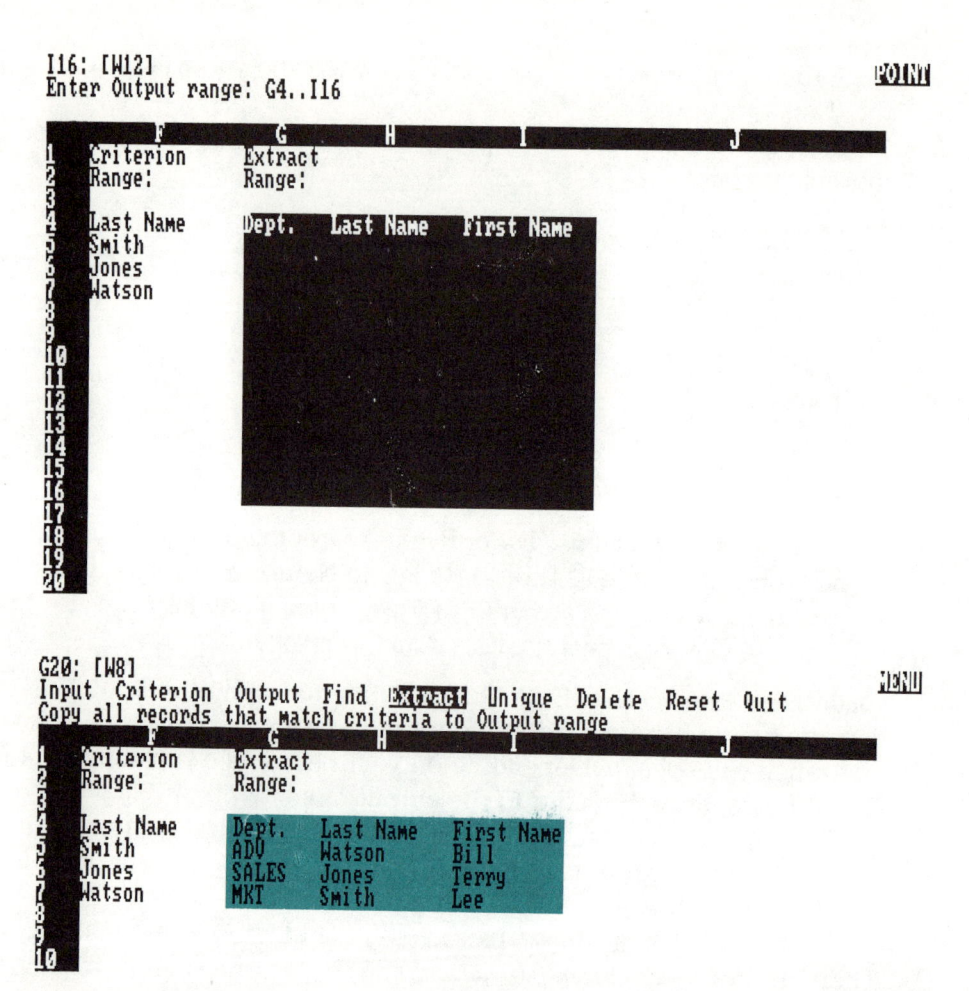

```
I16: [W12]                                                      POINT
Enter Output range: G4..I16
      F          G          H          I          J
 1  Criterion  Extract
 2  Range:     Range:
 3
 4  Last Name  Dept.      Last Name  First Name
 5  Smith
 6  Jones
 7  Watson
 8
 9
10
11
12
13
14
15
16
17
18
19
20
```

```
G20: [W8]                                                       MENU
Input  Criterion  Output  Find  Extract  Unique  Delete  Reset  Quit
Copy all records that match criteria to Output range
      F          G          H          I          J
 1  Criterion  Extract
 2  Range:     Range:
 3
 4  Last Name  Dept.      Last Name  First Name
 5  Smith      ADV        Watson     Bill
 6  Jones      SALES      Jones      Terry
 7  Watson     MKT        Smith      Lee
 8
 9
10
```

If the output range is not large enough to hold all the records, the computer will beep and 1-2-3 will display a message telling you of the problem. Press Esc and re-enter the command, this time including more rows of cells in the output range. If, as described earlier, you specified only the row of field names as the output range, remember that 1-2-3 will erase any data in the rows below.

/Data Query Unique: The /Data Query Unique command is the /Data Query Extract command, but does not repeat records that occur more than once in the database. The *Unique* part of this command ensures that duplicates are not copied to the output range you specify.

Just as with the /Data Query Extract command, you must specify the input, criterion, and output ranges *before* choosing /Data Query Unique. The same procedures otherwise apply to both commands.

Only one additional note need be made about /Data Query Unique: If you specify some, rather than all, of your database fields in the output range, this command will eliminate not only duplicate records, but also those that appear (to 1-2-3) to be duplicates because the fields containing unique data are not specified in the output range. In other words, if your database contains the following two records:

Last Name:	First Name:	Department:	Job Class.:	Date Hired:
Smith	Harry	Acctg	3	8/14/77
Smith	Harry	Acctg	3	12/11/80

and your output range only specifies the fields Last Name, First Name, Department, and Job Class., the /Data Query Unique command will eliminate the second record, because the field that distinguishes it from the first (Date Hired) is not part of your specified output range.

/Data Query Delete: The /Data Query Delete command offers you a quick and easy way to clean up or update an existing database. This is much like the /Data Query Find command, but instead of simply highlighting the records that match your criteria, it asks if you want to delete the record(s) it finds. As for /Data Query Find, you must specify the input range and a pre-established criterion range before selecting the command.

Once you select /Data Query Delete, 1-2-3 will find the records that match your criteria, and request confirmation of your intent to delete by offering two choices: *Cancel* and *Delete*. If you are certain you want to remove these records, select *Delete*. Once you press Return, however, the records will be gone: You get no second chance. If you decide not to delete, choose *Cancel* before pressing Return, to return to the /Data Query menu.

Note: When you delete records from a database, not only do you delete entries, the remainder of the input range moves up to fill the space. This can have unexpected side effects if the cells in the area referred to, or were referenced by, formulas outside the input range. Before deleting records that contain or are referenced by formulas, be certain you know how those formulas will be affected.

You can use the F7 [Query] key with this command, so you can, if you wish, specify one set of criteria, delete the records that match, then change the criteria and press F7 to repeat the /Data Query Delete command with a different set of records.

Reset: 1-2-3 remembers, and saves with the file, the most recent input, criterion, and output ranges you specify when you choose one of the /Data Query commands. The next time you request the same command with the same database, 1-2-3 proposes the ranges you used in the last instance.

If you want to use the proposed responses, press Return to execute the command. If you want to change or modify any of these ranges, then select the *Reset* option to clear 1-2-3's "memory" of your prior choices and to specify new ranges.

Quit: If, during any /Data Query operation, you decide you do not wish to carry out the command, choose the *Quit* option to return to READY mode and begin again.

/Data Regression   /DR

```
Worksheet Range Copy Move File Print Graph Data System Quit
Fill Table Sort Query Distribution Matrix Regression Parse
X-Range Y-Range Output-Range Intercept Reset Go Quit
```

- **Description**

The /Data Regression command is in Release 2 of 1-2-3 only. It enables you to perform multiple regression analysis with 1 to 16 independent variables, each a column containing up to 8192 data values (the maximum number of rows in the worksheet).

/Data Regression

Regression is a statistical method that is used to determine whether two or more variables are interrelated—for example, whether athletic activity is related to job performance, or whether speed limits are related to number of traffic accidents. With regression analysis, a quantitative relationship can be established between (or among) the variables involved. Regression analysis very often is used to predict or estimate the value of one variable corresponding to a given value of another variable.

■ **Procedure**

When you choose the /Data Regression command, 1-2-3 displays the submenu that is shown at the beginning of this entry. To begin, select *X-Range* and enter the range, by address or by name, of the columns containing the data representing the independent variables. As noted earlier, you can include up to 16 independent variables, each with up to 8192 values.

Next, select *Y-Range*, and enter the range containing the column of data representing the dependent variable. This column must contain the same number of rows specified for the X range.

Third, select *Output-Range* and specify the range of cells that will receive the output of the command. The output range is required to be at least nine rows deep and two columns wider than the number of independent variables you selected. You can specify the output range either by name or address, or by entering the address of the cell that will become the top left-hand corner of the output range.

The next menu choice, *Intercept*, offers two choices: *Compute* and *Zero*. Select *Zero* to force the Y intercept to be 0; otherwise, press Return to accept the default, *Compute*.

To carry out the command, select *Go*. 1-2-3 will perform the analysis and display, in the output range:

- *Constant*, the Y intercept.
- *Std Err of Y Est*, the standard error of the estimated Y values.
- *R Squared*.
- *No. of Observations*, the number of values for any of the X or Y variables.
- *Degrees of Freedom*.
- *X Coefficient(s)*, the slope for each of the independent variables.
- *Std Err of Coef.*, the standard error for each of the X coefficients.

/Data Regression · /Data Sort

- **Comments**

    You can produce the estimated Y values by entering the following formula in a range of cells:

    coefficient of X1∗X1+coefficient of X2∗X2+...constant

/Data Sort /DS

```
Worksheet  Range  Copy  Move  File  Print  Graph  Data  System  Quit
Fill  Table  Sort  Query  Distribution  Matrix  Regression  Parse
Data-Range  Primary-Key  Secondary-Key  Reset  Go  Quit
```

- **Description**

    /Data Sort is a command that you use to sort database records or worksheet information, in ascending or descending order, on the field (column) that you specify.

- **Procedure**

    When you choose the /Data Sort command, 1-2-3 displays the menu of command options listed at the beginning of this entry. Before /Data Sort can be carried out, you must select and respond to at least three of these options, as described in the following steps:

    1. When you choose the /Data Sort command, *Data-Range* is highlighted. Press Return, and when 1-2-3 prompts *Enter Data range:*, specify the range of cells you want sorted. Include *all* records, but do not include any field names at the top of a database.

    2. After you enter the data range, 1-2-3 will return to the menu of options. The next step is to select *Primary-Key* from the menu. When 1-2-3 displays the prompt *Enter Primary sort key:*, enter the address of any cell in the field you want sorted.

    3. 1-2-3 will then prompt *Enter Sort order (A or D):*. Select *A* to sort in ascending order, *D* to sort in descending order. (The list at the end of this entry shows you the order in which 1-2-3 sorts.)

    4. When 1-2-3 returns again to the menu of options, specify a *Secondary-Key* if some of your primary entries appear in more than one record and you want to sort these in ascending or descending order on a secondary-key field. 1-2-3 uses this key to break "ties" in the primary-key field.

    5. Select the *Go* option to perform the sort.

6. Select the *Reset* option to cancel the current choices for the data range and the primary and secondary keys. If *Reset* is not used, the sort settings will be stored as part of the worksheet file.
7. Select *Quit* to return to READY mode without performing the sort.

When 1-2-3 carries out the /Data Sort command, it sorts the records in the range you specified, according to the keys and the order you requested.

Note: Once sorted, there is only one way to "unsort" your records and return them to their prior order. You do this by creating a separate index field in the data range *before* you specify the /Data Sort command. The index field need only be a few characters wide; in it, number your records—for example, from 1 to 100 (you can use the /Data Fill **56★** command to do this quickly).

If you take this precaution whenever you think you might want to return the records to their original order, you can easily do so by specifying the numbers in the index field as your primary sort key.

The following two examples show the same set of entries sorted twice. In the first example, the names are sorted in ascending alphabetic order according to department (the primary key); duplicate entries could also be sorted, as mentioned, in alphabetic order, by last name (the secondary key). In the second example, the same entries have been returned to their original order by sorting on the index field.

```
A5: [W3] 10                                                           READY

     A    B          C           D                    E
   ================================================================
   1     Employee Database
   2  ----------------------------------------------------------------
   3
   4      Dept.  Last Name   First Name  Address              Phone
   5      10 ADV  Jaworski    Steve       4025 54th NW         367-1280
   6       7 ADV  Watson      Bill        10245 E. Shelby      882-9716
   7       1 ADV  Williams    Chris       10849 NW 189th       224-6293
```

```
A5: [W3] 1                                                            READY

     A    B          C           D                    E
   ================================================================
   1     Employee Database
   2  ----------------------------------------------------------------
   3
   4      Dept.  Last Name   First Name  Address              Phone
   5       1 ADV   Williams    Chris       10849 NW 189th       224-6293
   6       2 MKT   Tramiel     Jan         317 Woodlawn Rd.     771-1503
   7       3 SALES Dallas      Dave        211 Garfield St.     783-8547
```

/Data Sort

- **Comments**

Although the /Data Sort command is straightforward in both intent and execution, you must be careful when you sort records or worksheet ranges that contain formulas. 1-2-3 will automatically adjust relative cell addresses in sorted formulas when it re-orders your information, but the new cell references will not necessarily be correct.

You do not need to worry if:

- The formula references are absolute. These addresses will remain the same.
- The formula references are relative, *and* they refer to other cells in the same row—all of which are included in the data-sort range. No matter whether these rows are moved up or down on the worksheet, these cell references will maintain the same relative positions.

You do need to consider the effects of sorting if:

- The formula references are relative, *and* they refer to cells in other rows of the data-sort range. Since all rows will probably be moved to new positions, these relative references will most likely not point to the correct record.
- The formula references are relative, and they are in a formula *outside of* the data-sort range. The references in the formula will not be adjusted to reflect the new location of the moved cell.

- **Sort order**

When sorting, 1-2-3 uses the following default system.

On an ascending sort:

- Blank cells.
- Label cells from A to Z (uppercase/lowercase differences are not considered).
- Special characters.
- Numeric cells from 0 to 9.

On a descending sort:

- Numeric cells from 9 to 0.
- Special characters.

- ☐ Label cells from Z to A (uppercase/lowercase differences are not considered).
- ☐ Blank cells.

Using the Install 182★ program, you can move numbers to the beginning of the ascending sort order, or to the end of the descending sort order.

Data table

Any worksheet that contains formulas contains two types of values: input values, which are the constants you enter, and output values, which are the results of your formula calculations. Output values are dependent on input values in one way or another: Either they use input values directly, or they use the results of other calculations that, in turn, depend on input values.

Sometimes, all you may need from a worksheet is a single set of output values, based on a single set of one or more input values. More often, however, you want to perform a "what if" analysis, changing an input value to see the effect of the change on your formula calculations.

You could, of course, change the input value, recalculate the worksheet and, for future reference, save the results to disk or print them. Or, each time you changed the input value, you could recalculate the worksheet and write the results on a piece of paper. Or...you could use a data table and let 1-2-3 tabulate the results for you, on the worksheet itself.

▪ What is a data table?

A data table is a range of cells you set aside in a blank area of your worksheet. In this table, 1-2-3 displays a calculated series of output values that show you the effects of different "what if" situations. Depending on the situation that you want to analyze, you can tell 1-2-3 to substitute a series of input values for either one or two variables used by the formula (or formulas) whose output values you wish to see and compare.

The results of the formula recalculations are recorded in table form on the worksheet, so you can think of a data table as something of a "summary" section of your model that groups the formula values you are interested in and lets you see the results of substituting a list of numbers into your model, one at a time.

Data table

1-2-3 allows you to create two types of data tables, Data Table 1 and Data Table 2. Data Table 1 allows you to specify a list of different input values for one variable; Data Table 2 allows you to specify two lists of different input values for two variables.

Both types of data tables can be used with either a worksheet or with a 1-2-3 database. In the latter case, you can use the database statistical functions (such as @DAVG) to analyze database records according to a list of specified criteria, and let 1-2-3 tabulate the results for you. The uses of data tables with 1-2-3 databases are discussed later in this entry, under the headings "Data Table 1 (or 2) and Database."

- **Data Table 1**

To create a Data Table 1, you need:

☐ One input cell to tell 1-2-3 where the list of values will be substituted, one at a time.

☐ A column (list) of different values for 1-2-3 to use in the input cell.

☐ A row of one or more formulas, or references to formula cells, that operate on the input cell and calculate the output values you wish to see.

When entered, a Data Table 1 looks like this:

Blank	Formulas
Input variables	Results

The input cell can be any cell on the worksheet whose value you want to play "what if" with. It's important to note that this cell's original value is unaffected by the /Data Table command. In the data table itself:

- The column of new input values must form the left-hand column of the table range.
- The row of formulas, or references to formulas, must form the top row of the table range.
- The cell in the top left corner of the table range cannot contain either an input value or a formula, because 1-2-3 ignores this cell in carrying out the /Data Table 1 command. If you wish, you can enter a label in this cell to serve as a title identifying the table contents.

The finished data table forms a matrix in which each calculated value is the result of using the input value to its left, in the formula directly above. The following simple example shows a completed Data Table 1.

```
B9: (C2) [W14] @DDB($B$4,$B$5,$B$6,$B$7)                         READY
```

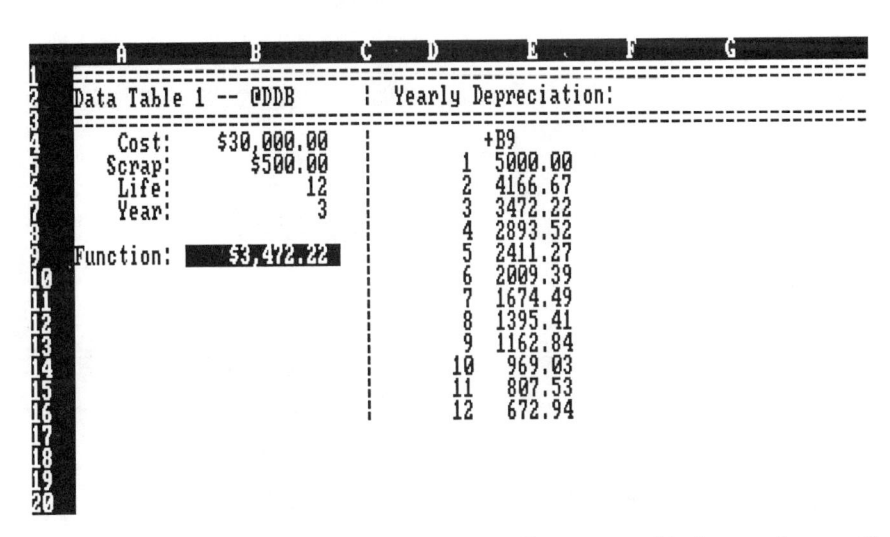

```
         A         B           C       D       E     F      G
 1  ============================================================
 2  Data Table 1 -- @DDB        ¦  Yearly Depreciation:
 3  ============================================================
 4       Cost:   $30,000.00     ¦         +B9
 5      Scrap:      $500.00     ¦     1   5000.00
 6       Life:           12     ¦     2   4166.67
 7       Year:            3     ¦     3   3472.22
 8                              ¦     4   2893.52
 9   Function:    $3,472.22     ¦     5   2411.27
10                              ¦     6   2009.39
11                              ¦     7   1674.49
12                              ¦     8   1395.41
13                              ¦     9   1162.84
14                              ¦    10    969.03
15                              ¦    11    807.53
16                              ¦    12    672.94
17
18
19
20
```

Data Table 1 and databases: Databases are collections of information, rather than models based on calculations, so data tables are used somewhat differently with databases. Instead of performing "what if" analyses, you can use data tables to:

- Analyze database values according to specified criteria.
- Summarize a large database.

Data table

When you use a Data Table 1 to analyze a database, the format of the table is the same as with a worksheet. However, because you are using database statistical functions, you must specify an input range, an offset, and a criterion range in your formulas. (If you are not familiar with these terms, they are explained in detail in the entry Database 44★.)

When you set up the data table:

□ The left-hand column must contain the list of values or labels you are using as criteria in your formulas; they must be typed exactly as they are entered in the database itself. Computed criteria cannot be used in the variable list.

□ The top row must contain the formulas that will calculate values for each of the criteria listed in the left-hand column.

□ The input cell is a blank cell in the criterion range, immediately below the name of the field whose values or labels will be compared against the criteria.

The following diagram illustrates the format of a Data Table 1, when used with a database.

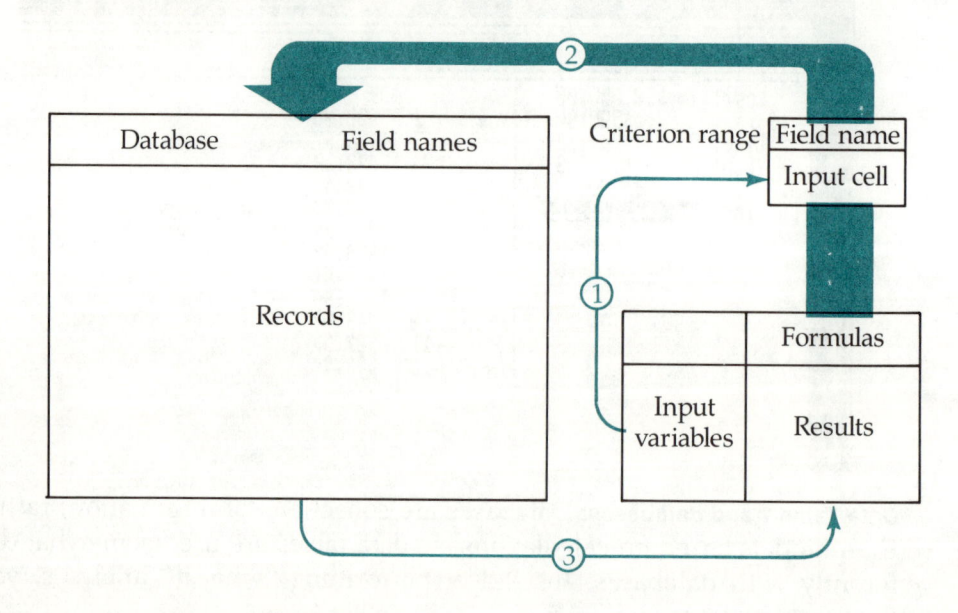

Data table

When the /Data Table 1 command is carried out, each of the values or labels you specify in the left-hand column will become the criterion for which 1-2-3 finds and calculates results according to the formulas in the top row of the table. The following example shows a completed Data Table 1, used to evaluate a simple database.

```
C15: (T) [W17] @DSUM(DB,3,CRIT)                                    EDIT
@DSUM(A3..D12,3,A15..A16)
```

	A	B	C	D	E
1		Test Food Database			
2	==
3		Day	Mouse #	Test Food	Amt. Eaten (oz.)
4		1	1	crunchies	1.00
5		1	2	chunkies	0.75
6		1	3	munchies	0.80
7		2	1	munchies	1.20
8		2	2	crunchies	0.50
9		2	3	chunkies	0.90
10		3	1	chunkies	0.20
11		3	2	munchies	0.60
12		3	3	crunchies	1.10
13					
14					
15	Test Food			@DSUM(DB,3,CRIT)	@DAVG(DB,3,CRIT)
16		crunchies		2.60	0.87
17		chunkies		1.85	0.62
18		munchies		2.60	0.87
19					
20					

■ **Data Table 2**

Data Table 2 is essentially the same as Data Table 1, in approach if not in effect. You use the /Data Table 2 command at times when a formula calculates the results based on two input values, and you want to see the effect of changing both—for example, when you want to see how loan payments vary according to interest rate and term of the loan.

A Data Table 2 differs from a Data Table 1 in the following ways:

☐ The table shows you the results of calculations in *one* formula, not more than one.

☐ The formula must be in the top left-hand corner of the table range—the cell you leave blank in a Data Table 1.

☐ The list of input values for one variable must be placed in the left-hand column of the table, as for Data Table 1, *but* the list of input values for the second variable must be placed in the top row of the table (where your formula or formulas appear in a Data Table 1).

As for Data Table 1, the input cells are *outside* the table range. They must be the addresses of the two variables that are used by the formula you are calculating.

The following diagram shows the format of a Data Table 2.

Formula	Input variables for input cell 2
Input variables for input cell 1	Results

When the formula in the data table is recalculated, 1-2-3 substitutes *pairs* of values for the two variables in the formula. As for Data Table 1, the result is a matrix, but in this case, each calculated value represents the output generated when the variable to its left *and* the variable directly above are both used as input values in the formula.

The following simple example shows the use of Data Table 2.

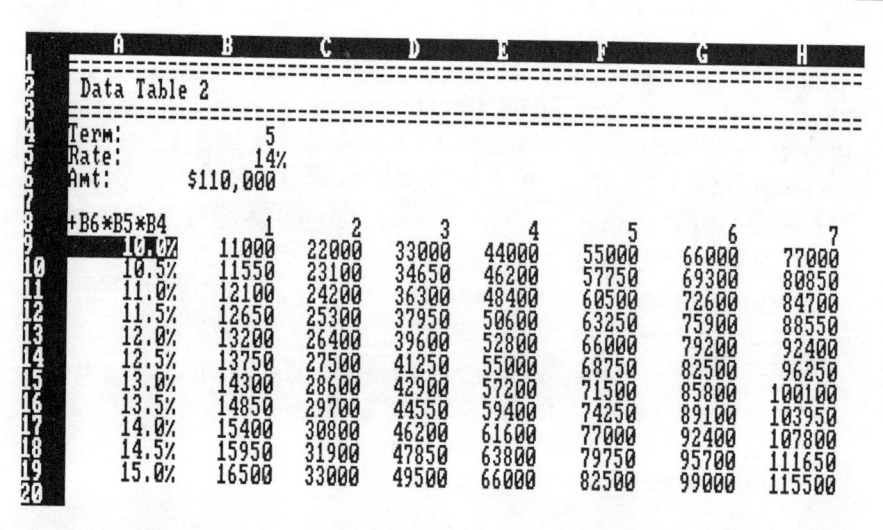

```
A9: (P1) [W10] 0.1                                              READY

         A          B       C       D       E       F       G       H
======================================================================
  1  Data Table 2
  2  ==================================================================
  3
  4  Term:           5
  5  Rate:          14%
  6  Amt:      $110,000
  7
  8  +B6*B5*B4       1       2       3       4       5       6       7
  9       10.0%  11000   22000   33000   44000   55000   66000   77000
 10       10.5%  11550   23100   34650   46200   57750   69300   80850
 11       11.0%  12100   24200   36300   48400   60500   72600   84700
 12       11.5%  12650   25300   37950   50600   63250   75900   88550
 13       12.0%  13200   26400   39600   52800   66000   79200   92400
 14       12.5%  13750   27500   41250   55000   68750   82500   96250
 15       13.0%  14300   28600   42900   57200   71500   85800  100100
 16       13.5%  14850   29700   44550   59400   74250   89100  103950
 17       14.0%  15400   30800   46200   61600   77000   92400  107800
 18       14.5%  15950   31900   47850   63800   79750   95700  111650
 19       15.0%  16500   33000   49500   66000   82500   99000  115500
 20
```

Data Table 2 and databases: Using a Data Table 2 with a database combines the format of a typical two-variable data table with the setup requirements unique to using database statistical functions. As for Data Table 1, this means specifying an input range (the database itself), an offset (the number of the field you want to analyze, counting from the left-hand margin), and a criterion range (the field names of the two variables you wish to change). Computed criteria (for example, +A2>10) cannot be used in the variable lists.

The following diagram shows the format of a Data Table 2, when used with a database.

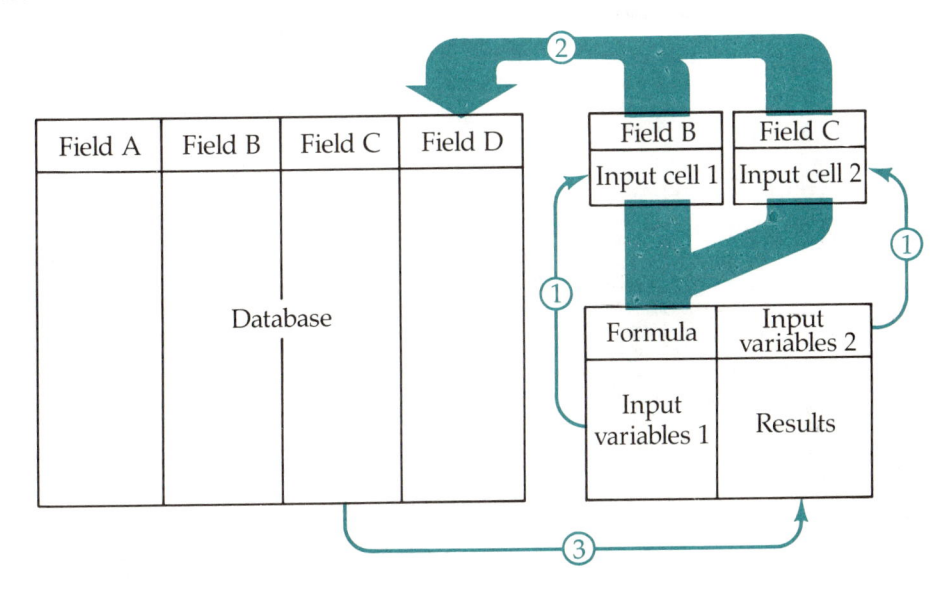

Note that:

- The database formula is in the top left corner cell of the table range.
- One list of value/label criteria, corresponding exactly to those in the database, is entered down the left-hand column of the table. These are the criterion values for input cell 1 (field B in the criterion range).
- A second list of value/label criteria, corresponding exactly to others in the database, is entered across the top row of the table. These are the different values for input cell 2 (field C in the criterion range).

Data table

When the /Data Table 2 command is carried out, 1-2-3 calculates the formula, using *pairs* of values from the top row and the left-hand column of the data table.

The results, as for other data tables, is a matrix in which each formula value is the product of using the criterion to the left *and* the criterion directly above, in the database formula.

A completed data table 2 is shown in the following illustration.

```
E4: (T) [W20] @DSUM(INPUT,2,CRIT)                              EDIT
@DSUM(A4..C19,2,F13..F14)
         A           B        C    D       E          F       G        H
    =================================================================
  1
  2   Widget Inventory
  3  ================================================================
  4       Color     Shape   Qty.      @DSUM(INPUT,2,CRIT) round square triangle
  5         red     round     12              red           49     49       49
  6        blue    square      9              yellow        54     54       54
  7       green  triangle     31              green         70     70       70
  8      yellow  triangle     14              blue          62     62       62
  9        blue    square      6
 10      yellow     round     21
 11         red     round     11
 12      yellow  triangle      9
 13        blue    square     18                     Color    Shape
 14       green    square     25
 15        blue  triangle     21
 16       green    square     14
 17        blue     round      8
 18      yellow     round     10
 19         red    square     26
 20
```

■ **Comment**

For step-by-step instructions, see the entries /Data Table 1 87★ and /Data Table 2 89★.

86

/Data Table 1 /DT1

```
Worksheet Range Copy Move File Print Graph Data System Quit
Fill Table Sort Query Distribution Matrix Regression Parse
1 2 Reset
```

■ **Description**

The /Data Table 1 command creates on your worksheet a table that records the results of recalculating a formula or series of formulas based on different values you want to assign to a variable. In effect, the /Data Table 1 command enables you to see the results of different "what if" situations without having to change the variable, recalculate the worksheet, change the variable to another value, recalculate the worksheet again...and so on. The data table also shows these results in a separate area of the worksheet, without changing any of the existing values in your model, so it is useful when you want to see only certain results, or test certain values without disturbing the remainder of your worksheet. Also, the results of a data table can be quite useful for graphing purposes.

■ **Procedure**

Before you choose the /Data Table 1 command, you must first create the "environment" in which it will operate. This means setting up a table area in a blank part of your worksheet.

When you create the table, bear the following in mind:

- The *top left corner cell* cannot contain either variable values or formulas, because it is ignored during the table calculation. This cell can, however, contain an identifying title if you wish to include one.

- The *input cell* can be any cell on the worksheet that contains the variable you wish to test. It cannot be part of the table itself. The value of this cell is unaffected by the table calculation.

- The *variables* must be the different values you wish to test. They must form the lefthand column of the data table.

- The *formulas* must be the top row of the table. If the formula or formulas you wish to recalculate already exist elsewhere on the worksheet, the formula row can contain the addresses of these formula cells. Formulas must contain the address of the input cell. You can also include values, labels, strings, or other cell addresses if you wish.

/Data Table 1

When you choose the /Data Table command, 1-2-3 first presents a menu of choices: *1*, *2*, and *Reset*. *1* selects /Data Table 1. (*2* selects /Data Table 2. For information on the differences, see Data Table **79★** and /Data Table 2 **89★**.)

Once you select /Data Table 1, 1-2-3 prompts *Enter Table range:*. Include the entire table in this range—everything from the blank cell in the top left corner to the row and column where the rightmost formula and the bottommost variable intersect.

1-2-3 next prompts *Enter Input cell 1:*. Here, you can either type the address of the input cell, or move the cell pointer to it.

When you press Return, 1-2-3 calculates the formulas in the first row of the data table, substituting, in turn, each of the values in the left-hand column for the variable you specified as the input cell. The resulting table is a matrix in which each calculated value represents using the variable to its left in the formula directly above.

▪ Using a database

As described in the extended entry Data Table, you can create a data table with a database, instead of with a worksheet. In this case, the top row of the data table must contain database statistical functions, rather than worksheet formulas, because you will be sorting and calculating information from specified *fields* of your database.

Thus, although the layout remains the same as for a worksheet, a database Data Table 1 differs from one for a worksheet in the following ways:

☐ You must specify an input range (the entire database), an offset (the column in which you are interested), and a criterion range (your selection parameters) in your formulas. (These are described in detail in the entry Database **44★**).

☐ You must create or use a pre-existing criterion range outside of the table; this consists of the database field name you wish to test, immediately *above* the blank cell that you will specify as the input cell for your data table.

☐ The left-hand column of the data table must contain some or all of the entries listed in the database under the field name you specify as your criterion. They must be entered in the data table *exactly* as they appear in the database. Formulas or computed criteria are not allowed.

When 1-2-3 carries out the /Data Table 1 command, it takes each entry from the left-hand column of the data table, places it in the input cell, and searches the database for all occurrences of that entry. It then takes the corresponding values from the offset (column) you specified in your formula, and uses them in calculating the formula in the top row of the data table. The result is then placed in the data table, in the cell beneath the formula and to the right of the criterion.

■ Comments

When you use a data table, 1-2-3 calculates the results of using each of the variables in the left-hand column of the table. It does not, however, automatically recalculate the table every time you change one of the variables or formulas. If you do make changes to your data table and wish to recalculate it, press the F8 [Table] 144♦ key when in the READY mode 249♦.

If you wish to start over, use the *Reset* option of the /Data Table command to cancel the table range and input cell. Or, use the /Range Erase 299★ command to eliminate the table entirely. If *Reset* is not used, the /Data Table settings are saved on disk with the worksheet.

/Data Table 2   /DT2

```
Worksheet Range Copy Move File Print Graph DATA System Quit
Fill  TABLE  Sort Query Distribution Matrix Regression Parse
1  2  Reset
```

■ Description

Like the /Data Table 1 87★ command, the /Data Table 2 command enables you to create, on your worksheet, a table that records the results of recalculations in a "what if" situation. With a Data Table 2, you can change values for two variables, to see how these changes affect the results of a worksheet formula. Like /Data Table 1, the /Data Table 2 command lets you see and compare the results of changing variables without having to make the changes, recalculate the worksheet, make other changes, recalculate again, and so on.

/Data Table 2

■ **Procedure**

You must create the data table on a blank area of your worksheet before you choose the /Data Table 2 command.

When you create the table, remember that:

☐ You must have two *input cells* on the worksheet—outside the table range—that will contain the variables you want to test.

☐ You must enter the values for *one input cell* down the left-hand column of the data table, directly below the cell that contains the formula you wish to recalculate.

☐ You must enter the values for *the second input cell* across the top row of the data table, to the right of the cell that contains the formula you wish to recalculate.

☐ The *top left corner cell* of the table must contain a formula that references the two input cells. The formula can contain strings, values, labels, and cell addresses, as long as it contains the addresses of the two input cells.

When you choose the /Data Table command, 1-2-3 first presents a menu of choices: *1, 2,* and *Reset.* Select *2* to create the two-input data table.

1-2-3 then prompts you to *Enter Table range:*. Specify the area you have set aside for the data table, including all cells from the upper left (formula) cell to the bottom right—the cell at which the bottom-most row of values for the first variable intersects the rightmost column of values for the second.

You will then be prompted sequentially to enter the addresses of input cell 1 and input cell 2. Type the addresses, or point to the appropriate cells, then press Return.

1-2-3 will carry out the /Data Table 2 command. To recalculate the formula in the upper left corner of the data table, it will substitute *pairs* of variables from the left-hand column and the top row for the input cell addresses in the formula. It will then display the results, placing each new value in one cell of the table, to the right of and below the corresponding variables.

/Data Table 2

- **Using a database**

  As described in the extended entry Data Table 79★, you can create a data table with a database, instead of with a worksheet. In this case, however, your formula must use the database statistical functions, rather than worksheet formulas, because you will be analyzing specified *fields* of your database, according to the criteria you define.

  The layout of a database Data Table 2 thus remains the same as that for a worksheet, but its contents differ in the following ways:

  ☐ You must specify an input range (the entire database), an offset (the column you are interested in), and a criterion range (your selection parameters) in your formula. (These terms are described in detail in the entry Database 44★.)

  ☐ You must create or use a pre-existing criterion range outside of the table; this consists of the database field names you wish to test, immediately *above* the blank cells that become your input cells 1 and 2.

  ☐ The left-hand column of the data table must contain some or all of the labels or values listed in the database under the field name you specify as your first criterion. They must be entered in the data table *exactly* as they appear in the database.

  ☐ The top row of the data table must contain some or all of the labels or values listed in the database under the field name you specify as your second criterion. They must be entered in the data table *exactly* as they appear in the database.

  ☐ Formulas or computed criteria are not allowed.

  When 1-2-3 carries out the /Data Table 2 command, it will take pairs of variables from the left-hand column and the top row of the data table, search the specified database fields for records that match both, find the offset entry or entries for those records, and then perform the calculation specified in your formula. Finally, 1-2-3 will place the calculated result in the data table, to the right of and below its corresponding variables.

/Data Table 2 · @DATE()

■ **Comments**

Once you have created a data table, 1-2-3 does not automatically recalculate its values if you change any of the variables or formulas. To update a modified data table, press the F8 [Table] key **144♦** when the mode **248★** indicator says READY. 1-2-3 will recalculate the table, using the last specified table range and input cells.

To cancel the definition of a data table, choose the *Reset* option of the /Data Table command. To eliminate a data table completely, use the /Range Erase **299★** command. If the *Reset* option is not used, data table settings will be stored on disk with the worksheet.

@DATE()

■ **Format**

@DATE(year,month,day)

■ **Description**

The @DATE function converts the date entered in the argument into a five-digit serial number, which is a value that can be formatted to a standard date appearance with the /Range Format **300★** command and can be used in other formulas—for example, sorting according to date parameters.

■ **Procedure**

The @DATE function requires three numeric values, which can be entered as numbers, cell names or addresses, or formulas:

☐ Year, which can be any number between 0 (for the year 1900) and 199 (for the year 2099).

☐ Month, which can be any number between 1 (January) and 12 (December).

☐ Day, which can be any number between 1 and 31, as long as it is valid for the month in which it occurs—for example, 30 would not be valid for February, 31 would not be valid for June.

If any of these three numbers is invalid, the function returns the value ERR. Thus:

@DATE(81,3,30)

returns the serial number 29665. But:

@DATE(81,2,30)

returns the value ERR, because there were not 30 days in February 1981 (or any other year).

- **Example**

The @DATE function can be used when you want to subtract one date from another, to determine the number of days elapsed. In the following worksheet, @DATE has been used to enter the serial numbers for August 26, 1986 and December 25, 1986 in cells B4 and B5. The formula in B6 subtracts B4 from B5 to give the number of days between the two dates:

```
B4: (D1) [W20] @DATE(86,8,26)                                READY

            A                      B           C
   ============================================
 1
 2 Contract #66342B
 3 ============================================
 4       First day of contract period:    26-Aug-86
 5       Last day of contract period:     25-Dec-86
 6  Number of days in contract period:          121
 7
```

Date-related analyses

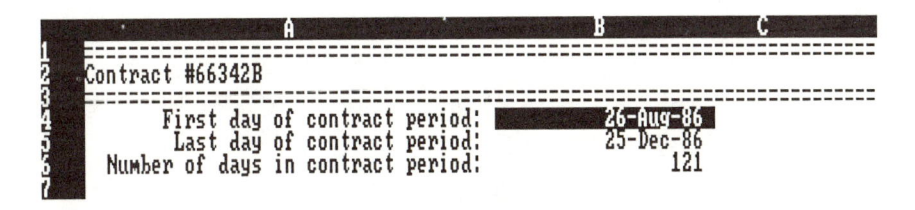

1-2-3's date functions can be used to perform date-related analyses, or calendar arithmetic. These analyses are performed by converting numeric values to five-digit serial numbers. In Release 2 of 1-2-3, the function @DATEVALUE 96★ also enables you to translate text strings or labels that specify a date into corresponding serial numbers.

- **Serial numbers**

The serial numbers that are used in date calculations span the years between January 1, 1900 and December 31, 2099. The beginning value is 1, the highest is 73050. Although serial numbers may, at first glance, seem like confusing arrays of digits, it is not necessary for you to know that 31048 is the serial number for January 1, 1985. The real value of serial numbers is that they can be added, subtracted, sorted, and otherwise analyzed.

To *display* serial numbers as recognizable dates, you can use the /Range Format Date command. To *convert* serial numbers into calendar dates, or calendar dates into serial numbers, you can use 1-2-3's date functions.

■ The date functions

Both Release 1a and Release 2 of 1-2-3 provide the following date functions:

- ☐ @DATE **92★**, which returns the serial number for a date entered as three numeric values—year, month, and day.
- ☐ @DAY **98★**, which returns the day number (1 to 31) of the date represented by a serial number.
- ☐ @MONTH **250★**, which returns the month (1 to 12) of the date represented by a serial number.
- ☐ @YEAR **382★**, which returns the year (0 for 1900 to 199 for 2099) of the date represented by a serial number.

In addition, Release 1a has the function @TODAY, which returns the serial number for the date you enter when you start your computer. With Release 2, the comparable function is @NOW, which returns the current time in addition to the current date. The serial number in this instance is a decimal fraction, in which the integer portion is the date, and the fraction is the time.

Note: When loaded into Release 2, any existing @TODAY functions in a Release 1a file will automatically be replaced with @NOW.

In Release 2 only, there is also the @DATEVALUE function mentioned earlier, which enables you to convert date strings to serial numbers.

■ Date calculations

There are many different ways that serial numbers and date functions can be used in worksheets. They can, for example, be used to generate appointment calendars or "tickler" files. Or they can be used with logical functions, such as @IF—perhaps to return the message *Account overdue* if today's date minus the date of last payment is greater than 30.

The @NOW (or @TODAY) function is particularly useful in date calculations based on the current date. Any cell in which it is entered can be formatted to *display* the date serial number in any of the forms acceptable to 1-2-3 (for a table of these formats, refer to the entry @CELL **18★** or the entry /Range Format Date **302♦**). You will thus never need to concern yourself with the serial number itself, but 1-2-3 will automatically update the function cell with today's date (and time in Release 2, if you choose) whenever you recalculate the worksheet. Furthermore, if you need to use the date in any calculations, 1-2-3 will be able to use the serial number in "calendar arithmetic."

Date-related analyses

Examples: The following examples illustrate two ways in which you might find date-related analyses useful. The first shows a way to generate a daily calendar with the @NOW function and the /Copy command. The second shows a bond calculation.

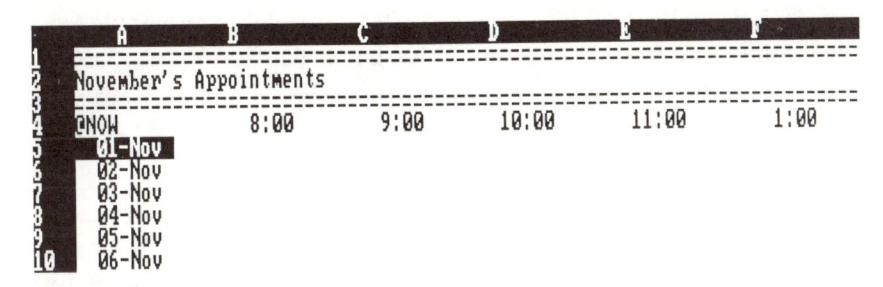

```
A5: (D2) +A4+1                                                    READY
```

```
        A           B           C           D           E           F
   ==========================================================================
 1
 2   November's Appointments
 3  ==========================================================================
 4  @NOW            8:00        9:00       10:00       11:00        1:00
 5  01-Nov
 6  02-Nov
 7  03-Nov
 8  04-Nov
 9  05-Nov
10  06-Nov
```

Note: To create the preceding calendar, you would enter @NOW in cell A4 and copy the formula in A5 down the column. To avoid having the @NOW function change the date in A4 each time you load the file, convert the @NOW function from a formula to a value. To do this, first you highlight the cell with the pointer, press the F2 [Edit] 144♦ key, then press the F9 [Calc] 144♦ key and press Return.

```
B13: [W13] ((1+R/M)-(P+(A/E)*(R/M)))*(M*E/DSM)/(P+(A/E)*(R/M))     READY
```

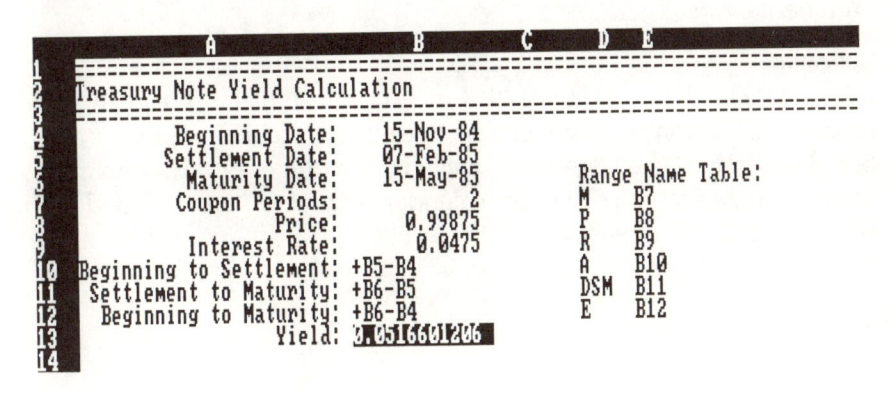

```
          A                B           C           D        E
   ==========================================================================
 1
 2   Treasury Note Yield Calculation
 3  ==========================================================================
 4          Beginning Date:  15-Nov-84
 5         Settlement Date:  07-Feb-85
 6           Maturity Date:  15-May-85             Range Name Table:
 7          Coupon Periods:          2             M       B7
 8                   Price:    0.99875             P       B8
 9           Interest Rate:     0.0475             R       B9
10   Beginning to Settlement: +B5-B4               A       B10
11    Settlement to Maturity: +B6-B5               DSM     B11
12    Beginning to Maturity:  +B6-B4               E       B12
13                    Yield:  0.0516601206
14
```

95

@DATEVALUE()   A Release 2 date function

- **Format**
@DATEVALUE(date string)

- **Description**
The @DATEVALUE function translates a text string into a five-digit date serial number that can be used in formulas. @DATEVALUE is comparable to @DATE in returning a date value between 1 (for January 1, 1900) and 73050 (for December 31, 2099). It differs, however, in using a character string instead of numeric values as the basis of its calculations.

- **Procedure**
The date string required as the argument to the @DATEVALUE function must be in one of 1-2-3's date formats, D1 to D5, each of which is a different way of presenting the year, month, and day (not all are included in some formats). For example, the date December 25, 1986 is represented as 25-Dec-86 in D1 format, 25-Dec in D2 format, and Dec-86 in D3 format (complete tables can be found in the entries @CELL 18★ and /Range Format 300★). If the year is not displayed in a date format, it is assumed to be the current year; if the day is not displayed, it is assumed to be the first day of the month.

The date string can be entered in the argument, enclosed in double quotation marks, or it can be a cell reference. Thus, @DATEVALUE("25-Dec-86"), @DATEVALUE(A1), and @DATEVALUE(Christmas) would all be appropriate arguments.

- **Comments**
Like @DATE, the @DATEVALUE function is useful in converting calendar dates to serial numbers that can be used in calculations. For example, number of days since the last visit to a client, or number of days remaining on a project. Some examples of such "calendar arithmetic" are included in the entry Date-Related Analyses 93★.

@DAVG()

- **Format**

    @DAVG(input range,offset,criterion)

- **Description**

    @DAVG is a statistical function **146♦** that calculates the average (mean) of selected values in a database. @DAVG is the database equivalent of @AVG, but is more selective because it processes values within a specified field, and only for records that match the criteria you establish.

- **Procedure**

    Like the other database statistical functions, @DAVG requires three arguments: an input range, an offset, and a criterion range.

    □ The input range is the database to be evaluated. It must include the field names in the first row of the database, and can be specified as either a cell range or a range name.

    □ The offset is the field (column) to be evaluated for the records specified by the criterion range. The offset is a number from 0, which is the leftmost column, to n, the rightmost column of the database.

    □ The criterion range establishes the conditions under which records from the input range will be selected for processing. A criterion range must be a range of cells in which the top row contains the field name(s) exactly as spelled in the database and the row or rows below contain the criteria for evaluation. The criterion range can be specified as a range name or the two corner addresses of a range.

    Note: Input ranges, offsets, and criterion ranges are also discussed in the entries titled Functions **145★**, Database **44★**, and /Data Query **65★**. Refer to those entries for more details. You can also see an example of their use in the formula and illustration on the next page.

@DAVG() · @DAY()

■ **Example**

In the following example, @DAVG is used with a Personnel database to find the average monthly salary of employees in the Accounting department of a small company.

```
B17: (C2) [W13] @DAVG(A4..D14,3,A17..A18)                           READY
```

```
            A                    B           C              D
 1  ===========================================================
 2  Personnel Database
 3  ===========================================================
 4  Name                       SSN        Department      Salary
 5  Smothers, Tom           386558833       shipping    $22,000.00
 6  Wellington, George      376524251     accounting    $27,994.00
 7  Smithfield, Sue         293832302          admin    $26,888.00
 8  Robinson, Glenda        142990957       shipping    $19,982.00
 9  Westerhaus, Arnie       385558857          sales    $29,976.00
10  Flakburton, Frank       376558863       shipping    $17,970.00
11  Bauman, Eddie           387562109     accounting    $39,994.00
12  Mains, Clair            222489672          admin    $26,888.00
13  Featherstrom, Joyce     243176543     accounting    $31,982.00
14  Nostrum, Pat            425897761          admin    $29,976.00
15
16       Criterion Range:    Function:
17           Department       ██████████  = Average Salary in Accounting
18           accounting
19
20
```

■ **Comments**

Although it is a database function, @DAVG works not only with a database, but with a worksheet as well. As long as the arguments are entered correctly and the criterion range does not exceed 32 columns, @DAVG makes no distinction between a worksheet and a database.

@DAY()

■ **Format**

@DAY(date)

■ **Description**

The @DAY function returns the day number of a date specified as a five-digit serial number that is the number of days elapsed since December 31, 1899, where 00001 is January 1, 1900. The highest possible serial number is 73050, for December 31, 2099.

Procedure

The value returned by @DAY is a number between 1 and 31. The argument can be the serial number of a given date, or it can be a reference to a cell containing the serial number.

To generate the appropriate serial number, you can use:

- ☐ @DATE 92★ to convert numeric values that represent a date.
- ☐ @DATEVALUE 96★ to convert a character string (Release 2 only).
- ☐ @NOW 258★ to convert the date you entered when you started your computer (the equivalent of @NOW in Release 1a is @TODAY).

Example

1-2-3's date functions are useful when you want to perform "calendar arithmetic" (see the entry Date-Related Analyses 93★). Several date functions can be combined in a single formula. For example:

@DATE(@YEAR(@NOW)−1,@MONTH(@NOW)+1,@DAY(@NOW))

would return the serial number for one month from today, last year. If the function cell were formatted to a standard appearance (with the /Range Format 300★ command), the serial number would be displayed in the date format specified by the command.

@DCOUNT()

Format

@DCOUNT(input range,offset,criterion range)

Description

@DCOUNT is the database equivalent of the statistical function @COUNT 42★, which counts the number of items in a list. @DCOUNT performs the same operation, but counts the number of non-blank cells in a specified field (column) and in records that match a given criterion or set of criteria.

Procedure

@DCOUNT requires three arguments: an input range, an offset, and a criterion range.

- ☐ The input range is the database to be evaluated. It must include the field names in the first row of the database, and can be specified as either a cell range or a range name.

@DCOUNT()

- The offset is the field (column) to be evaluated for the records specified by the criterion range. The offset is a number from 0, which is the leftmost column, to n, the rightmost column of the database.
- The criterion range establishes the conditions under which records from the input range will be selected for processing. A criterion range must be a range of cells in which the top row contains the field name(s) exactly as spelled in the database and the row or rows below contain the criteria for evaluation. The criterion range can be specified as a range name or the two corner addresses of a range.

Note: Input ranges, offsets, and criterion ranges are also discussed in the entries titled Functions **145★**, Database **44★**, and /Data Query **65★**. Refer to those entries for more details.

■ Example

This example presents a small database of employee attendance records. The @DCOUNT function finds the number of people in the shipping department whose records show less than five days of absence due to illness.

```
D17: [W12] @DCOUNT(A4..G14,4,A17..B18)                           READY

          A                   B           C            D         E    F
    ====================================================================
  1 
  2  Personnel Database
  3 ====================================================================
  4  Name                    SSN      Department    Salary     Vac. Sick Days
  5  Smothers, Tom        386558833     shipping   $22,000.00   10    3
  6  Wellington, George   376524251   accounting   $27,994.00   10    2
  7  Smithfield, Sue      293832302        admin   $26,888.00    5    7
  8  Robinson, Glenda     142990957     shipping   $19,982.00    6    0
  9  Westerhaus, Arnie    385558857        sales   $29,976.00   10    1
 10  Flakburton, Frank    376558863     shipping   $17,970.00    4    6
 11  Bauman, Eddie        387562109   accounting   $39,994.00    7    2
 12  Mains, Clair         222489672        admin   $26,888.00   22    0
 13  Featherstrom, Joyce  243176543   accounting   $31,982.00   12    3
 14  Nostrum, Pat         425897761        admin   $29,976.00    9    1
 15
 16  Criterion Range:                             Function:
 17  Sick Days            Department                        2
 18  +F5<5                shipping
 19
 20
```

- **Comments**

Although it is a database command, @DCOUNT works not only with a database, but with a worksheet as well. As long as the arguments are entered correctly and the criterion range does not exceed 32 columns, @DCOUNT makes no distinction between a worksheet and a database.

@DDB()   A Release 2 financial function

- **Format**

@DDB(cost,salvage,life,period)

- **Description**

The @DDB function is one of three functions in Release 2 of 1-2-3 that calculate the depreciation of an asset. @DDB uses the double-declining balance method; the other functions, @SLN **327★** and @SYD **336★**, calculate straight-line and sum-of-the-years' digits depreciation, respectively.

With the double-declining balance method, the depreciation allowance for each year is a constant percent of the undepreciated balance (book value) of the asset. Since the book value decreases each year, the depreciation allowance is greatest at first and becomes progressively smaller later on. The depreciation calculation continues until book value of the asset equals the salvage value.

1-2-3 uses the following formula to calculate depreciation by the double-declining balance method:

$$(book\ value * 2)/n$$

where: book value for any given period is equal to the total asset minus the sum of previous depreciation; n is the life of the asset.

- **Procedure**

The arguments to the @DDB function are values, which can be entered either as numbers or as references to cells containing the values. The cost of the asset is its original price; the salvage value is the amount the asset will be worth at the end of its useful life; the life of the asset is the number of periods until the asset is depreciated to salvage value; the period is the particular period whose depreciation allowance is to be calculated.

@DDB() · @DMAX()

■ **Comments**

Release 1a of 1-2-3 does not have an @DDB function. The following illustration shows the steps that would be used in calculating depreciation with the double-declining balance method.

```
B18: (C2) [W14] @DDB(B13,B14,B15,B16)                                    READY

       A           B              C                D
  1  =====================================================================
  2  Double Declining Balance Calculation
  3  =====================================================================
  4       Cost:    $20,000.00
  5       Year 1    $5,000.00  +$B$4*(2/8)
  6       Year 2    $3,750.00  ($B$4-@SUM($B$5..$B5))*2/8
  7       Year 3    $2,812.50  ($B$4-@SUM($B$5..$B6))*2/8
  8       Year 4    $2,109.38  ($B$4-@SUM($B$5..$B7))*2/8
  9
 10  ---------------------------------------------------------------------
 11  Release 2 -- @DDB
 12  ---------------------------------------------------------------------
 13       Cost:    $20,000.00
 14       Scrap:          400
 15       Life:             8
 16       Year:             3
 17
 18   Function:    $2,812.50
 19
 20
```

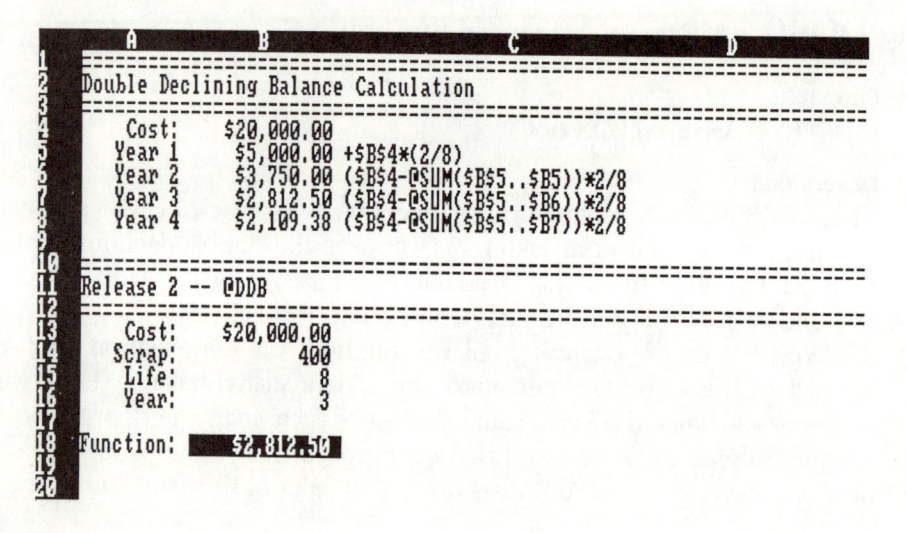

@DMAX()

■ **Format**

@DMAX(input range,offset,criterion range)

■ **Description**

@DMAX is a statistical function 146♦ that returns the maximum (largest) of selected values in a single field (column) of a database. @DMAX is the database equivalent of @MAX, but processes values within a specified field, and only for records that match the criteria you establish.

■ **Procedure**

@DMAX requires these three arguments: an input range, an offset, and a criterion range.

  □ The input range is the database to be evaluated. It must include the field names in the first row of the database, and can be specified as either a cell range or a range name.

102

@DMAX()

- The offset is the field (column) to be evaluated for the records specified by the criterion range. The offset is a number from 0, which is the leftmost column, to n, the rightmost column of the database.
- The criterion range establishes the conditions under which records from the input range will be selected for processing. A criterion range must be a range of cells in which the top row contains the field name(s) exactly as spelled in the database and the row or rows below contain the criteria for evaluation. The criterion range can be specified as a range name or the two corner addresses of a range.

Note: Input ranges, offsets, and criterion ranges are also discussed in the entries titled Functions **145★**, Database **44★**, and /Data Query **65★**. Refer to those entries for more details.

■ **Example**

The following example uses @DMAX to find the highest daily sale in a specified time period. The input range is a database named Jan_Sales.

```
D9: (C2) [W28] @DMAX(JAN_SALES,1,D5..D6)                        READY
```

	A	B	C	D
1	Sales for January 1986			
2	==			
3	Date	Amount		
4	20-Jan	$13,625.29		
5	23-Jan	$25,019.00		Criterion Range:
6	17-Jan	$11,626.75		Date
7	29-Jan	$20,441.37		@DAY(A5)>20#AND#@DAY(A4)<29
8	27-Jan	$11,254.75		
9	31-Jan	$3,546.00		Function:
10	16-Jan	$10,000.00		$36,990.75
11	24-Jan	$10,825.25		
12	19-Jan	$5,537.75		Explanation:
13	21-Jan	$25,377.50		
14	28-Jan	$36,990.75		Find the largest sale
15	25-Jan	$8,550.66		between the 20th and the 29th
16	22-Jan	$15,169.50		
17	18-Jan	$19,681.15		
18	30-Jan	$14,168.17		
19	15-Jan	$10,179.25		
20	26-Jan	$7,267.41		

■ **Comments**

Although it is a database command, @DMAX works not only with a database, but with a worksheet as well. As long as the arguments are entered correctly and the criterion range does not include more than 32 columns, @DMAX makes no distinction between a worksheet and a database.

@DMIN()

@DMIN()

- **Format**

  @DMIN(input range,offset,criterion range)

- **Description**

  @DMIN is a statistical function 146♦ that returns the minimum (smallest) of selected values in a database. @DMIN is the database equivalent of @MIN, but is more specific because it allows you to set conditions, so that only certain values are selected for processing.

- **Procedure**

  @DMIN requires these three arguments: an input range, an offset, and a criterion range.

  □ The input range is the database to be evaluated. It must include the field names in the first row of the database, and can be specified as either a cell range or a range name.

  □ The offset is the field (column) to be evaluated for the records specified by the criterion range. The offset is a number from 0, which is the leftmost column, to n, the rightmost column of the database.

  □ The criterion range establishes the conditions under which records from the input range will be selected for processing. A criterion range must be a range of cells in which the top row contains the field name(s) exactly as spelled in the database and the row or rows below contain the criteria for evaluation. The criterion range can be specified as a range name or the two corner addresses of a range.

  Note: Input ranges, offsets, and criterion ranges are also discussed in the entries titled Functions 145★, Database 44★, and /Data Query 65★. Refer to those entries for more details.

- **Example**

  The following example uses @DMIN to determine the lowest daily sale in a specified time period. The input range is a database named Jan_Sales.

@DMIN() · @DSTD()

```
D9: (C2) [W28] @DMIN(JAN_SALES,1,D5..D6)                      READY
```

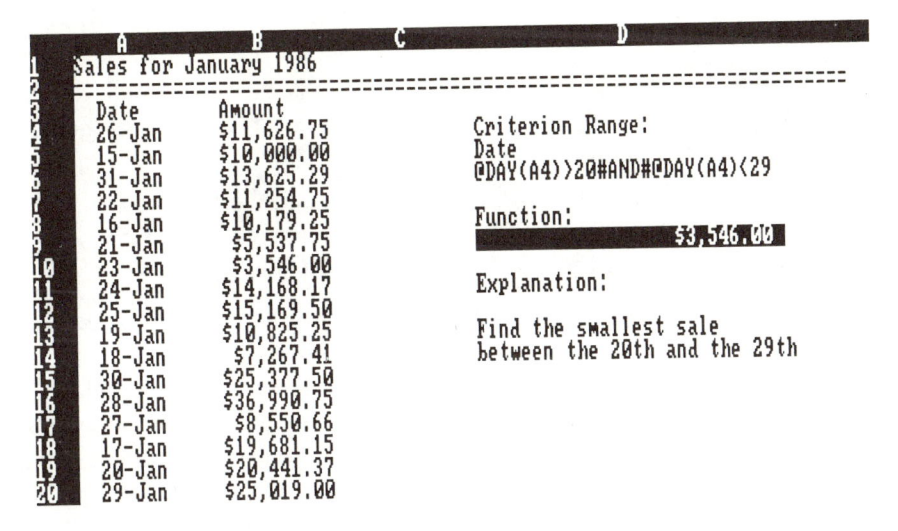

```
        A          B           C                D
  1  Sales for January 1986
  2  ================================================================
  3     Date       Amount
  4    26-Jan     $11,626.75        Criterion Range:
  5    15-Jan     $10,000.00        Date
  6    31-Jan     $13,625.29        @DAY(A4)>20#AND#@DAY(A4)<29
  7    22-Jan     $11,254.75
  8    16-Jan     $10,179.25        Function:
  9    21-Jan      $5,537.75                      $3,546.00
 10    23-Jan      $3,546.00
 11    24-Jan     $14,168.17        Explanation:
 12    25-Jan     $15,169.50
 13    19-Jan     $10,825.25        Find the smallest sale
 14    18-Jan      $7,267.41        between the 20th and the 29th
 15    30-Jan     $25,377.50
 16    28-Jan     $36,990.75
 17    27-Jan      $8,550.66
 18    17-Jan     $19,681.15
 19    20-Jan     $20,441.37
 20    29-Jan     $25,019.00
```

- **Comments**

  Although it is a database command, @DMIN works not only with a database, but with a worksheet as well. As long as the arguments are entered correctly and the criterion range does not exceed 32 columns, @DMIN makes no distinction between a worksheet and a database.

@DSTD()

- **Format**

  @DSTD(input range,offset,criterion range)

- **Description**

  @DSTD is a statistical function 146♦ that returns the population standard deviation of selected values in a single field (column) of a database. @DSTD is the database equivalent of @STD, but allows you to set the conditions under which values are to be chosen for processing.

@DSTD()

- **Procedure**

  @DSTD requires these three arguments: an input range, an offset, and a criterion range.

  □ The input range is the database to be evaluated. It must include the field names in the first row of the database, and can be specified as either a cell range or a range name.

  □ The offset is the field (column) to be evaluated for the records specified by the criterion range. The offset is a number from 0, which is the leftmost column, to n, the rightmost column of the database.

  □ The criterion range establishes the conditions under which records from the input range will be selected for processing. A criterion range must be a range of cells in which the top row contains the field name(s) exactly as spelled in the database and the row or rows below contain the criteria for evaluation. The criterion range can be specified as a range name or the two corner addresses of a range.

  Note: Input ranges, offsets, and criterion ranges are also discussed in the entries titled Functions **145**★, Database **44**★, and /Data Query **65**★. Refer to those entries for more details.

  Even though it uses selected samples from a database, @DSTD calculates a *population* standard deviation, and not a *sample* standard deviation. For the latter, use the following formula (for brevity, input range=i; offset=o; criterion range=c):

  @SQRT(@DCOUNT(i,o,c)/@DCOUNT(i,o,c)−1)) ∗ @DSTD(i,o,c)

- **Comments**

  Although it is a database command, @DSTD works not only with a database, but with a worksheet as well. As long as the arguments are entered correctly and the criterion range does not exceed 32 columns, @STD makes no distinction between a worksheet and a database.

@DSUM()

■ **Format**

@DSUM(input range,offset,criterion range)

■ **Description**

@DSUM is a database statistical function 146♦ that returns the sum of selected values in a specified field (column) of a database. The @DSUM function is the database equivalent of the @SUM 335★ function, and operates in the same way, but allows you to set conditions under which values are selected for processing.

■ **Procedure**

@DSUM requires these three arguments: an input range, an offset, and a criterion range.

- ☐ The input range is the database to be evaluated. It must include the field names in the first row of the database, and can be specified as either a cell range or a range name.

- ☐ The offset is the field (column) to be evaluated for the records specified by the criterion range. The offset is a number from 0, which is the leftmost column, to n, the rightmost column of the database.

- ☐ The criterion range establishes the conditions under which records from the input range will be selected for processing. A criterion range must be a range of cells in which the top row contains the field name(s) exactly as spelled in the database and the row or rows below contain the criteria for evaluation. The criterion range can be specified as a range name or the two corner addresses of a range.

Note: Input ranges, offsets, and criterion ranges are also discussed in the entries titled Functions 145★, Database 44★, and /Data Query 65★. Refer to those entries for more details. You can also see an example of their use in the formula and illustration on the next page.

@DSUM() · @DVAR()

- **Example**

In the following example, @DSUM is used to find the sum of all salaries in column 3 (offset) of a Personnel database (input range) in which Department is Accounting (criterion).

```
B17: (C2) [W13] @DSUM(A4..D14,3,A17..A18)                          READY
```

```
         A                    B           C             D
1  ================================================================
2  Personnel Database
3  ================================================================
4  Name                      SSN      Department      Salary
5  Smothers, Tom          386558833    shipping      $22,000.00
6  Wellington, George     376524251    accounting    $27,994.00
7  Smithfield, Sue        293832302    admin         $26,888.00
8  Robinson, Glenda       142990957    shipping      $19,982.00
9  Westerhaus, Arnie      385558857    sales         $29,976.00
10 Flakburton, Frank      376558863    shipping      $17,970.00
11 Bauman, Eddie          387562109    accounting    $39,994.00
12 Mains, Clair           222489672    admin         $26,888.00
13 Featherstrom, Joyce    243176543    accounting    $31,982.00
14 Nostrum, Pat           425897761    admin         $29,976.00
15
16    Criterion Range:          Function:
17       Department             $99,970.00  = Total Accounting Payroll
18       accounting
19
20
```

- **Comments**

Although it is a database command, @DSUM works not only with a database, but with a worksheet as well. As long as the arguments are entered correctly and the criterion range does not exceed 32 columns, @DSUM makes no distinction between a worksheet and a database.

@DVAR()

- **Format**

@DVAR(input range,offset,criterion range)

- **Description**

@DVAR is a statistical function 146◆ that returns the population variance (square of the standard deviation) of selected values in a single field (column) of a database. @DVAR is the database equivalent of @VAR. It operates in the same way as @VAR, but allows you to set the conditions under which values are chosen for processing.

■ Procedure

@DVAR requires these three arguments: an input range, an offset, and a criterion range.

- ☐ The input range is the database to be evaluated. It must include the field names in the first row of the database, and can be specified as either a cell range or a range name.
- ☐ The offset is the field (column) to be evaluated for the records specified by the criterion range. The offset is a number from 0, which is the leftmost column, to n, the rightmost column of the database.
- ☐ The criterion range establishes the conditions under which records from the input range will be selected for processing. A criterion range must be a range of cells in which the top row contains the field name(s) exactly as spelled in the database and the row or rows below contain the criteria for evaluation. The criterion range can be specified as a range name or the two corner addresses of a range.

Note: Input ranges, offsets, and criterion ranges are also discussed in the entries titled Functions **145★**, Database **44★**, and /Data Query **65★**. Refer to those entries for more details.

@DVAR uses selected samples from a database, but nonetheless calculates a *population* variance, not a *sample* variance. To calculate the latter, use this formula (for brevity, input range=i; offset=o; criterion range=c):

(@DCOUNT(i,o,c)/@DCOUNT(i,o,c)−1)) ∗ @DVAR(i,o,c)

■ Comments

Although it is a database command, @DVAR works not only with a database, but with a worksheet as well. As long as the arguments are entered correctly and the criterion range does not exceed 32 columns, @DVAR makes no distinction between a worksheet and a database.

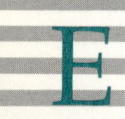

Editing cell entries

Cells on a worksheet generally contain any of three types of information: numbers (values), labels (text), or formulas (including functions). With advanced applications, they can also contain simple to complicated macros.

With any of these, if your entries are correct but you wish to change something about them, you can do so at any time by highlighting the appropriate entry and pressing the F2 [Edit] key to tell 1-2-3 you wish to move into EDIT **249♦** mode.

You can correct errors in numbers or labels (including macros) either before or after you press Return to complete the entry. Formulas are a bit different: If you press Return after entering a formula that contains an error, 1-2-3 will cause the computer to beep and will automatically put you into EDIT mode so you can correct the problem.

- **Editing keys**

If you notice a typographical or other error while typing a short entry, it is probably simpler just to backspace (and thus delete) characters until you reach and can correct the error. With long or complex entries, however, you may prefer to erase everything and start over, or, especially when editing a macro, you may want to jump back and forth, inserting and deleting characters here and there. The following keys enable you to do this:

Key:	Action:
F2 [Edit] key	Toggles back and forth between EDIT and VALUE or LABEL mode when pressed
Backspace	Deletes the preceding character
Del	Deletes the character at the cursor location
Esc	Closes the edit line, but leaves the cell intact
Ins	Toggles between inserting new characters and overtyping existing text
Home	Moves the cursor to the beginning of an entry
End	Moves the cursor to the end of an entry

Key:	Action:
Right arrow	Moves the cursor one character right
Left arrow	Moves the cursor one character left
Tab (Big Right) or Ctrl-right arrow	Moves the cursor five characters right
Backtab (Big Left) or Ctrl-left arrow	Moves the cursor five characters left
Return	Completes an entry and leaves the pointer on the same cell
Up arrow	Completes an entry and moves the pointer up one cell
Down arrow	Completes an entry and moves the pointer down one cell
Pg Up	Completes an entry and moves the pointer up one screen
Pg Dn	Completes an entry and moves the pointer down one screen

- **Comments**

Related information can be found in the following entries: Formulas 136★, Functions 145★, Keyboard 194★, Labels 199★, Macro 211★, Mode Indicators 248★, Numbers 261★, and Operators 263★.

@ERR

- **Format**

@ERR

- **Description**

@ERR is a special function that returns the value ERR in a formula. The function takes no argument.

@ERR

■ **Procedure**

The @ERR function is simply entered, in either upper- or lowercase, as *@ERR*. It is often used in formulas or functions, such as @IF, that test one or more cells to determine whether they contain acceptable values. The following example illustrates this type of usage.

```
C6: (F2) @IF($B6>0,@SUM($B$4..$B6),@ERR)                           READY
```

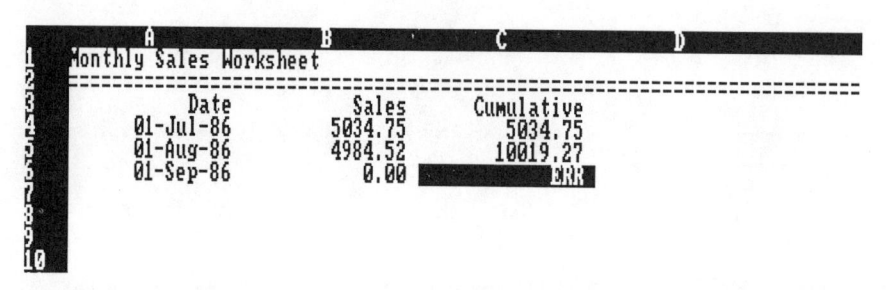

```
      A              B            C            D
 1  Monthly Sales Worksheet
 2  ================================================================
 3              Date         Sales     Cumulative
 4         01-Jul-86       5034.75       5034.75
 5         01-Aug-86       4984.52      10019.27
 6         01-Sep-86          0.00           ERR
 7
 8
 9
10
```

Since 1-2-3 displays ERR not only in the function cell, but in cells containing formulas that depend on the value calculated in the function cell, @ERR is also a useful tool for finding and correcting errors in a worksheet. In the following illustration, for example, it is easy to see that the formula in cell C8 is dependent on the ERR value in cell C6.

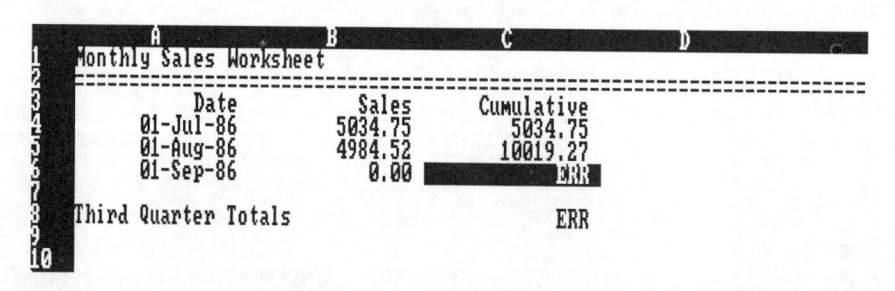

```
C6: (F2) @IF($B6>0,@SUM($B$4..$B6),@ERR)                           READY
```

```
      A              B            C            D
 1  Monthly Sales Worksheet
 2  ================================================================
 3              Date         Sales     Cumulative
 4         01-Jul-86       5034.75       5034.75
 5         01-Aug-86       4984.52      10019.27
 6         01-Sep-86          0.00           ERR
 7
 8  Third Quarter Totals                          ERR
 9
10
```

112

@ERR · Error messages

You can control the propagation of ERR with one of the following functions: @ISERR 185★, or @ISNA 186★. With Release 2 of 1-2-3, you can also use @CELL 18★, @CELLPOINTER 21★, @ISNUMBER 186★, or @ISSTRING 187★.

For example, the following formula:

@IF(@ISERR(A1),0,A1)

would prevent an error in A1 from propagating throughout the worksheet.

■ **Comments**

The value ERR is also displayed by 1-2-3 itself when errors occur in formulas, either because they attempt an unacceptable operation, such as division by zero, or because they contain a cell reference that has been invalidated by a move, copy, or delete operation. Although ERR has the same value, whether it is returned by the @ERR function or by 1-2-3, the two possible sources of the error value are distinct.

@NA 257★ is a function that is related to @ERR. It produces the value NA in a formula.

Error messages

Whenever 1-2-3 encounters a problem (such as a range name it does not recognize within a macro) or an obstacle to carrying out a command, it causes your computer to beep and it displays an error message at the bottom left corner of the screen.

1-2-3 has a large number of these error messages. Many of them are self-explanatory and indicate problems that are easily corrected. Others may be more difficult to understand, or you may not know how to solve the problems they indicate. If you encounter an error message you do not understand, simply press the F1 [Help] 144♦ key. As illustrated on the following page, 1-2-3 will display a list of error messages, along with brief descriptions of each. If you are still uncertain, highlight the message that concerns you and press Return. 1-2-3 will display an additional screenful of information describing the message in more detail.

Note: Help with error messages is available only in Release 2 of 1-2-3.

```
A1:                                                              HELP

Error Message Index
Break
Cannot create file
Cannot delete file
Cannot find COMSPEC
Cannot hide all columns
Cannot invert matrix
Cannot invoke DOS
Cannot justify text if Worksheet protection enabled
Cannot read Help file
Column hidden
Directory does not exist
Disk drive not ready
Disk error
Disk full
Disk is write-protected
Expanded memory error -- Press [HELP]

Continued            Help Index
```

@EXACT()   A Release 2 string function

- **Format**
  @EXACT(string1,string2)

- **Description**
  The @EXACT function compares two strings to determine whether they match precisely—not only in the letters they contain, but also in capitalization and equivalence of accent marks. If the two strings are exact matches, the function returns 1 (true); if they are not exact matches, the function returns 0 (false).

- **Procedure**
  The @EXACT function allows string arguments only; numeric values produce the value ERR. The strings can be specified either directly, by inclusion in the argument, or indirectly, as a cell reference.

  If either or both of the strings are included in the argument, each must be enclosed in double quotation marks. For example:

  @EXACT("A","a")

(This argument would return the value 0, because "A" and "a" are not an exact match.)

If either or both of the strings are designated by cell references, they need not be enclosed in quotation marks, within the cells where they occur. For example, if cell A1 contains the label Smith, Joe, and cell B20 contains the label Joe Smith, you could enter the @EXACT function in any one of the following forms:

@EXACT(A1,B20)

@EXACT(A1,"Joe Smith")

@EXACT("Smith, Joe",B20)

(Again, all functions would return the value 0, because the two strings are not exact matches.)

The @EXACT function is particularly useful in conditional statements that test for an acceptable value. For example:

@IF(@EXACT(B20,"Joe Smith"),B25,@NA)

would return the value in cell B25 if the label in cell B20 is exactly equal to the string Joe Smith; otherwise, it would return the value @NA.

■ **Comments**

For a less exacting comparison of two strings, use the equal (=) operator, which will ignore upper- and lowercase, and the presence or absence of accent marks. To perform a comparison of this sort, enter the strings as a formula. An example would be:

+"bon appetit"="bon appétit"

This formula would produce the value 1 (true), despite the accent mark over the *e* in the second string. The formula would also return the value 1 for either of the following:

+"Bon Appetit"="bon appetit"

+"BON APPETIT"="Bon Appetit"

More details on using strings in formulas are in the entry String 332★.

@EXP()

■ **Format**

@EXP(x)

■ **Description**

The function @EXP returns the value of the constant *e* raised to the power specified by *x*. *e* is the mathematical constant 2.7182818..., the base of the natural logarithm. Thus, @EXP is the inverse of the function @LN **205★** (natural logarithm).

■ **Procedure**

The argument of @EXP must be either a numeric value or a reference to a cell containing a numeric value. You could enter the function as either:

@EXP(25)

or as:

@EXP(A1)

if, in the second instance, cell A1 contained a numeric value, such as 15.

The argument can be a decimal fraction, but cannot be a number greater than 709, because 1-2-3 would not be able to store the result of the calculation. If the argument is greater than 230, the result can be calculated, but cannot be displayed.

■ **Examples**

The following examples illustrate the use of @EXP:

@EXP(123.456)

returns the value 4.1E+53.

@EXP(1)

returns the value 2.718281... (*e*). You can use this to generate the value *e* in other calculations.

@EXP(@LN(3))

returns the value 3. This example demonstrates the inverse relationship between the @EXP and @LN functions.

@FALSE

- **Format**

    @FALSE

- **Description**

    @FALSE is a logical function that can be used in a formula to return the numeric value 0. Although you don't ever *need* to use the @FALSE function (you can use 0 in a formula instead), this function is useful in making the purpose of a formula easier to understand.

    No argument is used with @FALSE.

- **Procedure**

    The @FALSE function is usually used inside the functions @CHOOSE **23★** and @IF **179★**. Its logical companion is @TRUE **347★**, which returns 1.

    The following two examples demonstrate the same situation. The first example uses the @FALSE and @TRUE functions; the second uses the values 0 and 1. In both instances, the formula returns 0 (false) if the value in cell A1 is not less than the value in A4, and it returns 1 (true) if the value in A1 is less than the value in A4:

    @IF(A1<A4,@TRUE,@FALSE)

    @IF(A1<A4,1,0)

Both formulas accomplish the same purpose, but to someone unfamiliar with a worksheet, the first might be much easier to interpret.

File

When you create or change a worksheet, database, or graph with 1-2-3, your work is held in your computer's random access memory (RAM). As you add to, modify, or delete from your efforts, your changes are made only in RAM. Since RAM is volatile, its contents disappear whenever the power is shut off. To guard against losing your work in case of a power outage, or to save your work for another 1-2-3 session, you must store it in a file on disk.

Like any other software, 1-2-3 saves both programs and data in disk files. Each file is identified by a unique combination of an eight-character file name and a three-character extension.

File

■ **File names**

1-2-3 file names compatible with Release 1a can be any combination of the following characters:

- ☐ The letters A through Z.
- ☐ The digits 0 through 9.
- ☐ The underline character, _.

Spaces are not permitted; punctuation marks and other symbols are allowed, if your operating system accepts them. With Release 2, 1-2-3 now permits the use of any character in the LICS character set, except the space. You must precede the file name with a drive identifier (such as a:) or a path name (such as \REGION_5\EXPENSES\JULY) if you are storing or retrieving a file in a directory or drive other than the one that is currently active.

There is also one special file name, AUTO123, which 1-2-3 looks for at the beginning of every session. If a file with this name exists in the startup directory (see /Worksheet Global Default Directory 363◆), it is retrieved from disk and becomes the current worksheet. Thus, if you want to load a particular worksheet in your next 1-2-3 session, you can save it as AUTO123 for automatic retrieval later on. The file name can always be changed to a more descriptive one, either when you save the worksheet in 1-2-3, or at another time (use the DOS Rename command).

Note: Path names and directories are treated somewhat differently in Releases 1a and 2 of 1-2-3. This entry is based primarily on Release 2; specific differences between the two versions are noted in the entries on the /File commands. Also, depending on the version of DOS and the release of 1-2-3 you are using, you may need to consult either your DOS or 1-2-3 manual for specifics (version 1 of DOS, for example, does not support subdirectories, so you cannot use path names, even though 1-2-3 allows you to specify them). Release 2 of 1-2-3 requires DOS 2.0 or higher on the IBM PC.

File

- **Extensions**

    Depending on the type of file you create, 1-2-3 adds one of the following extensions when you save the file:

    ☐ .WK1 (.WKS in Release 1a) if the file is a worksheet.

    ☐ .PIC if the file contains data for a graph.

    ☐ .PRN if the file is a *print*, or text file—in other words, an ASCII file (such as one from another program) that contains no special "program-specific" characters. You use .PRN files with the 1-2-3 /Print File **269★** and /File Import commands.

    With Release 2 of 1-2-3, you can also specify an extension of your own choice. For example, you can save a 1-2-3 worksheet as SCHEDULE.NOV. If you do this, however, you must remember to specify both the file name and the extension when retrieving the file, and you must choose the *Other* option of the /File Erase and /File List commands to have 1-2-3 erase or display it.

- **Managing files**

    To help you with general file management, 1-2-3 provides the /System **337★** command, which temporarily suspends the 1-2-3 program and enables you to use DOS commands, such as Format, Copy, and CheckDisk. In addition, the 1-2-3 System Disk contains a program called the Access System **3★**, which includes the Translate **342★** program. (The Access System is started by typing *Lotus* at the start of a session.) Translate lets you convert dBASE, VisiCalc, and other files to 1-2-3 worksheets, and vice versa.

    The following table lists the file-management aids you can reach from the Access System in Release 1a of 1-2-3:

Name:	What it does:
Disk-Manager	Lets you format, copy, compare, and check disks. (If the DOS files FORMAT.COM, DISKCOPY.COM, DISKCOMP.COM and CHKDSK.COM are in the 1-2-3 directory.)
File-Manager	Lets you copy, erase, rename, and sort the directory of files on a disk in the drive you specify.
Translate	Lets you convert files from dBASE, VisiCalc, and DIF formats to 1-2-3 worksheet files or vice versa.

File

The /System command is only in Release 2 of 1-2-3, and is the successor to File-Manager and Disk-Manager.

To enable you to manage individual files, 1-2-3 has a set of eight /File commands you use from within the worksheet. These commands are:

Command:	What it does:
/File Combine 121★	Lets you merge part or all of a .WK1 or .WKS file with the current worksheet.
/File Directory 123★	Lets you check on or change the current directory or (DOS Version 2.0 and above) subdirectory.
/File Erase 124★	Lets you erase one or more files (using wildcard characters).
/File Import 126★	Lets you transfer standard text (ASCII) files from another program into 1-2-3.
/File List 128★	Lets you see a list of files of a specified type and displays the size of the highlighted file, along with the time and date of the last modification.
/File Retrieve 128★	Lets you retrieve a worksheet file from disk.
/File Save 130★	Lets you save the current worksheet on disk.
/File Xtract 133★	Lets you save part of the current worksheet in a new file.

■ **Directories**

Release 2 of 1-2-3 displays subdirectories of the current directory in the file menu along with file names. They are identified by the backslash (\) which is appended to their name (for example, FILES\). To move into a subdirectory, highlight the subdirectory name and press Return. To move from a subdirectory to the directory one level above, press the backspace key.

■ **Program files**

1-2-3 consists of many separate program files stored on the six disks (one disk is a backup System Disk) that make up the 1-2-3 package. You need not be concerned with the contents of any of these files, but be careful not to alter or delete them. Whenever 1-2-3 needs a program file that is not on the disk in the currently active drive, it will prompt you to insert the appropriate disk.

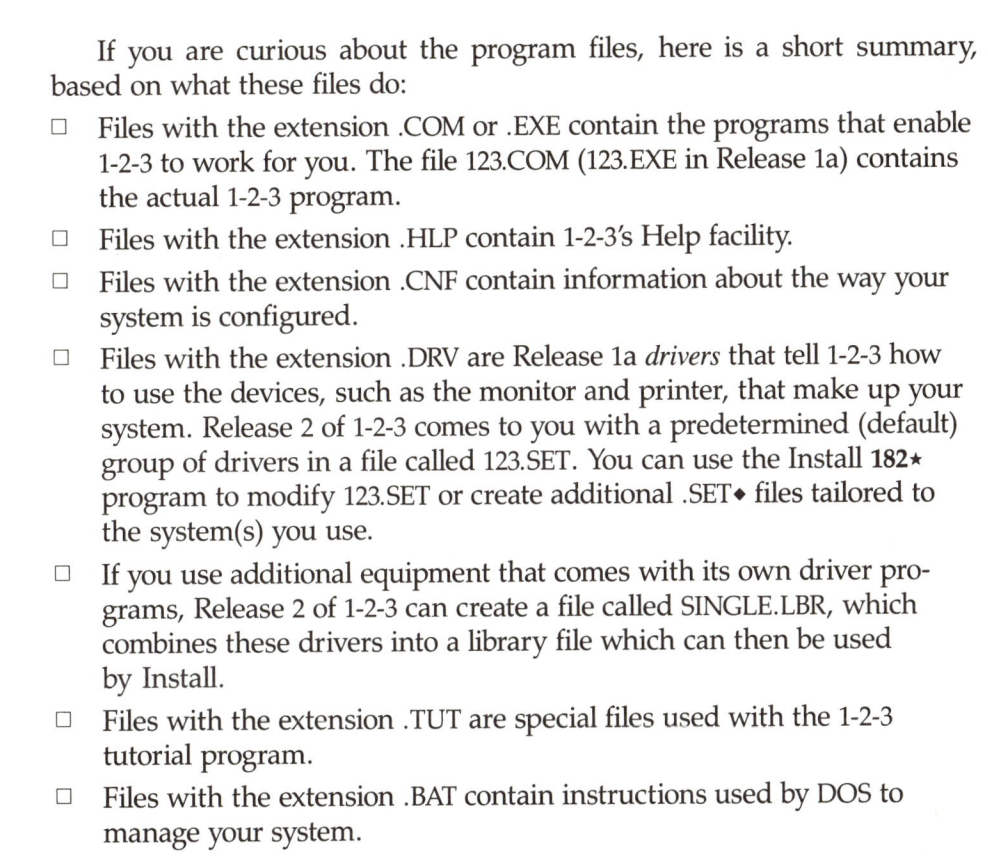

If you are curious about the program files, here is a short summary, based on what these files do:

- Files with the extension .COM or .EXE contain the programs that enable 1-2-3 to work for you. The file 123.COM (123.EXE in Release 1a) contains the actual 1-2-3 program.
- Files with the extension .HLP contain 1-2-3's Help facility.
- Files with the extension .CNF contain information about the way your system is configured.
- Files with the extension .DRV are Release 1a *drivers* that tell 1-2-3 how to use the devices, such as the monitor and printer, that make up your system. Release 2 of 1-2-3 comes to you with a predetermined (default) group of drivers in a file called 123.SET. You can use the Install **182★** program to modify 123.SET or create additional .SET♦ files tailored to the system(s) you use.
- If you use additional equipment that comes with its own driver programs, Release 2 of 1-2-3 can create a file called SINGLE.LBR, which combines these drivers into a library file which can then be used by Install.
- Files with the extension .TUT are special files used with the 1-2-3 tutorial program.
- Files with the extension .BAT contain instructions used by DOS to manage your system.

/File Combine   /FC

```
Worksheet  Range  Copy  Move  File  Print  Graph  Data  System  Quit
Retrieve  Save  Combine  Xtract  Erase  List  Import  Directory
Copy  Add  Subtract
```

■ **Description**

The /File Combine command is used to combine (merge) all or part of the data from a stored .WK1 (or .WKS) file with the current worksheet, at the location you specify with the cell pointer. You can thus consolidate several small worksheets or bring selected data from other files into the model you are currently building.

/File Combine

- **Procedure**

  Before selecting the /File Combine command, move the cell pointer to the *top left corner* of the area that will receive the transferred cells.

  Be careful to locate the pointer exactly where you want it. The new cells will overlay the area extending down and to the right of the pointer's location, and will replace, add to, or subtract from existing values, depending on your choice of options.

  Command options: Whenever you choose the /File Combine command, 1-2-3 presents the three options *Copy*, *Add*, and *Subtract*.

  ☐ *Copy* replaces current cell entries with incoming ones, including formulas and labels.

  ☐ *Add* adds incoming numbers, including calculated values, to numbers and empty cells in the current worksheet. Labels and formulas in the current worksheet are unaffected—any incoming values directed toward those cells are discarded.

  ☐ *Subtract* subtracts incoming numbers, including calculated values, from numbers and empty cells in the current worksheet. Again, existing labels and formulas are unaffected. Note, however, that the *Subtract* option treats empty cells as 0. Thus, if you subtract a positive number from an empty cell, the result will be a negative number (0−123=−123).

  Specifying the source: After choosing the option you want, 1-2-3 prompts you to select how much of the incoming file you want to combine: *Entire-File* or *Named-Range*.

  ☐ If you select *Entire-File*, 1-2-3 prompts *Enter name of file to combine:* and displays a list of the files on the disk in the current drive and directory.

  If you want to combine a file from a drive other than the current drive, or from a directory other than the current directory, precede the file name with the appropriate drive letter or path name.

  ☐ If you select *Named-Range*, 1-2-3 prompts *Enter range name:* before requesting the name of the file to combine. Unlike many other 1-2-3 commands, this one does not display a list of existing range names.

- **Example**

  The following example shows a small monthly expense form whose total cells are combined with a master worksheet that tracks year-to-date totals.

/File Combine · **/File Directory**

```
         A              B              C              D
  ╔════════════════════════════════════════════════════════════════
1 ║
2 ║ INDIVIDUAL EXPENSE RECORD -- Smith         First Quarter 1984
3 ║
4 ║                   January        February        March
5 ║ Lodging:
6 ║    04-Jan         $54.75
7 ║    06-Jan         $65.95
8 ║    09-Jan         $24.10
9 ║    TOTAL         $144.80          $0.00          $0.00
10║ Transportation:
11║    04-Jan         $36.00
12║    06-Jan        $101.00
13║    09-Jan         $64.00
14║    TOTAL         $201.00          $0.00          $0.00
15║ Meals:
16║    04-Jan         $21.55
17║    06-Jan         $18.10
18║    09-Jan         $44.25
19║    TOTAL          $83.90          $0.00          $0.00
20║
```

```
         A              B           C           D           E
  ╔═══════════════════════════════════════════════════════════════
1 ║
2 ║ COMBINED EXPENSE RECORD                First Quarter 1984
3 ║
4 ║                   QTR         Jan         Feb        March
5 ║ Total Expenses   $0.00       $0.00       $0.00       $0.00
6 ║
7 ║ Total -- Smith: $429.70      $0.00       $0.00       $0.00
8 ║      Lodging   $144.80
9 ║ Transportation $201.00
10║        Meals    $83.90
```

/File Directory /FD

```
Worksheet  Range  Copy  Move  File  Print  Graph  Data  System  Quit
Retrieve  Save  Combine  Xtract  Erase  List  Import  Directory
```

■ **Description**

Whenever you begin a session with 1-2-3, the program checks a file called 123.CNF for a standard (default) directory setting. Unless you have changed the original 1-2-3 default, the current directory is the main, or root, directory in drive A. (In Release 1a, the default is the root directory in drive B).

To change the current directory setting, you use the /File Directory command. This command is helpful when you wish to use a different drive to save or retrieve a file, or (with DOS Version 2.0 and above) to store or retrieve a file in a directory other than the current directory. /File Directory can also be used simply to check on which directory or subdirectory is current.

/File Directory · /File Erase

■ **Procedure**

Once you select the /File Directory command, 1-2-3 prompts *Enter current directory:* and displays the path name of the current directory.

If you are simply checking on the current directory, press Return (to accept the setting) or Esc (to cancel the command).

If you wish to change the directory, type a new disk-drive designator (if necessary) followed by a reverse slash (\) and the new path name.

If you are changing to a directory within the hierarchy of the current directory, you can start the path name with the current directory. For example, if the current directory is REGION_5 and you want to change to the lower-level directory SALES, you could type *SALES* (the name of the directory followed by a backslash), rather than, say, *c:\MIDWEST\REGION_5\SALES*. Or, if you prefer to be in the directory one level higher you could type .. (the DOS symbol for the preceding directory).

Once you change the current directory, all subsequent saving, listing, and retrieving file operations are interpreted as referring to the new directory setting. To use files in a different directory, you must specify the appropriate path name.

■ **Comments**

If you are working with Release 1a of 1-2-3 and with DOS 1.10, choose the /File Directory command if you want to save or retrieve a file on a disk in a different drive. In response to the prompt, type the letter of the drive containing the disk you wish to use.

/File Erase   /FE

```
Worksheet  Range  Copy    Move    File   Print  Graph  Data    System  Quit
Retrieve   Save   Combine Xtract  Erase  List   Import Directory
Worksheet  Print  Graph   Other
```

■ **Description**

The /File Erase command is used to erase any files on a disk that have the same extension or that match a pattern you provide. The 1-2-3 extensions are .WK1, .PRN, and .PIC. The two wildcard characters ? and * can be used to create a pattern that specifies more than one file.

Procedure

When you select the /File Erase command, 1-2-3 first prompts for the type of file you wish to erase: *Worksheet, Print, Graph,* or *Other.*

- *Worksheet* causes 1-2-3 to display all .WK1 and .WKS file names in the current directory along with any subdirectory names (Release 2 only).
- *Print* causes 1-2-3 to display a list of all .PRN file names in the current directory along with any subdirectory names (Release 2 only).
- *Graph*♦ causes 1-2-3 to display a list of all .PIC file names in the current directory along with any subdirectory names (Release 2 only).
- *Other* is a choice available only in Release 2; it causes 1-2-3 to display a list of all file names in the current directory along with any subdirectory names.

Select the option you want, and 1-2-3 will then prompt *Enter name of file to erase:*. Choose a file name by highlighting it with the cell pointer, or specify a group of files by using either of the two wildcard characters:

- Use the ? one or more times to specify single characters in the file name. For example, P?N would encompass PAN, PEN, PIN, and PUN.
- Use the * to specify all characters to the end of the file name. For example, J* would encompass JANUARY, JUNE, and JULY.

After you select the file(s) and press Return, 1-2-3 prompts for confirmation before carrying out your command, by displaying *No* and *Yes.*

Choose *No* to cancel, *Yes* to carry out the command.

Comments

Release 2 of 1-2-3 differs from Release 1a in the following ways:

- It offers the *Other* option discussed earlier.
- It allows you to erase files in a different directory by using the cursor to change directories or by preceding the file name with the appropriate path name. This can be accomplished in either Release 1a or 2 by changing the current directory with the /File Directory **123★** command.

/File Import

/File Import /FI

```
Worksheet Range Copy Move File Print Graph Data System Quit
Retrieve Save Combine Xtract Erase List Import Directory
Text Numbers
```

■ **Description**

The /File Import command allows you to transfer a file created by another program into a 1-2-3 worksheet. You can import the file as text only or as a combination of numbers (values) and labels (text).

■ **Requirements**

Because the /File Import command transfers data generated by another program, there are two requirements you must observe:

☐ The file you import must have the extension .PRN. If it does not, or if it has a different extension, you can use the /System 337★ command in order to suspend 1-2-3 temporarily. Then, use the DOS Rename command to change the extension. (With Release 1a of 1-2-3, use the File-Manager in the Lotus Access System to give the file the appropriate extension.)

☐ The file must be a print file. In other words, the program that creates the file must be able to save the document as a standard ASCII 5★ text file, containing no special characters that 1-2-3 will be unable to work with. Generally, programs that have this capability offer the option when you save a file; 1-2-3, for example, provides the /Print File 269★ command.

Exception: For files created with programs, such as VisiCalc and dBASE, that are supported by 1-2-3, use the Translate 342★ facility from the Lotus Access System, instead of the /File Import command.

■ **Procedure**

Before choosing the /File Import command, place the pointer in the cell that is to become the top left corner of the area into which you are importing the file. The imported file will be placed in the range of cells extending down and to the right of the location of the cell pointer. *Contents of existing cells are overwritten,* so be certain that the area to be occupied is either blank or contains no information you need to keep.

/File Import

When you select the /File Import command, 1-2-3 offers two options, *Text* and *Numbers*.

If you choose *Text*♦, 1-2-3 places each line of data in a single cell, then moves down one row to insert the next line, and the next.... Even though the text may be lines from a word-processed document, 1-2-3 treats each line as a label and begins it at the left edge of the cell to which it is transferred.

If you choose *Numbers*, 1-2-3 transfers numbers and also transfers characters that are enclosed in double quotation marks (for example, "December 25"). Numbers are placed in individual cells, in rows corresponding to the lines they occupy in the original file. Incoming numbers are mapped into existing range or global cell formats—number of decimal places, for example.

Characters in quotation marks are treated as left-aligned labels. Mixed numbers and labels are placed in successive columns and rows, to match their positions in the original file.

After you have selected *Text* or *Numbers*, 1-2-3 prompts *Enter name of file to import:*. If you are satisfied that the imported file will transfer properly, press Return, and the new file will then appear at the location specified by the cell pointer.

■ **Comments**

The maximum size of a file you can import is 240 characters by 8192 lines. (With Release 1a, the maximum size is 240 characters by 2048 lines.)

When 1-2-3 searches for numbers and character strings in importing a file, it treats blank spaces, punctuation marks, and all characters not enclosed in quotation marks as delimiters (separators) between entries. Because of this, imported numbers cannot contain commas—1,200, for example, is not allowed. If such punctuation is important, enclose the numbers in quotation marks before importing them, then edit the cells later to remove the label prefix 1-2-3 assigns them.

To "clean up" a file after importing it, you can use the /Range Justify **306★** command to adjust line lengths. With Release 2, you can use the /Data Parse **61★** command to break long labels into separate cell entries.

127

/File List · /File Retrieve

/File List /FL

```
Worksheet Range Copy Move File Print Graph Data System Quit
Retrieve Save Combine Xtract Erase List Import Directory
Worksheet Print Graph Other
```

- **Description**

The /File List command enables you to see a list of files and their sizes in the current directory.

- **Procedure**

When you choose the /File List command, 1-2-3 displays the same options as for /File Erase: *Worksheet*, *Print*, *Graph*, and (Release 2 only) *Other*.

Select *Worksheet* to see a list of .WK1 and .WKS file names; *Print* to see a list of .PRN file names; and *Graph* to see a list of .PIC file names. Select *Other* to see a list of all file names in the current directory. When you are through, press any key to return to your worksheet.

To move to a new subdirectory, move the highlight to the subdirectory name and press Return. To move up along the current path, you can press the backspace key.

/File Retrieve /FR

```
Worksheet Range Copy Move File Print Graph Data System Quit
Retrieve Save Combine Xtract Erase List Import Directory
```

- **Description**

The /File Retrieve command loads a previously saved worksheet, including all its settings, from disk into your computer's memory. The /File Retrieve command erases the current worksheet before it retrieves the new one, so remember to save any changes to your current work (with the /File Save 130★ command) before loading a new file.

/File Retrieve

■ **Procedure**

Whenever you issue the /File Retrieve command, 1-2-3 displays the names of the first five .WK1 files and/or subdirectories listed in the current directory. The names appear in a horizontal row in the third line of the Control Panel **29★**. If you want to see a complete listing, press the F3 [Name] **144◆** key. 1-2-3 will display all the worksheet files and/or subdirectories in the current directory, in the same form as for /File List **128★**. To see the size of a file and the date it was last changed, move the pointer to that file with the arrow keys. Press the F3 [Name] key again, when you have finished.

To move the highlight in the Control Panel from one file name or subdirectory to another, use the cursor-movement keys as follows:

Key:	Direction of movement:
Left arrow	Toward the first file name or directory currently displayed; circles through the file name menu if pressed repeatedly
Right arrow	Toward the last file name currently displayed; returns to the first five names if pressed when the highlight reaches the end of the list
Up arrow	To the previous five file names displayed
Down arrow	To the next five file names, if the list contains more than five
Home	To the beginning of the list
End	To the end of the list

To specify the file you want to retrieve, highlight it as described and press Return. If the file exists in another directory, type the path and file names or press the backspace key to move upward along the current path. To enter a subdirectory, highlight the name and press Return. If you assigned the file an extension other than .WK1 or .WKS, type both the file name and extension. If the file is not a .WK1 or .WKS file, use Translate to convert it, or use /File Import **126★** if it is a plain ASCII file.

If the file you specify has been saved with a password, as described in the entry /File Save, 1-2-3 will prompt for the password with the message *Enter password:* Type the password, exactly as you did originally, including upper- and lowercase. 1-2-3 will display a small box for each of the characters as you type them. If you do not enter the password correctly, 1-2-3 will refuse to retrieve the file.

/File Retrieve · /File Save

■ **Comments**

The /File Retrieve procedure in Release 1a of 1-2-3 is essentially the same as described here, with the following exceptions:

- ☐ Release 2 displays a list of five file names, with extensions, and includes directories within the current directory. Release 1a displays eight file names, no extensions, and no directories.

- ☐ Release 1a does not provide for password protection.

/File Save /FS

```
Worksheet  Range  Copy  Move  File  Print  Graph  Data  System  Quit
Retrieve  Save  Combine  Xtract  Erase  List  Import  Directory
```

■ **Description**

The /File Save command saves a complete copy of the current worksheet on disk. The file is saved with all its current settings, and is automatically given the extension .WK1, unless you specify a different extension.

The file is saved to the current disk and directory. To specify a different (non-current) drive, precede the file name with the appropriate drive prefix, such as a:. To save the file in a different directory, precede the file name with the appropriate path name, beginning with the \ (root) directory.

■ **Procedure**

When you choose /File Save, 1-2-3 prompts *Enter save file name:*.

If you are saving a new worksheet for the first time during the current session, type a file name and press Return to create a new file.

If you have retrieved an existing file, press Return when 1-2-3 proposes the previously assigned file name. 1-2-3 will then replace the previous version with the current version.

Alternatively, type or point to the name of an existing file in the list 1-2-3 automatically displays, in groups of five at the bottom of the Control Panel, the first time you save. To see more names, or to move forward or backward in the list, use the arrow, Home, and End keys, which are described in more detail in the entry on /File Retrieve.

If you use the name of an existing file, 1-2-3 prompts you to *Cancel* or *Replace*. If you choose *Replace*, 1-2-3 overwrites the old file with the version that is being saved. If you choose *Cancel*, 1-2-3 cancels the /File Save command sequence.

Note: Be certain that you want to overwrite the old file when you choose *Replace*. 1-2-3 does not make automatic backup copies of your files, so any data you replace is lost to you, unless you have an archive copy stored elsewhere.

If you have already saved a worksheet file during the current session, 1-2-3 displays the last file name you used with a /File Save command. To accept 1-2-3's proposed choice, just press Return. To save the file under a different name, type the file name of your choice and press Return. To see a menu of existing file names, press Esc.

Regardless of the way you choose a file name, 1-2-3 displays a *Disk Full* message if there is not enough room on the current disk for your entire worksheet file. If you see this message, press Esc. You can then replace the full disk with another formatted data disk, or use the /File List **128★** command to see a list of existing files and perhaps pick a few unneeded ones for erasure. Depending on how much room you estimate your worksheet requires (there are no guidelines for this, unfortunately, other than your own experience), you may be able to make more room on the disk by erasing old or unneeded files with the /File Erase **124★** command, or you may decide to save a key portion of the active worksheet with the /File Xtract **133★** command.

Passwords: With Release 2 of 1-2-3, you have the ability to protect a file from casual retrieval by assigning it a password. Unless the password is entered correctly during the /File Retrieve procedure, 1-2-3 will refuse to load a protected file. As with any other use of "secret" passwords:

☐ Remember it.
☐ Don't leave it lying around in full view.

To assign a password, choose the /File Save command and type the file name; press the spacebar and the letter P, then press Return. 1-2-3 will prompt for the password with the message *Enter password:*. Type a password of up to 15 characters (including any LICS **203★** characters you wish). Do not use spaces, pay attention to case, and in general try to avoid passwords that are either too obvious or so complicated you must write them down to remember them. Both extremes defeat the purpose of password protection.

/File Save

When you create your password, 1-2-3 displays a small box on-screen for each character you type. It does not display the password itself. Press Return when you finish entering the password, and 1-2-3 will display the prompt *Verify password:*. Type the password again and press Return to complete the procedure.

Once you have assigned a password to a file, you can continue using the same password each time you retrieve and save the file, or you can choose to change or delete the password.

To use an existing password again, choose the /File Save command, and press Return.

To change the password, choose the /File Save command, press the backspace key, press the spacebar and the letter P, then press Return, and create a new password.

To delete the password, choose the /File Save command, then press the backspace key, and press Return again. The file will be saved without password protection.

- **Comments**

In Release 1a of 1-2-3, the /File Save command works much as described here, with the following exceptions:

☐ Path names are not allowed. To save the current worksheet to a different directory, you must first change the current directory with the /File Directory **123★** command.

☐ As mentioned, password protection is not available.

☐ The menu displayed the first time you save a file shows eight, not five, file names, and includes no extensions or directories.

With any release of 1-2-3, and regardless of whether you choose to save a file under the same or a different file name, take the same conservative approach that you would with any other valuable files: Save often—whenever the work you stand to lose due to a power failure or an error of judgment is worth more than the time it would take to re-create your efforts.

Likewise, if you are making changes to an existing worksheet and you would like to keep the original for historical or comparison purposes, consider using related, but descriptive file names and saving each as a separate file. You can always bring relevant information from many different worksheets into a single "master" copy with the /File Combine **121★** command. Your files will be even more accessible and easy to use if you are careful to set the correct date each time you start a session with 1-2-3. Later, if you need to check on the date, you can use the /File List **128★** command.

132

/File Xtract /FX

```
Worksheet  Range  Copy  Move  File  Print  Graph  Data  System  Quit
Retrieve  Save  Combine  Xtract  Erase  List  Import  Directory
Formulas  Values
```

■ **Description**

The /File Xtract command lets you extract part of the current worksheet and save it in a separate worksheet (.WK1) file. This command is useful when you have created a large or a modular worksheet that you either cannot save on a single disk or that you prefer not to save in its complete form—perhaps because part of your current worksheet, if extracted, could form the basis for the next in a series of models, or perhaps because you would like to save your formula values as numbers for use as data in another worksheet.

■ **Procedure**

Before you begin the /File Xtract command sequence, determine exactly which rows and columns of cells you wish to extract. You will name them as a separate file, but you will *refer* to them as a range of cells.

Also, clear any Titles or Windows settings before you use /File Xtract. These settings are saved with the extracted file and could cause problems if you try to combine the extracted file with an existing worksheet.

When you choose the /File Xtract command, 1-2-3 presents you with two options, *Formulas* and *Values*. This means you can either extract the formulas in your worksheet, or you can extract the values they calculate. If you choose *Formulas*, bear the following in mind:

☐ Relative addresses will retain their original meanings in the new file: A current relative address that refers to a cell three rows above and one column to the right will carry that reference into the new worksheet.

☐ Absolute addresses will be adjusted just as relative addresses are, despite the $ sign. Thus, an absolute reference to a cell ten rows up and three columns left will retain that meaning when extracted.

/File Xtract

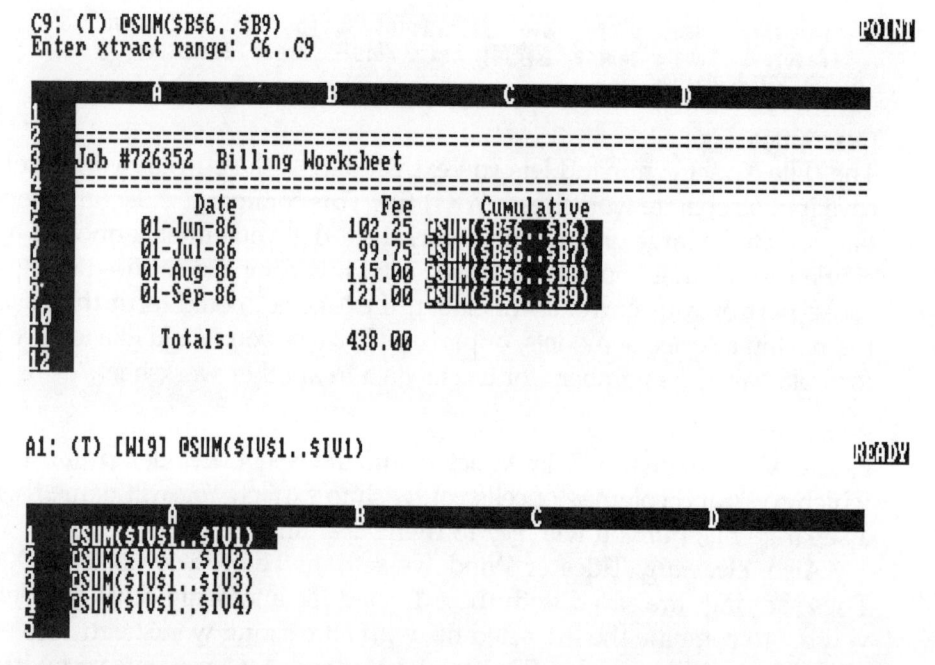

You can see these adjustments in the following two illustrations:

```
C9: (T) @SUM($B$6..$B9)                                          POINT
Enter xtract range: C6..C9
```

```
            A              B           C              D
 1
 2  ================================================================
 3  Job #726352  Billing Worksheet
 4  ================================================================
 5              Date           Fee     Cumulative
 6          01-Jun-86       102.25    @SUM($B$6..$B6)
 7          01-Jul-86        99.75    @SUM($B$6..$B7)
 8          01-Aug-86       115.00    @SUM($B$6..$B8)
 9          01-Sep-86       121.00    @SUM($B$6..$B9)
10
11          Totals:         438.00
12
```

```
A1: (T) [W19] @SUM($IV$1..$IV1)                                  READY
```

```
            A              B           C              D
 1  @SUM($IV$1..$IV1)
 2  @SUM($IV$1..$IV2)
 3  @SUM($IV$1..$IV3)
 4  @SUM($IV$1..$IV4)
 5
```

Once you have selected *Formulas* or *Values*, 1-2-3 prompts *Enter Xtract file name:*. Type a file name or choose one from the list that 1-2-3 displays. Next, 1-2-3 prompts for the range you wish to extract. Highlight the range, type a range name, or type the addresses of the two opposite corner cells of a range, and press Return.

If you selected a file name already assigned to a .WK1 file in the current directory, 1-2-3 will prompt you to *Cancel* or *Replace*. Choose *Cancel* if you do not wish to overwrite (and thus erase) the existing file; otherwise, choose *Replace* if you do wish to overwrite the file.

The range, along with the current formats, column widths, and Worksheet settings that relate to it, will be extracted to the new file.

Comments

You must be very careful when extracting named ranges or formulas that refer to cells outside the extracted range. Either can cause serious problems if they are combined into another worksheet. For example, suppose a series of formulas in cells B1..B10 contain references to values in cells A1..A10. B1..B10 are extracted:

- If they become a new file, cell B1 becomes the top left corner cell of the new worksheet—it becomes cell A1. Since the old references to cells A1..A10 must still point somewhere, the references "wrap" around the entire width of the worksheet and become references to cells IV1..IV10, 256 columns to the right, but one column to the left.

- If they are extracted to an existing worksheet, the old references may or may not be correct. If cells B1..B10 become G5..G15, for example, the original references now will point to cells F5..F15. Unless cells F5..F15 contain data you want the extracted formulas to calculate, the result will be either incorrect calculated values or an array of error messages that might be perpetuated throughout dependent formulas.

@FIND()   A Release 2 string function

Format
@FIND(search string,string,start number)

Description
@FIND is a string function that searches a specified string of characters (string) to determine whether another (search string) appears within it. The search begins at the character location within the string that is defined by the start number. The function returns a numeric value that pinpoints the location at which the search string begins. The function returns ERR:

- If the search string does not occur in the specified string.
- If the start number is a negative number.
- If the start number is greater than the number of characters, minus 1, in the string to be searched.

■ **Procedure**

When you enter the @FIND function, both the search string and the string to be searched can be entered either as character strings or as cell references or single-cell range names. If entered as character strings, they must be enclosed in double quotation marks. If the arguments are cell references, the cells must contain labels, but the labels need not be enclosed in quotation marks.

The string to be searched can be up to 240 characters long.

The start number begins at 0, the leftmost character of the string. Thus, the start number can be any number up to 1 less than the number of characters in the string to be searched. The start number can be a decimal fraction, but if so, 1-2-3 uses only the integer portion of the number.

The @FIND function is case-sensitive, so it will only return the location of the search string if all specified characters match in terms of upper- and lowercase letters.

The following examples demonstrate the capabilities of @FIND.

@FIND("mark","the marketplace shows our ads are hitting the mark",0)

returns the value 4, indicating the first occurrence of the string *mark*.

@FIND("mark","the marketplace shows our ads are hitting the mark",80)

returns the value ERR, because the start number is greater than the number of characters in the string to be searched.

@FIND("MARK","the marketplace shows our ads are hitting the mark",0)

returns the value ERR because the search string MARK does not occur in all capitals within the string being searched.

Formulas and formula calculation

A formula is a cell entry that tells 1-2-3 to perform a calculation. The result of the calculation is a value that can be used, just like the data you enter, in any operation appropriate for that type of value.

Note: Release 2 of 1-2-3 provides expanded capabilities over Release 1a for manipulating dates, times, and character strings in formulas. For ease of reference, this entry discusses "traditional" number-based formulas. Details on time-and-date formulas and string formulas can be found in the entries Date-Related Analyses 93★ and String 332★.

Starting a formula

A formula can be up to 240 characters long. It must begin with one of the following:

- A plus or minus sign (+ or −).
- One of the digits 0 through 9.
- A decimal point (.).
- An opening parenthesis, (.
- An @ character.
- A # character.
- A $ sign.

When you type one of these characters at the beginning of a formula, 1-2-3 puts you into VALUE **249♦** mode and prepares to receive a formula. If you do not begin with one of these characters, 1-2-3 assumes you are entering text and puts you into LABEL **249♦** mode. The results are quite different:

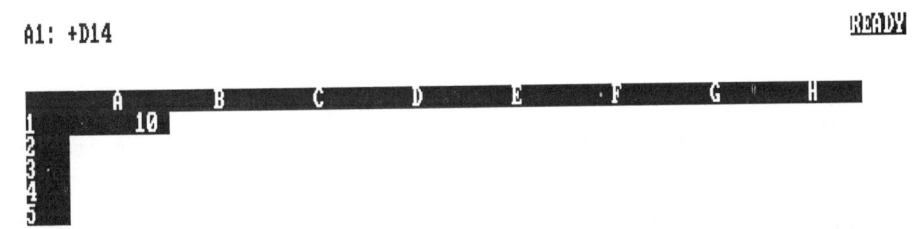

A1: +D14   READY

```
        A      B      C      D      E      F      G      H
1      10
2
3
4
5
```

This result is a number (the value in cell D14) that can be used in calculating other numeric values.

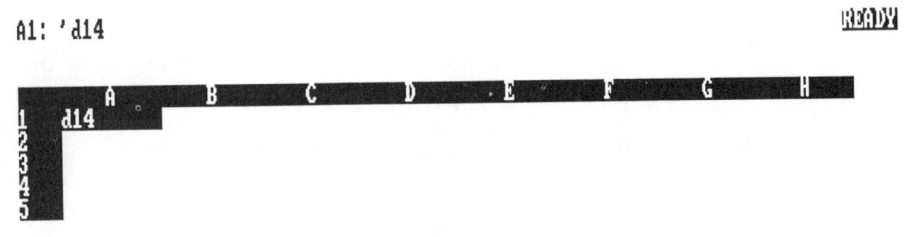

A1: 'd14   READY

```
        A      B      C      D      E      F      G      H
1  d14
2
3
4
5
```

This result is text. It can be used in string **332★** operations, but not in calculating numeric values.

Formula components

Formulas can include:

- Numbers.
- Operators.
- Single cell addresses and cell ranges.
- Range names.
- Functions or other formulas.

Spaces are not allowed in formulas, unless they occur in range names or in character strings enclosed in double quotation marks.

Numbers: Numbers in formulas can be either positive or negative, written as whole numbers, decimal fractions, or in exponential form. For example, 123, −123, 123.456, −123.456, and 12.34E5 are all allowable numbers.

Operators: 1-2-3 uses the following arithmetic and logical operators, and calculates them in the order of precedence shown in the following table. If two or more operators of the same precedence occur in a formula, they are handled in sequence from left to right.

Symbol:	Meaning:	Order of precedence:
^	Exponentiation	First
−,+	Negative, positive	Second
*, /	Multiplication and division	Third
+,−	Addition and subtraction	Fourth
=, <>	Equal, not equal	Fifth
<, >	Less than, greater than	Fifth
<=	Less than or equal to	Fifth
>=	Greater than or equal to	Fifth
#NOT#	NOT in a logical comparison, as in saying, "If NOT this...."	Sixth
#AND#	AND in a logical comparison, as in saying, "If this AND this...."	Seventh
#OR#	OR in a logical comparison, as in saying, "If this OR this...."	Seventh

In Release 2 of 1-2-3, there is also a concatenation operator, the ampersand (&), which is used exclusively in string 332★ operations. Like the logical #AND# and #OR#, it is seventh in order of precedence.

Use of parentheses: You can tell 1-2-3 to calculate parts of a formula in other than its normal order of precedence by enclosing segments in parentheses. 1-2-3 calculates entries in parentheses first, beginning with the innermost set of parentheses if several segments are "nested," one inside of the other, as in the following example:

1000*((A1+100)/(B1−B2))

In this instance, 1-2-3 would first calculate the value of A1+100, then the value of B1−B2, even though addition and subtraction normally have a lower order of precedence than multiplication and division. After calculating the values in the innermost sets of parentheses, 1-2-3 would then calculate the value in the next set of parentheses, A1+100/B1−B2, and, finally, would multiply the entire result by 1000.

Cell references: The entries Cell 13★ and Range 291★ discuss cell references in detail. The following discussion applies primarily to cell references as they are used in formulas. For more details, see Cell, Range, /Copy 31★, and /Move 250★.

Cell references in formulas can either be to single cells or to cell ranges. Ranges, however, are included only in function 145★ arguments. You would not, for example, enter the formula:

1000+A1..B10

although you could enter it as:

1000+(@SUM(A1..B10))

Cell references can be entered in formulas in either of two ways, regardless of whether they refer to single cells or to cell ranges. The first is by highlighting the appropriate cell(s) with the cell pointer; the second way is by typing the cell address(es).

Formulas and formula calculation

Pointing: To indicate a cell by pointing to it, all you need do is move the pointer. The address of the cell will appear in the formula, which 1-2-3 displays in the third line of the Control Panel at the top of the screen.

If all you wish to reference is a single cell, typing the next character in the formula (or pressing Return if you are finished) causes the address to become part of the formula and causes the cell pointer to jump back to the formula cell.

If you wish to reference a range of cells, you can move the highlight to one corner cell of the range, type a period (.) to anchor that cell, and extend the highlight to cover the remainder of the range. As with a single cell, 1-2-3 displays the appropriate cell addresses in the Control Panel.

Typing: Typing cell addresses accomplishes the same goal as pointing. To type a range reference, type the address of one corner cell of the range, then type a period and the address of the diagonally opposite corner cell.

Relative, absolute, and mixed references: 1-2-3 has three methods of referring to cells. The differences in these methods are described briefly here, but are primarily of importance when you copy or move formulas, and so are covered in more detail in the entries /Copy and /Move.

Each of the three types of cell reference has its own meaning and its own appearance:

- A relative reference is positional, telling 1-2-3 to use the contents of a cell x number of columns and y number of rows away from the formula cell. A relative reference looks like this: A1, and always points to a cell at a certain relative distance from the formula cell. If the formula is copied or moved, the reference is adjusted to indicate whichever cell occupies the same position, relative to the formula's new location, as the cell originally referenced. For example, suppose a formula in cell A1 contains a relative reference to cell B1. If the formula is copied to cell A2, 1-2-3 will change the relative reference to B2, so the formula continues to refer to a cell in the same row, one column to the right of the formula cell.

- An absolute reference is fixed and unchanging. No matter where the formula is copied or moved, an absolute reference always refers to one particular cell on the worksheet. An absolute reference is indicated by $ signs before both the column and row coordinates: $A$1. You can make a cell reference absolute by pressing the F4 [Absolute] **144♦** function key while you are in POINT **249♦** or EDIT **249♦** mode.

- A mixed reference tells 1-2-3 to treat one part of the cell reference as absolute, the other as relative. This type of reference is used when the column must remain the same, but the row coordinate may change, or vice versa. The absolute part of the reference is preceded by a $ sign, the relative part is not: $A1 or A$1, for example. Pressing the F4 [Absolute] key cycles a cell reference through the various combinations of relative and absolute coordinates during POINT or EDIT mode.

Range names: You can include range names in place of addresses for either single cells or multiple-cell ranges. Range names can be either relative or absolute (type a $ sign before the range name or press the F4 [Absolute] key). You cannot make a range name a mixed reference.

■ Editing formulas

When you press Return to indicate that you have completed entering a formula, 1-2-3 checks the entry for input errors it can recognize. If it finds an error, it causes the computer to beep, puts you in EDIT mode, and places the cursor at its best guess of the problem spot in the formula.

To correct the error, you can use any of the editing keys described in Editing Cell Entries **110★**.

ERR and NA: Sometimes, however, a formula will contain other types of errors. It might, for example, refer to a cell or range that you later delete. Or it might refer to a cell containing an ERR value. In either of these instances, 1-2-3 displays *ERR* in all affected cells, and your only recourse is to backtrack, find the error, and correct it. You can control the propagation of ERR by testing for acceptable values with the following functions: @IF **179★**, @CHOOSE **23★**, @ISERR **185★**, @ISNA **186★**, @ISSTRING **187★**, and @ISNUMBER **186★**.

Formulas and formula calculation

Circular references: If you create a formula that refers to itself (directly or indirectly), 1-2-3 displays *CIRC* (for circular) at the lower right corner of the screen if recalculation is set to Natural order (described in the next section). A circular reference may or may not be deliberate—an example of its deliberate use is shown in the entry Iteration 188★. An example of an indirect CIRC reference would be entering +A1*10 in B1 when A1 contained +B1+5. If the reference is not deliberate, again your only recourse is to edit the formulas involved.

■ **Calculating formulas**

1-2-3's default settings for worksheet recalculation are the *Natural* and *Automatic* options of the /Worksheet Global Recalculation 371★ command. This means a worksheet is recalculated each time a value is changed or a new entry is made, and that the formulas are recalculated in the order in which their values are required—values needed first are calculated first (formulas which depend on other formulas are calculated after the non-dependent ones).

At times, however, especially when you are entering data or editing formulas in a large worksheet, you may prefer to speed the process by turning off automatic recalculation. Or, you may build a worksheet that requires recalculation by row or by column, rather than in natural order. Or, you may want the worksheet recalculated several times in a row.

All of these options are selected through the /Worksheet Global Recalculation command and are discussed under that entry.

In terms of the formulas on your worksheet, however, you can set recalculation to *Manual* and recalculate when you wish by pressing the F9 [Calc] 144◆ key. Each new formula you enter will still be calculated, even in Manual mode, but you can also recalculate the entire worksheet by pressing the F9 function key.

Managing formulas: You can include formulas within formulas, functions within functions within formulas. Because of this, formulas can become extremely complex—especially given the 240-character length to which they can grow.

When you create complex formulas, especially on a large or complicated worksheet in which many formulas depend on the results of other formulas, good documentation is an enormous asset. Not only can you backtrack more easily, to see what you have done, you can also find errors more quickly if a string of ERR values suddenly proliferates throughout your worksheet, or you try to recalculate and 1-2-3 presents you with the message CIRC at the bottom of the screen.

Frequency distribution

A frequency distribution is a table that shows how values in a list fall into a set of specified intervals defined by a bin **12**★ range. A frequency distribution is created with the /Data Distribution **52**★ command, which returns the number of values in a list that fall into each of the intervals (bins) you specify.

Frequency distribution tables are useful in demographic studies, business reports, summaries of sales figures, analyses of test scores—any time you have a large number of data values that you wish to condense. Frequency distribution tables are also very useful in creating a list of data points that you can chart with the /Graph **148**★ commands.

Function keys

Note: The following description applies to the IBM personal computers and compatibles that use the same function-key designations. If your computer differs, refer to your manual for the equivalent keys on your keyboard.

The function keys on a computer keyboard are, in a way, "free" keys that can be used to perform application-specific tasks. For example, whereas a word-processing program might use the F5 function key to turn the overtype feature on and off, another program might use the F5 key for an entirely different task.

Function keys

1-2-3 assigns the following tasks to the function keys (labeled F1, F2, and so on) on the IBM keyboard:

Key◆:	Function performed:
F1 [Help]	Calls up the Help facility.
Alt-F1 [Compose]	Enables you to create accented and other special characters in the Lotus International Character Set (LICS) 203★.
F2 [Edit]	Toggles you in and out of EDIT 249◆ mode.
Alt-F2 [Step]	Turns on single-step mode for macro 211★ execution; causes macros to be carried out a step at a time, pausing after each; used for debugging macros.
F3 [Name]	In POINT 249◆ mode, displays a list of currently defined range names.
F4 [Absolute]	In POINT and EDIT modes, cycles through absolute, mixed, and relative referencing, or makes a range name absolute.
F5 [Goto]	Moves the cell pointer to the cell you specify; useful for moving the pointer long distances on the worksheet. This key is often used with the F3 [Name] key to move to a range.
F6 [Window]	Moves the pointer from one window to the other on a screen split with the /Worksheet Window 378★ command.
F7 [Query]	Causes 1-2-3 to repeat the last /Data Query 65★ command used.
F8 [Table]	Causes 1-2-3 to repeat the last Data Table 79★ operation.
F9 [Calc]	In READY 249◆ mode, recalculates the entire worksheet; in VALUE 249◆ or EDIT mode, calculates the value of the highlighted formula.
F10 [Graph]	Displays the last specified graph.

Functions

Functions are prewritten formulas built into 1-2-3 to perform standard calculations without your having to create the formulas to do so. Essentially, you provide the values the function requires, and 1-2-3 does the work.

■ Format

Every 1-2-3 function begins with an @ character, followed by the function name, followed (often, but not always) by one or more arguments, which are the details you must provide, enclosed in parentheses. Thus, you must enter a function in the following format:

@function name(argument 1,argument 2,...argument n)

where:

- ☐ The first character is the @ character optionally preceded by a standard formula character, + or (.
- ☐ The second character begins the function name. No spaces are allowed between the two. You can type the function name in uppercase characters, lowercase characters, or any combination of upper- and lowercase.
- ☐ If the function requires an argument, the function name is followed immediately by an open parenthesis.
- ☐ The open parenthesis is followed immediately by one or more arguments, separated by commas. Again, no spaces can be included, unless they occur in range names or character strings enclosed in double quotation marks—for example, Jan Sales or "Jan Sales".
- ☐ The last argument is followed immediately by a closing parenthesis.

■ Arguments

Function arguments are single numeric values, range references, or character strings (which you use depends on the function involved). Cell references, whether they are to single cells or ranges, can be entered either by pointing or by typing the appropriate name or address(es). Details on cell references are included in the entries Cell **13★**, Formulas and Formula Calculation **136★**, and Range **291★**.

Single numeric values: A single numeric value can be a number, a single-cell reference, or the calculated value of one or more formulas or functions. For example:

@ABS(−10)
@SQRT(D15)
@INT(B1/B2∗2)
@SQRT(@SQRT(16))

Ranges: A range reference can either be the addresses of two diagonally opposite corner cells of a range, or it can be a range name. For example:

@SUM(A1..A10)
@SUM(Sales)

Strings: A string can be an actual string of characters enclosed in double quotation marks, a cell reference, a cell name, or a string formula using the & concatenation operator. For example:

@EXACT("Jan Sales","JAN SALES")
@FIND("Smith",A1,0)
@FIND("Smith",Emp Name,0)
@LOWER("NOW IS THE "&"TIME FOR ALL GOOD MEN")

Note: String operations are a feature of Release 2 of 1-2-3.

- **Database statistical functions**◆

Certain functions are designed specifically for use with databases. These are @DSUM, @DAVG, @DCOUNT, @DMIN, @DMAX, @DSTD, and @DVAR. They are the database equivalents of the functions @SUM, @AVG, @COUNT, @MIN, @MAX, @STD, and @VAR, and accomplish much the same objectives, but are tailored to use with database fields and records.

Each of the database statistical functions requires an argument that takes the following form:

@function name(input range,offset,criterion range)

where:

☐ The input range is the database itself, including the field names, which are required in the first row of the database.

☐ The offset is the column (field) on which the function is to operate.

□ The criterion range is a range of cells, separate from the database, in which you specify the criteria against which 1-2-3 evaluates each value in the offset, and from which 1-2-3 chooses the values that are included in calculating the value of the function. The criterion range is a way for you to analyze records and include only those that meet your requirements. Examples are included in the entries on each of the database statistical functions, and on the entries Data Table **79★**, /Data Table 1 **87★**, and /Data Table 2 **89★**.

- **Comments**

1-2-3 offers many different functions for performing a wide variety of arithmetic, trigonometric, logical, financial, and string operations. Details are included in the entries on the individual functions.

@FV()

- **Format**

@FV(payment,interest,term)

- **Description**

The @FV function is a financial function that returns the future value of an investment made in equal amounts (payment), at a fixed periodic interest rate, over a specified number of periods (term). @FV answers the question: Is a given investment strategy adequate to meet a future cash liability or obligation? The future value is calculated according to the formula:

$$FV = payment * ((((1+int)^n)-1)/int)$$

where: payment is the payment per period; int is the periodic interest rate; and n is the number of periods.

The arguments can be numeric values, cell addresses, other functions, single-cell range names, or formulas. So, for example, any of the following would be valid: @FV(2000,.12,24), @FV(A1,A2,A3), or @FV(Payment,Rate,Term).

@FV() · /Graph

- **Example**

  Like 1-2-3's other financial functions, the @FV function assumes an ordinary annuity—in other words, an investment of periodic equal payments in which the payments are made at the end, not the beginning, of each period. To calculate an annuity due—one in which payments are made at the beginning of each period—you can use the formula:

  @FV(payment,interest,term) * (1+interest)

  Whether for an ordinary annuity or an annuity due, the term and the interest rate must match in terms of the period specified. Thus, if the term is given in years, and the interest rate is monthly, multiply the term by 12.

  The following two examples illustrate the differences between the projected future value of an ordinary annuity and an annuity due, based on monthly payments of $100 over a term of five years, with 8.5 percent annual interest paid at the end of each month.

  @FV(100,.085/12,60)

  gives $7444.24, the value of an ordinary annuity.

  @FV(100,.085/12,60) * (1+.085)

  gives $8077.00, the value of an annuity due.

  A popular use of @FV is to plan for a child's college education. With @FV you enter what you can afford to save each month, the interest you can earn, and how much time you have, to see how much money will result.

/Graph

- **Description**

  The /Graph commands enable you to use 1-2-3's graphing facility to create several different types of charts to display the results of your worksheet data or calculations. This entry discusses graphs in general, and provides an overview of the ways in which you use the /Graph commands. Individual entries on each of the commands give details on how and when to use them.

- **What is a graph?**
A graph is a visual representation of the numeric data in a worksheet, so by creating a graph, you can easily see relationships between and among sets of values. This facility is especially useful in preparing summaries of data for presentation. If your computer has graphics capability, you can also use graphs to see on screen the effects of changing values in a "what if" situation, simply by telling 1-2-3 to plot (and label) the results of using different variables on a single graph. (This latter application is particularly effective if you first calculate the "what if" values in a data table 79★.)

The /Graph commands enable you to prepare graphs and, if your computer has graphics capability, to display those graphs on the screen. The PrintGraph 271★ program, a set of related commands available through the 1-2-3 Access System 3★, enables you to print the graphs you create, as well as add special formatting to them and choose other features, including size, orientation, type style, degree of quality, and position on the page.

- **Creating a graph**
Since a graph is a two-dimensional picture of a set of data values, there are certain pieces of information 1-2-3 needs before it can translate your values into a graph. At the very minimum, it must know what *type* of graph you want, and what *ranges of values* are to be graphed. Optionally, and for your own ease of understanding, you can tell 1-2-3 to add *enhancements*—legends, titles, labels, crosshatching, and so on.

Graph types: Using the /Graph commands, you can create five different types of graph: line, bar, XY, stacked bar, and pie charts. Line graphs plot a set of data values over time; bar and stacked bar graphs show quantitative relationships of individual values; XY graphs show the points at which values in two sets of data coincide; and pie charts show values as percentages (slices) of a whole (pie). The illustrations on the following pages show examples of each, and the values they represent. In sequence, they are a line, bar, XY, stacked bar, and pie chart.

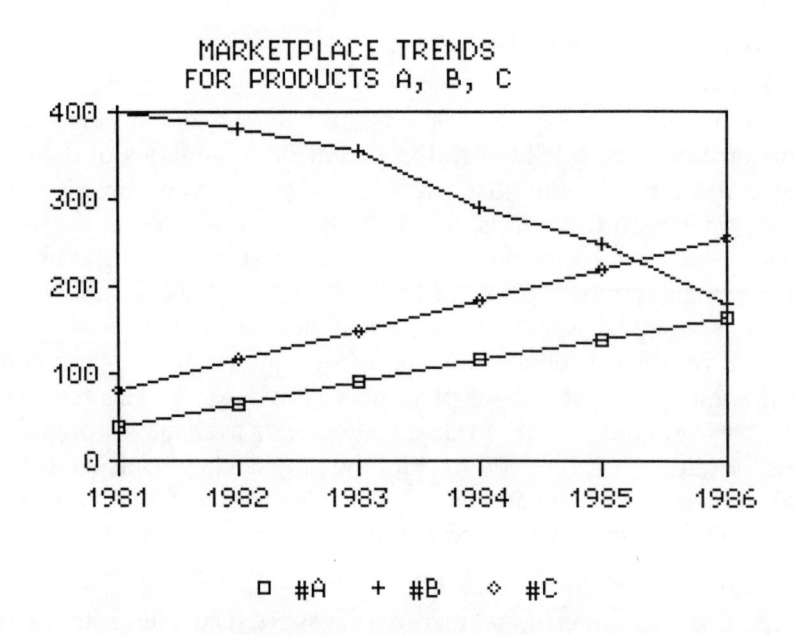

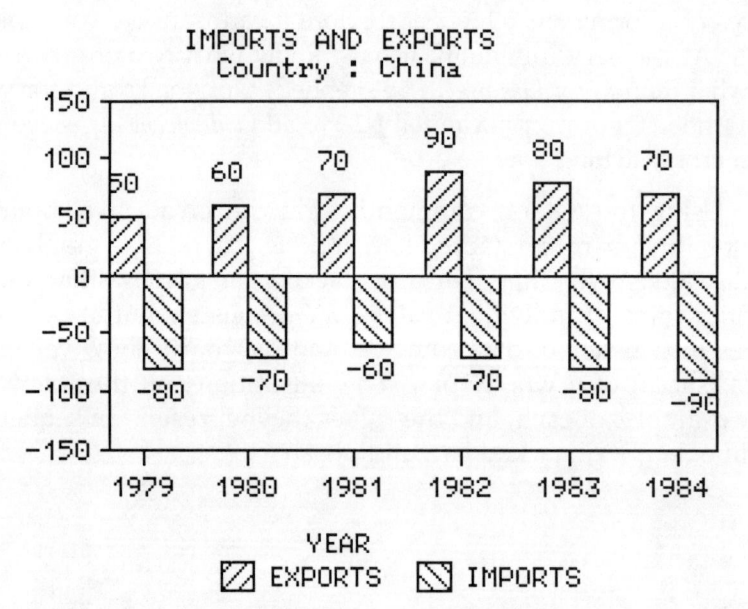

/Graph

MARKETPLACE TRENDS
FOR PRODUCTS A, B, C

□ #A   + #B   ◇ #C

IMPORTS AND EXPORTS
Country : China

YEAR
▨ EXPORTS   ▧ IMPORTS

/Graph

Gasoline Consumption vs. Price (1973-1982)

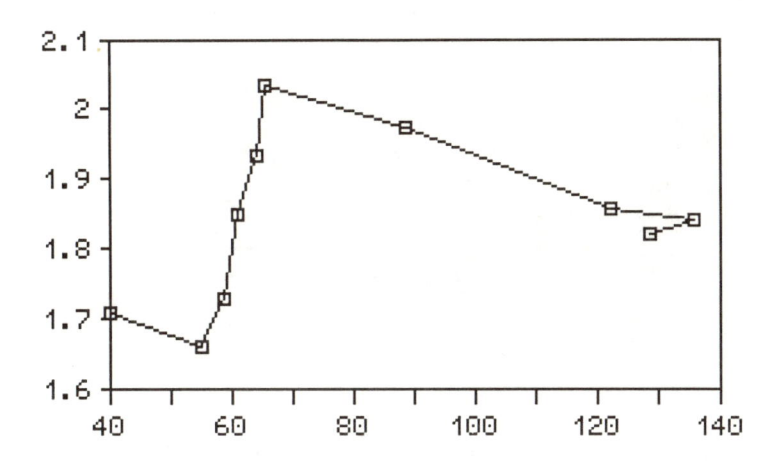

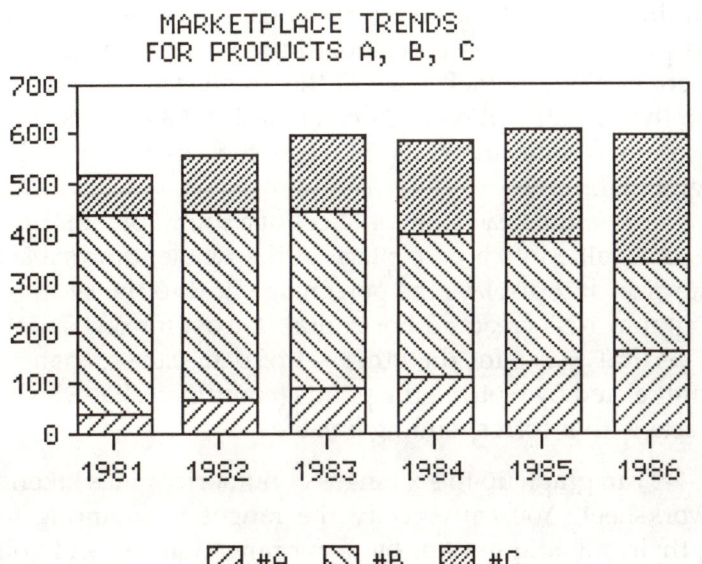

MARKETPLACE TRENDS
FOR PRODUCTS A, B, C

#A #B #C

151

/Graph

```
         MARKETPLACE TRENDS - 1985
            FOR PRODUCTS A, B, C
```

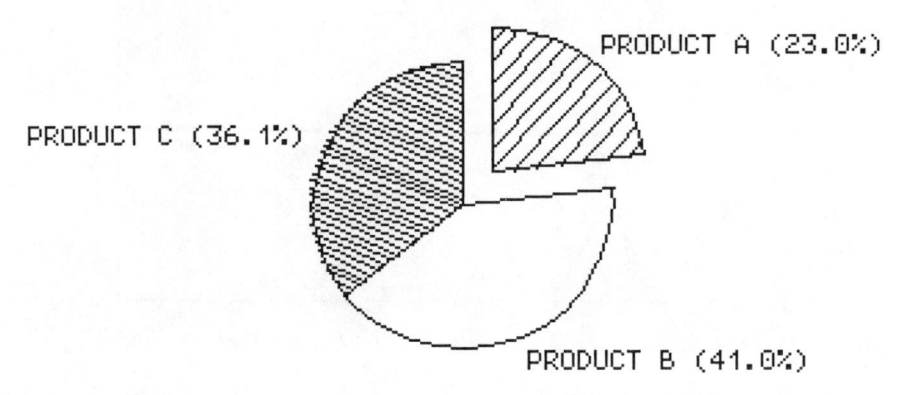

                                PRODUCT A (23.0%)

           PRODUCT C (36.1%)

                                PRODUCT B (41.0%)

Data points: On line, bar, and stacked bar graphs, data values are always represented as points or as bars corresponding to a vertical scale (the Y axis) 1-2-3 generates along the left edge of the graph. Unless you specify otherwise with the /Graph Options **162★** command, 1-2-3 automatically divides the Y axis into equal intervals between the smallest and largest values being graphed.

A pie chart represents data values as slices of a round pie. In this case, 1-2-3 converts each value into a percentage of the whole, draws a slice of the appropriate size, and displays the percentage next to the slice.

On an XY graph, 1-2-3 creates a horizontal (X axis) for one set of data values, and a vertical Y axis for the other set of data values, then shows how the two are related by plotting the points (coordinates) at which each X value intersects with a corresponding Y value.

Graph ranges: 1-2-3 can graph up to six ranges of numeric values taken from the current worksheet. You can specify the ranges by pointing to the range, typing their cell addresses or by using range names, and you can enter or change data either before or after you have defined the ranges with a /Graph command.

The data ranges can include any values you care to have graphed—1-2-3 will graph them to the appropriate scale. However, it is important to make certain that all ranges you specify are the same size. You cannot, for example, use one range of 10 cells and another of 100 on the same graph.

To tell 1-2-3 you want to specify a range of values, you choose one of the letter options, *X* or *A* through *F*, on the /Graph menu:

```
Type X A B C D E F Reset View Save Options Name Quit
```

A represents your first set of data values, *B* represents the second, *C* represents the third, and so on.

- In line and bar graphs, each value from each data range is plotted individually.
- In stacked bar graphs, values from successive ranges (B through F) are *built on top of* the bars generated for the A range.
- In pie charts, you specify only a single A range. The B range is optional, for designating crosshatching and exploded sections.
- In XY graphs, you specify A to F ranges and, as described next, an X range as well.

The definition of an X range varies, according to the type of graph you tell 1-2-3 to draw.

- On a line, bar, or stacked bar graph, the X range can include numbers, labels, or even formulas. 1-2-3 displays the entries from this range as labels for points along the X axis of the graph. For example, if you specify the six columns of sales figures in the worksheet on the following page as ranges A through F, you can specify the row of column headings (1981 through 1986) as the X range, and 1-2-3 will display those headings along the X axis of the graph, as shown.

/Graph

```
A10: 'TOTAL                                                          READY
```

	A	B	C	D	E	F	G
1		MARKETPLACE TRENDS					
2		FOR PRODUCTS A, B, C					
3							
4		1981	1982	1983	1984	1985	1986
5							
6	PRODUCT A	40	65	90	115	140	165
7	PRODUCT B	400	380	356	290	250	180
8	PRODUCT C	80	115	150	185	220	255
9							
10	TOTAL	520	560	596	590	610	600

MARKETPLACE TRENDS
FOR PRODUCTS A, B, C

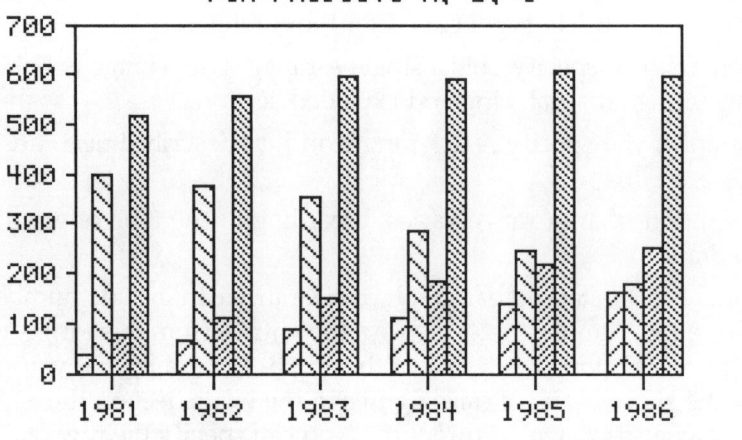

[bar chart showing #A, #B, #C, Total across years 1981–1986]

- In a pie chart, each entry in the X range is displayed as a label for its corresponding piece of pie.
- In an XY graph, as described earlier, the X range must be a range of values. 1-2-3 displays those values along the X axis of the graph.

Symbols, shaded patterns, and color: When graphing different ranges of values, 1-2-3 can differentiate individual ranges by using symbols (in line and XY graphs) or by indicating shading with different types of crosshatching (in bar and stacked bar graphs, and in pie charts). 1-2-3 can also use color, if your computer is equipped to display it. There are eight different types of shading (or color) available, 0 (no shading) through 7. Adding 100 to a shading value causes the corresponding pie slice to be "exploded" away in a pie chart. These options are chosen through the *Color* and *B&W* options of the /Graph Options command.

The methods for differentiating ranges are preset in 1-2-3, as shown in the following chart:

Range order:	Letter:	Symbol:	Pattern:	Color:
First	A	□	/ / /	White
Second	B	+	\ \ \	Red
Third	C	◇	////////	Blue
Fourth	D	△	\\\\\\\\	White
Fifth	E	×	XXX	Red
Sixth	F	▽	XXXX	Blue

Enhancements: There are a number of ways you can enhance your graphs, to make them easier to understand or, simply, to make them look nicer. As with specifying colors or patterns, you make these selections through the /Graph Options command. These choices are described briefly here, and in more detail in the /Graph Options entry.

Legends: You can tell 1-2-3 to include a legend with a graph, to identify any of the following:

- ☐ Data ranges.
- ☐ Symbols in a line or XY graph.
- ☐ Colors or patterns in a bar or stacked bar graph.

1-2-3 ignores legends in pie charts, because it uses labels in the X range for the same purpose.

When entering a legend, you can either type one of up to 19 characters or you can specify a cell address or range name *preceded by* the backslash (\). (If you omit the backslash, 1-2-3 will display the address or name, instead of the cell contents.)

Legends are placed beneath the X axis of the graph so, obviously, the shorter the better. You can, if you wish, enter a legend of more than 19 characters by entering it in a cell and then referencing that cell by typing a backslash and a cell reference or range name in response to the prompt.

Sometimes, the screen will display a legend with overlapping characters. This does not, however, necessarily mean that the legend will be printed the same way. The PrintGraph program may correct the situation; to be certain, use the PrintGraph Image-Select 272★ command to preview the graph before you print it.

Formats: With line and XY graphs, you can choose the *Format* option of the /Graph Options command and do one of the following:

- ☐ Connect data points with lines only.
- ☐ Display data points as symbols only.
- ☐ Display data points with *both* lines and symbols.
- ☐ Replace lines and symbols with identifying labels.

These choices can be applied either to individual ranges of values or to the graph as a whole.

If you choose to replace lines and symbols with labels, you use the *Data-Labels* option of the /Graph Options command to specify the range of cells whose contents are to be used to label the corresponding data points of the graphed ranges. You use this same option to specify the alignment (left, center, right, above, or below) you want for the labels. A label range can contain either text or values.

Titles: 1-2-3 lets you specify up to four different titles: two at the top of the graph, one along the X axis, and another (which is displayed and printed sideways) along the Y axis. Titles at the top of the graph are centered; on paper, the first is printed in larger characters and, if you choose (through the PrintGraph program), in a different font.

Titles can be up to 39 characters long. They can either be typed in directly or, if you want to use the contents of an existing cell, they can be selected by typing a backslash and a cell address or range name.

Grid lines: Grid lines create the on-screen equivalent of lines on graph paper. 1-2-3 displays them for each scale marker on either the X axis, the Y axis, or both axes. You can specify grid lines for any type of graph other than a pie chart.

Scales: 1-2-3 will automatically determine a numeric scale that allows all values in your data ranges to be displayed on-screen. On the Y axis, this scale corresponds to either the height of the bars in a bar or stacked bar graph, or to the coordinates in an XY graph.

If you wish, however, you can choose *Scale* from the /Graph Options menu to tell 1-2-3 to use an X or Y scale (and, optionally, the upper and lower scale limits) you specify. You can also use this option to tell 1-2-3 not to display all intervals on the X axis—in other words, to skip some and display only every other interval, or every third one, or whichever marker you specify.

You can also use the *Scale* option to format numbers. The choices are the same as those for standard numeric formatting (see /Worksheet Global Format 366★ or /Range Format 300★ for details). You can format numbers on either the X or the Y axis, but bear in mind that numeric formatting on the X axis is cosmetic only except on XY graphs, because only these graphs treat numbers on the X axis as actual numeric values.

- **Viewing a graph**

    As long as you have entered enough information for 1-2-3 to create a graph, you can view that graph at any time. If you are in the /Graph menu, select the *View* option. If you are in READY mode 249◆, press the F10 [Graph] 144◆ key and 1-2-3 will display the graph most recently drawn.

    Since 1-2-3 remembers the data ranges rather than the cell contents when it stores graph specifications, you can change the data in defined ranges again and again, and view the resulting graph immediately.

- **Saving graphs**

    When you have created a graph, you can store it for future use in two ways:

    ☐ Use the /Graph Save 172★ command to tell 1-2-3 to save the graph as a special file with the extension .PIC. Once saved, you can print the graph with the PrintGraph program mentioned earlier. This type of graph cannot have its values changed.

□ Use the /Graph Name 160★ command to assign a unique name (of up to 15 characters) to the graph *and to save its settings with the current worksheet*. This method enables you to create a number of different graphs from the same worksheet, save each graph under its own name, and "file" all of them with the worksheet from which they are derived. This type of graph can be viewed and modified whenever you want. The graph settings are kept with the worksheet when you use the /File Save 130★, /File Retrieve 128★, or /File Xtract 133★ command. The /File Combine 121★ command, however, does not carry graph settings with a combined file.

In essence, when you save a graph as a .PIC file, you are telling 1-2-3, "This graph is complete; store it as a separate document that I can print with PrintGraph." When you name a graph, however, you are telling 1-2-3, "This graph may or may not be complete; save its settings with my worksheet so I can refer to it later."

The difference between the two methods is substantial. Depending on what you intend to do with your graph, make your choice according to both your current and future needs.

■ **Comments**
Related entries are: /Graph A...F 158★, /Graph X 174★, /Graph Type 173★, /Graph Reset 171★, /Graph View 174★, /Graph Save 172★, /Graph Options 162★, /Graph Name 160★, and /Graph Quit 171★.

/Graph A...F   /GA...F

```
Worksheet Range Copy Move File Print Graph Data System Quit
Type X A B C D E F Reset View Save Options Name Quit
```

■ **Description**
The /Graph A...F commands let you specify up to six data ranges on the current worksheet for graphing. Each range is defined with one of the letters A through F and each can contain either calculated or numeric values. Values in these ranges are graphed so that they correspond to program-generated points on the Y axis of all but pie charts. With the latter, you can specify only a single *data* range, A, in which each value represents one slice (percentage) of the pie (an optional B range is for formatting; X is for labels).

Note: The /Graph X **174★** command also lets you specify a range, but differs from the A through F choices in two respects:

- It represents the X, not Y, axis of the graph.
- It can refer to either labels or data values, depending on the type of graph you are creating.

■ **Procedure**

When you choose the /Graph command to specify one or more data ranges, it is best to enter the ranges in sequence, beginning with A. To begin, highlight the letter A in the /Graph menu and press Return.

1-2-3 will prompt *Enter first data range:*. If you have not specified a range before, 1-2-3 displays the current address of the cell pointer. If you have already specified a range, 1-2-3 highlights and displays the addresses of the range you last specified.

Depending on circumstances, you can:

- Press Return to accept the proposed range.
- Type a period (.) to anchor the current cell and then expand the pointer with the arrow keys.
- Change the proposed range or specify a new one either by typing the addresses of two diagonally opposite corner cells or by moving the cell pointer, then anchoring and expanding it as explained in the preceding step.
- Type a range name or press the F3 [Name] **144♦** key to display a list of existing names to choose from.

After any of these steps, press Return to execute the command.

There are no limits (other than the worksheet's dimensions) on the number or size of the values you can specify—1-2-3 will graph them to an appropriate scale whenever possible. It automatically generates a scale that covers the interval between the smallest and largest values in the range(s). Nor are you restricted to using all positive numbers or all negative numbers; if some values are positive and others are negative, 1-2-3 will graph them all according to scale, above and below a 0 point on the Y axis.

Note: If a range contains widely varying values—5 to 5,000,000, for example—the limitations of your screen and printer may prevent 1-2-3 from displaying values at one or the other extreme. When this happens, 1-2-3 will graph whichever extreme contains the most data values.

If values are equal to or greater than 1000, 1-2-3 displays them as units with the explanatory label *(Thousands)*. Similarly, if values are equal to or greater than 1,000,000, 1-2-3 displays them as units with the explanatory label *(Millions)*. You can, however, change this default format with the /Graph Options **162★** command.

Specifying subsequent ranges: If you wish to specify more than one range of data values, simply follow the same procedure, choosing, in turn, the letters B, C, D, and so on. It is important to remember that each subsequent range you specify must contain the same number of cells as those you have already defined. 1-2-3 creates multiple-range graphs by plotting the contents of corresponding cells, so you cannot tell it to graph one range of 10 values and another of 12, 15, 2000, or whatever.

- **Comments**

Once you have defined data ranges, you can use the /Graph Reset **171★** command to cancel any or all of them. To see what a graph looks like, use the /Graph View **174★** command or, if you are in READY mode **249◆**, press the F10 [Graph] **144◆** function key.

For additional details on naming and specifying cell ranges, see the entry Range **291★**.

/Graph Name   /GN

```
Worksheet  Range  Copy  Move  File  Print  Graph  Data  System  Quit
    Type  X  A  B  C  D  E  F  Reset  View  Save  Options  Name  Quit
         Use  Create  Delete  Reset
```

- **Description**

The /Graph Name command is used to name, view, and delete specified graphs as part of the current worksheet. Because the /Graph Name command stores graph settings in much the same way range addresses are stored with range names, many different graphs can be stored with the worksheet from which they are created, and you can easily switch back and forth among them, simply by calling each by name.

- **Procedure**

When you choose the /Graph Name command, 1-2-3 displays the menu shown at the beginning of this entry.

Create: Choose *Create* to assign a name to a graph and store its settings in the worksheet. 1-2-3 will prompt *Enter graph name:*. You can type a name of up to 15 characters.

Note: If the name already exists for another graph, 1-2-3 will overwrite the settings for that graph without prompting for confirmation. You can quickly check existing graph names by pressing Esc to move back one step in the command sequence, then choosing *Use* from the /Graph Name list of options. 1-2-3 will display a menu of all graph names associated with the worksheet.

Although you can create many graph names with the /Graph Name command, the settings are not permanently saved with the worksheet until you use either the /File Save **130★** or the /File Xtract **133★** command to store your work on disk. Once saved, the graphs can be brought back with the /File Retrieve **128★** command.

To print a graph that has been named and stored with the /Graph Name command, you must save it to disk as a separate file with the /Graph Save **172★** command. It can then be printed from the PrintGraph **271★** program.

Using a named graph: Choose *Use* to view a graph previously named with /Graph Name Create and make its settings the currently active ones.

When you specify this command, 1-2-3 prompts *Enter name of graph to make current:*, and displays a menu of existing graph names. You can choose from these by pointing or typing. When you press Return, 1-2-3 makes the named settings current and draws the graph they specify.

Note: When you use this command, any current graph settings are replaced by those of the incoming graph. If you want to reuse your current settings, be sure to save them with the /Graph Name Create command before you choose /Graph Name Use.

/Graph Name · /Graph Options

Deleting a graph: Choose *Delete* to erase a graph you previously named with /Graph Name Create.

When you choose this command, 1-2-3 prompts *Enter name of graph to delete:* and displays a menu of existing graph names. Select the one you want, either by typing or pointing, and press Return.

Note: 1-2-3 does not prompt for confirmation before deleting the graph you select, so be certain you have no further need for the graph.

Since the /Graph Name Delete command removes unwanted graph settings from the worksheet itself, you can use this command as a quick way to reduce the size of a file or to free memory for other uses.

To delete a graph saved to disk (.PIC file), use the /File Erase Graph 125◆ command.

Resetting graph names: Choose *Reset* to erase all graphs previously named with /Graph Name Create.

Note: When you choose this command, 1-2-3 offers no prompt and no menu. As soon as you press Return, all named graphs associated with the current worksheet cease to exist. Since 1-2-3 does not request confirmation, be certain you wish to remove all graphs. If there are any you want to keep, either delete the graphs one by one with the /Graph Name Delete command, or save finished graphs for printing with the /Graph Save command (The current settings are not affected.)

/Graph Options   /GO

```
Worksheet  Range  Copy  Move  File  Print  Graph  Data  System  Quit
Type  X  A  B  C  D  E  F  Reset  View  Save  Options  Name  Quit
Legend  Format  Titles  Grid  Scale  Color  B&W  Data-Labels  Quit
```

■ **Description**

The /Graph Options command allows you to choose enhancements for the graphs you create. Using this command, you can add legends, titles, formats, labels, and grids; you can create graphs in color or with shaded patterns; and you can control the scale of the X and Y axes, as well as format the numbers and labels on them.

Procedure

When you choose the /Graph Options command, 1-2-3 displays the menu of choices shown at the beginning of this entry.

Legends: Choose *Legend* to tell 1-2-3 to include a legend below a graph, as in the following illustration:

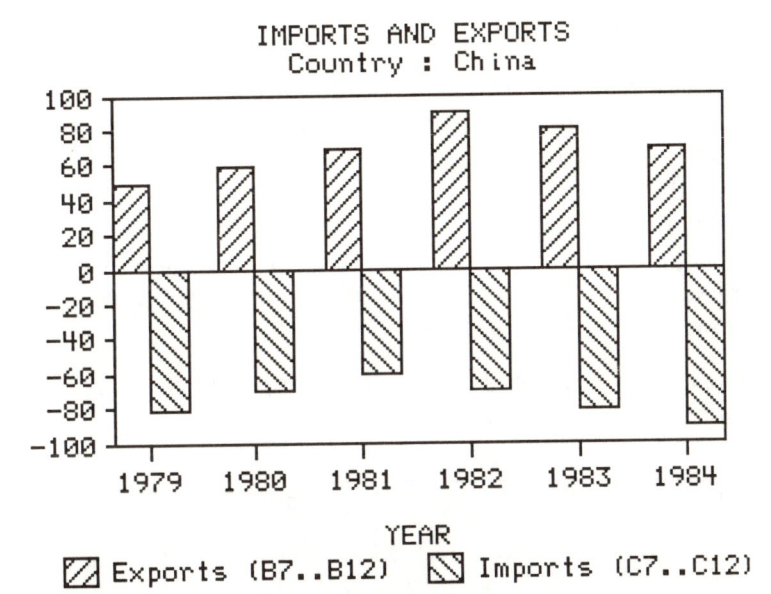

IMPORTS AND EXPORTS
Country : China

[Bar graph showing values from 1979 to 1984, with Exports (B7..B12) and Imports (C7..C12) legend]

A legend can identify any of the following:

☐ A data range.
☐ A symbol in a line or XY graph.
☐ A color or pattern in a bar or stacked bar graph, as shown.

1-2-3 ignores legends in pie charts, because it uses labels in the X range for the same purpose.

When entering a legend, you can either type one of up to 19 characters or you can specify the contents of a cell anywhere on the worksheet by typing a backslash (\), followed by either a cell address or a single-cell range name.

If you specify a cell address on the worksheet, 1-2-3 will not automatically update your graph if you happen to move the cell with the /Move 250★ or the /Worksheet Insert 373★ or /Worksheet Delete 357★ command. Thus, if you think you may be rearranging a graph-related worksheet, you should consider using a cell name, rather than address, as a reference for a legend. 1-2-3 will automatically redefine the name if the cell is moved, so the name will always refer to the correct location.

Since legends are placed below the X axis of the graph, the shorter they are, the more easily read your graph will be. If, however, your legend must be longer than the 19 characters you can type directly, enter the text of the legend in a cell and use the backslash-cell reference method to display it.

Sometimes, the screen will display a legend with overlapping characters. This does not necessarily mean the legend will be printed the same way. The PrintGraph program may correct the situation; to see a more accurate portrayal of a graph's printed appearance, use the PrintGraph Image-Select 272◆ command to preview it before printing.

Formats: Choose *Format* to specify a particular appearance for either a line or an XY graph's data values, as in the following illustration:

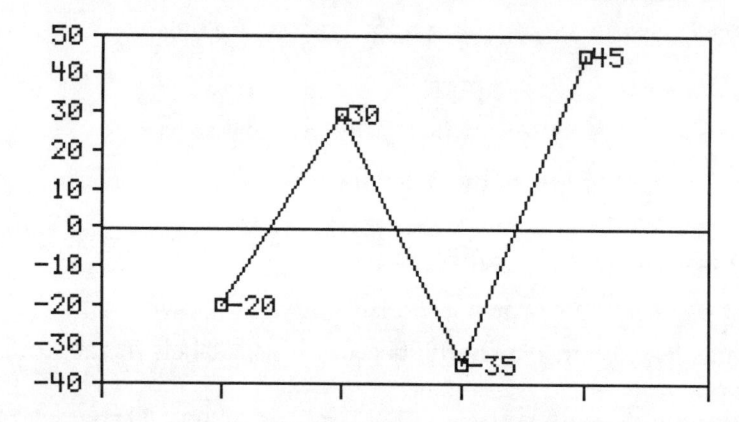

When you choose *Format*, 1-2-3 first offers the following choices: *Graph, A, B, C, D, E, F,* and *Quit*.

Select *Graph* to format all data ranges in the graph; select *A* through *F* to format an individual data range; or select *Quit* to exit the command.

After you select either all or part of the graph for formatting, 1-2-3 offers four more choices: *Lines, Symbols, Both,* and *Neither.* Select:

- *Lines* to connect data values with lines only.
- *Symbols* to show data values as symbols only.
- *Both* to show both lines and symbols. (This is the choice illustrated on the preceding page, and is the default format 1-2-3 uses.)
- *Neither* to show neither lines nor symbols. (Since this can make your graph invisible, choose this format only if you want to use the *Data-Labels* option to label the data points on the graph.)

If you choose to display symbols in your graph, 1-2-3 uses a predetermined set of six, one for each of the possible data ranges, as illustrated in the following table.

Data range:	A	B	C	D	E	F
Symbol:	□	+	◇	△	×	▽

Titles: Choose *Titles* to add descriptive titles to a graph, as illustrated here:

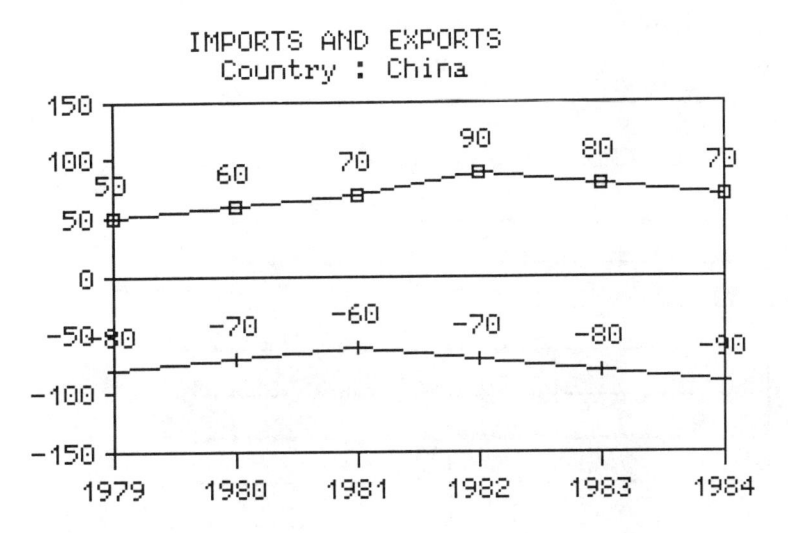

```
              IMPORTS AND EXPORTS
                Country : China
   150 ┬
                               90
   100 ┤           60    70    ┌──────80        70
      50┐                      └──────┐─────────┐
    50 ┤─────────────────────────────────────────
        
     0 ┤─────────────────────────────────────────
                        -60
         -50-80  -70           -70
              ┤                        -80      -90
   -100 ┤
   
   -150 ┴────┬─────┬─────┬─────┬─────┬─────┬
         1979  1980  1981  1982  1983  1984
```

165

/Graph Options

When you select *Titles*, 1-2-3 offers four options: *First*, *Second*, *X-axis*, and *Y-axis*. Choose:

- *First* to add a centered title at the top of the graph.
- *Second* to add a second centered title line beneath the first. When printed, the second title will be in smaller type and can, if you wish, be printed in a different font as well.
- *X-axis* to add a centered title below the horizontal X axis of the graph.
- *Y-axis* to add a title (which will be printed sideways) along the vertical Y axis of the graph. This choice does not apply to pie charts.

A title can be up to 39 characters long. Just as for legends, you can either type a title or use the contents of a cell anywhere on the worksheet by typing a backslash followed by either a cell address or a cell name. If you use the name of a multiple-cell range, 1-2-3 will consider the title to be the contents of the top left-hand cell of the range. You can use this backslash-cell reference method to include a title longer than 39 characters.

Grid: Choose *Grid* to create a grid of lines on any type of graph except a pie chart. Just as when you use graph paper, you may find that creating a grid makes it easier to compare separate graphed values, as you can see in the following illustration:

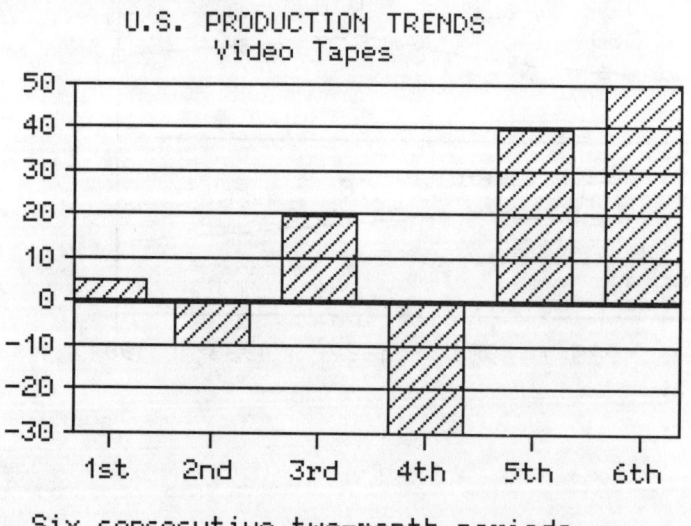

U.S. PRODUCTION TRENDS
Video Tapes

Six consecutive two-month periods

/Graph Options

When you select *Grid*, 1-2-3 offers four choices: *Horizontal, Vertical, Both,* and *Clear.* Choose:

- *Horizontal* to create a grid across the graph, beginning at each scale mark, as shown on the preceding page.
- *Vertical* to create a grid up and down the graph, beginning at each scale mark.
- *Both* to create horizontal and vertical grid lines from all scale marks.
- *Clear* to delete grid lines.

To see a grid, use the /Graph View **174**★ command.

Scale: 1-2-3 automatically determines a numeric scale so that your data can be presented on-screen, within the preset height and width of 1-2-3's graph display. Choose *Scale* to override 1-2-3's choices and set your own scale along the X and Y axes of a graph, or to specify a skip factor to display every nth scale mark along the X axis.

When you choose *Scale*, 1-2-3 displays three initial choices: *Y Scale, X Scale,* and *Skip.* Choose:

- *Y Scale* to set your own scale along the Y axis.
- *X Scale* to set your own scale along the X axis.
- *Skip*♦ to specify the intervals between scale marks on the horizontal axis. This option is useful when the X axis is overcrowded and you want to reduce the number of scale marks 1-2-3 displays and prints. The skip factor does not affect your graphed data, as you can see in the illustration here and on the next page.

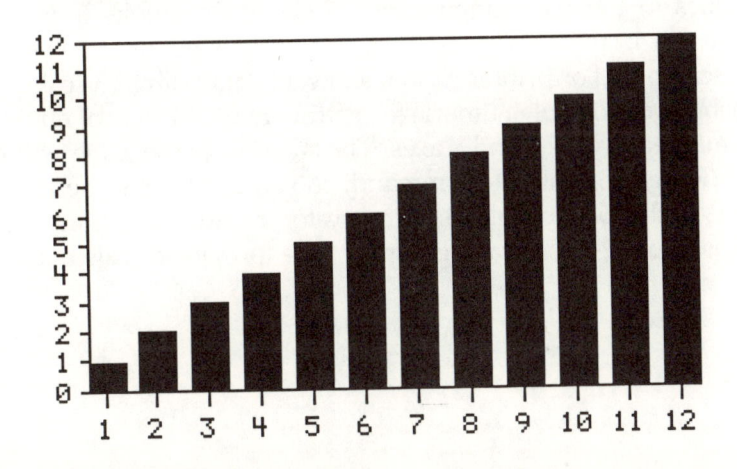

/Graph Options

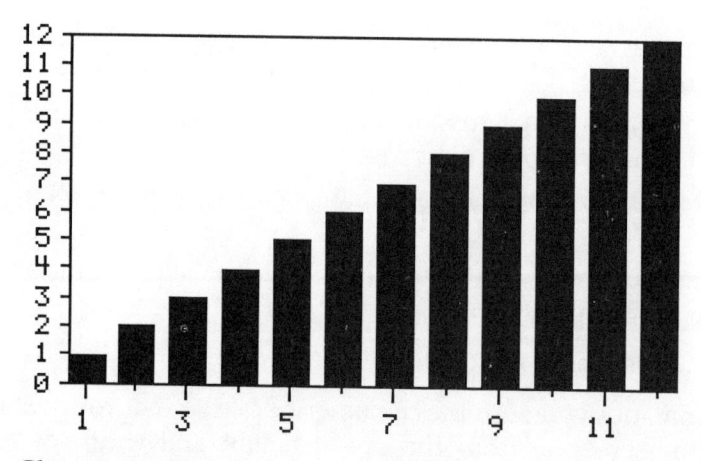

```
12
11
10
 9
 8
 7
 6
 5
 4
 3
 2
 1
 0
    1    3    5    7    9    11
```

Choosing either *Y Scale* or *X Scale* causes 1-2-3 to display an additional list of choices: *Automatic, Manual, Lower, Upper, Format, Indicator,* and *Quit.*

Automatic is the default setting. Choose this only if you have previously set scaling to *Manual* and you now wish to return to automatic scaling.

Manual lets you set scale limits of your own. If you select this option, you must then choose *Lower* and *Upper* to tell 1-2-3 the highest and lowest data values you want it to display.

When you choose manual scaling, 1-2-3 still fills the screen with your graph, but it will not show values that fall outside the limits you set. There is one exception to this rule: 1-2-3 ignores positive upper and lower limits for bar and stacked bar graphs; in these graphs, the baseline is always 0, and the entire bar is displayed.

In other instances, upper and lower limits may be rounded somewhat, and if the values in the data range vary widely (for example, 5, 50, and 50,000,000 all appear in the same range), extreme values may not be plotted because your screen and/or printer cannot show all data points to scale.

Format enables you to apply numeric formatting to the display of numbers used as scale markers on the X and Y axes. The choices are the same as those offered in the /Range Format **300★** command, so you can format these numbers for a fixed number of decimals, as currency, for scientific notation, and so on. With Release 2 of 1-2-3, you can also apply time formats to scale markers.

X-scale formatting, however, is meaningful only for XY graphs. All other graphs treat numbers on the X axis as labels, not numeric values.

Indicator is a Release 2 option that enables you to turn off 1-2-3's automatic indication of the size of the units displayed as scale markers on the X and Y axes. Normally, when scale markers exceed three digits (for example, when the Y scale is marked off in thousands), 1-2-3 shortens the numbers and displays an indicator that tells you what units are represented. Thus, the numbers 5000, 6000, 7000, and 8000 will be displayed as 5, 6, 7, and 8 on the axis, with the notation *(Thousands)* alongside.

If you wish, for the sake of appearance or because you have annotated the scale intervals in a legend, you can turn off 1-2-3's automatic display of the indicator. The choices are *No* and *Yes* (the default).

Color: The *Color* option of the /Graph Options command enables you to display a graph in color, if you have a color monitor. This option is not related to printing a graph in color, because 1-2-3 automatically stores preset color assignments for your data ranges, even if the graph is created on a monochrome monitor. The choice of printing in color is made through the PrintGraph **271★** program, and depends on the printer or plotter you use, not on a /Graph Options Color setting.

B&W: The *B&W* option is used to change from a color fill display to a line pattern fill for bar and stacked bar graphs.

Data-Labels: Choose the *Data-Labels*♦ option to specify a range of cells whose contents you want to use to label data values within a graph. These labels are like X-range labels, but appear inside the graph as an adjunct to, or replacement for, data-point symbols. (Pie charts use the X range for labels and ignore the *Data-Labels* option.)

When you choose *Data-Labels*, 1-2-3 prompts with the letters of the six possible data ranges, A through F. Choose the range to which you want to apply data labels. 1-2-3 will then prompt you to enter the range of cells whose contents are to be used as labels. Enter the range, making certain

/Graph Options

that there is a label cell for each of the data values you want to label in the graph. If you want to label only some of the values, include one blank cell in the range for each non-labeled value in the graph. This same procedure can be used, as shown in the following two illustrations, to position a label where you want it within a graph.

```
D12: 'prisons
Enter label range for A-range data: D3..D12                          POINT
         A           B         C         D         E         F         G
  1   State Budget Prisons  Welfare
  2
  3              Aug-81   1250000   1000000
  4              Feb-82   1325867   1025000
  5              Aug-82   1401734   1050000
  6              Feb-83   1477601   1075000
  7              Aug-83   1553468   1100000
  8              Feb-84   1629335   1125000
  9              Aug-84   1705202   1150000
 10              Feb-85   1781069   1175000
 11              Aug-85   1856936   1200000
 12              Feb-86   1932803   1225000   prisons   welfare
 13              Aug-86   2008670   1250000
 14              Feb-87   2084537   1275000
 15              Aug-87   2160404   1300000
 16              Feb-88   2236271   1325000
 17              Aug-88   2312138   1350000
 18
```

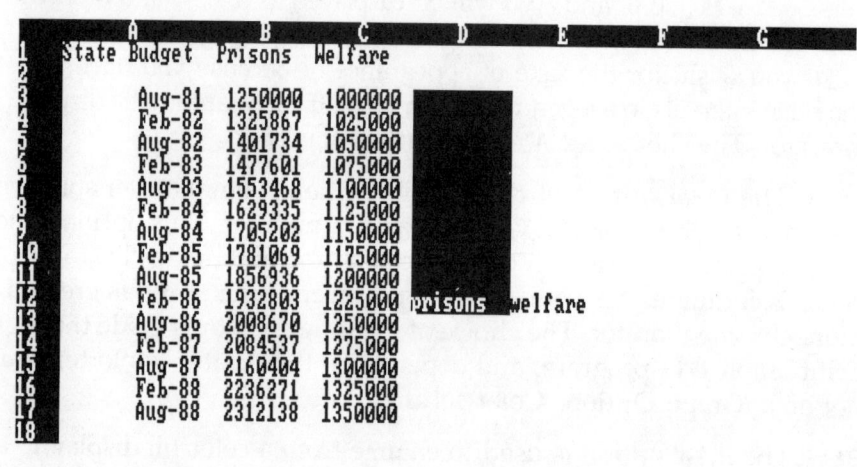

State Budget

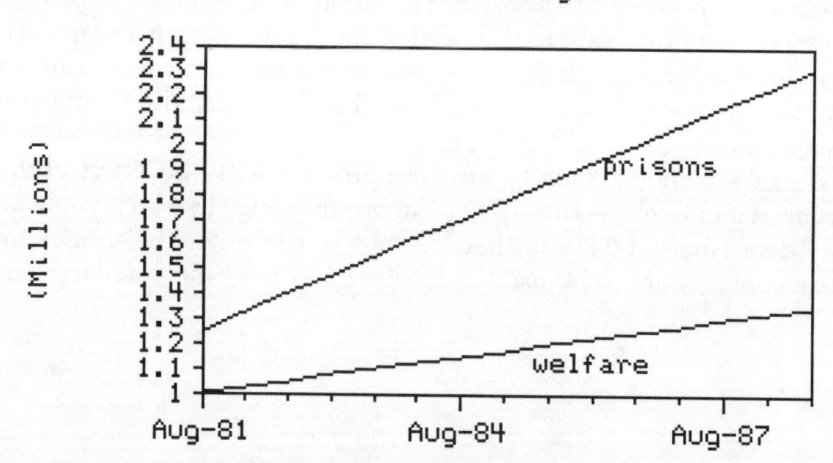

[Line graph showing prisons and welfare values from Aug-81 to Aug-87, Y-axis in Millions from 1 to 2.4]

Quit: Choose the *Quit* option from within the /Graph Options menu to exit the command and return to READY **249◆** mode.

/Graph Quit /GQ

```
Worksheet Range Copy Move File Print Graph Data System Quit
Type X A B C D E F Reset View Save Options Name Quit
```

- **Description**

    The /Graph Quit command enables you to leave the /Graph commands menu and return to READY 249♦ mode without saving any graph settings you may have specified.

- **Procedure**

    If the menu of /Graph commands is displayed in the Control Panel at the top of the screen, simply choose /Graph Quit to return to READY mode.

    If you have selected one of the /Graph commands, either press Esc to return to the /Graph menu or, if the command offers the option, choose *Quit* to exit the command and then choose the /Graph Quit command.

/Graph Reset /GR

```
Worksheet Range Copy Move File Print Graph Data System Quit
Type X A B C D E F Reset View Save Options Name Quit
Graph X A B C D E F Quit
```

- **Description**

    The /Graph Reset command allows you to cancel either individual range settings or *all* settings for the current graph.

- **Procedure**

    When you choose the /Graph Reset command, 1-2-3 displays the menu of choices shown at the beginning of this entry. Depending on what it is you wish to do:

    ☐ Choose *Graph* to cancel all settings for the current graph. This is the equivalent of erasing a graph so you can start all over, but it works only if you have not yet named the graph with the /Graph Name Create 161♦ command. If the graph has already been named, you must use the /Graph Name Delete or Reset command, instead.

/Graph Reset · /Graph Save

- Choose *X* to reset, and thus prevent the display of, the X range. With all but XY graphs, choosing *X* eliminates the descriptive labels you specified with the X range for display along the X axis or (for pie charts) alongside each slice of pie. You must have a numeric X range in an XY graph.
- Choose one of the options lettered *A* through *F* to reset and thus suppress the specified data range from being displayed. Choosing one of these options also resets any corresponding data labels you have specified with the /Graph Options 162★ command. If you later specify the same range, 1-2-3 will reinstate corresponding labels.
- Choose *Quit* to return to the menu of /Graph commands.

/Graph Save /GS

```
Worksheet Range Copy Move File Print Graph Data System Quit
Type X A B C D E F Reset View Save Options Name Quit
```

- **Description**

The /Graph Save command tells 1-2-3 to save the current graph on disk as a separate file for later printing with PrintGraph 271★. When you save a graph with this command, 1-2-3 stores it with all its current settings. You cannot bring the file back into 1-2-3 if you decide you want to change it. To save graph settings with the worksheet, use the /Graph Name 160★ command.

- **Procedure**

When you choose the /Graph Save command, 1-2-3 prompts *Enter graph file name:* and displays a list of any existing file names and subdirectories.

If you wish to assign the file a new, as-yet-unused file name, type one, with up to eight letters or numbers (no spaces or special symbols, other than the underscore character).

If you want to save the graph with one of the existing file names 1-2-3 displays, highlight the appropriate file name and press Return. Since using an existing file name means that 1-2-3 will overwrite the old file with the new one, it prompts for confirmation by offering the choices *Cancel* and *Replace* before carrying out your command.

When you save a graph, 1-2-3 creates a file as a graphic on disk, and assigns it the extension .PIC for "picture." The file is saved in the current directory, unless you specify otherwise by: preceding the file name with the letter or name of a different disk or directory; moving into another directory by selecting a subdirectory name in the file menu; or backspacing up through the current path when in the file menu.

/Graph Type   /GT

```
Worksheet  Range  Copy  Move  File  Print  Graph  Data  System  Quit
Type  X  A  B  C  D  E  F  Reset  View  Save  Options  Name  Quit
Line  Bar  XY  Stacked-Bar  Pie
```

- **Description**

The /Graph Type command enables you to tell 1-2-3 which of the following types of graph you want to create: line (default), bar, XY, stacked bar, or pie.

- **Procedure**

When you choose the /Graph Type command, 1-2-3 displays the menu of choices shown at the beginning of this entry.

- ☐ Select *Line* to compare one or more series of values over time.
- ☐ Select *Bar* to see relationships among one or more series of values.
- ☐ Select *XY* to plot the relationship of one or more series of values to those in another series.
- ☐ Select *Stacked-Bar* to sum and compare corresponding values from two or more series.
- ☐ Select *Pie* to see each value in a single series diagramed as a percentage of the sum of all values in the series.

When you press Return, 1-2-3 returns to the /Graph commands menu. You can then specify the ranges of values to be graphed, as described in the entries /Graph A...F **158★** and /Graph X **174★**. The range requirements of each type of graph are as follows:

- ☐ Line, bar, or stacked bar graph: One to six ranges (A to F) of values.
- ☐ XY graph: One to six ranges (A to F) of values to be plotted along the Y axis; one X range of values to be plotted along the X axis.
- ☐ Pie chart: One (A) range of values only; one X range for labels to be displayed alongside each slice of the pie; an optional B range for shading and explosions.

/Graph View · /Graph X

/Graph View /GV

```
Worksheet Range Copy Move File Print Graph Data System Quit
Type X A B C D E F Reset View Save Options Name Quit
```

- **Description**

    If your computer is capable of displaying graphics, you can view the current graph by selecting the /Graph View command. 1-2-3 defines and remembers data ranges by cell locations, rather than actual values, so you can change cell contents repeatedly and view the results with /Graph View, without having to redefine data ranges each time.

- **Procedure**

    You select /Graph View directly from the /Graph menu. When you press Return, 1-2-3 displays the current graph, using the settings you most recently specified. To return to the /Graph menu, press any key.

- **Comments**

    An alternative means of viewing the current graph is to press the F10 [Graph] 144♦ function key while in READY mode 249♦. As with the /Graph View command, press any key when you wish to move on to another task. If you have two monitors, with one configured for graphics, you can leave the graph on the graphics monitor as you return to edit your worksheet.

    If your computer cannot display graphics, you cannot view your graphs unless you store them on disk with the /Graph Save 172★ command, then print them out with the PrintGraph 271★ program.

/Graph X /GX

```
Worksheet Range Copy Move File Print Graph Data System Quit
Type X A B C D E F Reset View Save Options Name Quit
```

- **Description**

    The /Graph X command, like the /Graph A…F commands 158★, lets you specify a range of cells whose contents you want placed in a graph. Its use varies, however, according to the type of graph you are creating:

    ☐ For line, bar, or stacked bar graphs use /Graph X to specify a range of *labels* to be displayed along the X axis of the graph.

    ☐ For pie charts, use /Graph X to specify a range of *labels* to be displayed alongside each slice of the pie representing the values in the A range.

□ For XY graphs, use /Graph X to specify the range of *values* or *formulas* to be plotted in pairs with the values specified in the A to F ranges.

Note that the X range has no numeric significance, *except* in XY graphs. Even though you can display numbers (dates, for example) as the X range in a line, bar, or stacked bar graph, or in a pie chart, those numbers are always descriptive labels with no mathematical relationship to the values plotted in the graph.

■ **Procedure**

The procedure for specifying an X range is the same as for specifying any A to F range.

To begin, you highlight the letter X in the /Graph menu and press Return. 1-2-3 will prompt *Enter X axis range:*. If you have not specified a range before, 1-2-3 displays the current address of the cell pointer. If you have already specified a range, 1-2-3 highlights and displays the addresses of the range you last specified.

Depending on circumstances, you can:

□ Press Return to accept the proposed range.

□ Type a period (.) to anchor the current cell and then expand the pointer with the arrow keys.

□ Change the proposed range or specify a new one either by typing the addresses of two diagonally opposite corner cells or by moving the cell pointer, then anchoring and expanding it.

□ Type a range name or press the F3 [Name] **144♦** key to display a list of existing names to choose from.

After any of these steps, press Return to execute the command.

■ **Comments**

As long as you have specified enough prerequisites for 1-2-3 to generate a graph, you can view the results at any time, either by choosing the /Graph View **174★** command or, if you are in READY mode **249♦**, by pressing the F10 [Graph] **144♦** function key.

If you find that the labels you specified for the X axis are crowded or overlapping, you may be able to refine the display by skipping some labels with the /Graph Options Scale Skip **167♦** command. If you are uncertain about the graph's appearance, or would simply like to see how the graph will look when printed, you can preview it with the PrintGraph **271★** program.

To cancel an X range, use the /Graph Reset **171★** command.

Help

1-2-3 offers an extensive, context-sensitive Help utility, which is available whenever you press the F1 [Help] key. The Help utility provides general information when you use it at the READY prompt, and tailored help when you use it inside a menu or in an error situation. When invoked, the Help utility saves the current session screen and presents its best guess as to the information you need. Use the pointer-movement keys to select a highlighted topic on a Help screen, then press Return to advance to a screen containing information on that topic. To review previous Help screens, press the backspace key. When you are ready to return to the worksheet, press Esc. Because the Help facility provides context-sensitive information, it can be used as a reference as you move through 1-2-3's tree-structured menu system, and will provide you with pertinent information on choosing command options or the right syntax or alternatives.

Unlike Release 1a, in which the Help utility was non-removable, Release 2 of 1-2-3 has its Help utility configured for a floppy disk system, in which the disk in drive A can be removed. This means, however, that the Help utility may be somewhat sluggish because it closes the Help file each time you exit the utility and reopens the file each time you invoke it. If you use 1-2-3 with a hard disk, change 1-2-3's method of accessing the Help file to *Instant* rather than the preconfigured removable access. To do this, use the /Worksheet Global Default Other Help 365♦ command, then the /Worksheet Global Default Update 363♦ command to update 1-2-3's configuration file to reflect the change. With the *Instant* option, 1-2-3 will open the Help file the first time you press F1 [Help], then leave it open for rapid access.

@HLOOKUP()

- **Format**
@HLOOKUP(x,range,row number)

- **Description**
@HLOOKUP is a special function that searches for, and returns, a value located within a table. Like the complementary function @VLOOKUP 351★, @HLOOKUP is useful when you have a number of alternative choices, such as tax rates, discounts, or commissions, from which you want to select different elements in different situations.

@HLOOKUP()

The function name is a reference to *horizontal* table lookup, and describes the order in which 1-2-3 searches the table range: First, 1-2-3 searches horizontally, comparing the value x, which you provide in the argument, to the comparison values you have entered in the top, or index, row of the table.

If 1-2-3 finds a value equal to x, it stops on that column and goes down to the row specified by the argument's row number, and then retrieves the value in the cell at the intersection of the column and row. If 1-2-3 does not find a value exactly equal to x, it stops at the first value greater than x, *backs up* one cell to the column headed by the preceding comparison value, then moves down that column to retrieve the value in the cell specified by the argument's row number.

Note: Horizontal and vertical lookup sequences are diagramed in the entry Lookup Tables **207★**.

■ **Procedure**

@HLOOKUP requires three arguments: x, range, and row number:

☐ x must be a numeric value or a reference to a cell containing a numeric value. If x is less than the smallest value in the index row, the function returns ERR. If x is greater than the largest value in the index row, 1-2-3 stops at the largest value. For example, if the index row contains the numbers 2, 4, 6, and 8, the function would return ERR if x=1, and would stop at 8 if x=9.

☐ The range is a reference to all cells in the lookup table, including the index row. The range can be specified by name or by cell addresses. The index row must contain numeric values, or references to cells containing numeric values, arranged in ascending order.

☐ The row number designates the row from which the lookup value is to be retrieved. The row number can be 0 or a positive number. If it is 0, 1-2-3 returns a value from the index row. If the row number is 1 or greater, 1-2-3 moves down the table to the row specified, and retrieves the value in that cell.

■ **Example**

The example on the following page illustrates the use of a horizontal lookup table. The three @HLOOKUP arguments can be seen in the formula at the top of the illustration.

@HLOOKUP() · @HOUR()

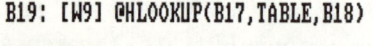

```
B19: [W9] @HLOOKUP(B17,TABLE,B18)                                    READY
         A     B       C       D       E       F       G
    ==================================================================
  1  Compound Interest -- Compounded Annually
  2  ==================================================================
  3
  4  Principal:    $100.00
  5
  6  Period (Yrs)    9%     10%     12%     14%     16%
  7         1      9.00   10.00   12.00   14.00   16.00
  8         2     18.81   21.00   25.44   29.96   34.56
  9         3     29.50   33.10   40.49   48.15   56.09
 10         4     41.16   46.41   57.35   68.90   81.06
 11         5     53.86   61.05   76.23   92.54  110.03
 12         6     67.71   77.16   97.38  119.50  143.64
 13         7     82.80   94.87  121.07  150.23  182.62
 14         8     99.26  114.36  147.60  185.26  227.84
 15         9    117.19  135.79  177.31  225.19  280.30
 16
 17  Interest:      10%
 18  Years:          5
 19  Function:    61.05
 20
```

Note: The lookup table illustrated here could be organized as a vertical lookup table, in which 1-2-3 would search down the first (index) column, then across to the designated column number. This format is illustrated in the entry @VLOOKUP.

With Release 2 of 1-2-3, rows and columns in a lookup table can be transposed with the /Range Transpose **316★** command.

@HOUR()   A Release 2 time function

- **Format**
@HOUR(time number)

- **Description**
@HOUR is a time function that returns a value between 0 and 23, representing the hour of the day indicated by a fractional serial number corresponding to a time of day. The serial number can be generated by the @TIME **340★**, @TIMEVALUE **342★**, or @NOW **258★** function.

- **Procedure**

    The argument of the @HOUR function can be either a fraction or a serial number, as long as it is less than .9 (for 11 p.m.). If a serial number, such as 32663, has no decimal fraction, 1-2-3 returns the value 0, indicating midnight. For example:

    @HOUR(.25)

would return the value 6, for 6 a.m.—one-quarter of the 24 hours in a day.

    @HOUR(1/4)

would also return the value 6.

    @HOUR(32663.5)

would return the value 12, for noon—half of the 24 hours in a day.

    @HOUR(@NOW)

would return the hour of the current time, accurate to the last time you recalculated the worksheet (1-2-3 updates the current date and time specified by the @NOW function whenever you recalculate, either by entering new information with recalculation set to automatic, by executing the macro statement {Calc}, or by pressing the F9 [Calc] 144♦ key).

@IF()

- **Format**

    @IF(condition,true value,false value)

- **Description**

    @IF is a logical function that is used to test a condition and return either the true or the false value specified in the argument. 1-2-3 evaluates the function as follows: First, it tests the condition to see whether it is non-zero (true) or zero (false). If the result of the test is non-zero, the true value is returned; if the result is zero, the false value is returned.

- **Procedure**

    When you use @IF, the condition must be a logical formula, a numeric value, a cell address or range name referring to a numeric value, or a formula that calculates a numeric value.

@IF()

Often, the condition is built with one of the logical operators 263♦: =, <, <=, >, >=, or <>. For example:

@IF(A1=0,NA,A4/A1)

returns the value NA if the value in cell A1 equals 0; otherwise, it returns the result of dividing the value in A4 by the value in A1.

1-2-3 also provides three additional operators, logical NOT (#NOT#), logical AND (#AND#), and logical OR (#OR#) that enable you to construct compound statements that test several conditions at once. For example:

@IF(#NOT#B1=C1,@ABS(B1−C1),C1)

returns the absolute value of B1 minus C1 if the value in B1 does *not* equal the value in C1; otherwise, it returns the value in C1.

@IF(C1=4#OR#B1<>12,A1,A2)

returns the value in cell A1 if the value in C1 equals 4 *or* the value in B1 is not equal to 12; otherwise, it returns the value in cell A2.

@IF(C1<=4#AND#B1>12,D6,D7)

returns the value in cell D6 if the value in C1 is less than or equal to 4 *and* the value in B1 is greater than 12; otherwise, it returns the value in cell D7.

The true and false values in the argument can be either numeric values or (Release 2) character strings. If strings are used, they must be enclosed in double quotation marks, as in the following example:

@IF(A1>0,"Paid","Unpaid")

- **Comments**

1-2-3 allows you to nest @IF statements (place one within another) to extremely complex levels. You can use this nesting to enable your @IF statements to do more work, by inserting an @IF in the true value argument, the false value argument, or both. Each of the added @IF statements can then contain @IF statements of their own. For an example that uses a series of nested @IF statements, refer to the entry @@() 1★.

@INDEX()   A Release 2 special function

- **Format**

    @INDEX(range,column,row)

- **Description**

    The @INDEX function returns the value of the cell at the location specified by column and row in the designated range. This function is useful with 1-2-3 databases.

- **Procedure**

    You can enter the range as the addresses of diagonally opposite corners, by pointing, or as a range name. The column and row must be designated as numeric values. If you specify either as a decimal fraction, 1-2-3 uses the integer portion as the index value.

    The @INDEX function counts the top left-hand corner cell of the specified range as row 0 and column 0. If either the row or column is a negative number or a number greater than the number of columns or rows in the range you specify, the function returns ERR.

- **Example**

    The following illustrations show the @INDEX function used both correctly and incorrectly with a small database (the second illustration attempts to use a nonexistent row).

```
B11: (,0) [W9] @INDEX(B5..F9,4,0)                                    READY
```

	A	B	C	D	E	F	G
1	==
2	Road Mileage Between Cities
3	==
4		Atlanta	Boston	Chicago	Detroit	Houston	
5	Atlanta	0	1,037	674	699	789	
6	Boston	1,037	0	963	695	1,804	
7	Chicago	674	963	0	266	1,067	
8	Detroit	699	695	266	0	1,265	
9	Houston	789	1,804	1,067	1,265	0	
10							
11	Function:	789					
12							

181

@INDEX() · Install

```
B11: (,0) [W9] @INDEX(B5..F9,0,5)                                    READY
```

```
        A           B        C        D        E        F        G
 1  ===================================================================
 2   Road Mileage Between Cities
 3  ===================================================================
 4               Atlanta  Boston  Chicago  Detroit  Houston
 5   Atlanta         0    1,037      674      699      789
 6   Boston      1,037        0      963      695    1,804
 7   Chicago       674      963        0      266    1,067
 8   Detroit       699      695      266        0    1,265
 9   Houston       789    1,804    1,067    1,265        0
10
11   Function:        ERR
12
```

Install

The Install program is a Release 2 utility that sets up 1-2-3 for the specific pieces of equipment in your computer system. Install presents lists of equipment options, and you choose from them by moving a highlight bar. Unlike 1-2-3 itself, the Install program does not let you select an option by typing the first letter of its name.

You do not need to use Install before using 1-2-3, but until you do use it, 1-2-3 will not know what type of monitor or printer you use. Since these pieces of equipment can differ considerably, depending on type (a color/graphics versus a monochrome monitor, for example) and special requirements (such as printer-specific setup codes), you will not be able to display graphs on your monitor, nor will you be able to use a printer to print worksheets or graphs.

Install works by bringing the separate *driver* (control) programs for your equipment into a single file called a driver set. 1-2-3 creates this set for you and assigns it the extension .SET 121♦. Before you leave Install, 1-2-3 prompts you to provide a file name for the driver set, but in most instances you will want to accept the file name 1-2-3 proposes: 123.SET. This is the driver set that 1-2-3 automatically looks for when it is started. If you are using 1-2-3 on different computer systems or with different equipment configurations, you may need to create more than one driver set. In this case, you can use 123.SET for the system you use most often, and assign a unique file name to each additional driver set you create. All, however, must have the extension .SET.

If you do create more than one driver set, you will need to specify an alternative set (other than 123.SET) when you start 1-2-3. For example, you would type *lotus alt1* at the DOS command prompt to start the Access System with the alternate driver set named ALT1.SET. Or, you could start the 1-2-3 worksheet program with the alternate driver set by typing *123 alt1* at the DOS command prompt.

To begin creating a driver set, you can start the Install program in either of two ways: from DOS, by typing *Install* when the Utility disk is in drive A, or from inside the 1-2-3 directory, if you have a hard disk. For a step-by-step guide to installing drivers, you should refer to the Lotus Development Corporation's booklet *Getting Started*, which comes with your documentation.

@INT()

- **Format**

  @INT(x)

- **Description**

  The @INT function returns the integer portion of a number (x). In effect, @INT removes the decimal portion of the argument.

- **Procedure**

  The argument of @INT can be either a positive or a negative number, specified either as a numeric value or a reference to a cell containing a numeric value. 1-2-3 will return the integer portion of the number, without rounding decimal fractions up to the next value. For example:

  @INT(123.456)

returns the value 123.

  @INT(−123.456)

returns the value −123.

  If cell A1 contains the value 55.55:

  @INT(A1)

returns the value 55.

Comments

If you simply wish to display numbers as integers, or you wish to see only a portion of a number's decimal fraction, use the /Range Format 300★ command and set the decimals to a fixed number. If you do this, numbers will be displayed in their shortened form, but any calculations will be based on the full precision of the decimal value.

To round numbers, use the @ROUND 322★ function.

@IRR()

Format
@IRR(guess,range)

Description

@IRR is a financial function that calculates the internal rate of return (profit) on a series of payments. It is a measure of the interest rate returned by the money invested, and calculates a percentage based on future cash flows received regularly. The @IRR function assumes that the income from the investment is reinvested at the internal rate of return interest rate. But often this cannot be done, and the real internal rate of return is far less than the function indicates.

Procedure

The @IRR function uses an iterative process to arrive at its results. There is no exact formula that calculates the internal rate of return. Instead, 1-2-3 relies on a trial-and-error process that gives a very close approximation. Since the calculations are based on approximations that are refined each time the values are recalculated, the function requires an initial guess as to the correct rate of return. Usually, a guess anywhere between 0% (0) and 100% (1) will work. Your guess should be close to what you think the actual answer will be. For example, if your internal rate of return will be an annual rate between 5% and 15%, a guess of about 10% will probably work.

In cases where there are multiple sign changes in cash flows (the range part of the argument), the internal rate of return can have more than one value. When this is true, different results can occur when different guesses are tried out.

The range part of the @IRR argument includes the future cash flows, both positive and negative, resulting from the investment. Cash outflows are indicated as negative values; the first value in the range must be negative.

■ **Example**

The following example calculates the internal rate of return on a six-year investment in which the initial investment and a balloon payment in the third year are represented as negative cash flows, and returns for the other years are positive.

```
B6: (P0) [W9] @IRR(B4,B5..G5)                                      READY

         A         B         C         D         E         F         G
   ==========================================================================
 1
 2    @IRR
 3  --------------------------------------------------------------------------
 4       Guess:       8%
 5       Flows:    -2000      1000       900      -300       400       400
 6    Function:       9%
 7
```

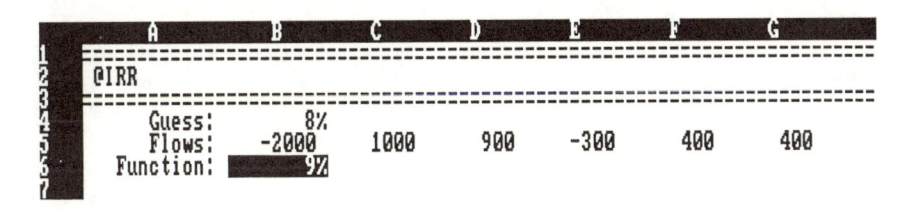

@ISERR()

■ **Format**

@ISERR(x)

■ **Description**

@ISERR is a logical function that tests its argument (x) to determine whether its value is ERR. (To 1-2-3, ERR is a numeric value.)

■ **Procedure**

The argument of the @ISERR function can be a formula or any reference to a single cell. The function returns one of two possible values: 0 when the test of the argument is false and the cell does not contain an ERR value; 1 when the test is true and the cell does contain an ERR value.

1-2-3 does not care *how* an ERR value occurs. Thus, the argument:

@ISERR(@ERR)

in which ERR is deliberately placed in the argument, is no different from:

@ISERR(3/0)

in which 1-2-3 returns the value ERR because you cannot divide by 0.

185

@ISERR() · @ISNA() · @ISNUMBER()

The @ISERR function, like @ISSTRING or @ISNUMBER, can be used to prevent ERR messages from propagating through a worksheet. For example:

@IF(@ISERR(A1),0,A1)

traps an error value in cell A1 by returning 0 if A1 contains ERR, and returning the value of A1 if the cell does not contain ERR.

@ISNA()

- **Format**
@ISNA(x)

- **Description**
@ISNA is a logical function that tests its argument to determine whether its value is NA. (To 1-2-3, NA is a numeric value.)

- **Procedure**
The argument of the @ISNA function can be a formula or any reference to a single cell. The function returns one of two possible values: 0 when the test of the argument is false and the cell does not contain NA; 1 when the test is true and the cell does contain NA.

Similar to the @ISERR 185★ function and others, the @ISNA function is useful in preventing NA values from propagating throughout a worksheet. For example:

@IF(@ISNA(A1),0,A1)

traps the value NA in cell A1 by returning 0 if the cell contains NA, and returning the value of A1 if the cell contains a value other than NA.

- **Comment**
The value NA is generated with the @NA 257★ function.

@ISNUMBER()   A Release 2 logical function

- **Format**
@ISNUMBER(x)

- **Description**
The @ISNUMBER function tests its argument for a numeric value. If the test is true, the function returns 1; if the test is not true, the function returns 0.

- **Procedure**
  The argument to @ISNUMBER can be a number, a reference to a cell containing a number, or a formula or formula reference that returns a numeric value. For example:

   @ISNUMBER(200)

  returns 1, for true, as does:

   @ISNUMBER(A5)

  if cell A5 contains a number or a calculated value, such as @SUM(A1..A4), and cells A1 to A4 contain numeric values.

  Like @ISERR **185**★ and other functions, the @ISNUMBER function is useful in preventing errors from propagating throughout a worksheet. For example:

   @IF(@ISNUMBER(A1),A1+A4,"No number")

  would return the value of cell A1 plus A4 if A1 contained a number; otherwise, it would return the message *No number.*

  @ISNUMBER is useful in macros for such purposes as testing keyboard input. Its complement is the function @ISSTRING .

@ISSTRING() A Release 2 logical function

- **Format**
  @ISSTRING(x)

- **Description**
  The @ISSTRING function tests its argument for a string value. If the test is true, the function returns 1; if the test is not true, the function returns 0.

- **Procedure**
  The argument to @ISSTRING can be a string enclosed in double quotation marks, a reference to a cell containing a string, or a formula or formula reference that returns a string value. For example:

   @ISSTRING("John Doe")

  returns 1, for true, as does:

   @ISSTRING(A1)

  if cell A1 contains a label, such as John Doe.

@ISSTRING() · Iteration

The & concatenation operator 263♦ can be included in the @ISSTRING argument, as in:

@ISSTRING("John "&A1)

The @ISSTRING function is useful for validating worksheet entries or keyboard input. For example:

@IF(@ISSTRING(A1),"OK","A1 is numeric")

returns *OK* if the entry in A1 is a label, but returns *A1 is numeric* if the entry in A1 is numeric or a formula that returns a numeric value or if it is blank (blank cells equal 0 in 1-2-3). The logical complement of @ISSTRING is the Release 2 function @ISNUMBER 186★.

Iteration

Iteration is the repeated recalculation of a formula or set of formulas that form a circular reference.

■ Definition of circular references

In general, every worksheet formula that contains a reference depends on another cell that contains a constant value. For example, if cell A2 contains the formula +A1∗1.10, and cell A1 contains the constant value 100, the formula in A2 depends directly on the constant value in A1.

In other cases, a formula may refer to another cell that, in turn, contains a formula that depends directly on the constant value. For example, if, in the preceding example, cell A3 contains the formula +A2∗2, that formula indirectly depends on the constant value in cell A1, via the formula in A2.

It is possible, however, to create formulas that do not depend, directly or indirectly, on a constant value, but rather depend ultimately on themselves. For example, suppose that cell A1 contains:

+A3−4

cell A2 contains:

+A1∗2

and cell A3 contains:

+A2∗2

In order to calculate the value in A3, 1-2-3 first must calculate the value in A2. But A2 depends on A1, so in order to calculate the value in A2, 1-2-3 first must calculate the value in A1. But A1 does not contain a constant value. It contains a formula that depends on A3; so in order to calculate the value in A1, 1-2-3 first must calculate the value in A3. The references in the formulas for A3, A2, and A1 form a circle—a circular reference.

Most circular references are created by mistake. If 1-2-3 were to try and calculate the values of the formulas in a circular reference, it would have to continuously calculate the value of each formula over and over again. Instead of recalculating the formulas in a circular reference, however, if 1-2-3 is in Natural recalculation mode (see /Worksheet Global Recalculation 371★) it displays CIRC at the lower right corner of the screen to alert you to the situation, and then stops calculating the formulas.

With Release 2 of 1-2-3, you can use the /Worksheet Status 374★ command to find a circular reference in your worksheet. If the CIRC indicator has appeared on your screen, the *Circular Reference:* field of the Worksheet Status screen displays the address of one cell where a formula refers to itself. If you remove the circular reference from the worksheet, 1-2-3 either displays *(None)* in that field or points to the next circular reference it has found.

STAT

```
Available Memory:
   Conventional.....  384933 of 385072 Bytes (99%)
   Expanded.........  (None)

Math Co-processor:  (None)

Recalculation:
   Method..........  Automatic
   Order...........  Natural
   Iterations......  1

Circular Reference:  B2

Cell Display:
   Format..........  (G)
   Label-Prefix....  '
   Column-Width....  9
   Zero Suppression.  Off

Global Protection:  Off
```

CIRC

Iteration

- **Using circular references**

  For some worksheet models, it is necessary to use a circular reference to obtain the results you need. For example, the following illustration shows a simple model for computing the net profit and bonus for a given gross profit:

  ```
  A3: [W22] " Bonus (0.1*B2):                                    READY
  ```

  ```
            A         B         C         D         E         F
  1     Gross profit:
  2   Net profit (B1-B3):
  3      Bonus (0.1*B2):
  4
  ```

  In this model, the net profit is the gross profit minus the bonus. The bonus is 10 percent of the net profit. So the net profit and bonus formulas in B2 and B3 form a circular reference.

  Suppose you build this model by entering 1000 in B1 and the formulas in B2 and B3. When you enter the formula in B2, B3 is blank, so the value of the formula is 1000−0, or 1000. When you enter the formula in B3, its value is equal to 0.1 ∗ 1000, or 100. At this point, you have a a circular reference, and 1-2-3 displays CIRC and stops recalculating:

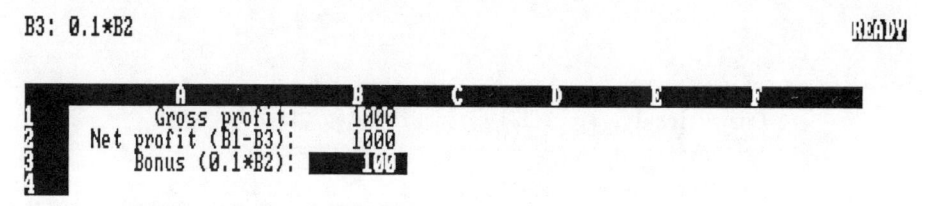

  ```
  B3: 0.1*B2                                                    READY
  ```

  ```
            A         B         C         D         E         F
  1     Gross profit:   1000
  2   Net profit (B1-B3): 1000
  3      Bonus (0.1*B2):   100
  4
  ```

  Note that, having entered the formula in B3, you now have an "incorrect" value in B2. Its formula says the value should be 1000−100, or 900, but because calculation was stopped, its value is still 1000. If you press the F9 [Calc] key, 1-2-3 computes the formulas in B2 and B3 again. First, the value of B2 becomes 1000−100, or 900. Then, the value of B3 becomes 0.1 ∗ 900, or 90:

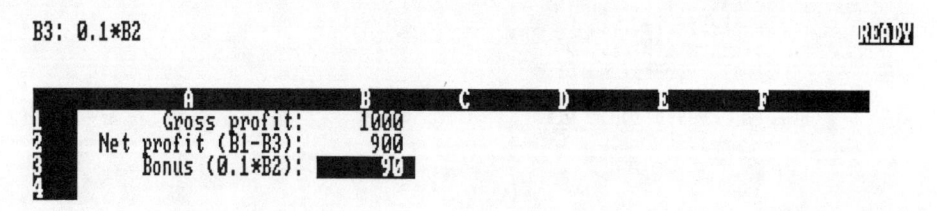

  ```
  B3: 0.1*B2                                                    READY
  ```

  ```
            A         B         C         D         E         F
  1     Gross profit:   1000
  2   Net profit (B1-B3):  900
  3      Bonus (0.1*B2):    90
  4
  ```

Again the value of B2 is incorrect. Its formula says the value should be 1000−90, or 910.

The true solutions to the formulas in B2 and B3—the values that make B2 equal to B1 minus B3, and B3 equal to 10 percent of B2—are 909.0909... and 90.90909.... Suppose you press the F9 [Calc] key four more times. The values in B2 and B3 become, respectively, 910 and 91; 909 and 90.9; 909.1 and 90.91; 909.09 and 90.909. Note that the amounts by which the values change from one pass, one *iteration*, to the next become smaller and smaller. The values are refined each time, and become closer and closer to the true solutions of 909.0909... and 90.90909....

This is the process of iteration: the repeated calculation of formulas in a circular reference. Although this example has stepped through the process "manually," you can use the /Worksheet Global Recalculation command to tell 1-2-3 to perform the procedure a set number of times (between 1 and 50).

For example, suppose you enter the preceding worksheet and enter the value 1100 in cell B1. This time, choose the /Worksheet Global Recalculation command, select *Iteration*, and set the iteration count to 10. As soon as you press the F9 [Calc] key, 1-2-3 recalculates the formulas ten times, to produce the true solutions:

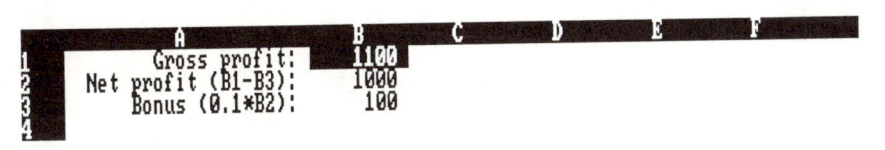

```
B1: 1100                                                          READY

        A              B         C         D         E         F
  1     Gross profit:  1100
  2     Net profit (B1-B3):  1000
  3     Bonus (0.1*B2):  100
  4
```

Now that iteration is turned on, each time you change the value of cell B1, 1-2-3 will iterate ten times to find the true solutions. The number of times you want 1-2-3 to iterate is determined by the accuracy to which you want 1-2-3 to calculate the true solutions.

- **Convergence and divergence**

In the preceding example, the values in B2 and B3 came closer and closer to the true solutions with each iteration. Such a circular reference is said to converge. It is also possible, however, to create a circular reference that diverges.

Iteration

For example, suppose you enter the formula +A2+1 in cell A1, and the formula +A1+1 in cell A2. With each iteration, the values will become, respectively: 1 and 2; 3 and 4; 5 and 6; 7 and 8; and so on. They will continue to grow with each iteration because there are no true solutions to this circular reference. There are no two values in which the first is equal to the second, plus one, and the second is equal to the first, plus one.

Not all models that diverge do so because they have no true solutions, however. Whether a circular reference converges or diverges depends on the formulas involved. And, sometimes, there are two ways of creating the same circular reference—one that converges and one that diverges. For example, the following sequence shows convergence:

```
A1: (T) [W13] (8-2*A2)/3                                          READY
         A              B        C        D        E        F        G
    1  (8-2*A2)/3
    2  (7-A1)/5
    3
```

```
A1: [W13] (8-2*A2)/3                                              READY
         A              B        C        D        E        F        G
    1  2.6666666667
    2  0.8666666667
    3
```

```
A1: [W13] (8-2*A2)/3                                              READY
         A              B        C        D        E        F        G  *
    1                  2
    2                  1
    3
    4
    5
    6
    7
    8
    9
   10
   11
   12
   13
   14
   15
   16
   17
   18
   19
   20
                                   CIRC
```

192

and this sequence shows divergence:

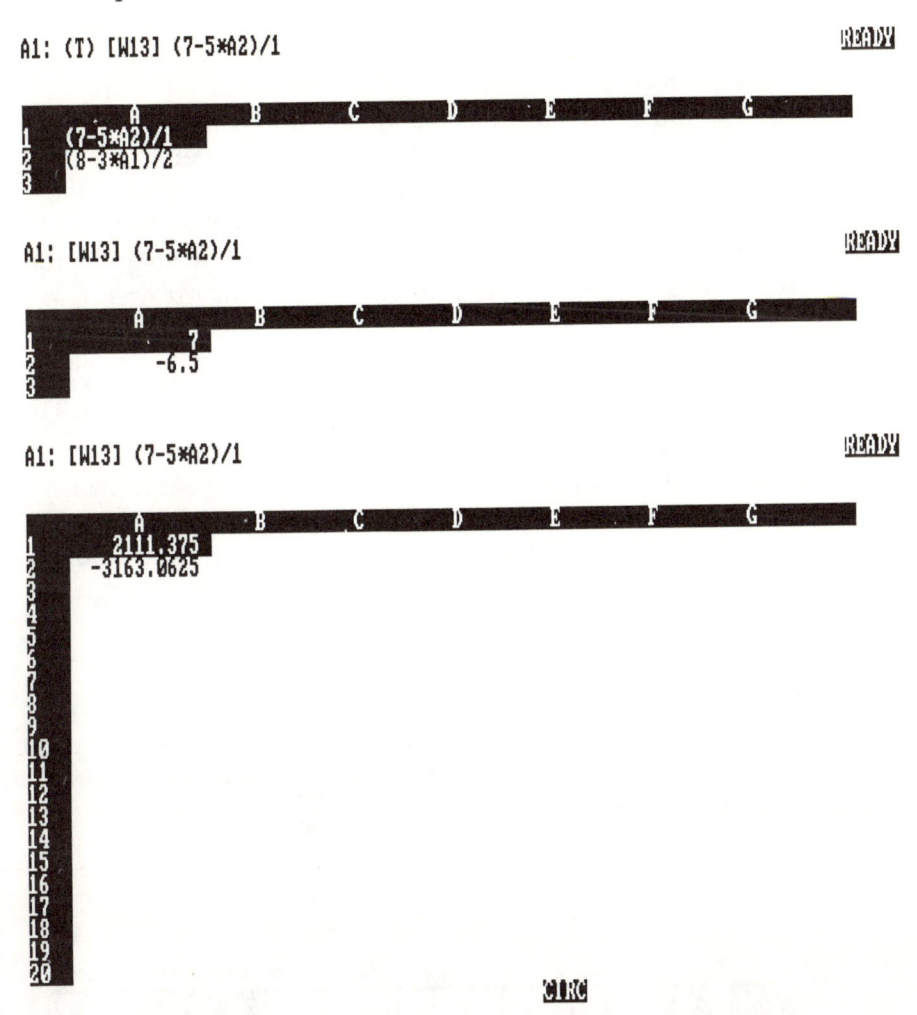

```
A1: (T) [W13] (7-5*A2)/1                                    READY
        A           B        C        D        E        F        G
1  (7-5*A2)/1
2  (8-3*A1)/2
3
```

```
A1: [W13] (7-5*A2)/1                                        READY
        A           B        C        D        E        F        G
1       7
2      -6.5
3
```

```
A1: [W13] (7-5*A2)/1                                        READY
        A           B        C        D        E        F        G
1    2111.375
2   -3163.0625
3
4
5
6
7
8
9
10
11
12
13
14
15
16
17
18
19
20                                      CIRC
```

Both of the circular references in the preceding examples have the same solution of A1 equal to 2 and A2 equal to 1. The first model, however, will converge to those solutions within ten iterations but, in the second model, the values of A1 and A2 will grow by larger and larger amounts and never converge, even though it has the same solutions.

Iteration · **Keyboard**

Both of these models represent the set of equations A1*3+A2*2 equals 8 and A1*1+A2*5 equals 7. The first model uses the first equation as the formula for A1 and the second equation as the formula for A2, while the second model does the reverse.

Although you need not understand how these models represent the equations, the point you should bear in mind is that often there are several ways to build the same set of circular references, and that some of these ways may converge while others diverge. If you find yourself with iterated values that don't seem to be solutions to your formulas, look again at the formulas and see if there is another way to construct your circular reference.

- **Calculation order**

In a very few circular references, not only does the iteration depend on the formulas involved and the number of iterations specified, it also depends on the order in which the formulas are calculated. When creating a circular reference, be certain you know exactly the order in which your formulas will be calculated. If necessary, change the order with the *Natural*, *Rowwise*, and *Columnwise* options of the /Worksheet Global Recalculation command. You can use /Worksheet Status to display the current recalculation settings.

K

Note: The following discussion is based on the IBM Personal Computer keyboard. If you use a different keyboard with 1-2-3, please check your manual regarding any differences.

Keyboard

In addition to the number, character, and symbol keys on your keyboard, 1-2-3 uses such keys as the arrow, Pg Up, Pg Dn, Home, End, and function (Fx) keys to simplify or accomplish many different tasks. Some of these keys are used for moving the pointer about the worksheet or through menus of options, or for editing cell entries. Others (the function keys) are dedicated to or toggle in and out of specific tasks. The tables included in this entry are designed as a quick reference for those times when you may need to refresh your memory.

- **Pointer-movement keys**

Use the following keys when you are in READY or POINT mode.

Key ♦:	Action:
Left arrow	Moves the pointer left one cell.
Right arrow	Moves the pointer right one cell.
Up arrow	Moves the pointer up one cell.
Down arrow	Moves the pointer down one cell.
Tab or Ctrl-Right arrow	Moves the pointer right one screen.
Backtab (Shift-Tab) or Ctrl-Left arrow	Moves the pointer left one screen.
Pg Up	Moves the pointer up one screen.
Pg Dn	Moves the pointer down one screen.
Home	Moves the pointer to the top left-hand corner of the worksheet (Cell A1).
End-Home	Moves the pointer to the bottom right-hand corner of the active area of the worksheet (the intersection of the lowest row and rightmost column of your work area).
End-Up arrow	Moves the pointer upward to the end of a series of like cells; stops when series ends.
End-Down arrow	Moves the pointer downward to the end of a series of blank or non-blank cells; stops when series ends.

Keyboard

Key♦:	Action:
End-Right arrow	Moves the pointer right to the end of a series of blank or non-blank cells; stops when end of series is reached.
End-Left arrow	Moves the pointer left to the end of a series of blank or non-blank cells; stops when end of series is reached.

Use the following keys if you are in MENU or HELP mode.

Key♦:	Action:
Left arrow	Moves the pointer one selection left.
Right arrow	Moves the pointer one selection right.
Up arrow	Moves the pointer one selection up (HELP mode only).
Down arrow	Moves the pointer one selection down (HELP mode only).
Home	Moves the pointer to the first selection.
End	Moves the pointer to the last selection.
Backspace	Returns to the previous help screen (Release 2 only).

■ Editing keys

Use the following keys *before* pressing Return during data entry.

Key♦:	Action:
F2 [Edit]	Toggles you in and out of EDIT mode.
Backspace	Deletes the preceding character.
Esc	Cancels current entry; returns to READY.
Home	Completes the current entry and moves the pointer to the top left-hand cell of the worksheet.
End	Completes the current entry and toggles the END indicator off or on.
Left arrow	Completes the current entry and moves the pointer left one cell.

Key ◆:	Action:
Right arrow	Completes the current entry and moves the pointer right one cell.
Up arrow	Completes the current entry and moves the pointer up one cell.
Down arrow	Completes the current entry and moves the pointer down one cell.
Tab or Ctrl-Right arrow	Completes the current entry and moves the pointer right one screen.
Backtab or Ctrl-Left arrow	Completes the current entry and moves the pointer left one screen.
Pg Up	Completes the current entry and moves the pointer up one screen.
Pg Dn	Completes the current entry and moves the pointer down one screen.

Use the following keys to edit an entry while in EDIT mode.

Key ◆:	Action:
F2 [Edit]	Toggles you in and out of EDIT mode.
Backspace	Deletes the preceding character.
Esc	Removes entry from edit line (second line of Control Panel); remains in EDIT.
Del	Deletes the character at the cursor location.
Ins	Toggles between inserting and replacing text (OVR mode; overwrite).
Home	Moves the cursor to the first character in the entry.
End	Moves the cursor to the last character in the entry.
Left arrow	Moves the cursor one character left.
Right arrow	Moves the cursor one character right.
Up arrow	Completes the current entry and moves the pointer up one cell.

Keyboard

Key♦:	Action:
Down arrow	Completes the current entry and moves the pointer down one cell.
Tab or Ctrl-Right arrow	Moves the cursor five characters right.
Backtab or Ctrl-Left arrow	Moves the cursor five characters left.
Pg Up	Completes the current entry and moves the pointer up one screen.
Pg Dn	Completes the current entry and moves the pointer down one screen.

- **Special keys**

Use the following keys to perform specific tasks.

Key♦:	Action:
Alt-alphabetic character	Invokes a macro 211★ named *character*.
F1 [Help]	Calls up the Help facility.
Alt-F1 [Compose]	Enables you to create accented and other special characters in the Lotus International Character Set (LICS) 203★.
F2 [Edit]	Toggles you in and out of EDIT mode.
Alt-F2 [Step]	Turns on single-step mode for macro 211★ execution; causes macros to be carried out a step at a time, pausing after each for the user to press any key; used for debugging macros.
F3 [Name]	In POINT mode, displays a list of currently defined range names.
F4 [Absolute]	In POINT and EDIT modes, cycles through absolute, mixed, and relative referencing, or makes a range name absolute.

Keyboard · **Labels**

Key♦:	Action:
F5 [Goto]	Moves the cell pointer to the cell you specify; useful for moving the pointer long distances on the worksheet. This key is often used along with the F3 [Name] key to move to a named range.
F6 [Window]	Moves the pointer from one window to the other on a screen split with the /Worksheet Window 378★ command.
F7 [Query]	Causes 1-2-3 to repeat the last /Data Query 65★ command used.
F8 [Table]	Causes 1-2-3 to repeat the last Data Table 79★ operation.
F9 [Calc]	In READY 249♦ mode, recalculates the entire worksheet; in VALUE 249♦ or EDIT mode, calculates the value of the currently highlighted formula.
F10 [Graph]	Displays the last specified graph.

Labels

Whenever you enter information into a worksheet cell, 1-2-3 interprets it as a numeric value, a formula, or a label. Most labels are descriptive text, such as Third-Quarter Sales, but a label can consist not only of text, but also of numbers, special symbols—in fact, any character in the 1-2-3 LICS 203★ character set. Thus, a label can look like this:

123

or this:

2+2

or this:

@SUM(A1..B15)

But when any such numeric expressions are entered as labels, rather than as numbers or formulas, they cannot be used in mathematical calculations, and they must be preceded by a label-prefix character, as described in the following section.

- **Entering labels**

Whenever you begin a cell entry with a character other than one of the digits 0 through 9 or one of the characters that indicate the beginning of a formula (such as +, @ or an open parenthesis), 1-2-3 automatically assumes you are entering a label and puts you into LABEL 249◆ mode. Unless you have changed the global label-prefix setting (with the /Worksheet Global Label-Prefix 368★ command), it assigns the entry the label prefix ', which indicates a left-justified label.

If you wish to begin a label with a number or a character that would normally indicate the beginning of a formula, you must enter the label prefix yourself, to tell 1-2-3 to interpret the following entry as text. In addition to the ' label prefix, you can also use a double quotation mark ("), to specify a right-justified label, or you can use a caret symbol (^), to indicate a centered label. You can also use a backslash (\) to repeat a label across the width of a cell; for example, you can enter \= to create a double-dashed line across a cell.

You do not see the label-prefix character in the cell itself, but when the cell pointer is on a cell containing a label-prefix, 1-2-3 does display it at the beginning of the cell-entry display in the Control Panel at the top of the screen.

Labels can be up to 240 characters long, and can include blank spaces. If the label is longer than the cell is wide, 1-2-3 continues the label into any blank cells to the right. If there are no blank cells, 1-2-3 truncates the display of the label, but remembers the entire label and will display it completely if you widen the cell, erase the contents of the cells to the right, or move the label to a blank area of the worksheet.

- **Label alignment**

Label prefixes can be changed with either the /Worksheet Global Label-Prefix command or the /Range Label 308★ command (/Range Label-Prefix in Release 1a of 1-2-3).

The /Worksheet Global Label-Prefix command is used to change the current default setting for the entire worksheet. This command affects all labels you enter after changing the setting, but not existing label prefixes.

The /Range Label command is used to change the alignment of existing labels in a particular range of cells. However, even though you format a range for left, right, or centered alignment, only labels already in the range are affected. Any labels you enter later will be given the current global default alignment.

- **Label commands**

  There are a number of different commands that enable you to use and manipulate labels in a worksheet. For example, you can:

  □ Use ranges of worksheet labels in graphs to clarify or describe the data values you chart (see /Graph Options Data-Labels **169♦**).

  □ Use worksheet labels as single-cell range names for macro cells immediately adjacent to them (see /Range Name Labels **312♦**).

  □ Search for, match, add together, extract from, and change labels to upper- or lowercase characters with the Release 2 string **332★** functions.

  □ Import ASCII text files (from a word processor, perhaps) as columns of long labels with the /File Import **126★** command, then edit and realign the text in paragraph form with the /Range Justify **306★** command.

  □ Break long labels into rows and columns of information with the Release 2 /Data Parse **61★** command.

  □ Use labels as search criteria in a database to select and process information in selected records.

  □ Create special labels that can help you automate tasks by storing command or menu keystrokes (see Macros **211★**).

@LEFT()   A Release 2 string function

- **Format**

  @LEFT(string,n)

- **Description**

  The @LEFT function searches a string and extracts n number of characters (a substring) from the beginning of the string. The @LEFT function complements the functions @RIGHT **321★**, which returns n characters from the end of the string, and @MID **244★**, which returns n characters from a specified point within a string.

Procedure

The @LEFT function allows a string argument only; a numeric value will produce the value ERR. The value n must be either a number or a reference to a cell containing a numeric value.

The string can be specified either directly, by inclusion in the argument, or indirectly, as a cell reference. If the string is included in the argument, it must be enclosed in double quotation marks. For example:

@LEFT("Alas, poor Yorick",4)

(This would return *Alas* because the second part of the argument (4) specifies the first four characters of the string.)

When using the @LEFT function, remember that blank spaces and punctuation count as characters. Thus:

@LEFT("04/12/72",2)

would return *04*, while

@LEFT("04/12/72",5)

would return *04/12*.

Note also that leading blank spaces will be counted as characters. For example, if cell A1 contains a label, YTD Sales, preceded by four blank spaces, the function:

@LEFT(A1,9)

would return four blanks and the characters *YTD S*.

@LENGTH() A Release 2 string function

Format
@LENGTH(string)

Description
The @LENGTH function returns the number of characters that are contained in a string.

- **Procedure**

The @LENGTH function allows string arguments only; numeric values produce the value ERR. The string can be specified either directly, by inclusion in the argument, or indirectly, as a cell reference. You can use the concatenation operator (&) in either instance, to have the function return the combined lengths of more than one string. For example:

>@LENGTH("one"&"two"&"three")
>@LENGTH(A1&B1&C1)

for cell references. Or:

>@LENGTH(one&two&three)

for range names.

If the string is included in the argument, it must be enclosed in double quotation marks. For example:

>@LENGTH("The tortoise "&"and the hare")

(This argument would return the value 25, for each character and blank space enclosed in the two sets of double quotation marks.

Strings designated by cell references need not be enclosed in quotation marks, but must be entered as labels in the cells where they occur.

- **Comments**

Uses of the @LENGTH function might include validating input or determining the length of a line (perhaps for setting print margins) with a formula such as:

>@LENGTH(A1&B1&C1&D1&E1)

LICS

LICS is an acronym for Lotus International Character Set, the system used by Release 2 of 1-2-3 for coding all the characters (including control functions) in a worksheet, print, or graph file.

The LICS character set is based on the ASCII 5★ system, which includes 256 possible codes, 128 of which are considered the standard ASCII set, and the remainder the extended ASCII set. The first 128 LICS codes correspond to standard ASCII codes; the remaining 128 are used for creating special characters, such as accented letters and international currency symbols.

LICS

Some LICS characters, such as the British pound symbol, are not represented on a standard keyboard. To enter them, you press Alt-F1 [Compose] and a predetermined sequence of characters (listed in Appendix 2 of the 1-2-3 manual). The pound symbol, for example, is created by pressing Alt-F1, then L, and then the equal sign (=).

These special characters may or may not be reproducible on your monitor or printer. If your display is limited to the standard text characters, you can still type LICS special characters, however. Your monitor will simply display a "fallback" representation (an e without an acute accent, for example), but if you use a printer capable of reproducing the character, it will be printed as é. The following two illustrations show the international LICS characters (codes 128 through 255), as they are displayed on an IBM color/graphics monitor, and as they appear when typeset.

LICS Code:	Character:	LICS Code:	Character:	LICS Code:	Character:	LICS Code:	Character:
128	`	160	ƒ	192	À	224	à
129	´	161	¡	193	Á	225	á
130	^	162	¢	194	Â	226	â
131	¨	163	£	195	Ã	227	ã
132	~	164	"	196	Ä	228	ä
133		165	¥	197	Å	229	å
134		166	Pts	198	Æ	230	æ
135		167	§	199	Ç	231	ç
136		168		200	È	232	è
137		169	©	201	É	233	é
138		170	ª	202	Ê	234	ê
139		171	«	203	Ë	235	ë
140		172	∆	204	Ì	236	ì
141		173	π	205	Í	237	í
142		174	≥	206	Î	238	î
143		175	÷	207	Ï	239	ï
144	`	176	°	208	Ð	240	ð
145	´	177	±	209	Ñ	241	ñ
146	^	178	2	210	Ò	242	ò
147	¨	179	3	211	Ó	243	ó
148	~	180	"	212	Ô	244	ô
149	ı	181	µ	213	Õ	245	õ
150	–	182	¶	214	Ö	246	ö
151	▲	183	•	215	Œ	247	œ
152	▼	184	™	216	Ø	248	ø
153	■	185	¹	217	Ù	249	ù
154	●	186	º	218	Ú	250	ú
155	←	187	»	219	Û	251	û
156		188	¼	220	Ü	252	ü
157		189	½	221	Ÿ	253	ÿ
158		190	≤	222		254	
159		191	¿	223	ß	255	

@LN()

- **Format**

    @LN(x)

- **Description**

    The function @LN returns the natural logarithm, or logarithm base e of x. e is the mathematical constant 2.7182818.... Thus, @LN is the inverse of the function @EXP 116★.

- **Procedure**

    The argument of @LN must be either a numeric value greater than 0, or a reference to a cell containing such a value. For example, you could enter the function as either:

    @LN(10)

    or as:

    @LN(A1)

    if, in the second instance, cell A1 contained a numeric value.
    If x is 0 or a negative number, the function returns ERR.

- **Examples**

    In the following examples:

    @LN(2.7182818)

    returns the value 1. This demonstrates *e* as the base of the natural logarithm.

    @LN(@EXP(3))

    returns the value 3. This demonstrates the inverse relationship between @LN and @EXP.

    @LN(8)/@LN(2)

    returns 2, the base-2 logarithm of 8. You can use this method to find logarithms in other bases with the @LN function.

@LOG()

- **Format**

    @LOG(x)

- **Description**

    The @LOG function returns the logarithm base 10 of *x*. @LOG is the inverse of base-10 exponentiation, or the letter E in scientific notation.

- **Procedure**

    The argument of @LOG must be either a numeric value greater than 0, or a reference to a cell containing such a value. For example, you could enter the function as either:

    @LOG(100)

or as:

@LOG(A1)

if, in the second instance, cell A1 contained an appropriate numeric value.
If x is 0 or a negative number, the function returns ERR.

- **Examples**

In the following examples:

@LOG(10)

returns the value 1. This demonstrates what it means for 10 to be the base of the logarithm.

@LOG(1E5)
@LOG(10^5)

return the value 5. These examples demonstrate the meaning of E in scientific notation and show what it means for @LOG to be the inverse of base 10 exponentiation.

@LOG(8)/@LOG(2)

returns the value 3, the base-2 logarithm of 8. You can use this method to find logarithms in other bases with the @LOG function.

Lookup tables

A lookup table is a range of cells on a worksheet that contains a table of values, from which you can select the most appropriate one for a given situation. In form and function, a lookup table is no different from an income-tax table, a table of sales taxes, discount rates, commission percentages—or, for that matter, a child's multiplication table.

In any and all of these tables, the values are grouped logically, in a pattern determined by an identifying row and/or column at the top or left of the table entries. To find a particular value, you can either scan horizontally to find the category you want, then search vertically to find the value you need, or you can scan vertically and then horizontally.

Lookup tables in 1-2-3 work on the same principle. Once you have created a table of values, 1-2-3's two lookup functions, @HLOOKUP (for horizontal lookup table) and @VLOOKUP (for vertical lookup table), can search the table either horizontally or vertically and retrieve the value you need, for a given situation.

■ The lookup table

To create a lookup table, you need to set aside a range of cells large enough to hold the values you want to include. Across the top row, or down the left column, enter a list of numeric values representing intervals or reference points you can use in the function argument to uniquely identify the row or column 1-2-3 will use in searching for the value you want to find. These intervals are the comparison values in the *index* row or column of the table. For example, if commission rates were based on $1000 increments, the comparison values could be $1000, $2000, $3000, and so on.

The comparison values must be numeric and must be entered in ascending order. The remainder of the table is simply a matrix of cells containing the values for which you want to search.

■ Lookup functions

Both of 1-2-3's lookup functions require three arguments in order to operate. The functions and their arguments are:

@HLOOKUP(x,range,row number)
@VLOOKUP(x,range,column number)

In both functions, x represents a numeric value you provide, which 1-2-3 compares against the values in the index row (or column) of the lookup table. The range is the range of cells occupied by the lookup table, including the index row (or column).

The row (or column) number is the number of a row (or column) you designate; regardless of whether the lookup is horizontal or vertical, 0 represents the index row or column; the first actual row or column of data values begins with 1. If the row or column number is equal to, or greater than, the number of cells in the table row or column, either lookup function returns ERR since it would otherwise reference a cell outside the table range.

In a horizontal (@HLOOKUP) table, 1-2-3 searches the top (index) row of the lookup table for a value equal to or greater than x. If it finds a value equal to x, it stops at that column. If it does not find a value exactly equal to x, it continues searching the index row until it encounters the first value greater than x; then, it stops and backs up one cell to the preceding value. If 1-2-3 does not find a value as great as x, it stops at the last column in the table.

Lookup tables

1-2-3 then proceeds to search down the selected column to the row designated by the row number in the argument. When 1-2-3 reaches the correct row, it retrieves the value in the cell at the intersection of the column and row, and returns that value in the function cell.

The @VLOOKUP function operates in exactly the same way, except that it searches *down* the leftmost column (index column) of the table, then searches *across* the selected row to find the value specified by the column number you designate in the function argument.

The following two diagrams illustrate the sequence and direction of the searches performed by the @HLOOKUP and @VLOOKUP functions:

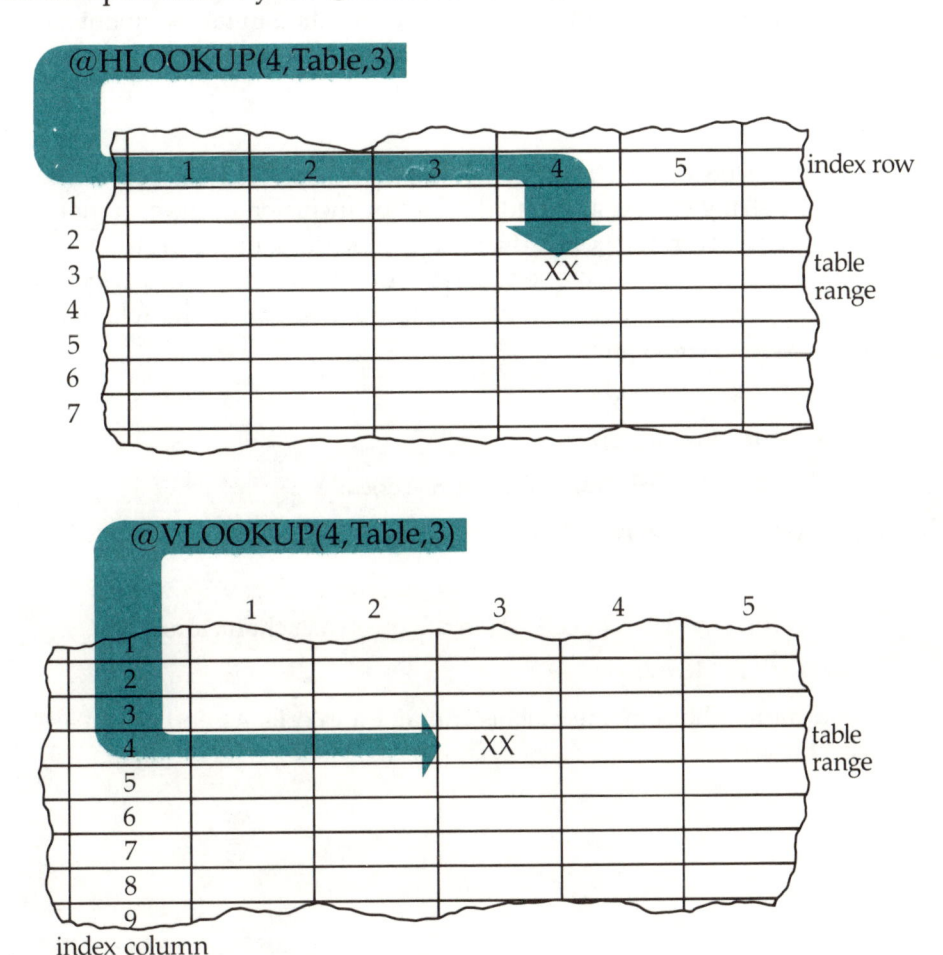

@HLOOKUP(4,Table,3)

index row

table range

@VLOOKUP(4,Table,3)

table range

index column

209

■ **Comments**

For more details on using the two lookup functions, refer to the entries @HLOOKUP **176★** and @VLOOKUP **351★**.

@LOWER()   A Release 2 string function

■ **Format**

@LOWER(string)

■ **Description**

The @LOWER function returns the string specified in its argument as lowercase letters only, whether or not the string contains all capital letters, only lowercase letters, or a mixture of the two.

■ **Procedure**

@LOWER allows string arguments only; numeric values produce the value ERR. The string can be specified directly, by inclusion in the argument, or indirectly, as a cell reference. If the string is included in the argument, it must be enclosed in double quotation marks. You can also use the & concatenation operator to combine two or more strings. Thus, any of the following arguments would be acceptable:

@LOWER("le Grand Prix")

would return *le grand prix*.

@LOWER("ABSOLUTELY NOT! "&"She cried.")

would return *absolutely not! she cried*.

@LOWER(A1)

would return the label in cell A1, in all lowercase characters.

@LOWER(A1&A2)

would return the combined labels contained in cells A1 and A2, in all lowercase characters.

Macro

A macro is a form of typing shorthand that enables you to store a series of keystrokes and worksheet commands in a cell or series of cells. In their most elementary form, macros are just collections of keystrokes that can be played back repeatedly, like duplicating a word several times with a word processor. Macros are keystroke processors, but much more besides. It is probably evident that macros can help automate your work and, in the process, open the way to savings in time and effort, as well as increased productivity. This is why macros were known as the *typing alternative* in the Release 1a manual.

When should you use macros? Because macros can be "played back" repeatedly, with ease, any repetitive worksheet task is a cue to use a macro. Consider the simple task of changing the width of 20 columns in the worksheet. The command sequence to change a column to a width of 15 characters is: /Worksheet Column Set-Width, 15, a press of the Return key, then a press of an arrow key to move to the next column. Not very difficult, but after trying this sequence for a few columns you begin to look for a better way. That way is a macro. Consider the following macro.

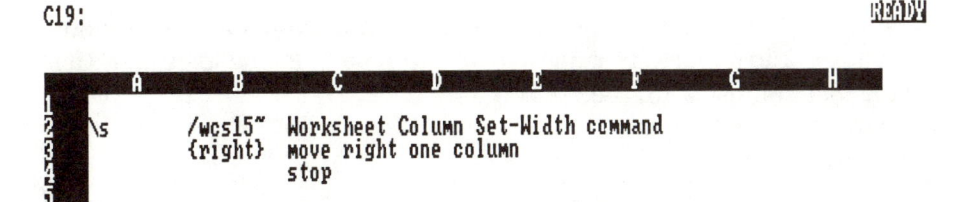

```
C19:                                                            READY

         A       B          C         D         E       F       G       H
    1
    2   \s     /wcs15~    Worksheet Column Set-Width command
    3          {right}    move right one column
    4                     stop
    5
```

Notice that the examples presented in this entry are written in three-column style. This is to provide a clear, structured format that makes macro text easier to read and design. The \s to the left is a label that reminds you what the macro's name is (see the following section, "Naming Macros"). The macro itself is the column in the center. The third column is for comments that explain the action of the macro.

The macro presented here is composed of two labels that store the keystrokes (or representations of keystrokes) you press when you execute the command yourself. The first label types the /Worksheet Column Set-Width sequence, then types the characters 1 and 5, then types a Return (the tilde, ~, is the macro representation of pressing the Return key). The cell below contains a "special-key" statement. The special-key statements are names enclosed in curly braces ({ }). This statement tells the macro interpreter (the control program that reads your macro labels and attempts to execute them) to move one column to the right. After executing that label, the macro interpreter stops because it has come to a blank cell.

When 1-2-3's macro interpreter finishes with the label in one cell, it looks at the following cell in the current column. If that cell contains a label, the interpreter will continue the macro's execution in that cell. This process continues until the interpreter finds a non-label cell (a blank cell or a cell that contains a numeric value).

With this small macro you can replace eight keystrokes with two: the [Macro]-S combination (on an IBM PC-type keyboard, the [Macro] key is equivalent to the Alt key). To adjust the widths of 20 columns, you move the cell pointer to the first column you want to adjust, then invoke the macro with the [Macro]-S keystrokes. To adjust the next column, press those two keys again. Over the course of 20 columns, you will save 120 keystrokes—a fair amount of time and repetition.

In addition to simple keystrokes, all of 1-2-3's commands, plus many sophisticated *interactive* operations are available through macros. For example, if you needed to enter a series of labels in your worksheet, you might put a "pause" into a macro that allowed you to type a unique identifier, then have the macro finish with the "boilerplate."

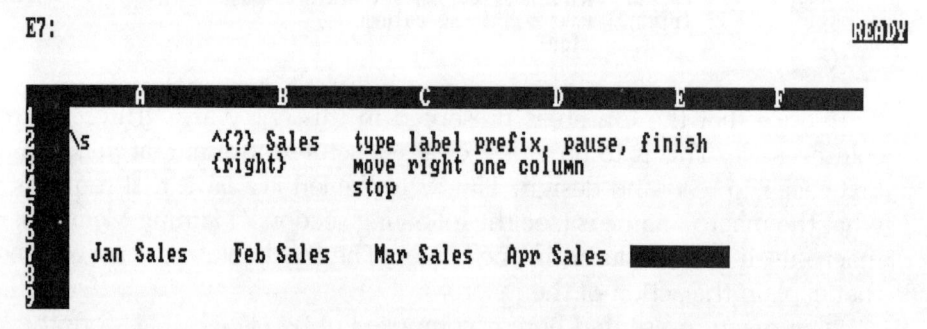

```
E7:                                                              READY

        A          B            C          D          E         F
1
2      \s        ^{?} Sales    type label prefix, pause, finish
3                {right}       move right one column
4                              stop
5
6
7      Jan Sales  Feb Sales    Mar Sales  Apr Sales
8
9
```

The macro representation of a pause is {?}. In the preceding illustration, the macro in the center column does the following:

1. Types the caret (^) label prefix to center the new label.
2. Stops and waits for keyboard input. The macro will accept any series of standard characters (up to the cell limit of 240 characters) and will continue with the remainder of the macro after you press Return.

3. Finishes the label by typing a space, then the word *Sales*.
4. Moves to the next column and stops.

In the lower half of the illustration, you can see that the macro has been used four times. Each time the macro was invoked, a unique identifier was typed at the pause.

By now, you can see that it is fairly easy to create a macro that enters labels into the worksheet or changes column widths. It is just as easy to create macros that perform specialized tasks, such as applying a special format to a cell, erasing a cell, updating a worksheet file, or carrying out any repetitive or time-consuming task.

Somewhat more complex are macros that prompt for string or numeric input, or deal with ranges. You could write macros that present an input form for data entry use, or automate long command sequences for printing. In short, nearly any task that you commonly do can be written as a macro.

■ Creating macros

Macros are labels, so they begin with a label **199★** prefix and are entered on a worksheet just as any other label is. Macros are unique, however, because of the work they perform: They tell 1-2-3 to do something. In this respect, the keystrokes and commands you include in macros resemble a programming language, such as BASIC. You use them to put together sets of instructions that 1-2-3 can interpret and execute to provide the result you want, as often as you want, without your having to repeatedly type long command sequences.

Although macros are, essentially, labels, you must follow certain rules to make certain they are executed properly and do the job you want them to do.

Getting ready: Macros can be very powerful conveniences when they are written correctly, but they can be disastrous when they aren't. Because macros are storehouses of commands, a macro could destroy data, or even erase your worksheet before you realized what was wrong. It always pays to plan ahead and to have a backup copy of the worksheet you are experimenting with. Since a macro is essentially replacing the effort of entering commands via the keyboard, the best way to plan a macro is to manually step through the sequence of commands you want to include in the macro (using the keyboard) one keystroke at a time. You should take notes on each step. Once you have the steps in the task written down, you are prepared to translate them into a macro.

Entering a macro: Before you begin typing a macro, place the pointer in an out-of-the-way section of your worksheet, to avoid bumping into other labels or into your data. 1-2-3 reads macro instructions down a column, not across a row, so you can enter a sequence of instructions:

- In a single cell, which can contain up to 240 characters.
- In a series of adjacent cells in a single column.

1-2-3 is not particular about which of these options you choose, but it is usually best to have one cell dedicated to one task. For example, a simple macro to format the current cell as a fixed decimal can be entered like this:

'RFF~

or like this:

'RF
'F~

Since macros are labels, they are preceded by a label prefix. If your macro performs a simple task, such as typing characters, you won't need to type the label prefix, 1-2-3 automatically adds the default label prefix when you enter character data into a cell. For example, if your macro types the label *Sales*, it will look like this: '*Sales*. When this macro is executed, 1-2-3 will ignore the macro's label prefix and instead use the current default label prefix as it types out the characters in the word *Sales*. If you wanted to center that label, however, you would need to type both the macro's label prefix and the label's label prefix: ' as the standard beginning, then the label prefix for centered text (^), then type the rest of the label. In this case, you would end up with '^*Sales*, which would produce a centered label when the macro was invoked.

If your macro does something more complex, it probably will start with a command, and to invoke commands, the slash (/) must be typed. To enter the slash into a macro, as the first entry, you must precede it with a label prefix, or else 1-2-3 will start executing the commands instead of storing them in the cell. This is why macros are entered as labels. For example, if you entered this macro:

'/RFF~B1..B10

and did not include the label prefix, 1-2-3 would assume that your first keystroke (/) meant "I want to use a command," and would automatically take you to the menu of /Range Format command options.

Naming macros: A macro name is a special type of range name. However, only the first cell of a macro need be named. If you name the entire range of cells that a macro occupies, 1-2-3 will still use only the first cell of the range to determine where it is to start. Because a macro name is a range name, you use the /Range Name command to give a name to a macro. Macro names are unique among range names because they always begin with the backslash character. The backslash is followed by a single alphabetic character or a zero (the zero designates an auto-execute macro which cannot be invoked from the keyboard).

These are legal macro names: \A, \a, \z, \0.

These are illegal macro names: \off, \on, \%, \8.

Macros that you can invoke from the keyboard are distinct from macro subroutines, which can be given any name (up to 14 characters) but must be called from within a macro.

Two methods: There are two standard methods of creating macro range names: The /Range Name Create 310♦ command sequence and the /Range Name Labels Right 312♦ command sequence. The second method allows for efficient documenting of macro names and is preferable. The following example shows how a simple macro to erase the current cell is named with the /Range Name Labels command.

'\E   '/RE~

To apply the name \E to the macro above you would simply move the cursor to the cell containing '\E, issue the /Range Name Labels Right sequence and press Return. 1-2-3 will apply the label contained in the highlighted cell to the cell on its immediate right, as a range name. This method also allows a macro to be easily identified when other macros are nearby.

- **The auto-execute macro**

One special macro name (\0) indicates that a macro is an auto-execute macro and should be started immediately after the worksheet is retrieved from its file. This type of macro is often used to present a menu of options, such as a list of directories, or a list of standard worksheets or worksheet templates. When it is used with 1-2-3's auto-loading worksheet (AUTO123.WK1 or AUTO123.WKS) this macro makes it possible to customize 1-2-3 completely. However, the \0 macro is strictly limited to execution when a worksheet is retrieved. It cannot be executed from the keyboard as a standard macro.

- **Executing macros**

Until you invoke your macro by name, the instructions it contains cannot be carried out; the macro is "inert," even though it represents 1-2-3 commands that can be executed just as if you had typed them. To carry out (invoke) your macro at the appropriate time, you press the Alt [Macro] key and, at the same time, press the letter you used as the macro name.

When you do this, the macro interpreter tells 1-2-3 that a macro has been invoked and should be executed immediately.

Here is the difference between typing keystrokes and including them in a macro. If, while doing something on a worksheet, you type /WEY and press Return, 1-2-3 interprets the keystrokes as a command and erases the current worksheet. If, on the other hand, you store the same keystrokes as the label '/WEY, and save them as a macro named \E, your worksheet will remain untouched until you press the Alt-E key combination. Only then will 1-2-3's macro interpreter come into play and execute the /Worksheet Erase command sequence represented by the macro named \E.

When you invoke a macro, 1-2-3 first searches for a range with the name *character*. When this is found, it then checks the upper left-hand corner cell of that range for a label. If this cell contains a label, 1-2-3 begins executing the macro there. It starts with the first character in the label, executes that keystroke, moves to the next character, executes that keystroke, and continues in this way. If it encounters a tilde, it executes a Return; if it finds a left brace, it reads the following characters to determine which special keystroke or command is to be carried out.

When 1-2-3 reaches the end of the label, it moves to the cell directly below. If this cell contains a label, 1-2-3 continues executing the macro. When 1-2-3 finally encounters either a blank cell or one containing a number or a formula, it considers the macro completed and stops execution. The macro is, of course, carried out at rapid speed—much faster than you could type the same commands individually.

During execution of a macro, you cannot use the keyboard for other instructions. You can, however, stop the macro completely by pressing Break (Ctrl-Break on an IBM PC-type keyboard).

Note: It is important to remember that cell references within a macro are not updated when the worksheet is reorganized or modified with the /Move 250★, /Copy 31★, /Worksheet Insert 373★, or /Worksheet Delete 357★ commands. As a result, they may work improperly or not at all after you use one of these commands.

Macro

■ **Debugging macros**

When a macro doesn't perform as intended, it's time to "debug." This phrase is adopted from the programming field, where problems in programs are called bugs and removing them is called debugging. When macros are executed they run very rapidly and are extremely difficult to follow. To help you catch and solve problems, 1-2-3 has a built-in macro-debugging tool called single-step mode. In single-step mode a macro is executed a keystroke at a time. To enter single-step mode, you press Alt-F2 (Alt-F1 in Release 1a). Once you are in single-step mode, 1-2-3 pauses after executing each macro keystroke and waits for you to press a key. To continue, press any key other than Alt-F2 (or Alt-F1 with Release 1a); pressing this key combination causes you to exit single-step mode and usually stops execution of the macro.

While you are in single-step mode, 1-2-3 displays STEP at the bottom of the screen, unless you are between steps—at those times, it replaces STEP with a flashing SST (the SST appears in the upper right-hand corner if you are using Release 1a).

As you are stepping through your macro, if you find an error (either because 1-2-3 displays an error message or because you notice a misplaced or omitted keystroke), you can correct the problem on the spot. If the problem results in an error message, press Return or Esc. If the problem does not cause an error message, but you want to correct it anyway, press Break. You can then edit the macro, just as you would edit any other label. As you are still in the STEP mode, you can now invoke the macro again and proceed as before. To execute the macro normally, turn STEP mode off by pressing STEP again (the Alt-F2 key combination). Among the most common causes of errors in macros are: misspelled words, tildes omitted, and overwritten cell contents. Oftentimes, too, people forget what a macro does, confuse range names, get lost in the MENU mode, and so on.

■ **Special keys**

Very often, you will need to include non-character keys in a macro: the Return key, for example, or one of the function keys. Unlike command keystrokes, you cannot simply type the word *Return* or *right arrow* to tell 1-2-3 to use these keys.

Macro

The Return key, which is one of the most frequently used on the keyboard, is always represented by a tilde (~) in a macro. Whenever 1-2-3 encounters this symbol, it automatically issues a Return keystroke. The other non-character keys are described by alphabetic or numeric characters enclosed in braces, { and }.

Although tildes and left and right braces have special meanings in macros, you can also use them as standard characters (in Release 2) by surrounding them in braces: {~}, {{}, or {}}.

The following tables identify other special keys:

Key:	Symbol:	Meaning:
Home	{Home}	Moves pointer to A1
End	{End}	In EDIT mode, moves pointer to end of entry; in READY mode, used with a direction key to move pointer to end of a series of cells
Left arrow	{Left}	Moves pointer left one cell
Right arrow	{Right}	Moves pointer right one cell
Up arrow	{Up}	Moves pointer up one cell
Down arrow	{Down}	Moves pointer down one cell
Pg Up	{PgUp}	Moves pointer up one screen
Pg Dn	{PgDn}	Moves pointer down one screen
Tab	{Bigright}	Moves pointer right one screen
Backtab (Shift-Tab)	{Bigleft}	Moves pointer left one screen
Esc	{Esc}	In EDIT or VALUE mode, cancels the current entry; in POINT mode, cancels the current range; in MENU mode, backs up to the next higher menu
Backspace	{Bs}	In EDIT or VALUE mode, deletes one character to the left; in POINT mode, cancels the current range
Del	{Del}	Deletes the character at the cursor location

Note: In Release 2 of 1-2-3, the preceding keys also accept a numeric argument within the braces to specify repetitive uses of that key. For example, {Up 8} is the equivalent of eight up-arrow keystrokes; {Bigright 2} is the same as two tab keystrokes.

Key:	Symbol:	Meaning:
Alt-F1	{Compose}	Creates accented and other special LICS 203★ characters
F2	{Edit}	Enters/exits EDIT mode
F3	{Name}	In POINT mode, displays range-name menu
F4	{Abs}	In POINT mode, establishes absolute cell reference; used repeatedly, cycles through mixed relative/absolute references for cell addresses
F5	{Goto}	Moves pointer to a specified cell
F6	{Window}	Moves pointer to next window
F7	{Query}	Repeats last /Data Query command
F8	{Table}	Repeats last /Data Table command
F9	{Calc}	Updates worksheet calculations
F10	{Graph}	Draws last specified graph
?	{?}	Pauses for keyboard input

Although 1-2-3 is generally not fussy about where you break macro instructions, you cannot break keywords between cells. If, for example, you were to enter this:

'1233{bs
'}456

1-2-3 would be unable to execute the macro and would display *Syntax error in macro key/range {...}* when it reached {bs and did not find the closing brace.

Macro

■ **Mode indicators**

The execution of a macro always begins in the READY mode. Depending on the instructions it carries out, however, it will not necessarily return you to READY mode. For example, if your macro invokes the /Range Format command, 1-2-3 will be in POINT mode, waiting for a range to be specified, just as it would be if you had typed the keystrokes for /Range Format yourself. When creating macros, especially those that involve a sequence of instructions, be certain to pay attention to the mode indicator at the top of the screen. If necessary, include an extra {Esc} instruction in your macro to bring 1-2-3 back to READY mode.

Note: If you have used the {PANELOFF} or {INDICATE} keyword (see the entry Macro Commands **225★**) available with Release 2, 1-2-3 will not redraw the Control Panel as your macro executes. Be certain you check your macro thoroughly before adding keywords that reduce your control over the macro: {BREAKOFF}, {WINDOWSOFF}, {PANELOFF}, and {INDICATE}.

■ **Using macros**

All of the preceding sections have covered general aspects of creating and executing macros. The remainder of this entry will cover ways of visualizing and creating intermediate to advanced macros you may be able to apply directly, or with modification, to your own worksheets. If you have not used macros before, you may want to experiment a bit on a "scratchpad" worksheet, creating macros containing commands and formulas you are comfortable with, before moving on to the next sections.

Because Release 2 of 1-2-3 offers an enhanced macro facility, much of the following discussion is based on its capabilities. However, much of this information is also applicable to Release 1a. If you use this earlier version, you might find it helpful to refer to the entry on macro commands, to see how macro commands in your version are handled in Release 2.

■ **Evaluating your needs**

A well-designed macro can not only help you to become more productive, it can help others who may be unfamiliar with 1-2-3 or your worksheets. Macros can help others use your worksheets quickly, easily, and with less room for error. In order to put macros to work, however, you must do some advance planning and ensure that your macros do the job they are meant to do.

This means that, before you can enter a macro, you must define the task or problem it is intended to solve, and then design the necessary set of instructions to do the work effectively.

Problem-solving of this sort can be made manageable if you take a structured approach, much as programmers do: Define the problem, then break it into logical steps that can be written up as separate procedures. Once the groundwork is done, you then manually execute each procedure, keeping track of *everything* you do with the keyboard. From there, you can write the macro in stages, testing and correcting each "subroutine" individually before combining all of them in a finished macro. An additional advantage to working in this way is that you can share useful subroutines with others, or you could parcel out a large problem among several people, each of whom can then concentrate on one part of the whole. This approach is particularly useful, because most macros are written to smooth out or automate operations, such as input and output routines, menu presentations, or specific types of calculations, that are easily broken into smaller segments.

■ **Macro commands**

Release 2 of 1-2-3 includes a special language, similar to the special key notation, called the advanced macro commands. These commands consist of keywords and, sometimes, arguments (similar to function arguments). Like special keys, these keywords and their arguments are enclosed in braces. For example, the command {OPEN file_name} contains the keyword OPEN and the argument *file_name*. The keyword identifies the command's function; the argument is the item on which the command operates.

■ **Some intermediate macros**

Release 2 of 1-2-3 offers several keywords that make it easy to prompt for information and to enter that information into a worksheet. Two such keywords are {GETLABEL} and {GETNUMBER}. These two 1-2-3 commands temporarily halt the execution of a macro and, optionally, display a message in the Control Panel that prompts for data. For example, the macro segment:

'{GETLABEL "Enter first search criterion: ",M24}~

displays the prompt *Enter first search criterion:* in the second line of the Control Panel and waits for a response. When the user presses Return, the macro continues, taking the keystrokes typed by the user and placing them as a left-aligned label (the keyword assigns the label prefix) in cell M24.

Each of 1-2-3's pause commands has its own strengths, however. For instance, the simple pause {?} can prompt the user for nearly any information:

'\r	'/PPR{?}~	Prompt for a print range
	'OML{?}~	Prompt for left margin value
	'MR{?}~	Prompt for right margin value
	'QGQ~	End options, and Go

issues the /Print Printer command, chooses the *Range* option, and waits for a range to be specified. It then goes on to prompt for left and right margins before finally issuing the *Go* command.

Another important use of macros is manipulating data that is currently in the worksheet. Macros can be used to convert a range of numbers to their string equivalents and back again, to round a series of numbers, to format and otherwise alter the appearance of worksheet values, or to compare user input against acceptable values. For example, the following macro prompts for a department name to work with, compares it against a list of acceptable values, and responds with an error message if a match is not found.

```
B8: [W16] @VLOOKUP(INPUT,TABLE,1)                                    READY
```

	A	B	C	D	E	F	G
1							
2	\t	{GETLABEL "Enter Department Name: ",input}~					
3		{LET input,@UPPER(input):value}~					
4		{IF @ISERR(@VLOOKUP(input,table,0))}{BRANCH error}					
5		{DISPATCH addr}~					
6							
7	input	SHIPPING					
8	addr	K12					
9							
10	error	{GETLABEL "That name is not found (press return) ",input}~					
11		{BRANCH \t}					
12							
13	table	ADMINISTRATION	K14				
14		FACILITIES	K11				
15		PRODUCTION	K10				
16		SHIPPING	K12				
17		WAREHOUSE	K13				

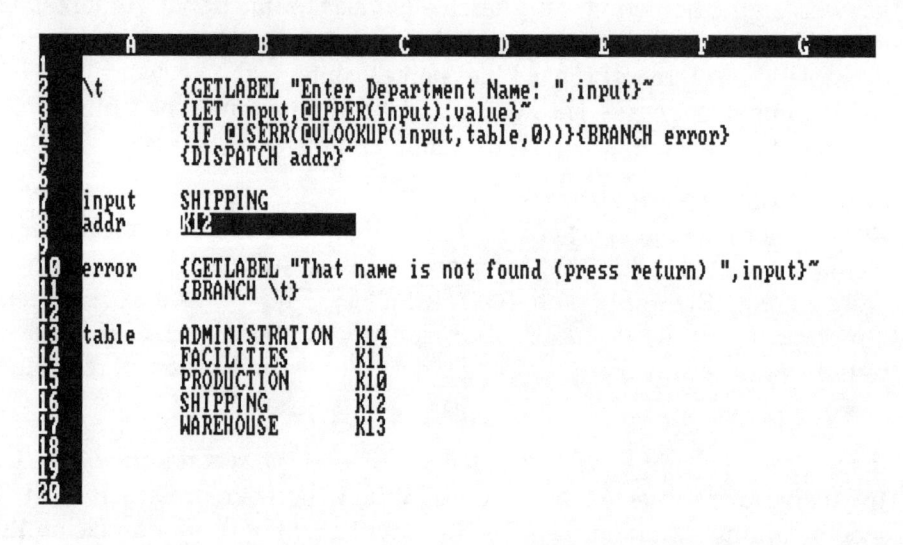

The macro works like this: the [Macro]-T keystrokes invoke the macro that starts at cell B2. The first command prompts for a department. The second command converts the input to all uppercase. The third command does a table lookup on the first column of the range *table* (cells B13..C17). If the @VLOOKUP function returns an error, that means the department wasn't found and macro program flow is routed to the error routine. If the department was found, the {DISPATCH} command routes program control to the address calculated at *addr* (which is an @VLOOKUP function on the second column of *table*).

Note: Release 2 of 1-2-3 offers automatic range-table generation, which was used to generate the table at the bottom of the illustration.

- **Advanced use of macro keywords**

With Release 2 of 1-2-3, you have a number of advanced options that make it possible to automate the movement of data to and from the storage devices in your system by writing characters to and reading them from ASCII files created within a macro. This opens the way to developing automatic audit-trail routines, as well as archiving systems.

Some other advanced options available with macros are macro menus created with the {MENUBRANCH} and {MENUCALL} keywords, customized input forms for data-entry, automated data table operations, and worksheet links with automated /File Xtract **133★** and /File Combine **121★** operations.

Perhaps the most exciting aspect of advanced use of macro commands is the ability to combine Release 2's label arithmetic with macro applications to create code that varies, depending on other values in your worksheet. For example, the function:

@IF(Sales>10000,"{BRANCH bonus}","{BRANCH next}")

returns the label {BRANCH bonus} if the worksheet cell named *Sales* has a value greater than 10000. This bit of code could have been written in many ways, but this serves to demonstrate how customized macro commands can be created with label arithmetic.

There is one problem with label arithmetic in macros, however. Release 2 does not necessarily update the worksheet while a macro is running. This means that macro code containing formulas is not always up to date. To help with this, Release 2 includes several very useful commands to calculate portions of the worksheet. Instead of calculating the entire worksheet with the {Calc} special-key statement, Release 2 offers {RECALC} and {RECALCCOL}, which operate on ranges. To ensure that a macro runs as intended, place a {RECALC} command in the cell preceding a formula and specify the formula cell in the {RECALC} argument. For example, the following macro uses a string formula:

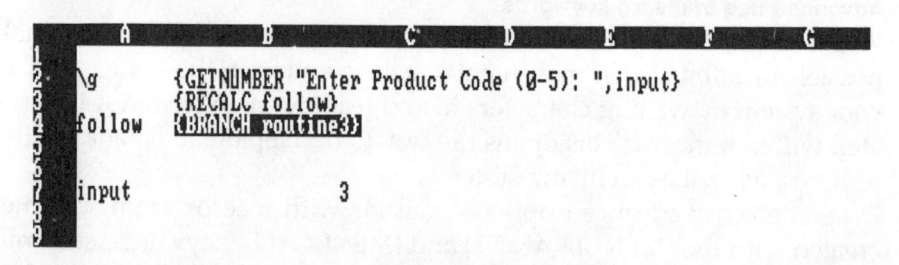

```
B4: [W17] +"{BRANCH routine"&@CHOOSE(INPUT,"0","1","2","3","4","5")&"}"        READY

           A          B              C          D        E       F       G
1
2        \g          {GETNUMBER "Enter Product Code (0-5): ",input}
3                    {RECALC follow}
4        follow      {BRANCH routine3}
5
6
7        input                       3
8
9
```

The string formula in B4 (and displayed in the Control Panel) calculates a label based on the value of the worksheet cell *input*. In this situation *input* has been given a value of 3 by the {GETNUMBER} command. The {RECALC} command updates the cell named *follow* (which is the string formula); the string formula uses the value to calculate the label, and returns *{BRANCH routine3}*. In this situation it would have been possible to include a tilde (~) after the {GETNUMBER} command and dispense with the {RECALC}, since the tilde emulates pressing the Return key and, in the default calculation mode, the entire worksheet is recalculated after a cell value is altered and Return is pressed. But if the worksheet were a large one, recalculating it entirely would lead to time-consuming macro code when, instead, your objective is efficient macro code.

Macro commands

Release 2 of 1-2-3 provides a set of advanced macro commands that can be used as a programming language to create complex and powerful macros and macro subroutines. Because many of these commands are interrelated, they are grouped together in this entry for ease of reference.

■ Syntax

1-2-3's advanced macro commands require that you follow a certain syntax—rules of organization and usage. This syntax is comparable in many respects to the format you use with 1-2-3 functions, because many of the macro keywords, such as {GETNUMBER}, require arguments you must supply in order for them to perform the tasks they are designed to do. The parallel is not complete, however, and differs sharply in one important respect: Formulas and cell references in macros are *not* updated automatically when you move, insert, or delete cells on the worksheet, either in a macro command or by editing the worksheet itself. Thus, any of these actions can invalidate a macro, whereas a function would be automatically adjusted to reflect such changes.

Format: Macro commands are always enclosed in braces, { and }. If they do not require an argument, they look like this:

{KEYWORD}

If they do take one or more arguments, they look like this:

{KEYWORD argument1,argument2,...argumentn}

The keyword (which can be entered in upper- or lowercase characters) is separated from the first argument by a blank space; the arguments are separated by a comma—no spaces—or, optionally, a semicolon.

Arguments: 1-2-3 allows four argument types:

- Number—a numeric value, a reference to a cell containing a numeric value, or the result of an expression that calculates a numeric value.
- String—any string up to 240 characters long, including the length of the keyword and braces, but generally not in the form of a string formula.
- Location—the name or address(es) of one cell or a multiple-cell range.
- Condition—any logical expression containing numbers or formulas.

Some keywords, such as {LET} allow you to specify an argument type as either a string or a value. In these instances, you separate the argument and type with a colon, and no spaces—for example, {KEYWORD argument:type}.

Macro commands

■ **Subroutines**

A subroutine is a macro that can be branched to, and returned from, by another macro. Subroutines are generally used for tasks that are performed frequently and from different locations in a worksheet. They are also ideally suited for creating large and complex macros from smaller components that can be entered, tested, and refined individually before being linked together by subroutine calls.

For example:

'{subroutine1 A1+B1}

calls subroutine1 and passes the value of A1+B1 to it (via the {DEFINE} command discussed later in this entry.

'{menucall menu1}

calls the menu named menu1.

Menus in macros: One application for macros that is both useful and very well suited to the modular approach that subroutines encourage is the creation of your own Control-Panel menus like the following:

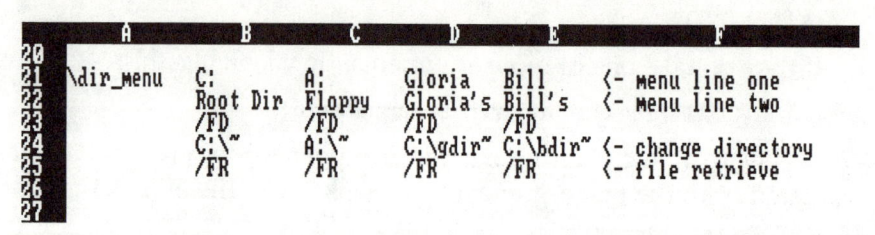

```
D39:                                                                    READY

          A           B          C           D           E             F
    20
    21   \dir_menu   C:         A:          Gloria      Bill      <- menu line one
    22               Root Dir   Floppy      Gloria's    Bill's    <- menu line two
    23               /FD        /FD         /FD         /FD
    24               C:\~       A:\~        C:\gdir~    C:\bdir~  <- change directory
    25               /FR        /FR         /FR         /FR       <- file retrieve
    26
    27
```

If your worksheet models involve a great deal of user entry or have very specific requirements, menus can aid both you and less experienced users in using the worksheet correctly.

To create a menu, you must enter three rows of information:

- □ In the first row, enter short, descriptive command names, such as Choose, String, Value, and Quit, for your menu choices. Use words that begin with different letters, so the user has the usual 1-2-3 option of either typing the first letter or highlighting the appropriate command.

Enter each command name in a separate cell. 1-2-3 allows up to eight commands. Bear in mind that your display is limited to 80 characters per line. No blank cells are allowed within the row, but 1-2-3 does require one blank cell at the right end of the row.

- In each menu cell of the second row, enter a descriptive label corresponding to each command name in the first row. Each command must have a descriptive label of some sort; if you don't want 1-2-3 to display a command description, enter blank spaces in the appropriate cell.
- In each menu cell of the third row, enter the appropriate macro instructions that carry out the menu command. These cells can contain subroutine calls to instructions integrated in a macro program, or calls to other menus, or regular macro instructions.

The three menu commands are {MENUCALL} (a subroutine call), and {MENUBRANCH} and /XM, both "goto"-type commands.

■ Commands

The following list of macro commands is in alphabetic order. Optional items are shown in angle brackets, < and >.

{?}: A keyboard-interaction command, {?} pauses the macro for keyboard input and resumes the macro immediately after the Return key is pressed. For example:

'{GOTO}{NAME}{?}~

prompts the user with a menu of range names and waits for the selection.

'{?}~{DOWN}

waits for input, enters the response in the current cell, and moves the pointer down one cell.

{BEEP <number>}: A way of providing the user with a warning or a reminder, this command creates a beep. If you specify a number between 1 and 4, you hear one of four beep sounds. '{BEEP 4}~ creates a long beep. 1 and 4 are deep-sounding beeps, 2 and 3 are high.

{**BLANK location**}: A data-manipulation command, {BLANK} erases the contents of the cell or cells specified by the location. {BLANK} is equivalent to /Range Erase, but is more convenient because it can be invoked when other menus are in use. For example:

'{BLANK Input Area}~

will erase the contents of the cells in the range named Input Area. Using {BLANK} on itself will cause an error message.

{**BRANCH location**}: A program-control command, {BRANCH}♦ transfers control to the location specified, and executes the macro keystrokes stored there. {BRANCH} is equivalent to /XG 380♦, and works like a Goto command in BASIC. The new location can be specified as a reference to a single cell or to a range. If the location is a range, execution begins in the top left-hand corner cell.

The {BRANCH} command is not the same as a subroutine call, which automatically returns control to the calling routine. To return from the called to the calling location, you must specify another {BRANCH} command. Because of this distinction, a subroutine call may be more appropriate in some circumstances.

{BRANCH} is often combined with the {IF} statement for conditional execution, as in {IF input<1#OR#>5}{BRANCH error}~.

{**BREAKOFF**}: A keyboard-interaction command, {BREAKOFF} turns off the Break key and prevents interruption of either macro execution or printing from within a macro. Break stays off until the macro ends or {BREAKON} is issued. On IBM and compatible keyboards, Break is the Ctrl-Break key combination.

This keyword should be avoided until macros have been thoroughly tested, but it is useful in preventing deliberate or inadvertent interruption while a macro is executing.

{**BREAKON**}: A keyboard-interaction command, {BREAKON} complements {BREAKOFF}. It cancels {BREAKOFF} and turns the Break key on. If Break is pressed after {BREAKON} takes effect, macro execution will be ended.

{**CLOSE**}: A file-manipulation command, {CLOSE} closes a file that has been opened ({OPEN}). If no file is open, the command is ignored.

{CONTENTS destination-location,source-location,<width>,<format>}: A data-manipulation command, {CONTENTS}♦ assigns the contents of one cell to another as a label. The contents of the source location are placed in the destination location. If you specify a width number, the source location is treated as if it had that width. For example, if cell A1 contains the label Cost Estimation Worksheet, then {CONTENTS A2,A1,4} will place 'Cost in cell A2, because cell A1 is treated as if it were only four characters wide. Practically, this means it is possible to truncate the source value (if it is a label) or alter the value's appearance without using the format option (if it is a number).

The format option can only be used if a width number is specified. The formats are those you would assign with the /Range Format command, but are given the following numbers for use with this command:

Number:	Format:
0 to 15	fixed, 0 to 15 decimals
16 to 31	scientific, 0 to 15 decimals
32 to 47	currency, 0 to 15 decimals
48 to 63	percent, 0 to 15 decimals
64 to 79	comma, 0 to 15 decimals
112	+/−
113	general
114	D1 date (DD-MMM-YY)
115	D2 date (DD-MMM)
116	D3 date (MMM-YY)
117	literal
118	hidden
119	D6 time (HH:MM:SS, a.m./p.m.)
120	D7 time (HH:MM, a.m./p.m.)
121	D4 date (full international)
122	D5 date (partial international)
123	D8 time (full international)
124	D9 time (partial international)
125 to 127	default numeric display

{DEFINE location1:type1,location2:type2...}: A program-control command, the {DEFINE} command specifies worksheet cells as storage locations for variables passed to a subroutine, and assigns a type to the variable stored there. Each location can be a single or multiple cell name or address; each type can be either :string or :value. The type :value tells 1-2-3 to evaluate the variable and store it as either a string or a number, depending on the result of the evaluation. If you do not specify a type, the default is :string (a left-aligned label).

Not all subroutines require a {DEFINE} command, but if any variables are passed to the subroutine, a {DEFINE} command must be the first statement in the subroutine. It is through {DEFINE} that you assign cells to contain any variables passed by the subroutine call. When the subroutine is invoked, the cells specified in the {DEFINE} command are filled with the variables, which are entered as either string or numeric values. For example, the command:

'{SUBROUTINE1 A1*10,"Sales",+"Total for "&G48,I2}~

invokes subroutine 1 and passes four variables to it. To be able to use those variables, subroutine 1 must define four cell locations to hold the variables and must also define whether the variables are to be treated as text or numbers. For example:

{DEFINE AB50:value,AB51:value,AB52:value,AB53:value}~

produces two strings and two numbers.

{DEFINE AB50,AB51,AB52,AB53}~

produces four string values.

{DISPATCH location}: A program-control command, {DISPATCH} branches to a cell that, in turn, contains a reference to another cell that is the ultimate destination of the command. {DISPATCH} is somewhat like the @@ function in this respect, because it moves to a cell indirectly, via an intermediate cell reference.

The location specified in the command must be a single cell; if it is not, the {DISPATCH} command behaves like the {BRANCH} command does and transfers execution control to the range, rather than extracting a reference to a new point of control. If the location is a blank cell or a number, macro execution is terminated. If you use a single-cell range name, enclose it in double quotation marks.

The {DISPATCH} command is useful in setting up a single cell that can act as a pointer to other locations on the worksheet, depending on varying conditions. For example, in:

'{IF input<1#OR#INPUT>5}{LET A1,"Error_Routine1"}~
'{IF input>1#AND#INPUT<5}{LET A1,"Input_OK"}~
'{DISPATCH A1}~

the {DISPATCH} command would place the single-cell range name Error_Routine1 in cell A1 if input is less than 1 or greater than 5; otherwise, the command would put the single-cell range name Input_OK in cell A1.

{FILESIZE location}: A file-manipulation command, {FILESIZE} finds the number of bytes in the currently {OPEN}ed file (one byte can be considered the same as one character) and places the information in the cell specified as the location. The location must be specified as a single cell, either by address or by a single-cell range name. The file size is recorded as a numeric value. If no file is currently open, the command is ignored.

{FOR counter-location,start-number,stop-number,step-number,starting-location}: A program-control command, {FOR} loops through a subroutine that begins in the cell specified by the starting location. The number of times the subroutine is executed is defined by the start number and the stop number, divided by the step number (increment). The counter location is a cell in which the cycle count is displayed as the {FOR} command is executed. Arguments can be values, formulas, or cell names or addresses. If multiple-cell ranges are specified, the {FOR} command refers to the top left-hand corner cell. Control returns to the {FOR} statement when the subroutine encounters either a non-label cell or {RETURN}.

{FOR} is the 1-2-3 equivalent of the FOR-NEXT loops in BASIC and other programming languages. It operates as follows: first the {FOR} statement is evaluated, before the subroutine is called. On the first pass, the counter location is given the start-number value and is compared to the stop number. If the value in the counter location is less than the stop number, the subroutine is invoked. If the counter number is equal to or greater than the stop number, the subroutine is not called. On each return from the subroutine, the value in the counter location is increased by the value of the step number and the {FOR} statement is again evaluated. If the start number is still less than the stop number, the subroutine is invoked and executed again. When the value in the counter location is equal to or greater than the stop number, the {FOR} command is completed and macro execution continues with the statement immediately following the {FOR}. For example:

'{FOR Times,1,5,1,subroutine1}

will execute subroutine1 five times and display the count in the cell named Times. In contrast:

{FOR Times,5,1,5,subroutine1}

will never execute subroutine1 because the start number is already greater than the stop number.

{FORBREAK}: A program-control command, {FORBREAK} ends the current {FOR} statement immediately. The macro continues executing in the cell immediately following the {FOR} command.

The {FORBREAK} command takes no argument, and the only legal location for this command is in the subroutine invoked by the {FOR} statement. {FORBREAK} is used with a conditional statement, as follows:

'{GETLABEL "Continue with input (Y/N) ",A1}~
'{IF A1="N"#OR#A1="n"}{FORBREAK}~

where an upper- or lowercase N typed into A1 executes the {FORBREAK} command and ends execution of the current {FOR} statement.

{GET location}: A keyboard-interaction command, {GET} instructs 1-2-3 to wait for the user to press any key and then place the keystroke in the cell specified as the location. If the location is a multiple-cell range, the keystroke is stored in the top left-hand corner cell of the range.

The keystroke can be either a single keystroke or a special key, such as F1 through F10. For a special key, the keystroke is stored as a label, such as 'Name, 'Edit, and so on.

{GET} does not accept more than one character, and does not display a prompt in the Control Panel, as {GETNUMBER} and {GETLABEL} do.

{GET} has the useful feature of not requiring the user to press the Return key in addition to typing a keystroke.

{GETLABEL prompt,location}: A keyboard-interaction command, the {GETLABEL} ♦ command displays your prompt in the second line of the Control Panel, waits for input of up to 80 characters followed by the Return key, and places the input as a left-aligned label in the cell specified as the location. The prompt must be enclosed in double quotation marks if a colon, semicolon, or comma is used in the prompt. For example:

{GETLABEL "[Save] Enter worksheet name: ",A1}~

prompts for a file name and places the response in cell A1.

{GETLABEL} is the Release 2 equivalent of the /XL **381♦** command.

{GETNUMBER prompt,location}: A keyboard-interaction command, the {GETNUMBER} ♦ command is the complement to {GETLABEL} and requires the same types of arguments. {GETNUMBER} displays a prompt and waits for input of up to 80 characters, then places the input in the cell specified as the location.

Input to the {GETNUMBER} command must always be a numeric expression—a number, a formula that calculates a numeric value, or a range name. {GETNUMBER} provides no validation of input, as the equivalent /XN **381♦** command does. A non-numeric response to a {GETNUMBER} results in the ERR value being placed in the specified location.

{GETPOS location}: A file-manipulation command, {GETPOS} returns the current position of the file pointer and stores it in the location cell. The file pointer is a byte number; 0 indicates the first position. {GETPOS} is useful for saving a record of the last position of the file pointer in a data-entry or editing session. If no file is open, the command is ignored; no error is generated.

{IF condition}: A program-control command, {IF}♦ provides conditional execution of the commands that follow in the same cell, depending on the result of a true/false evaluation. {IF} is analogous to the @IF **179★** function in using the if/then/else logic common to most programming languages, but should not be confused with the use or syntax of @IF. The {IF} command causes branching to another macro statement; the @IF function returns a value that exists in one cell or another on the worksheet.

The condition evaluated by the {IF} command can be any numeric or string value or expression. If the condition returns a non-zero value, it is true, and macro execution continues *in the same cell*, with the statement immediately following the {IF} statement. If the condition returns the numeric value 0, it is false, and macro execution continues *in the cell below* the cell containing the {IF} statement. Blank cells, strings, and the values ERR and NA are considered false. {IF} is the equivalent of /XI **380♦**.

The {IF} command is useful in validating input or for causing conditional branching in any situation that requires a logical test.

{INDICATE <string>}: A screen-control command, {INDICATE} changes the mode indicator **248★** in the upper right-hand corner of the Control Panel to a string of your choice. The string argument is optional. If used, it can be up to five characters long; if not used, the {INDICATE} command resets the indicator to its appropriate status.

When you use the {INDICATE} command with a string argument, the indicator you set remains on-screen, regardless of any subsequent mode changes. Unlike 1-2-3's built-in mode indicators, update is not automatic. {INDICATE} has no effect after a {PANELOFF} command is executed. To change or reset the indicator, you must use another {INDICATE} command. For example:

{INDICATE Enter}

could be used to announce a data entry situation;

{INDICATE Outln}

could be displayed while an outlining macro is running.

In either case, however, to restore the mode indicator to normal, you must include the statement {INDICATE} with no argument, in your macro.

To suppress the mode indicator entirely, use the statement:

{INDICATE ""}

{**LET location,number:type**}: or {**LET location,string:type**}: A data-manipulation command, {LET} places a number or a string in the cell specified as the location, without moving the cell pointer.

A number can be any numeric or calculated value or formula and can be stored as either a value or a string, depending on the type you specify. A string can be any label or string formula you specify. For example:

{LET A1,123+123}

will place the calculated value 246 in cell A1.

{LET A1,123+123:string}

will place the label '123+123 in cell A1.

If cell B22 contains the label John Doakes:

{LET A1,+"Total Sales: "&B22}

will place the string *Total Sales: John Doakes* in cell A1.

If you specify a multiple-cell range as the location, the command will place the results in the top left-hand cell of the range.

{**LOOK location**}: A keyboard-interaction command, {LOOK} examines the keyboard buffer during macro execution. If one or more characters have been typed and stored in the buffer, the first character is copied to the cell specified as the location, and macro execution continues. If a keystroke is not found, the location reference is erased. The character remains in the type-ahead buffer.

{LOOK} is similar to the BASIC Inkey statement, and can be used as an optional means of stopping a macro without resorting to the Break key or testing for input without pausing. For example:

{LOOK A1}
{IF A1<>""}{FORBREAK}

{**MENUBRANCH location**}: A keyboard-interaction command, the {MENU-BRANCH}♦ command pauses macro execution, goes to the location specified, and then displays the menu of choices entered there. Depending on the choice made, the macro then branches to the appropriate instructions, and execution continues. {MENUBRANCH} is a specialized form of the {BRANCH} command and, like {BRANCH} terminates macro execution when the last instruction in the branch routine is encountered. It is equivalent to the /XM 381♦ command. Unlike {MENUCALL}, {MENUBRANCH} requires a {BRANCH} or a /XG statement to return to the main macro.

{MENUCALL location}: A keyboard-interaction command, {MENUCALL} is similar to {MENUBRANCH} in pausing macro execution, going to the location specified, and displaying the menu entered there. {MENUCALL}, however, treats the menu like a subroutine and returns to the main macro when the menu instructions are completed. With {MENUCALL}, you can include a {RETURN} statement if you wish, but the statement is not required. Control will return to the main macro as soon as a non-label cell is encountered in the called routine.

{ONERROR branch-location,<message-location>}: A program-control command, {ONERROR} enables error trapping during macro execution and prevents inadvertent interruption by branching to the location specified if a 1-2-3 error occurs. The optional message location tells 1-2-3 to store the error message, so that you can see the cause of the problem. In effect, this command is similar to a {BRANCH}.

The {ONERROR} command is canceled as soon as an error occurs, the macro ends, or another {ONERROR} command is encountered. To continue trapping errors after an error arises, another {ONERROR} command must be executed.

By planning ahead for contingencies, you can use the {ONERROR} command to design an error handler that checks the error message and deals with the situation at hand.

{OPEN filename,access-mode}: A file-manipulation command, {OPEN} opens the file specified by the file name, and allows the type of operation specified by the access mode: R for read; W for write; or M for modify.

The file name specified with this command must be a string or a reference to a cell containing a string, and must be the path name, including extension, of the file to be opened. Altogether, the path name can be up to 64 characters long.

The access mode is always a single character: R, W, or M:

- If you specify R, an existing file can be read with the {READ} and {READLN} commands, but cannot be added to or modified. If this access mode is chosen, but the specified file does not exist, the command is invalid, but macro execution continues in the same cell, with the statement immediately following the {OPEN} command.

- If you specify W, the new file can be read, as described, and written to with the {WRITE} and {WRITELN} commands. Macro execution continues in the following cell. If the file already exists, it is erased.

□ If you specify M, an existing file can be read and written to. However, if the file does not exist, the command fails, although macro execution continues in the same cell, with the statement immediately following the {OPEN} command.

{PANELOFF}: A screen-control command, {PANELOFF} suppresses redisplay of the Control Panel while a macro is executing. This command takes no argument.

When {PANELOFF} is executed, the Control Panel is frozen in its current state until the macro ends or until a {PANELON} command is encountered. {PANELOFF} is useful in designing worksheets for people who may be confused or distracted by seeing 1-2-3 commands embedded in the macro being "played out" on-screen.

{PANELOFF} can be used along with {WINDOWSOFF} to freeze the entire screen during macro execution.

{PANELON}: A screen-control command, {PANELON} is the complement of {PANELOFF} and reinstates the display of the Control Panel during macro execution.

{PUT location,column-number,row-number,number}: or **{PUT location,column-number,row-number,string}:** A data-manipulation command, {PUT} places a number, string, or calculated value in a range (location), in the cell specified by the column and row numbers. The column and row numbers are offsets, beginning with 0, from the top left-hand corner of the range. For example:

{PUT Payroll,18,1,1000}

will put 1000 (a Christmas bonus, perhaps) into column 18, row 1, (the nineteenth column and second row) of the range named Payroll. To automate entry of all bonuses, the row offset (1) could be incremented after each {PUT} to advance to the next row.

If either offset is greater than the respective number of columns or rows in the range, the result is an error message.

The {PUT} command is similar to {LET}, but references a cell at a particular column/row intersection within a range, rather than a particular cell on the worksheet.

{QUIT}: A program-control command, {QUIT}♦ terminates the macro and returns control to the keyboard. {QUIT} does not take an argument. If used in a subroutine, it ends not only the subroutine, but the main macro, as well. {QUIT} is equivalent to the /XQ **380♦** command.

{READ bytecount,location}: A file-manipulation command, {READ} copies the specified number of characters (bytecount) from the file into the worksheet, as a left-aligned label in the cell you specify by location. The read begins at the current location of the file pointer and ends at bytecount plus the file-pointer location. The file pointer is updated automatically to reflect the new position. For example:

   {READ 10,A1}

will read ten characters, beginning at the current position of the file pointer, into cell A1 as a left-aligned label.

The bytecount must be between 0 and 240. If you specify a negative value, 1-2-3 uses the value 240.

{READLN location}: A file-manipulation command, {READLN} is similar to {READ}, but copies from the current location of the file pointer to the end of a line identified by a carriage return and line feed. The line is placed as a left-aligned label in the cell identified by the location, and the position of the file pointer is updated to point at the beginning of the next line.

The {READLN} command reads to, but does not copy, the carriage return at the end of the line.

{RECALC location,<condition>,<iteration>}: A data-manipulation command, {RECALC} recalculates part of the worksheet—the formulas in the range specified as the location. {RECALC} performs the recalculation downward on a row-by-row basis (the related command {RECALCCOL} performs the recalculation on a column-by-column basis).

The optional arguments, condition and iteration, determine whether recalculation is performed more than once. If a condition is specified, 1-2-3 evaluates it after each recalculation; if the condition is false (for example, A1<100), the recalculation is performed again. Similarly, iteration determines how many times recalculation takes place. If either or both of the options are included, recalculation continues until the condition is true or the number of iterations specified is completed.

Macro commands

There are several factors you must take into account when you use the {RECALC} (or {RECALCCOL}) command.

If your formula is:

☐ Below and to the left of its data formulas, use {RECALC}.

	A	B	C	D	E	F	G
1							
2				+D1+2			
3							
4		+D2+1					
5							
6							
7							

☐ Above and to the right of its data formulas, use {RECALCCOL}.

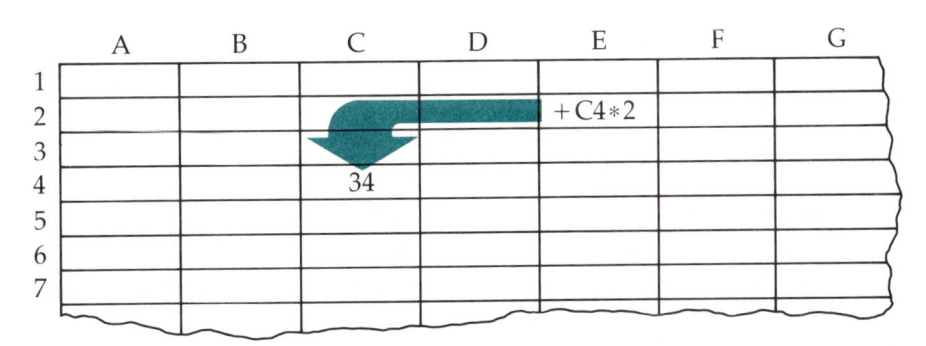

	A	B	C	D	E	F	G
1							
2					+C4*2		
3							
4			34				
5							
6							
7							

☐ Above and to the left of its data formulas, use {Calc}.

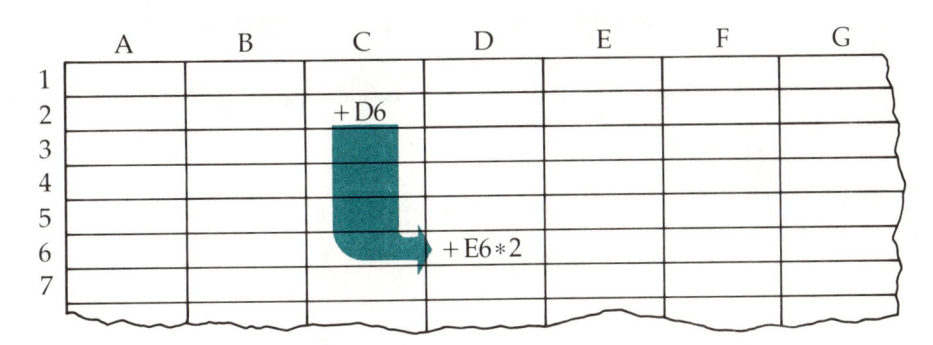

	A	B	C	D	E	F	G
1							
2			+D6				
3							
4							
5							
6				+E6*2			
7							

Formulas outside of the recalculation range must be updated before they are used in calculations. Use either the F9 [Calc] key or the {Calc} keystroke command in your macro before using formulas outside the recalculation range *and* before saving a worksheet in which you have used either {RECALC} or {RECALCCOL}.

{RECALCCOL location}: A data-manipulation command, {RECALCCOL} complements the {RECALC} command, but recalculates the formulas in the range specified by moving right, column by column. Except for the direction of recalculation, this command is identical to {RECALC}.

{RESTART}: A program-control command, {RESTART} cancels a subroutine call and erases return addresses from 1-2-3's internal log of calling routines (stack). Execution of the subroutine continues after a {RESTART} command, but macro execution ends when either the last statement or a {RETURN} instruction is encountered. {RESTART} takes no argument.

The {RESTART} command is useful inside a subroutine as a means of escaping a serious error. For example, you might want to call for a restart if important information were not found:

    {IF error-message="File not found"}
    {RESTART}
    {BRANCH \0}~

{RETURN}: A program-control command, {RETURN}♦ ends a subroutine call or a {MENUCALL} command and returns control to the calling macro. After a {RETURN}, execution resumes at the statement following the subroutine or {MENUCALL}. It is equivalent to the /XR 380♦ command.

The {RETURN} command is useful primarily within conditional statements. It is not required at the end of a subroutine or menu command, because control is automatically returned to the calling routine whenever the macro interpreter encounters a non-label cell. For example, the {RETURN} command can be used to exit a subroutine when a condition is not met:

    '{IF input_value<1}{RETURN}~

{**SETPOS file_position**}: A file-manipulation command, {SETPOS} sets the file pointer to a new position in the current file. The first character is at position 0. For example:

'{SETPOS 2}

moves the file pointer to the third character in the file.

Using this command, you can address any character in a 1-2-3 file. If no file is open, the command is ignored, but macro execution continues.

{**SUBROUTINE_NAME variable1,variable2,variable3...**}: A program-control device, {SUBROUTINE_NAME}♦ is a macro command in which any subroutine you design can be called by inserting its range name in braces. As described at the beginning of this entry, a subroutine is a special macro that executes a particular task or command. By enclosing its range name in braces and including the whole within the main macro, you enable 1-2-3 to branch to and from the subroutine. When a subroutine is called in this way, control returns to the main macro when 1-2-3 encounters a {RETURN} command or a non-label cell, whichever comes first. This command is similar to /XC **380**♦, but more powerful (see {DEFINE} for more information on variable passing).

{**WAIT time-number**}: A keyboard-interaction command, {WAIT} pauses macro execution until the time specified by the time serial number (a decimal fraction representing the time of day as a number between .000, for midnight, and .99999, for 11:59:59). The time need not be specified as a serial number, however. You can use one of the time functions (such as @NOW or @TIME) to generate the appropriate value. For example:

'{WAIT @TIME(8,00,00)}~

will halt macro execution until the computer's internal clock says it is 8 a.m. At that time, execution will continue with the next macro statement.

During the time the macro is halted, all keystrokes except the Break key (if {BREAKOFF} has not been executed) are buffered.

You can use this command to cause a macro to pause for a specified time period. For example:

'{WAIT @NOW+.0001}

will generate a 10-second pause before it will continue to the next macro statement.

{WINDOWSOFF}: A screen-control command, {WINDOWSOFF} freezes the worksheet window during macro execution. {WINDOWSOFF} has two advantages: First, it stops displays of worksheet changes as a macro executes and thus avoids confusing people who are unfamiliar with 1-2-3. Second, it allows a macro to run faster, because 1-2-3 does not have to pause and redraw the screen each time a change is made to the display.

The {WINDOWSOFF} command can be used in conjunction with the {PANELOFF} command to freeze the display of both the worksheet window and the Control Panel. Normal screen updating resumes when the macro ends or a {WINDOWSON} command is executed.

{WINDOWSON}: A screen-control command, {WINDOWSON} cancels the effect of the {WINDOWSOFF} command.

{WRITE string}: A file-manipulation command, {WRITE} copies the specified string to the current position of the file pointer in a file that has been opened in either write (W) or modify (M) access mode with the {OPEN} command.

The string can either be entered as the argument, enclosed in double quotation marks, it can be a reference to a cell containing a string, or it can be a string formula containing the & concatenation operator. For example:

{WRITE A1&B1&C1&D1}~

Similarly:

'{WRITE "If wishes were horses, "&"then beggars would ride"}~

would copy the string *If wishes were horses, then beggars would ride* into the open file at the current position of the file pointer.

All characters in the string are written in LICS **203★** code, and the file pointer is moved to the position in the string just past the last copied character. If the file pointer is at the end of the file, the string is added; otherwise, the string is inserted into the file.

{WRITELN string}: A file-manipulation command, {WRITELN} is similar to {WRITE}, but adds a carriage-return/line-feed to the end of the string.

'{WRITELN "If wishes were horses,"~}

would write the line *If wishes were horses*, to the current location of the file pointer, and end the line with a carriage return and a line feed, so that a second {WRITELN} command:

{WRITELN "Then beggars would ride."}

would result in two lines in the file:

If wishes were horses,
Then beggars would ride.

The {WRITELN} command is the complement of {READLN}. Together, the commands make reading and writing to files a simple task, as long as the lines involved do not exceed 240 characters. Given both {WRITELN} and {READLN}, there is no need to keep track of the number of characters being written to or read from a file during macro execution.

@MAX()

- **Format**
@MAX(list)

- **Description**
@MAX is a statistical function that returns the maximum (largest) value in the list specified as its argument. The complement of @MAX is @MIN **246★**, which returns the smallest value in a list.

- **Procedure**
The argument to @MAX is a single range reference or a list of items separated by commas, with no intervening blank spaces. Each item can be a numeric value, a single cell address, a range of cells, a range name, or a formula. Thus, any of the following would be valid arguments:

@MAX(A1..B1,C1,D1,E1)
@MAX(A1..A15)
@MAX(Sales)
@MAX(A1∗A2/A3,B2+C2,D11−D10)

@MAX ignores blank cells within a range, but treats label cells as 0. If the list is entirely empty (includes no numeric values or labels), @MAX returns the value ERR.

@MAX() · @MID()

■ **Example**
The following example uses the @MAX function to find the largest daily sale for a period.

```
E9: (C2) [W17] @MAX(B5..B20)                                    READY
```

	A	B	C	D	E
1					
2	Sales in January				
3					
4	Date	Amount			
5	16-Jan	$10,179.25			
6	26-Jan	$11,626.75			
7	17-Jan	$19,681.15			
8	22-Jan	$11,254.75			
9	27-Jan	$8,550.66		Function:	$36,990.75
10	31-Jan	$13,625.29			
11	30-Jan	$25,377.50		Explanation: Find the largest
12	28-Jan	$36,990.75		sale in the list
13	18-Jan	$7,267.41			
14	29-Jan	$25,019.00			
15	21-Jan	$5,537.75			
16	23-Jan	$3,546.00			
17	19-Jan	$10,825.25			
18	25-Jan	$15,169.50			
19	20-Jan	$20,441.37			
20	15-Jan	$10,000.00			

@MID()   A Release 2 string function

■ **Format**
@MID(string,start number,n)

■ **Description**
The @MID function searches a string and extracts n number of characters (a substring) from a specified point within the string. @MID complements the functions @LEFT, which returns n characters from the beginning of a string, and @RIGHT, which returns n characters from the end of a string.

■ **Procedure**
The @MID function allows a string argument only; a numeric value will produce the value ERR.

The start number specifies the number of characters into the string the extract begins, starting with 0, the leftmost character in the string.

The value n specifies the number of characters to be extracted. n must be either a number or a reference to a cell containing a numeric value.

@MID()

In the case of both the start number and the number of characters extracted, any blank spaces, punctuation marks, and symbols count as characters.

The string can be specified either directly, by inclusion in the argument, or indirectly, as a cell reference. If the string is included in the argument, it must be enclosed in double quotation marks. For example

@MID("04/12/72",3,2)

(In this instance, the function would return *12*, the two characters specified by n, beginning at the third character position.)

In either strings or cell references, you can use the & concatenation operator **263★** to retrieve characters from within two or more combined strings. For example:

@MID("roses "&"are red",6,3)

would return *are* the three characters beginning at position six in the combined string.

When you enter values for the start number and n, bear the following in mind:

- ☐ A start number larger than the number of characters in the string will result in an empty string—no characters.
- ☐ A value for n that is larger than the number of characters in the string will cause no problems. The function will simply stop when it reaches the end of the string. Specifying n as a large number is useful when you do not know the length of the string.
- ☐ If n is 0, the function will return an empty string—in other words, a string containing no characters. This is not the same as a blank space, however.

■ **Comments**

In working with strings and substrings, it is helpful to think of the string as an array of characters with an index that begins at 0. The characters within the string are accessed by varying the index. Thus, if the string is "John Smith", then the index number 0 returns the character J, and index number 4 returns the space character. (Note here that specifying 0 as the start number makes @MID the equivalent of the @LEFT function.)

245

@MIN()

@MIN()

- **Format**

    @MIN(list)

- **Description**

    @MIN is a statistical function that returns the minimum (smallest) value in the list specified as its argument. The complement of @MIN is @MAX **243★**, which returns the largest value in a list.

- **Procedure**

    The argument to @MIN is a single range reference or a list of items separated by commas, with no intervening blank spaces. Each item can be a numeric value, a single cell address, a range of cells, a range name, or a formula. Thus, any of the following would be valid arguments:

    @MIN(A1,B1,C1,D1,E1)
    @MIN(A1..A15)
    @MIN(Sales)
    @MIN(A1∗A2/A3,B2+C2,D11−D10)

    @MIN ignores blank cells within a range, but treats label cells as 0. If the list is empty (includes no numeric values or labels), @MIN returns ERR.

- **Example**

    The following example uses @MIN to find the lowest daily sale for a period.

```
E9: (C2) [W17] @MIN(B5..B20)                                READY
```

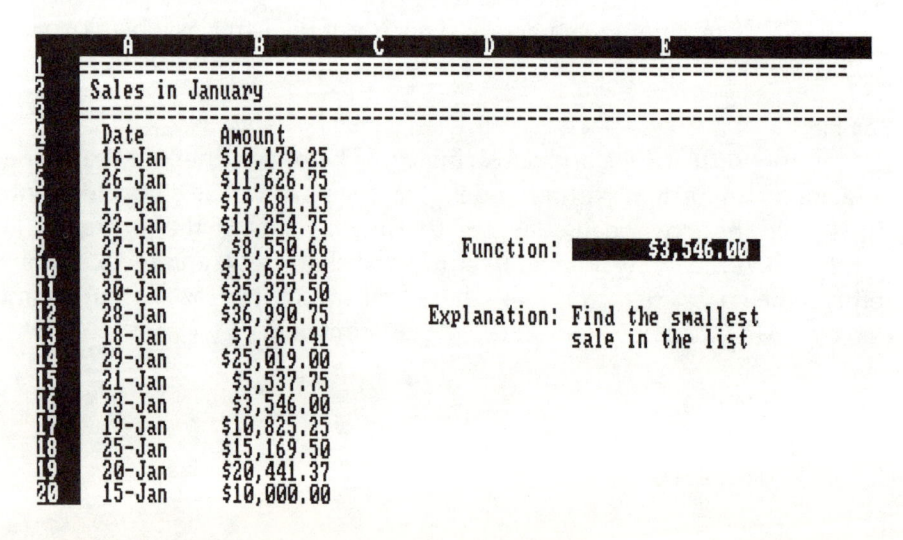

	A	B	C	D	E
1	===
2	Sales in January
3	===
4	Date	Amount
5	16-Jan	$10,179.25
6	26-Jan	$11,626.75
7	17-Jan	$19,681.15
8	22-Jan	$11,254.75
9	27-Jan	$8,550.66		Function:	$3,546.00
10	31-Jan	$13,625.29
11	30-Jan	$25,377.50
12	28-Jan	$36,990.75		Explanation: Find the smallest
13	18-Jan	$7,267.41			sale in the list
14	29-Jan	$25,019.00
15	21-Jan	$5,537.75
16	23-Jan	$3,546.00
17	19-Jan	$10,825.25
18	25-Jan	$15,169.50
19	20-Jan	$20,441.37
20	15-Jan	$10,000.00

@MINUTE() A Release 2 time function

- **Format**
  @MINUTE(time number)

- **Description**
  The @MINUTE function returns the minute of an hour, represented in standard format (0 to 59).

- **Procedure**
  The argument of the @MINUTE function can be a time serial number or a fraction. An integer returns 0, unless it is a time value, such as 08,14,08, that has been entered as part of the @TIME function. For example:

  @MINUTE(0.121154)

  would return 54.

  @MINUTE(@NOW)

  would return 37 if the current time were between 11:37:00 and 11:37:59.

  @MINUTE(10)

  would return 0, because the argument is not a time serial number, nor is it a fraction.

@MOD()

- **Format**
  @MOD(x,y)

- **Description**
  @MOD is a mathematical function that returns the remainder (modulus) of x divided by y. The formula used for calculating the modulus is:

  $x-(y*@INT(x/y))$

@MOD() · Mode indicators

- **Procedure**

    The arguments of @MOD can be any numeric values or references to single cells (x and y) containing numbers or calculated values. The values can be either positive or negative; if they are mixed, the sign of x determines the sign of the result. If y equals 0, the function returns ERR. Thus:

    @MOD(7,4)

    returns 3, but:

    @MOD(−7,4)

    returns −3. And:

    @MOD(5,2)

    returns 1. (In terms of the formula, this example would be calculated as: 5−(2∗@INT(5/2)).)

- **Example**

    The @MOD function is useful when you wish to determine what number best divides a known quantity. For example, if you have a supply of 138 basketballs, and you want to distribute them in lots of 7, the formula:

    @MOD(138,7)

    will tell you that five basketballs will remain when the last lot is distributed.

Mode indicators

The Control Panel **29**★ at the top of your screen displays a number of different types of information. The mode indicator is 1-2-3's way of telling you about itself. Located at the top right-hand corner of the Control Panel, the mode indicator is a one-word status report that changes as you work, to let you know what mode 1-2-3 is currently operating in. Usually, the mode indicator is under 1-2-3's control—for example, it displays READY when 1-2-3 is ready to accept a command or data, then changes automatically to MENU if you request a command menu. The following table lists and describes 1-2-3's built-in mode indicators.

Mode indicators

Mode ◆:	Description:
EDIT	Appears automatically if you make an error in entering a formula, and 1-2-3 moves the cursor to its "best guess" at the source of the problem. The formula will not be accepted until you have edited and corrected the error. Also, appears whenever you press the F2 [Edit] key to edit an entry.
ERROR	1-2-3 has detected a problem or has received a command it cannot carry out. Press Esc or Return or F1 [Help] and try again.
FILES	You have requested a list of files to be displayed.
FIND	1-2-3 is searching a database and executing a /Data Query Find **70**◆ command.
HELP	You have requested the Help **176**★ facility by pressing the F1 [Help] key.
LABEL	1-2-3 is interpreting your entry as text (a label), rather than numbers or a formula.
MENU	You have requested a command menu by pressing the / key.
POINT	A cell or cell range is highlighted and the pointer can be moved or expanded to include other cells.
READY	1-2-3 is waiting for you to enter a command or data.
VALUE	1-2-3 is interpreting your entry as numbers or a formula, rather than text (a label).
WAIT	1-2-3 is busy and cannot accept keyboard input at this time.

- **The {INDICATE} command**

In Release 2 of 1-2-3, you have the ability to create your own mode indicators by using the {INDICATE} macro command. A mode indicator you create must be no more than five characters long and differs from 1-2-3's built-in mode indicators in remaining on-screen even after the mode changes. For information on macros and the {INDICATE} command, see the entries Macro **211**★ and Macro Commands **225**★.

@MONTH()

■ **Format**

@MONTH(date number)

■ **Description**

@MONTH is a date function that returns the number of the month (1 to 12) represented by a specific date serial number.

■ **Procedure**

The argument of the @MONTH function must be a five-digit date serial number representing the number of days elapsed since December 31, 1899. The lowest number is 00001, for January 1, 1900, and the highest is 73050, for December 31, 2099. As with 1-2-3's other date functions, it is not necessary to try and determine the serial number of the date you wish to specify. The @DATE 92★, @DATEVALUE 96★, and @NOW 258★ functions will generate the number for you.

The argument must be numeric, but can be entered as a number, a cell reference or, as mentioned, a value calculated by another formula or function. For example:

@MONTH(29675)

returns 3, because 29675 is the serial number of March 30, 1981.

@MONTH(@DATEVALUE("Jan-84"))

returns 1, for January, after the @DATEVALUE function has converted the string "Jan-84" into its corresponding serial number.

/Move   /M

Worksheet Range Copy **Move** File Print Graph Data System Quit

■ **Description**

The /Move command enables you to move specified contents of a worksheet (values, labels, formats, and formulas) from one place to another. Moving cell entries is essential for editing or redesigning a worksheet, and with the ability to move cells and cell ranges on a worksheet, you have the ability to concentrate on what you put into a worksheet, not where you put it.

/Move

When you move cell contents, the cells you move from are called the source cells; the cells you move to are called the destination cells. 1-2-3 allows you to move as much of a worksheet as you wish, from one cell to a large block, as long as the source cells can be specified as a range 291★.

The /Move command is similar in effect to the /Copy 31★ command, but with one vital difference: /Move eliminates cell contents from their original locations and transfers them to a different part of the worksheet; /Copy duplicates cell contents.

■ **Procedure**

The general procedure for moving either one cell or many is as follows:

1. Place the cell pointer on the first cell you wish to move.
2. Type a slash (/) to display the Slash commands main menu.
3. Highlight the word *Move* and press Return, or type the letter M. 1-2-3 displays the *Enter range to move FROM:* prompt, including the address of the current cell.
4. Leave the pointer where it is to accept the current cell, or expand the highlight (using the arrow keys) to specify a range of cells. Alternatively, you can type a cell address or the name or addresses of a range. (If you wish to use 1-2-3's menu of existing range names, press F3 [Name] to display the list of current names, and highlight the appropriate name.) Press Return.

   1-2-3 then displays the *Enter range to move TO:* prompt, including the address of the current cell.
5. Specify the TO range either by pointing to the appropriate cells, typing the cell addresses, or typing the address of the top left-hand corner cell of the range (1-2-3 will still move the entire range, filling cells below and to the right of this corner cell). Press Return.
6. The contents of the source cells are moved to the new location and the cell pointer returns to its original position.

Warning: If the destination cells are not blank, the contents of those cells will be overwritten by the incoming cell contents. In addition, any formulas that reference the overwritten cells will have their address references replaced by ERR, and your only recourse will be to edit or delete the affected formulas. Be certain you know how the move will affect your worksheet before you carry out this command.

/Move

■ **Adjustments to address relationships**

You can use the /Move command to move labels, data, and formulas. Cell formats are also transferred intact. Whether you move a single cell or a range of cells, 1-2-3 automatically adjusts all formulas and ranges that reference those cells. 1-2-3 does not, however, make those changes in reverse. Thus, if you move a formula, the cell addresses in the formula remain as they were and continue to reference the original locations.

By way of example, the first of the following two illustrations shows a worksheet in which the formula in cell A1 refers to cells B1, C1, and D1. The second illustration shows a range name that refers to the same cells:

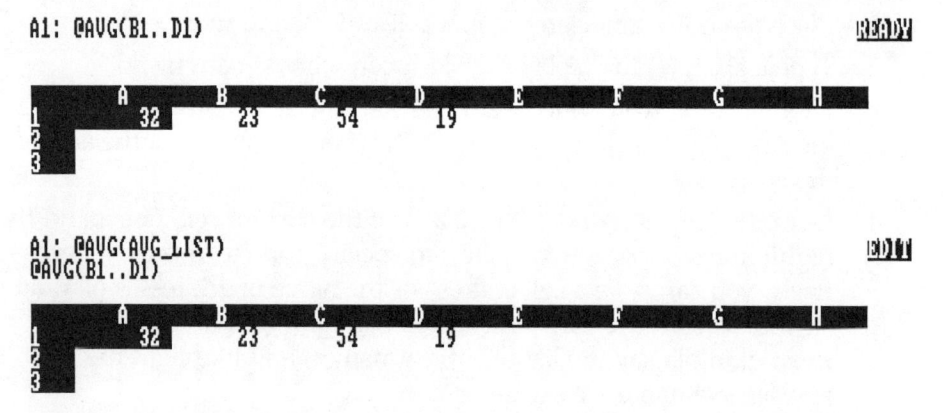

```
A1: @AVG(B1..D1)                                          READY

     A        B        C        D        E        F        G        H
1            32       23       54       19
2
3
```

```
A1: @AVG(AVG_LIST)                                        EDIT
@AVG(B1..D1)

     A        B        C        D        E        F        G        H
1            32       23       54       19
2
3
```

When the cells referenced by the formula and by the range name are moved to a new location, note that the formula and range name (addresses are shown in the Control Panel) are adjusted to reflect the cells' new location:

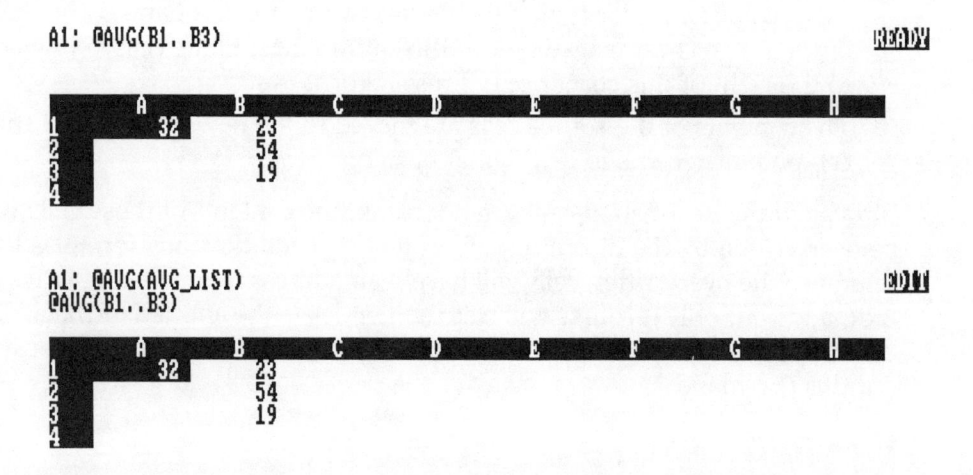

```
A1: @AVG(B1..B3)                                          READY

     A        B        C        D        E        F        G        H
1            32       23
2                     54
3                     19
4
```

```
A1: @AVG(AVG_LIST)                                        EDIT
@AVG(B1..B3)

     A        B        C        D        E        F        G        H
1            32       23
2                     54
3                     19
4
```

Suppose, however, that you move a formula that refers to unmoved cells. 1-2-3 maintains the original cell references, so that your moved formula still calculates the correct result.

However, as in the following two illustrations, if you move cells to an area containing existing values or formulas, 1-2-3 displays ERR in any formulas that refer to those overwritten cells:

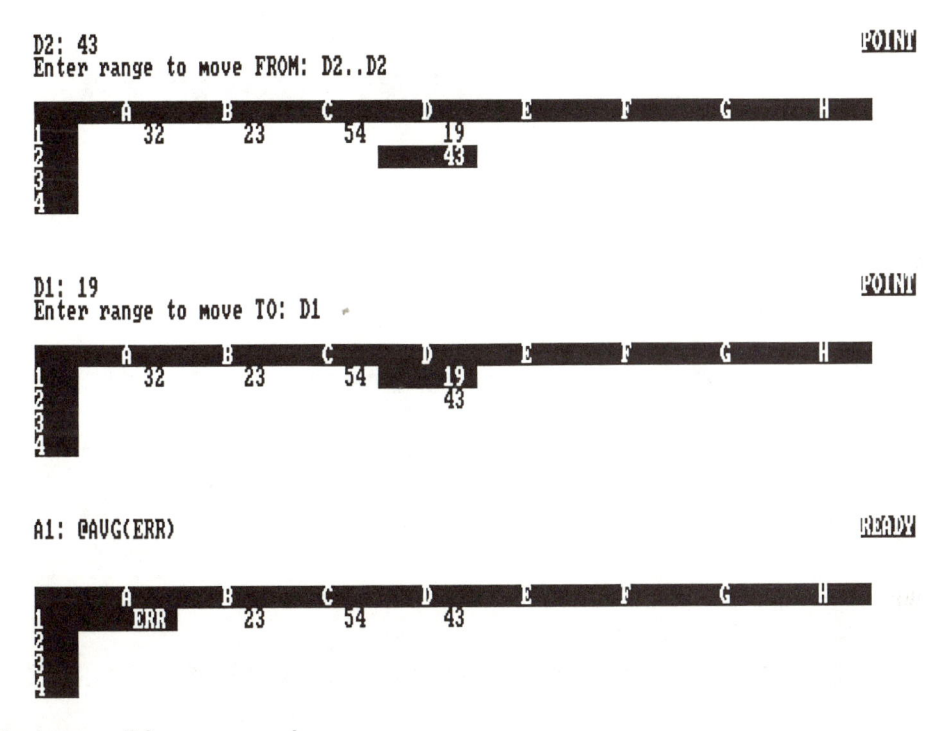

```
D2: 43                                                          POINT
Enter range to move FROM: D2..D2
        A       B       C       D       E       F       G       H
   1            32      23      54      19
   2                                    43
   3
   4
```

```
D1: 19                                                          POINT
Enter range to move TO: D1
        A       B       C       D       E       F       G       H
   1            32      23      54      19
   2                                    43
   3
   4
```

```
A1: @AVG(ERR)                                                   READY
        A       B       C       D       E       F       G       H
   1            ERR     23      54      43
   2
   3
   4
```

■ Moving a cell from a named range

There are two considerations when you are moving cells that are part of named cell ranges:

- ☐ If the cell you move is either the top left or bottom right corner cell of the range, 1-2-3 automatically adjusts the range definition to include the cell's new location. In this way, a range can be expanded or contracted to suit a new situation, without your having to re-create the range with a new size.

- ☐ If the cell you move is not the top left or bottom right corner cell, 1-2-3 moves the cell out of the defined range and adjusts any formulas that refer to that particular cell, but otherwise does nothing to the named range itself.

/Move

For example, the following worksheet contains a range named *prices*, which includes cells B5 to H6:

```
H6: [W1]                                                           POINT
Enter name: prices              Enter range: B5..H6

         A        B        C        D        E        F        G       H
   -------------------------------------------------------------------------
1
2     Models:   #451     #452     #453     #454     #455     #456
3  ----------------------------------------------------------------------
4  Prices
5  Standard:   14.95    19.95    25.95    29.95    34.95    41.95
6  Enhanced:   21.95    25.95    31.95    38.95    42.95    51.95
7
```

Suppose you want to extend the range, to make room for prices of additional items. You can simply move cell H6 to H7. 1-2-3 redefines the range name to include the new endpoint.

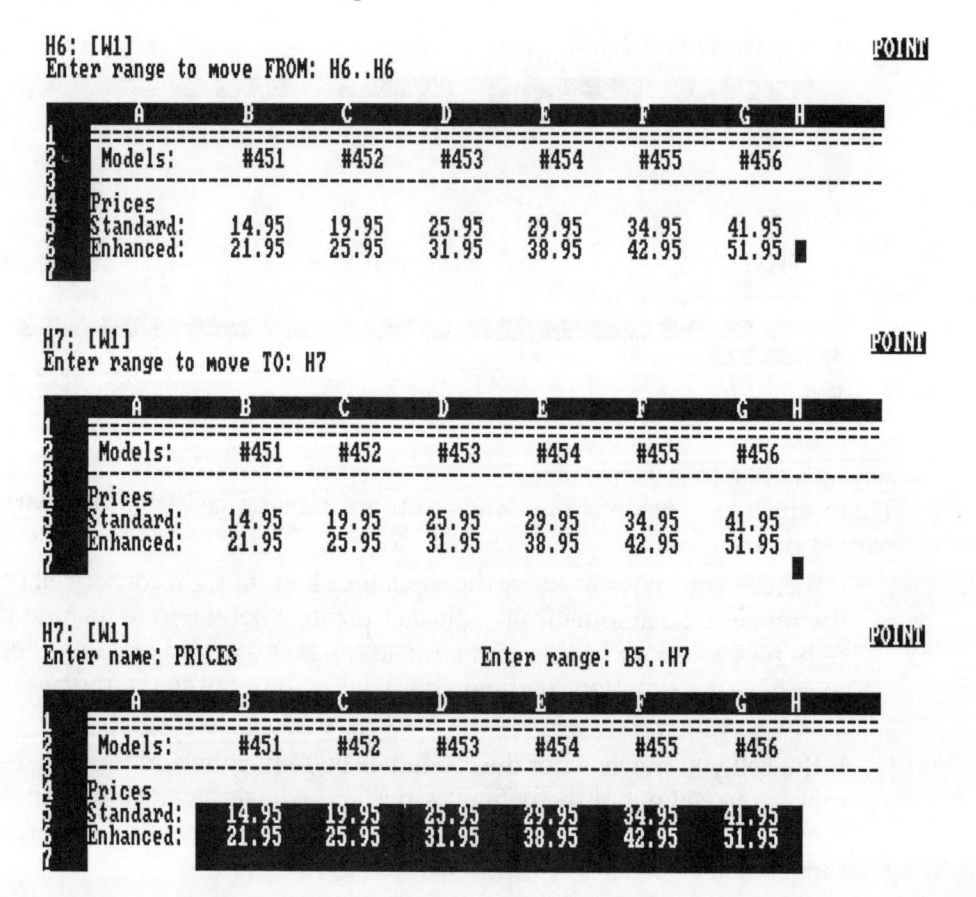

```
H6: [W1]                                                           POINT
Enter range to move FROM: H6..H6

         A        B        C        D        E        F        G       H
   -------------------------------------------------------------------------
1
2     Models:   #451     #452     #453     #454     #455     #456
3  ----------------------------------------------------------------------
4  Prices
5  Standard:   14.95    19.95    25.95    29.95    34.95    41.95
6  Enhanced:   21.95    25.95    31.95    38.95    42.95    51.95
7
```

```
H7: [W1]                                                           POINT
Enter range to move TO: H7

         A        B        C        D        E        F        G       H
   -------------------------------------------------------------------------
1
2     Models:   #451     #452     #453     #454     #455     #456
3  ----------------------------------------------------------------------
4  Prices
5  Standard:   14.95    19.95    25.95    29.95    34.95    41.95
6  Enhanced:   21.95    25.95    31.95    38.95    42.95    51.95
7
```

```
H7: [W1]                                                           POINT
Enter name: PRICES              Enter range: B5..H7

         A        B        C        D        E        F        G       H
   -------------------------------------------------------------------------
1
2     Models:   #451     #452     #453     #454     #455     #456
3  ----------------------------------------------------------------------
4  Prices
5  Standard:   14.95    19.95    25.95    29.95    34.95    41.95
6  Enhanced:   21.95    25.95    31.95    38.95    42.95    51.95
7
```

Note that column H, though blank, was included in the original range definition. Including a "dummy" cell makes modifying the range, without affecting range data, much easier.

- **Comments**

Like the /Copy command, the /Move command can be an enormous timesaver. Like /Copy, /Move can also be frustrating if you overlook the ways it operates. When using the /Move command, it is best to move either single cells or cell ranges to a blank area of the worksheet.

If you are reorganizing a worksheet, you may find it helpful to break the worksheet into sections and move each one out of the way before replacing it with another. The /Worksheet Insert 373★ command will also help by enabling you to insert additional columns or rows and thus create blank space into which you can move sections of the worksheet.

@N()   A Release 2 special function

- **Format**

    @N(range)

- **Description**

    The @N function returns the value of a single cell, the top left-hand corner cell of a range, as a numeric value. If the cell contains a string, the function returns the value 0.

- **Procedure**

    The @N function always references a single cell, but the argument must always be entered in the form of a range reference—either two cell addresses separated by one or more periods, such as A1..A4, or a single-cell address or single-cell range name preceded by an exclamation point—for example, !A1 or !Cell Name. When entering the function into a cell, 1-2-3 will automatically convert a single-cell reference to a range.

    If you are entering a range name, either make certain the range name refers to a single cell, or be sure that the top left-hand corner cell of the named range is the cell whose contents you want returned.

@N()

- **Example**

Suppose you had the following worksheet for tracking sales.

G7: @SUM(C6,@N(C7..C7),C8..C10)   READY

```
        A          B          C          D       E    F       G
 1 ========================================================================
 2  Region 5 Sales - January 1-15
 3 ========================================================================
 4                Model A    Model B    Model C
 5             -----------------------------------
 6  Jones          13         27          0
 7  Matteson    Vacation   Vacation   Vacation      Function:      59
 8  Albertson       9         11         32
 9  Hugo           17          5         19
10  Wilson          4         16         23
11
```

You could use the @N function in the following ways:

@N(!B6)

would return 13, the value in cell B6.

@N(!B7)

would return 0, because the cell contains a label, not a numeric value.

@N(D6..D10)

would return 0, the value in cell D6, the top left-hand corner of the range.

@SUM(C6,@N(C7..C7),C8..C10)

would return 59, the sum of cells C6 through C10, because the @N function referencing the label in cell C7 would return the value 0. If cell C7 were included without the @N, the function would return ERR.

As the preceding example shows, the @N function is useful for ensuring the valid result of calculations and preventing the occurrence of ERR values.

@NA

■ **Format**

@NA

■ **Description**

@NA is a special function that you can use to return the value NA in a cell for which a value is not yet available. The function takes no argument.

Since the NA value can only be entered via the @NA function, @NA is a useful device for annotating a worksheet in which some values remain to be gathered and/or entered. When you use the @NA function in a cell, the value NA is propagated throughout all formulas that depend on the value in that cell. Because 1-2-3 considers NA to be a numeric value, using this function does not produce a string of ERR values that might cause you to believe your formulas are incorrect. Once a required value is entered in the appropriate cell and the worksheet is recalculated, all dependent cells that contain NA will be updated to reflect the value in their calculations.

■ **Procedure**

The @NA function is simply entered, in either upper- or lowercase, as *@NA*. It is often used in formulas or functions, such as @IF, that test one or more cells to determine whether they contain usable values. The following example illustrates this type of usage.

@IF(@ISSTRING(A1),@NA,A1)

As mentioned, @NA is a useful tool for identifying absent values in a worksheet. In the following illustration, for example, it is easy to see which formula depends on a value that has not yet been provided:

```
F7: @SUM(B7..D7)                                                    READY
```

	A	B	C	D	E	F
1						
2	Region 5 Sales - January 1-15
3						
4		Model A	Model B	Model C		Totals
5						
6	Jones	13	27	0		40
7	Matteson	5	NA	40		NA
8	Albertson	9	11	32		52
9	Hugo	17	5	19		41
10	Wilson	4	16	23		43
11						

You can control the propagation of NA with the functions @ISERR **185★** and @ISNA **186★**. And with Release 2 of 1-2-3, you can also use @CELL **18★**, @CELLPOINTER **21★**, @ISNUMBER **186★**, or @ISSTRING **187★**.

For example, the following formula:

@IF(@ISNA(A1),0,A1)

would prevent ERR in cell A1 from propagating throughout the worksheet.

- **Comments**

@ERR **111★** is a related function that inserts the value ERR in a cell. Like NA, ERR is propagated throughout dependent formulas in a worksheet and can be kept from spreading by using one of the functions for controlling NA.

@NOW   A Release 2 date-and-time function

- **Format**

@NOW

- **Description**

The @NOW function returns a decimal serial number representing the current date and time as they are known to DOS.

The serial number is a decimal fraction in which the integer portion is a five-digit number representing the date as the number of days elapsed since December 31, 1899. The fractional portion is a time number between 0.000 (midnight) and 0.99999 (11:59:59 p.m.).

- **Procedure**

The @NOW function takes no argument. The serial number it returns is based on the date and time you entered when you started your computer or, if you have a built-in clock/calendar card, on the time and date it keeps. 1-2-3 will update the function value whenever you recalculate the worksheet.

If you wish to have the function return only the serial number for the current date, you can use:

@INT(@NOW)

to tell 1-2-3 to return only the integer portion of the number.

If you wish to see the date or time in a more recognizable format, you can use the /Range Format 300★ command to specify a particular date or time format. These formats are numbered D1 through D9, and tell 1-2-3 to display dates in such forms as Dec-25-86 or 25-Dec-86, and to display times in such forms as 11:30:55 or 23:30:55, and so on.

If you choose a particular date or time display, 1-2-3 will still record the complete serial number, but will display only the appropriately formatted integer or fractional portion, depending on whether you specify a date or a time format.

Thus, if the cell is formatted for the D1 date display, the @NOW function will cause 1-2-3 to calculate the entire serial number but display only the date, in the form DD-MMM-YY. If the cell is formatted for the D6 time display, 1-2-3 will display the time only, in the form HH:MM:SS (a.m. or p.m.).

For a complete list of these formats, refer to the entry on the /Range Format command.

- **Comments**

If, after entering the @NOW function, you notice that the current date or time is incorrect, select the /System 337★ command, which temporarily suspends 1-2-3 and provides access to DOS commands. Change the date or time by typing *date* or *time* and the correct entry when you see the DOS prompt.

@NOW is the Release 2 equivalent (with time added) of the @TODAY function in Release 1a. When a Release 1a worksheet is retrieved by Release 2, all occurrences of @TODAY are automatically converted to @NOW.

@NPV()

- **Format**

@NPV(interest,range)

- **Description**

The @NPV function is a financial function that uses a constant interest rate to calculate the net present value of a series of future cash flows, which can be either equal or unequal amounts. The function is useful for evaluating a long-term investment's potential for return on the money invested.

@NPV()

@NPV requires an interest rate and a range. The range is a row or column in the worksheet containing the values of the individual cash flows. The interest rate can be entered either as a percentage (10%) or as a decimal fraction (.10). The range can contain either numbers or calculated values, and can be entered as either cell addresses or a named range. Thus, the function could be entered in the worksheet as any variation of @NPV(10%,A1..A10) and @NPV(.10,Cash_flows).

Like other 1-2-3 financial functions, @NPV assumes that the cash flows occur at the ends of the periods, not at the beginning.

■ **Example**

Suppose that, over the course of the next year, you want to make some improvements to your property. You decide to spend $10,000 in the coming year and you want to set aside enough money now, in a separate account that pays 6.25 percent interest, to cover the monthly expenditures. You know that you will be working less on the improvements during the colder months, so the bulk of your spending will occur during the summer. You can use the @NPV function to determine the amount you will need to deposit in your home-improvement account, as shown in the following illustration:

```
E9: (C2) [W12] @NPV(0.0625/12,B4..B15)                              READY
```

	A	B	C	D	E
1	==
2	Improvement Schedule
3	==
4	Mar-86	$750.00
5	Apr-86	$750.00
6	May-86	$750.00
7	Jun-86	$800.00
8	Jul-86	$1,000.00
9	Aug-86	$1,200.00		Amount of deposit required:	$9,681.79
10	Sep-86	$1,200.00
11	Oct-86	$1,000.00
12	Nov-86	$800.00
13	Dec-86	$750.00
14	Jan-87	$500.00
15	Feb-87	$500.00
16		
17	Total:	$10,000.00

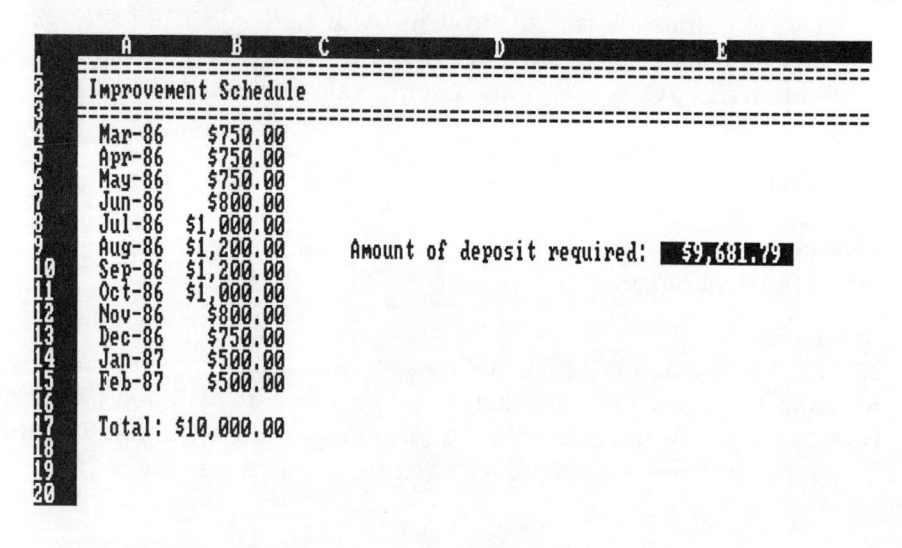

Numbers

Whenever you enter information into a worksheet cell, 1-2-3 interprets it as a number, a formula, or a label. Although the distinction among these may seem obvious, it sometimes is not. For example, any of the following will be interpreted as a numeric entry:

- 123
- 100+23
- @SUM(Numbers)

while any of these entries will be interpreted as text:

- ^123
- '100+23
- "@SUM(Numbers)

Although the same characters appear in both sets, the label prefixes (see Labels **199★**) in the second series tell 1-2-3 to treat those entries as text. (When used within a number, the caret (^) is interpreted as the exponentiation operator.) And the way in which an entry is interpreted determines what you can do with it. Numeric entries can be used in mathematical calculations; non-numeric expressions cannot.

■ Numeric entries

Numeric entries must either begin with a digit (0 through 9) or with one of the characters in the following set: [. + − $ ( ].

You can end a numeric entry with a percent sign if you wish, because 1-2-3 will convert it to the appropriate decimal fraction (for example, 6% will become .06 without your intercession).

No other characters are allowed in a number. Spaces or commas will result in an error.

(Functions and formulas **136★**, of course, can include text characters, as long as they represent function or range names, and the letter E can be used to indicate scientific notation.)

The size of a number you can enter is from 10^{-99} to 10^{99}. The size of a number 1-2-3 can calculate and store is in the range 10^{-308} to 10^{308}.

1-2-3 will store a number with up to 15 decimal places of accuracy.

Numbers are always aligned one character (to allow for a percent sign or a closing parenthesis) from the right edge of a cell. While in numeric form, they cannot be realigned, in the way labels can be left-aligned or centered. To change the alignment of a number, you must change it to a label either by preceding it with a label prefix or by converting it with the @STRING 334★ function or the macro command 225★ {CONTENTS}.

- **Numeric formats**

1-2-3 offers two commands, /Worksheet Global Format 366★ and /Range Format 300★, that control the appearance of numbers in a worksheet. The /Worksheet Global Format command controls the default display for all numbers throughout the worksheet; to override this default for individual numbers or ranges of numbers, you use the /Range Format command. The format of the currently highlighted cell is displayed in the first line of the Control Panel.

No matter which format command you use, however, it is important to remember that the format you select affects only the *displayed* value. The original stored value remains unchanged, and is used in all calculations. For example, you can format the number 3.123 to be displayed with no decimals, and 1-2-3 will show it as 3, but the value 3.123 will be used in any calculations.

- **Time and date**

1-2-3 uses numbers to represent date and (Release 2 only) time values as well as standard numeric values. The date is represented by a five-digit serial number indicating the number of days elapsed since December 31, 1899. The possible serial numbers range from 1, for January 1, 1900, to 73050 for December 31, 2099.

In Release 2, the date serial number is followed by a decimal fraction that represents the time. The possible values for the time number range from .000, for midnight, to .99999, for one second before midnight. Since time is represented as a decimal fraction, .25 indicates 6 a.m., .5 indicates noon, and .75 indicates 6 p.m.

Operators

Operators are the characters that tell 1-2-3 what type of calculation is to be performed. There are two basic categories of operators: arithmetic and logical. In Release 2, there is one other, the &, which is a concatenation operator for use in string 332★ formulas.

- **Arithmetic operators**

  The arithmetic operators are: + (addition), − (subtraction), * (multiplication), / (division), and ^ (exponentiation). Unless told otherwise, as discussed in the following section on parentheses, 1-2-3 calculates from left to right, and performs multiplication and division before addition and subtraction.

- **Logical operators** ◆

  The logical operators are used when you want 1-2-3 to evaluate an expression and return one of two possible values: 1 (true) or 0 (false). These operators include the symbols < (less than), <= (less than or equal to), > (greater than), >= (greater than or equal to), = (equal), and <> (not equal). In addition, there are the logical #NOT#, #OR#, and #AND#:

  ☐ #NOT#, in a logical comparison, is like saying, "If NOT this...."

  ☐ #OR#, in a logical comparison, is like saying, "If this OR this...."

  ☐ #AND#, in a logical comparison, is like saying, "If this AND this...."

- **Concatenation operator** ◆

  The concatenation operator is used exclusively in string (text) formulas to combine sets of characters. Within formulas, strings are enclosed in double quotation marks. Thus, the & could be used in a situation such as:

  @UPPER("when in the course "&"of human events")

  to combine the two strings and (in this example) convert the characters to uppercase letters.

- **Order of precedence**

  The arithmetic, logical, and concatenation operators are calculated in the order of precedence shown in the following table. When two or more operators of the same precedence occur in a formula, they are handled in sequence from left to right.

Symbol:	Order of precedence:
^	First
−,+(Negative, positive)	Second
*, /	Third
+,−(Add, subtract)	Fourth
=, <>	Fifth
<, >	Fifth
<=	Fifth
>=	Fifth
#NOT#	Sixth
#AND#	Seventh
#OR#	Seventh
&	Seventh

- **Overriding precedence**

  A calculation whose operator is higher in the precedence order is performed first, unless you use parentheses to override the normal order of calculation. For example, the formula 12+12/2 returns the value 18, because 1-2-3 performs the division first (12/2=6) and then the addition (12+6). In order to change the formula so that 12 and 12 are added together before the division takes place, you would write the formula as (12+12)/2.

  Parentheses must always be used in pairs (); if an open or close parenthesis is missing, 1-2-3 causes the computer to beep and refuses to accept the formula until you correct the error.

  Sets of parentheses can be nested within each other, sometimes to very complex levels—especially since 1-2-3 allows formulas to be as long as 240 characters. When a formula contains nested sets of parentheses, the calculations begin at the innermost set and are performed outward. If sets of parentheses are side by side in a formula, they are evaluated from left to right.

- **Comment**

  As with all 1-2-3 operations, a value included in a formula can be specified as a number, as a direct reference to a cell containing a value, or as a reference to a cell containing the result of another calculation.

@PI

- **Format**

    @PI

- **Description**

    @PI is a mathematical function that returns the value 3.14159..., the value of the mathematical constant π, which is the ratio between the circumference of a circle and its diameter. This ratio is constant for circles of all sizes.

- **Procedure**

    The @PI function does not take an argument. It operates on numeric values only, which can be entered either as numbers or references to cells containing numbers. For example:

    @PI*2^2

    returns the value 12.5664, the area of the circle whose radius is 2.

    @PI is useful in converting degrees to radians, and vice versa, for use as arguments with the trigonometric functions. For example:

    @PI/4

    returns 0.7854, one-fourth PI radians.

    45*@PI/180

    converts 45 degrees to radians (0.7854), while:

    0.7854*180/@PI

    converts radians to degrees, and:

    @SIN(45*@PI/180)

    returns 0.70711, the sine of 45 degrees.

@PMT()

- **Format**

    @PMT(principal,interest,term)

- **Description**

    @PMT is a financial function that calculates the amount of a loan payment per period, given the term of the loan, the per-period interest rate, and the amount of the principal.

The function uses the following formula:

principal * (interest/(1−(1+interest)^−n))

where n is the number of payment periods.

The @PMT function requires numeric arguments for principal, interest, and term. The arguments can be numbers, cell addresses, other functions, single-cell range names, or formulas. The interest rate can be entered either as a percentage (15%) or as a decimal fraction (.15). So, for example, any of the following formulas would be valid: @PMT(60000,.125,30), @PMT(A1,A2,A3), or @PMT(principal,rate,term).

The term is the length of the loan and should be entered in the same units of time used for the interest rate. Thus, if you wished to find the monthly payment for a 30-year loan of $60,000 at a 12.5 percent annual percentage rate, the argument would be: @PMT(60000,.125/12,360).

- **Example**

The following example shows the @PMT function used to calculate monthly payments on loan amounts ranging from $70,000 to $100,000, at annual interest rates of 11 percent to 12.5 percent, for a 30-year loan. Note that the terms are in months and the annual percentage rate is divided by 12.

```
F14: (C2) @PMT(F$6,$A14/12,360)                          READY
```

	A	B	C	D	E	F
1	@PMT					
2						
3	Interest			Loan Amounts		
4						
5		$70,000	$77,500	$85,000	$92,500	$100,000
6						
7	11.00%	$666.63	$738.05	$809.47	$880.90	$952.32
8	11.25%	$679.88	$752.73	$825.57	$898.42	$971.26
9	11.50%	$693.20	$767.48	$841.75	$916.02	$990.29
10	11.75%	$706.59	$782.29	$858.00	$933.70	$1,009.41
11	12.00%	$720.03	$797.17	$874.32	$951.47	$1,028.61
12	12.25%	$733.53	$812.12	$890.71	$969.30	$1,047.90
13	12.50%	$747.08	$827.12	$907.17	$987.21	$1,067.26

■ **Comments**

@PMT treats the loan like an ordinary annuity—one which is paid at the end, rather than the beginning (annuity due), of each period. To calculate payments on an annuity-due basis, you would divide by (1+interest).

This function is closely related to @FV **147★** and @PV **289★** in calculating results based on constant, rather than variable, cash flows.

Note: Banks and financial institutions have various methods of calculating payments that might yield slightly different results than @PMT returns.

Pointing

Many 1-2-3 commands require you to specify a cell or a cell range on which they are to act. Whenever the mode indicator **248★** at the top right corner of the screen displays either VALUE or POINT, you can specify cells by:

☐ Typing their address(es).

☐ Using a single- or multiple-cell range name.

☐ Pointing to them by expanding the highlight.

Cells and cell addresses are discussed in the entries Cell **13★** and Range **291★**. Range names are discussed in the entries Range and /Range Name Create **310◆**. This entry covers the basic elements of pointing to single cells or ranges of cells.

■ **Pointing to single cells**

Although some commands, including major worksheet-design tools such as /Copy **31★** and /Move **250★** allow you to specify either one cell or many, the process of pointing to a single cell is simple and easily mastered.

For single cells within the display area of the screen, you can use the arrow keys to move the pointer from cell to cell, and press Return when you have highlighted the cell you wish to reference.

For cells a fair distance away, you can scroll left or right one screen at a time by pressing the Tab (Big Right) or Backtab (Big Left, or Shift-Tab) key. Or, you can scroll up or down one screen at a time by pressing the Pg Up or Pg Dn key.

To move to the top left-hand corner of the worksheet, you can press Home; to move to the bottom right-hand corner of the active area, you can press End, then Home. To jump past blocks of like cells (data cells or blank cells), you can move in the appropriate direction by pressing End and then pressing one of the arrow keys.

■ **Pointing to ranges**

You can point to ranges in much the same way as you point to single cells. Ranges differ, however, in that you must point to a rectangular block of contiguous cells. You can begin pointing to a range by highlighting any corner cell of the range you want to specify. Under normal circumstances, however, the pointer jumps from cell to cell as you press the pointer-movement keys.

To specify a range, then, you must be able to "pin" one corner cell down so the highlight will expand, rather than move. This "pinning" is done by making one corner cell (it does not matter which corner) an anchor cell. When one cell is thus anchored, the pointer is free to travel to the left or right of the anchor, as well as to cells above and below the anchor cell, and the cell highlight will expand as it moves.

Whether or not you need to tell 1-2-3, "This is an anchor cell…don't let it move," depends on why you want to point to a range. If, for example, you are entering a formula, 1-2-3 cannot tell whether you intend to include a single cell reference or a range; in this case, you must anchor the cell yourself. If, on the other hand, 1-2-3 expects a range reference, the current cell will automatically be anchored and you can expand the pointer outward as you use the left, right, up, and down arrow keys. The cell diagonally opposite the anchor cell is called the free cell, because it can be moved to define the other endpoint of the range.

If the current cell is not anchored, 1-2-3 displays its address in the form *A1* in the Control Panel at the top of the screen. To anchor the cell, you can:

☐ Type a period. When you do this, 1-2-3 changes the displayed address to show it as a range reference; for example, A1..A1. (1-2-3 always displays two periods between the beginning and ending cells of a range, but you only need type one period.)

☐ Move the pointer to another cell, anchor it, and then expand the cell pointer.

☐ Press Esc to back out of a command or to eliminate the current cell from a formula and return the pointer to the formula cell.

If the current cell is anchored, 1-2-3 displays its address as a range reference (A1..A1) in the Control Panel. To point to a range, simply expand the pointer. You can also:

- Press Esc to cancel the range specification, but keep the pointer in the anchor cell and, at the same time, "un-anchor" it.
- Press the Backspace key to cancel a range you have pointed to and return the pointer to the original anchor cell.
- Type a period after pointing to a range, to rotate the anchor and free cells. This enables you to anchor a different corner of the range. Doing this does not alter the range definition, but does enable you to expand the pointer in a direction you could not go before, and also allows you to examine the corners of a range that is larger than the on-screen window.

/Print

The Print commands are used to create copies of your worksheets either on paper (the /Print Printer command) or on disk (the /Print File command).

To print graphs created from worksheets, you use the PrintGraph 271★ program rather than the /Print commands.

■ A note about printers

Printers, like people, differ widely. In many instances, they have requirements that are uniquely their own, so a discussion of printers as hardware and their potential variations is well beyond the scope of this book. The Epson and Hewlett-Packard LaserJet printers are mentioned as specifics where applicable, but for detailed information, you will need to refer to your own printer manual.

■ Before printing

1-2-3 (Release 2) cannot use your printer(s) unless you have used the Install 182★ program to specify the type of equipment, including printer(s), you use.

Printing depends not only on the /Print commands, but also on the settings of the /Worksheet Global Default Printer 361◆ command, which tells 1-2-3 about the printer connection (parallel, serial, or network) and the general page layout it is to use. Install and the /Worksheet Global Default Printer command create the path between 1-2-3 and your printer. The /Print commands send information along that path, and enable you to select different options or override the defaults.

/Print

■ **The /Print commands**

When you choose the /Print command from the main menu, 1-2-3 offers two options: *Printer* and *File*. Select *Printer* to create a hardcopy (paper) printout of a worksheet. Select *File* to print the file to disk. When you print a worksheet to disk, 1-2-3 creates a special file with the extension .PRN. This file is stored in ASCII/LICS **203★** format and can be printed from DOS or transported to a word processor or other program.

After you specify *Printer* or *File*, 1-2-3 presents its submenu of /Print commands. These are summarized in the following table and explained in more detail in separate entries.

Command:	*Function:*
/Print Printer (File) Range **287★**	Prints a specified range on paper or to a .PRN file.
/Print Printer (File) Line **280★**	Advances the printer by one line or adds a blank line to a .PRN file.
/Print Printer (File) Page **286★**	Advances the printer to the bottom of the page and prints a footer, if specified; adds blank lines and a footer to a .PRN file.
/Print Printer (File) Options **281★**	Allows you to specify page-layout options, including page length, margins, headers, footers, borders, and so on; also allows you to print formulas, rather than displayed values, or override page formatting if desired.
/Print Printer (File) Clear **278★**	Clears some or all existing print settings.
/Print Printer Align **278★**	Resets 1-2-3's internal line counter to top-of-page (line 1).
/Print Printer (File) Go **279★**	Starts printing the selected range on paper or to a .PRN file.
/Print Printer (File) Quit	Ends printing and returns to READY **249◆** mode.

PrintGraph

The PrintGraph program is a utility that enables you to print graph (.PIC) files created with 1-2-3's /Graph commands 148★ and saved with the /Graph Save 172★ command. To print graphs with PrintGraph, you must have a graphics printer or plotter installed in your current driver set (see Install 182★) and have one or more .PIC files that you wish to print.

■ Operation

You can start PrintGraph from the Access System menu by choosing the *PrintGraph* option, or you can start it from DOS by typing *pgraph* (if your PrintGraph disk is in drive A and the prompt is A>, or if the PrintGraph program has been copied to the 1-2-3 directory on a hard disk and you are in the 1-2-3 directory). This discussion of PrintGraph assumes you are using Release 2 of 1-2-3. The differences between the Release 2 version of PrintGraph and the previous version (1a) are primarily in the way menu choices are presented and in the increased number of fonts and graphics printers supported by Release 2. If you are a Release 1a user, you also have the option of upgrading to an expanded printer library; see your dealer for details.

When PrintGraph first starts, it presents a menu similar to the main menu of the worksheet. With PrintGraph, however, the menu line is always displayed and there is no need to press the slash (/) to request a command. Other than this one difference, PrintGraph's menus and command structure are the same as in the 1-2-3 program. PrintGraph's main menu presents the following options:

```
Select graphs for printing
Image-Select  Settings  Go  Align  Page  Exit
```

■ Using PrintGraph for the first time

When starting PrintGraph for the first time, you will need to configure the program so it knows where to find your .PIC files, where to find its font files, and which printer and connection will be used in printing the graphics. To do this, you need to choose the *Settings* command from the menu, then specify the appropriate information for the following options (each is described in later sections of this entry):

- ☐ Choose the *Hardware* option and tell PrintGraph which *Graphs-Directory*, *Fonts-Directory*, *Interface*, and *Printer* to use.

- ☐ When you have done this, choose *Settings Save* to make your specifications permanent.

PrintGraph

These are the minimum initial actions necessary to get PrintGraph ready to print a .PIC file. Once these settings are saved in the PGRAPH.CNF file (with the *Settings Save* command), it will not be necessary to repeat these steps unless some component of your setup changes (a new printer or connection, different paper size, and so on).

■ **Main menu summary**

These are the commands on the main menu, with a brief description of what each does:

- □ *Image-Select*: Chooses one or more graphs that have been created with the /Graph commands in the worksheet and saved to disk for printing.
- □ *Settings*: Configures PrintGraph for hardware and graph format needs.
- □ *Go*: Formats selected graphs for the current Settings options, and prints them on the current printer.
- □ *Align*: Informs the PrintGraph program that the printer is now set at the top of a new page.
- □ *Page*: Causes PrintGraph to issue an eject command, which advances the paper one page in the printer. This option is useful for removing graphs from the printer.
- □ *Exit*: Exits the PrintGraph program.

■ **Image-Select**

This main menu option presents a list of the graph (.PIC) files in the graph directory (specified in the hardware setup with the *Settings* command). Use the up and down arrow keys to move through the list of files. Press F10 [Graph] 144♦ to have the currently highlighted graph drawn on the screen.

To select graphs for printing, move the highlight to the graph name and press the spacebar. A pound sign (#) will appear at the beginning of the file name to indicate that it has been selected. If you want to print more than one graph, proceed to the next file name and press the spacebar again. The order in which the files are selected is the order in which PrintGraph will print them. To cancel a selection, select it again.

Press Return to exit to the main menu. If your settings are correct and you are ready, use the *Go* option to print the selected graphs.

Settings

To configure PrintGraph with the necessary information to work with your system, choose *Settings* (you must have run Install by this time). The following menu appears:

```
Specify colors, fonts and size
Image   Hardware  Action  Save  Reset  Quit
```

Image: The *Image* option provides the following menu:

```
Set size and orientation of graphs
Size  Font  Range-Colors  Quit
```

Size: This option determines the size and proportion of the printed graph. Your choices are:

- *Full:* This tells PrintGraph to size the graph so that it fills an 8.5- by 11-inch page (this is the default page size). Unless a rotation is chosen, the graph will be printed sideways; the X axis will be vertical. Margins and spacing are automatically adjusted by PrintGraph.
- *Half:* This option instructs PrintGraph to fill approximately half of an 8.5- by 11-inch page with the graph. Unless rotation is used, the X axis will be horizontal. Margins and spacing are automatically adjusted by PrintGraph.
- *Manual:* This option allows you to set the top and left margins, the width and height (size) of the graph, and the rotation of the graph.

  For *Left*, type the distance (in inches) from the left edge of the paper to the left edge of the graph. For *Top*, type the distance (in inches) from the top edge of the paper to the top edge of the graph.

  For *Width*, type the width (in inches) you want the graph to be (this creates an implicit right margin). For *Height*, type the height you want the graph to be (in inches), from the top to the bottom edge of the graph. For *Rotation*, type the amount of rotation (in degrees) of the X axis. Choose a number between 0 and 90. 0 causes no rotation; 90 will shift the X axis perpendicularly.

Note: 1-2-3 normally prints graphs sideways on the paper for larger size and higher resolution. Changing the rotation setting to 90 will cause the graph to be printed normally (as displayed on-screen) on the paper.

PrintGraph

Font: This option selects the fonts (typefaces) that will be used to letter your graph. The fonts are chosen and displayed for your selection from the fonts directory you specified in configuring PrintGraph for your system.

PrintGraph lets you use two different fonts for each graph. Font 1 is for the first line of the graph's title. Font 2 is for the rest of the text on the graph. If you want to use the same font for all the text on the graph, select only Font 1. The fonts with a 2 (BLOCK2) at the end of their names are of a heavier weight than the fonts which have a 1 at the end of their name.

After selecting *Font*, specify option *1* for Font 1 or option *2* for Font 2. Next, select a font from the list PrintGraph displays:

```
Copyright 1985 Lotus Development Corp.  All Rights Reserved.  Release 2    FONT
Select font 1

        FONT NAME       SIZE
        ----------------------
      # BLOCK1           5787         [SPACE] turns mark on and off
        BLOCK2           9300         [RETURN] selects marked font
        BOLD             8624         [ESCAPE] exits, ignoring changes
        FORUM            9727         [HOME] goes to beginning of list
        ITALIC1          8949         [END] goes to end of list
        ITALIC2         11857         [UP] and [DOWN] move cursor
        LOTUS            8679              List will scroll if cursor
        ROMAN1           6863              moved beyond top or bottom
        ROMAN2          11847
        SCRIPT1          8132
        SCRIPT2         10367
```

Range-Colors: This option assigns different colors to the graph data ranges. The colors that are available to you depend on your printer. If your printer doesn't support color, black is your only choice.

Select a range (X, A to F). Then, select the color you want to assign to that range by highlighting the color in the list that is displayed and pressing Return, or by typing the first character of the color name. Follow the same procedure for each range you want to assign a color. Choose *Quit* to return to the previous menu.

Quit: Returns you to the *Image* submenu.

274

Hardware: This *Settings* menu option allows you to define the printer, specify graph and font directories, identify the printer interface, and change the default paper size (8.5 by 11 inches). The *Hardware* option displays the following menu:

```
Set directory containing graphs
Graphs-Directory  Fonts-Directory  Interface  Printer  Size-Paper  Quit
```

Graphs-Directory: This option identifies the directory that contains your graph (.PIC) files. The default for this option is A:\.

To specify a graphs directory, choose *Graphs-Directory*. Type the name (including the path name) of the directory where the graph files you want to print are located. For example: *c:\accounting\bob\graphs*.

This is the directory where PrintGraph will look when you use *Image-Select* to indicate which graphs you want to print.

Fonts-Directory: This option specifies the directory that contains the font (.FNT) files that are used to letter your graph. The default directory is A:\.

To specify a fonts directory, choose the *Fonts-Directory* option. Type the name of the directory (including the path name) where the graph files you want to print are located. For example, *c:\123\fonts*.

Interface: Defines the printer interface (parallel or serial) that connects your computer to your printer. The eight possible options and their setting numbers are:

Interface:	*Setting number:*
Parallel	1
Serial	2
Second parallel	3
Second parallel	4
LPT1 (DOS device)	5
LPT2 (DOS device)	6
LPT3 (DOS device)	7
LPT4 (DOS device)	8

If you choose option 2 or 4 (serial printer), you must also indicate the speed (baud rate) at which it can receive the data sent by your computer. The choices are:

Baud rate:	Setting number:
110	1
150	2
300	3
500	4
1200	5
2400	6
4800	7
9600	8
19200	9

Printer: Chooses one of the graphic printers you installed with the Install program. If you installed only one printer, you still must use this option. The current printer (if any) has a pound sign (#) next to its name. To choose a printer from the list, highlight its name and press the spacebar. A pound sign (#) will appear next to the printer's name to indicate its choice as the current printer. Only one printer can be selected at a time. Be sure to use the *Interface* option to tell PrintGraph how the printer is connected.

Size-Paper: Specifies the default paper size. There are three size settings: *Length*, *Width*, and *Quit*. The default size is 8.5 by 11 inches. If you are using a wide-carriage printer with wide paper, you would probably want to change the width setting to 14.0 (inches).

Quit: Returns you to the *Settings* submenu.

Action: This *Settings* option controls printer actions after each graph is printed. When you choose the *Action* command, you are presented with three choices: *Pause*, *Eject*, and *Quit*. Defaults are no pause and no eject.

Pause: Choose this option to stop the printer between graphs. You need this option if your printer is a single-sheet printer. You'll have to change the paper between graphs.

Eject: Choose this option to advance the paper one page after each graph is printed. This option performs an automatic Page command for you. If you are printing your graphs on continuous-form paper, you will probably want to choose this option.

Save: This *Settings* option saves PrintGraph settings in a configuration file similar to 1-2-3's, in the same directory with the PrintGraph program. When PrintGraph is started, it retrieves the settings from the file, which is called PGRAPH.CNF. If you change PrintGraph's settings during a PrintGraph session, you must choose this option to SAVE those settings for a future session. When you press Return, the current settings are immediately written to the file.

Reset: This *Settings* option restores PrintGraph settings to the values found in the PGRAPH.CNF file. If you change some settings and want to restore the ones you had at the start of the session, use *Settings Reset*.

Quit: This option returns you to the main menu.

- **Go**

  This PrintGraph main-menu option tells PrintGraph to begin printing the graphs in the *Image-Select* list. Each graph is first formatted for the current settings, then printed. If your graphics printer is actually a plotter, you will be prompted to load the appropriate pens. After printing is finished, the main menu returns. To abort a graph, press the Break key (Ctrl-Break on IBM PC-style keyboards). Pressing the Break key may not have an immediate effect, but PrintGraph will eventually recognize the command.

- **Align**

  This PrintGraph main-menu option tells PrintGraph that the paper is currently at the top-of-page position. If the *Eject* option of the *Action* command is turned on, PrintGraph will return to this position after each *Eject* or *Page* command.

- **Page**

  This PrintGraph main-menu option advances the paper in the printer one page. This is often helpful for advancing continous-form paper so that the printed output can be removed.

Exit

This PrintGraph main-menu option is used to leave the PrintGraph program. You are asked to confirm whether you really do want to leave. If you have made any changes to PrintGraph's settings during the current session and you want to save them, be sure to use *Settings Save* before exiting.

/Print Printer Align /PPA

```
Worksheet Range Copy Move File Print Graph Data System Quit
Printer File
Range Line Page Options Clear Align Go Quit
```

■ **Description**

The /Print Printer Align command is one of three page-adjustment options 1-2-3 provides. Use this command to set the page line count to 0 whenever you reposition the paper in the printer at the top of a new page. If you do not use the /Print Printer Align command, and you adjust the paper in the printer, 1-2-3's internal line count may not match the page you are printing, and the page may end at some point above the actual bottom margin.

1-2-3's other page-adjustment options are /Print Printer (File) Line **280★**, which advances the printhead to the beginning of the next line, and /Print Printer (File) Page **286★**, which tells the printer to advance to the top of the next page.

/Print Printer (File) Clear /PPC or /PFC

```
Worksheet Range Copy Move File Print Graph Data System Quit
Printer File
Range Line Page Options Clear Align Go Quit
All Range Borders Format
```

■ **Description**

The /Print Printer Clear and /Print File Clear commands cancel specified print settings. You should use these commands to clear 1-2-3's memory of any range specifications or print options settings you do not wish to retain.

■ **Procedure**

When you choose the /Print Printer (File) Clear command, 1-2-3 offers four additional choices: *All, Range, Borders,* and *Format*.

Select *All* to clear the currently specified print range, as well as all specified borders, headers and footers, formats, and printer options. Choosing this option restores the *Formatted* and the *As-Displayed* settings of the /Print Printer (File) Options 281★ command.

Select *Range* to clear the current print-range specification. Alternatively, use the /Print Printer (File) Range 287★ command to modify or redefine a print range.

Select *Borders* to clear all previously specified border settings. This option is useful in eliminating a border if you inadvertently specify one by choosing the /Print Printer Options Borders 283♦ command and press Return, instead of Esc, to try and cancel the command. You can also use this option to prevent or eliminate duplication of borders on the first page of a multiple-page worksheet printout.

Select *Format* to clear margin, page-length, and setup-string settings and restore the defaults, which are:

☐ Top and bottom margins, 2 lines from the edge of the paper.
☐ Left and right margins, 4 and 76 spaces, respectively, from the left edge of the paper.
☐ Page length, 66 lines.

/Print Printer (File) Go   /PPG or /PFG

```
Worksheet  Range  Copy  Move  File  Print  Graph  Data  System  Quit
Printer  File
Range  Line  Page  Options  Clear  Align  Go  Quit
```

- **Description**

The /Print Printer Go command sends a specified print range to the printer; alternatively, the /Print File Go command sends the print range to disk, for storage as a .PRN ASCII/LICS 5★ file.

- **Procedure**

Before selecting /Print Printer (File) Go, you must specify, at the least, the range to be printed. If you are sending output to a printer and you have repositioned the paper so the printhead is at the top of the page, you should also use the /Print Printer Align 278★ command to set 1-2-3's line counter to 0 and ensure that the line count will match the printed page.

If 1-2-3 displays the message *Printer error* after you have selected /Print Printer Go and pressed Return, it means your printer is not ready—it is turned off or disconnected, or you may have specified the wrong connection. Press Esc to clear the message, then correct the problem and specify the command sequence again to restart the printing process.

Sometimes, even after your best efforts at matching the print range and page formatting to the paper size and layout you wish to use, you will find that the actual printed output is not what you wanted or expected. If this happens, you can stop the current print operation on many systems by pressing Break (the Ctrl-Break key combination). Do not be concerned if your printer continues after you press Break; it is simply printing the remaining characters in its buffer—the storage area where it holds incoming information until it can be printed. If you do interrupt printing, turn the printer off and then on again to start anew. Use the other /Print **269★** commands if need be to redefine your print specifications. Position the paper at the top of a new page and reset the line counter with the /Print Printer Align command before beginning the printing process again.

If you are printing to a disk file instead of to paper, select *Quit* when the process is complete, in order to terminate the current printing operation.

/Print Printer (File) Line   /PPL or /PFL

```
Worksheet  Range  Copy  Move  File  Print  Graph  Data  System  Quit
Printer  File
Range  Line  Page  Options  Clear  Align  Go  Quit
```

■ **Description**

The /Print Printer Line command advances the paper one line and positions the printhead at the left margin. If advancing one line causes the printer to reach the bottom of the current page, the command moves the paper to the top of the next page.

The /Print File Line command inserts a blank line in a .PRN disk file.

/Print Printer (File) Options /PPO or /PFO

```
Worksheet Range Copy Move File Print Graph Data System Quit
Printer File
Range Line Page Options Clear Align Go Quit
Header Footer Margins Borders Setup Pg-Length Other Quit
```

- **Description**

    The /Print Printer Options and /Print File Options commands enable you to specify printing options, such as page length, margins, headers, footers, and so on. In addition, the *Other* option of these commands allows you to print a cell-formula list, rather than displayed values; to override page formatting if you wish (useful when creating a file for other applications); or to suppress page breaks, headers, and footers.

- **Procedure**

    When you choose the /Print Printer (File) Options command, 1-2-3 displays the list of choices illustrated at the beginning of this entry.

    Header: Choose *Header* to print a one-line running head at the top of each page, on the first line below the top margin. 1-2-3 allows headers up to 240 characters long, including blank spaces. You can also number and date the pages automatically:

    ☐ Include a # in the header to tell 1-2-3 to number the pages sequentially, beginning with 1.

    ☐ Include an @ in the header to tell 1-2-3 to date each page with today's date. (To use a date other than the current date, use the /System command to temporarily suspend 1-2-3, then change the date with the DOS Date command. If you do this, remember to change the date back when you are finished.)

    Headers can also be justified in segments separated by the character ¦ (split vertical bar). The first segment is aligned at the left margin; the second

/Print Printer (File) Options

segment is centered on the line; and the third segment is aligned at the right margin. Thus, to center a header, you would precede it with |, as follows:

|BUDGET WORKSHEET

to align it with the right margin, you would enter it as something like:

||BUDGET WORKSHEET-Page #

to space three segments across the header line, you would enter:

BUDGET WORKSHEET|Page #|@

1-2-3 automatically inserts two blank lines between a header and the first printed line on a page. To increase the space below a header, insert blank rows on the worksheet and include them in the print range you specify.

As with all aspects of printing worksheets, pay attention to the number of characters you can print on a single line.

Footer: Choose *Footer* to print a one-line footer at the bottom of each page, on the line above the bottom margin. Footers are just like headers, except for location, and follow the same rules, including page numbering with the # sign, dating with the @ sign, and division of the footer into three segments with the | symbol.

Margins: Choose *Margins* to override the default margin settings. When you select this option, 1-2-3 prompts you with *Left, Right, Top,* and *Bottom.* When you select the margin you wish to change, 1-2-3 displays the current margin width. 1-2-3 allows left and right margins of up to 240 characters, and top and bottom margins of up to 32 lines.

Unless you have changed the default margin settings with the /Worksheet Global Default Printer 361♦ command, the margin settings that come with 1-2-3 are:

Margin:	*Setting:*
Top	2 lines from the top edge
Bottom	2 lines from the bottom edge
Left	4 spaces from the left edge
Right	76 spaces from the *left* edge (equivalent to 4 spaces from the right edge, assuming 80 characters across the page)

If you try to print lines that are longer than the margins allow, 1-2-3 will break the lines at the right margin and print the remainder at the end of the document. You can use this facility when printing wide worksheets by adjusting column widths and margin settings to "break" the worksheet between columns. For example, if the line you wish to print is 120 characters and includes 12 columns, each 10 characters wide, you could set the left and right margins to allow for a 60-character line length, select the entire 120 characters in your print range, and let 1-2-3 print each line in two segments, on two separate pages you can later tape together.

If, however, you set a right margin that extends beyond the right edge of the paper in your printer, 1-2-3 will not print the remainder of the line on another page. It will "wrap" the end of the line and print it on the following line of the same page.

Borders: Choose *Borders* ◆ to specify rows or columns (of headings, for example) that you want printed on each consecutive page. When you choose this option, 1-2-3 prompts you with *Rows* and *Columns* and, if you have already specified a border, highlights your earlier selection. Press Return to accept the proposed border, specify a new border by expanding the cell pointer or typing the range addresses, or delete the border specification with the /Print Printer Clear 278★ command. To specify both a row and a column border, issue this command once for each.

Note: When you choose the *Borders* option, 1-2-3 records the current location of the cell pointer. If you press Return without specifying a border range, 1-2-3 will use the current cell as a border specification and print its contents on each page. Use Esc or Break to exit this menu without making a choice.

Also, be sure not to specify the border cells as part of your print range. 1-2-3 will print the border automatically, so if you include them in your print range, they will be duplicated on your printout. Specify the first page as a separate range before selecting borders, if necessary.

Setup: Choose *Setup* to use different type sizes or fonts, or to change the line spacing of the text in your document.

/Print Printer (File) Options

When you use the *Setup* option, you tell 1-2-3 what type of printing or line spacing you want by entering setup strings that represent such elements as italic type, boldfacing, compressed print, and the like. These setup strings represent printer-control codes (for example, a \027 in the setup string for Escape, followed by a single 0, \0270, tells an Epson printer to set line spacing to eight lines per inch). Setup strings can vary from one printer to another, however, and for this reason 1-2-3 cannot offer you a menu of codes from which to choose. You must refer to your printer manual to find the codes that your printer requires.

To enter a setup string in a form that 1-2-3 will recognize, you must precede it with a backslash (\). The string can be up to 39 characters long. To replace an existing setup string with another, choose *Setup*, then press Esc and type the new setup string.

If you wish to use a setup string within a worksheet—for boldfacing a title, perhaps—precede the backslash with two ¦ symbols (do not use a label prefix) and type the code into the cell where you want the type change to begin. In this case, you do not choose the *Setup* option: You enter the setup string just as you would any other cell entry. To turn off the type change, enter another setup string where you want it to stop. In printing the worksheet, 1-2-3 will read the setup codes you entered and change the type size or font accordingly.

If you have a widely used printer, such as an Epson or IBM model, the following setup strings will probably work for you:

Setup string:	*Operation:*
\015	Change to compressed print (132 characters per line)
\018	Stop compressed print
\0270	Print eight lines per inch
\0272	Print six lines per inch (normal line spacing)

/Print Printer (File) Options

Here are some additional codes for the Epson and Hewlett-Packard LaserJet:

Setup string:	Operation:
\027G	Turn on double-strike printing (Epson)
\027H	Turn off double-strike printing (Epson)
\027E	Turn on emphasized printing (Epson)
\027F	Turn off emphasized printing (Epson)
\027&dD	Turn on automatic underlining (LaserJet)
\027&d@	Turn off automatic underlining (LaserJet)
\027&llO	Turn on landscape printing (sideways print) (LaserJet)
\027&0O	Turn off landscape printing (turn portrait on) (LaserJet)

Pg-Length: Choose *Pg-Length♦* to specify the number of lines to be printed on each page. Unless you have changed the default page length or top or bottom margins, 1-2-3 assumes a page is 66 lines long. Allowing space for margins, header, and footer, that setting allows you 56 printed lines of text per page, with a vertical spacing of six lines per inch. If you wish, you can change the page length to any number of lines between 10 and 100.

If you are considering changing page length because your worksheet is slightly too long to fit on one page, you might want to consider using the *Unformatted* option described in the next section to print your worksheet without allowing for page breaks, headers, or footers.

Other: Choose *Other* to specify the overall appearance and content of your document's printout or .PRN disk file. When you select Other, 1-2-3 displays four choices: *As-Displayed, Cell-Formulas, Formatted,* and *Unformatted.*

As-Displayed: The *As-Displayed* option prints your document as you see it on the screen. The *As-Displayed* setting is the default, and when you clear all print settings with the /Print Printer (File) Clear command, printing is reset to this specification. You should reset printing to the *As-Displayed* option after you have specified *Cell-Formulas.*

If you are using a split screen, *As-Displayed* prints the column widths of the current window. Thus, if you want to print a worksheet on which you cannot see the complete contents of one or more columns, you can open a second window, widen columns to display entries that are truncated on the screen, print the document, and then close the window to return to more compact column widths.

285

Cell-Formulas: The *Cell-Formulas*◆ option prints the contents of the cells specified in the print range—numbers, formulas, labels, and so on—exactly as they are displayed in the Control Panel. In addition, this option prints the address of the cell, its format, and its protection status. The contents of each cell are printed on a separate line, so the row and column orientation of the original worksheet is not reproduced.

This option is useful in creating a hardcopy record of the formulas you entered into a worksheet, and can also be used to print worksheets that contain long labels.

Formatted: The *Formatted* option prints worksheets with the page breaks, headers, and footers you have specified. This is the default and should be restored after you have chosen *Unformatted* for printing a particular range or document.

Unformatted: The *Unformatted* option, as mentioned earlier, causes 1-2-3 to ignore page breaks, headers, and footers. It is useful for printing worksheet ranges that barely spill over onto another page.

You should also choose the *Unformatted* option whenever you print a file to disk and you expect to use it with another program, such as a word processor. An unformatted file transports your data directly, without carrying over unnecessary page formatting.

/Print Printer (File) Page   /PPP or /PFP

```
Worksheet Range Copy Move File Print Graph Data System Quit
Printer File
Range Line Page Options Clear Align Go Quit
```

■ **Description**

The /Print Printer Page command advances the printer to the bottom of the current page and prints a footer, if you have specified one (with the /Print Printer Options 281★ command). At the end of the document, a footer is printed at the bottom of the page and the paper is advanced to the top of a new page.

The /Print File Page command adds blank lines and a footer, if specified, to a .PRN file.

■ Comments

With Release 2 of 1-2-3, the /Worksheet Page **374★** command allows you to insert page breaks where you wish in a document. When printing long worksheets that cover several consecutive pages, you can use the /Worksheet Page command to tell 1-2-3 to break the worksheet at the points you specify, then use the /Print Printer Options command to add a footer, such as *(Continued)*, at the bottom of each page.

/Print Printer (File) Range   /PPR or /PFR

```
Worksheet  Range  Copy  Move  File  Print  Graph  Data  System  Quit
   Printer  File
   Range  Line  Page  Options  Clear  Align  Go  Quit
```

■ Description

The /Print Printer Range and /Print File Range commands enable you to specify a range to be printed on paper or to a .PRN file.

■ Procedure

When you choose either the /Print Printer Range or /Print File Range command, 1-2-3 prompts you to *Enter Print range:*. It displays the current location of the cell pointer or, if you printed a range earlier, it highlights the last specified range. Press Return to accept the proposed range or press the Backspace key to define a new range.

You can specify a range by:

☐ Pointing to it.

☐ Typing the addresses of two diagonally opposite corner cells.

☐ Typing a range name.

☐ Pressing the F3 [Name] **144♦** key and choosing a range name from the list displayed.

End-Home takes you from the current anchor cell to the bottom right corner of the active worksheet area.

When you specify a range to be printed, do not include any cells you used to create a border along the top or left-hand edge of the worksheet. Borders are printed automatically, and including them in a range specification causes them to be printed twice. Also, if you are printing *As-Displayed* and your worksheet includes long labels that are not completely displayed on-screen, adjust the column width so they can be completely seen, or include extra columns in the range so they can be printed in their entirety.

After you have specified the range to be printed, specify any special formatting or choose the /Print Printer (File) Go **279★** command.

@PROPER() A Release 2 string function

- **Format**

@PROPER(string)

- **Description**

@PROPER converts upper-, lower-, and mixed upper- and lowercase characters and words in a string into "initial-capped" words in which the first letter is capitalized and the remaining characters are lowercased.

- **Procedure**

The @PROPER function requires a string of characters, which can be specified in the argument enclosed in double quotation marks or as a reference to a cell containing a label. The function does not affect non-alphabetic characters, such as periods, commas, numbers, and special symbols. The & concatenation operator can be used to combine strings within the argument or as a reference to more than one cell. Thus:

@PROPER("lotus development corporation")

will return *Lotus Development Corporation.*

@PROPER("tristan &"&" isolde")

will return *Tristan & Isolde.*

If cell A1 contains the label *snips and snails* and cell B1 contains the label *and puppy-dog tails*, then:

@PROPER(A1&B1)

will return *Snips And Snails And Puppy-dog Tails.* Note that blank spaces and punctuation are important in separating the words to be capitalized.

- **Comments**

The @PROPER function is useful in situations that involve typing proper names, company names, titles, and so on. Used with macros, @PROPER can speed data entry by eliminating concern for correct capitalization.

@PV()

- **Format**

  @PV(payment,interest,term)

- **Description**

  @PV is a financial function that computes the present value of a series of equal payments invested at a fixed interest rate, occurring at regular intervals over a fixed period. The function assumes that payments are made at the end, rather than the beginning, of each time period.

  The calculation performed by the @PV function is similar to that performed by @NPV, except that the latter calculates the net present value of a series of cash flows of either equal or *unequal* amounts.

  @PV requires three numeric arguments: payment, interest, and term. All three can be numbers or references to cells that contain either numbers or calculated values. The interest rate can be entered either as a percentage (10%) or as a decimal fraction (.10); if entered as a percentage, 1-2-3 will automatically convert and display the rate as a decimal value.

- **Example**

  The @PV function is useful for comparing the relative merits of different payment plans. For example, suppose you are planning to buy a new car and the dealer offers you a choice of different payment plans, each based on a different term and interest rate. You would like to determine which plan is the least costly to you, in terms of today's dollars.

```
D12: (C2) [W20] @PV(C12,A12/12,B12)                                    READY
```

	A	B	C	D
1				
2	@PV			
3				
4	Interest	Term	Monthly Payment	Present Value
5				
6	13.50%	24	$500	$10,465.28
7	13.25%	28	$465	$11,147.23
8	13.00%	32	$430	$11,575.85
9	12.75%	36	$395	$11,765.17
10	12.50%	40	$360	$11,727.49
11	12.25%	44	$325	$11,473.50
12	12.00%	48	$290	$11,012.45
13				

/Quit /Q

```
Worksheet  Range  Copy  Move  File  Print  Graph  Data  System  Quit
```

- **Description**

The /Quit command ends the current 1-2-3 session and returns you to DOS, if you started from DOS, or to the Access System, if you started from the Access System.

- **Procedure**

To choose the /Quit command, all you need to do is type /q. 1-2-3 will prompt for confirmation: *Yes* or *No*.

Before you choose *Yes*, take a moment to make certain that:

☐ You have saved your current document (with the /File Save **130**★ command).

☐ Or, you do not want to preserve the current document, with any modifications you have made.

1-2-3 does not automatically save your work when you quit, so ending a session without saving your file to disk means that you lose whatever entries and changes you have made.

@RAND

- **Format**

@RAND

- **Description**

@RAND is a mathematical function that returns a random number uniformly distributed between 0 and 1, with 15 decimal places of precision.

- **Procedure**

The @RAND function takes no argument, and each time the worksheet is recalculated, a new random number is generated for each @RAND function. Thus, if recalculation is automatic, the value of each @RAND function will change with each worksheet entry (each recalculation).

To increase the range of values for which a random number will be calculated, you can multiply the @RAND function by the required interval and, if you wish, add to it a lower limit other than 0. For example:

@RAND*50

will yield random numbers between 0 and 50.

@RAND*50+10

will yield random numbers between 10 and 60.

Copies of @RAND yield unique values, so you can use this function and the /Copy **31★** command to fill a range with unique numbers. For example, to fill a range with unique values between 1 and 100, you could enter:

@RAND*99+1

in one cell and copy the function to the other cells in the range. To have the function return integer values, you could enter it as:

@INT(@RAND*100)+1

Note: To convert a formula to its value, use /Range Value **318★** and specify the same FROM and TO ranges.

Range

A range is a rectangular block of cells **13★** identified by the addresses of any two opposite corners of the rectangle. A range can be any size you wish, from a single cell to (theoretically) the maximum size of a 1-2-3 worksheet. The only requirement is that each cell in a multiple-cell range must be adjacent—you cannot specify or define a range that contains non-contiguous cells. For example, these are all valid ranges of cells:

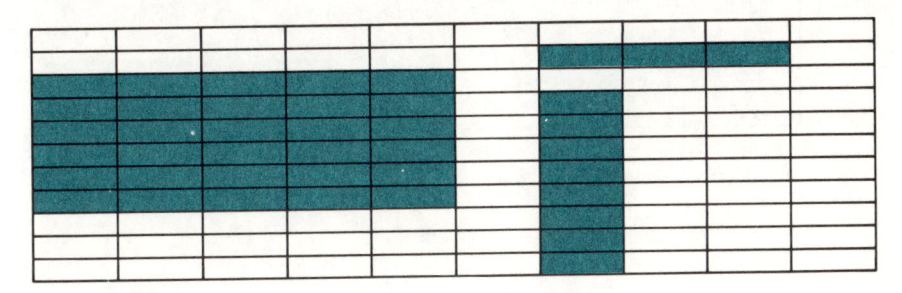

Range

These, however, are not ranges:

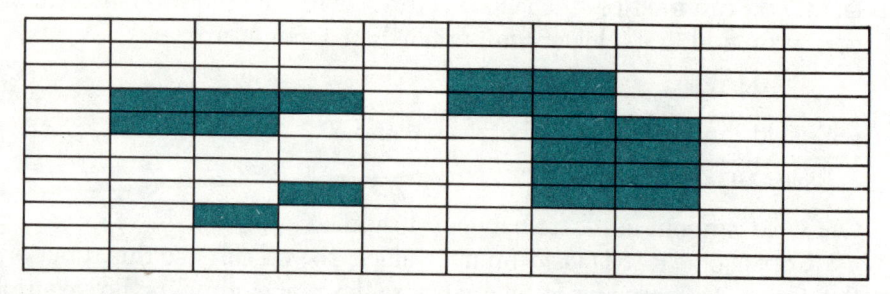

■ Referring to Ranges

1-2-3 always keeps track of specified ranges by "remembering" the addresses of their upper left and lower right corners. However, you can refer to ranges either by the addresses of any two opposite corners, or by a descriptive name of your choice. Any one of these types of reference can be used with any range, and you can, if you wish, refer to the same range by name in one command or formula, but by address in another. The following sections describe the various options 1-2-3 offers you for specifying ranges.

Range addresses: As mentioned earlier, you refer to a range by two diagonally opposite corners. If, for example, you want to refer to the block of cells from A1 to D4 as a range, you can use any pair of corners:

- ☐ A1 and D4.
- ☐ D1 and A4.
- ☐ D4 and A1.
- ☐ A4 and D1.

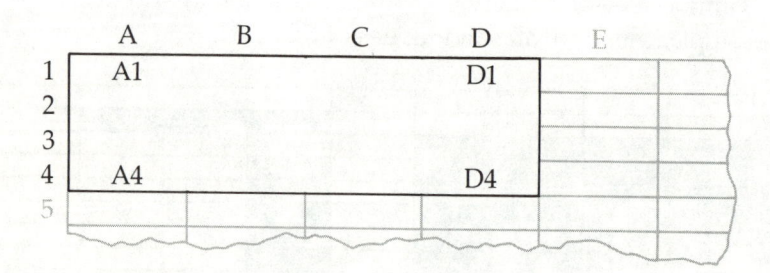

Depending on whether you are entering a formula or using a command that accepts or requires a range, you could specify the block of cells A1 to D4 as a range by:

- Typing addresses (in EDIT 249♦ or VALUE 249♦ mode).
- Highlighting the range (in POINT 249♦ mode).
- Naming the range (in EDIT, VALUE, or POINT mode).

Note: 1-2-3 displays the mode 248★ you are in at the upper right corner of the screen. The POINT mode is for moving the cell pointer to indicate a range. 1-2-3 usually moves you in and out of these modes automatically, as the situation requires. You can, however, choose to enter the EDIT mode by pressing the F2 (Edit) 144♦ key.

Typing range addresses: When typing ranges, you separate the addresses of the opposite corner cells with a period (.). 1-2-3 always displays ranges with two separating periods (such as A1..D4), but you do not need to type both of them.

To type the range as a relative 17♦ reference, type the cell references like this: A1..D4. To type the range as an absolute 17♦ reference, type it as: $A$1..$D$4. To type the range as a mixed 18♦ (relative/absolute) reference, type it as: $A1..$D4 or A$1..D$4 or $A$1..D$4 or any other combination of relative and absolute cell referencing you require.

Highlighting ranges: In POINT mode, the two corners that delimit a range are called the anchor cell and the free cell. The anchor cell is the first cell address specified, and it serves to "pin down" one corner. The free cell is the second corner address, and can be identified by the flashing underscore 1-2-3 displays in its center. Unlike the anchor cell, the free cell can be moved up, down, left, or right and so enables you to expand or contract the range.

In specifying a cell range by expanding the highlight, you can press the F4 (Absolute) 144♦ key to tell 1-2-3 you wish the range reference to be absolute. Press F4 again, and a mixed reference is proposed by 1-2-3. You can continue to press F4 to cycle through the various matched options.

When you use the cell pointer to highlight a range, you may or may not need to anchor the current cell before expanding the cell pointer. If, for example, you are entering a formula, 1-2-3 cannot anticipate whether you intend to include a single cell reference or a range, and so you must anchor the first corner cell yourself. In other instances (depending on the command you are using), 1-2-3 may propose one of the following in the second line of the Control Panel:

- The address of the current cell, as a free cell. This happens when you choose one of the /Data commands. For example, if you place the cell pointer on A1 and choose one of the /Data commands 51★, 1-2-3 proposes A1 as the first cell in the range to be defined. The cell is not anchored, however, and you are free to move the cell pointer to whichever new location you wish.
- The address of the current cell, as both the anchor and free cell. For example, if the cell pointer is on A1 and you choose a /Range command, 1-2-3 displays A1..A1 as the range to be affected. In this case, A1 is anchored, and you can expand the highlight as you wish.
- The address of the last range you specified, regardless of the current location of the cell pointer. For example, if you choose the /Data Fill 56★ command once and specify the range G1..K5, then choose the /Data Fill command again, 1-2-3 will propose the range G1..K5, no matter where the cell pointer happens to be.

Although these variations in free versus anchored cells may sound confusing, 1-2-3 works very logically, and there are only a few rules you need to remember about expanding the cell pointer to specify ranges.

If the highlighted cell is *not* anchored:

- You can type a period to anchor it. 1-2-3 responds by displaying the cell address as a range, for example, A1..A1.
- You can move the cell pointer to another location with the pointer-movement keys.
- You can press the Escape key to: back out of a command and/or move one step closer to the main menu; or eliminate the cell address from a formula and return the cell pointer to the formula cell.

- You can press the backspace key while specifying a range, in order to cancel your action and return the pointer to the cell you started in.

If the highlighted cell *is* anchored:

- You can type a period to rotate the anchor and free cells (in a clockwise direction). For example, in the range A1..D4, typing one period would rotate the anchor and free cells to become D1..A4. Typing another period would rotate them to D4..A1. Another period would rotate them to A4..D1. The advantage to rotating the anchor and free cells is in gaining the ability to expand the range in several directions—in effect, "pinning down" a different corner and stretching the range in a direction you could not go before:

- You can press Esc to cancel a range specification, return the pointer to the anchor cell, and at the same time "un-anchor" the cell.

- You can use the backspace key as described for cells that are not anchored.

Range names: You assign a name to a range with the /Range Name 310★ command, and you can use that name in any situation—whether a command or a macro or a formula—in which 1-2-3 either requires or allows a range to be specified.

You have a great deal of flexibility in naming a range. The name can be 1 to 15 characters long, and it can contain punctuation marks, other symbols, or numbers. You can type it in upper- or lowercase letters, although 1-2-3 will always display it in uppercase only. Like a file name, a range name should be as descriptive as possible. When naming a range, don't use a name, such as A1 or D33, that looks like a cell address. 1-2-3 will allow you to use it, but whenever you type the name, 1-2-3 will interpret it as a cell address, not a range name.

When naming ranges, you don't need to worry about keeping those ranges separate. You can assign two names to the same range or to overlapping ranges with equal ease. 1-2-3 will keep track of which name refers to which cells, and use the appropriate ranges in commands and formulas. You could, for example, name blocks of cells as shown in this diagram:

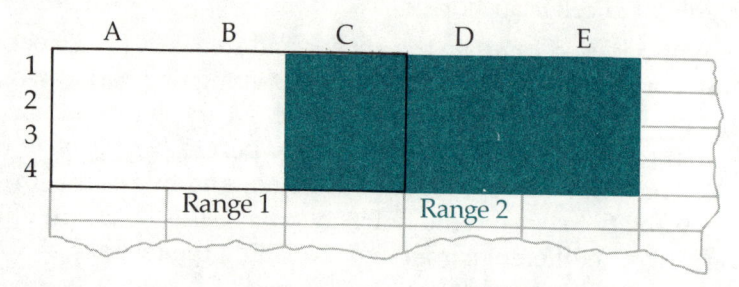

To 1-2-3, range names are no different from the cell ranges to which they refer. You can thus use range names in any situation in which you can use cell ranges—in commands or in formulas. Even if you are in POINT mode, 1-2-3 will allow you to type the name of a range you have already defined. You should keep the following distinction in mind, however, if you assign names to single-cell ranges as well as multiple-cell ranges:

- If the named range is a single cell, you can use that name in any formula, or as the argument to any function, that 1-2-3 offers. All operators and all functions accept single-cell addresses.
- If the named range refers to more than one cell, you can use that name only where 1-2-3 accepts or allows range references. You cannot, for example, use a multiple-cell range name in the function @SQRT, because the function requires a single value as an argument.

You can make a range name absolute simply by typing a $ in front of it, just as you would with a cell address. For example, if you named A1..D4 Profits, you would use Profits in a formula as a relative address, but $Profits as an absolute address. As with ranges you specify by expanding the highlight, however, you cannot specify a mixed relative/absolute named range. $Profits could never refer to $A1..D$4, for example.

If you create a number of named ranges for a worksheet, you need not be concerned about forgetting what they are, how the names are spelled, or what cells they refer to. To see a menu of all the names you have defined, simply select the *Create* option of the /Range Name command. To see which cells the name refers to, select the name from the menu; 1-2-3 will display the range in the Control Panel and will expand the cursor to highlight the range.

■ Adjusting ranges

Sometimes, especially with named ranges, you will want to change the size of the range—eliminate some cells or add new ones. Other times, you will indirectly change range references by moving cell ranges or by inserting or deleting columns or rows. 1-2-3 adjusts all affected cell references for you, according to the following three rules:

- If you redefine a named range, 1-2-3 adjusts every reference to that range, no matter whether you referred to the range by name or by address. You can think of this as comparable to a search-and-replace operation that affects every occurrence of the range in your worksheet. The only exception to this rule is when you redefine a single named cell as a multiple-cell range. 1-2-3 leaves all original formulas unchanged and replaces the name of the cell with its address in your formulas.

- If you adjust a range specification in a command or formula, 1-2-3 adjusts that range reference only, even if the original specification was to a named range. You can think of this as a search-and-replace of a selected occurrence only.

- If you delete the upper left or lower right corner of a range, 1-2-3: cancels all names you have given to the range; eliminates "remembered" references to the range from prior commands; and displays *ERR* in all formulas that refer to the range.

Note: Because 1-2-3 does automatically adjust all references that match a named range, it is wise to pay some attention to the ranges you specify as cell addresses. Even if you specify those addresses as absolute cell references, 1-2-3 will change them if:

1. They match a named range exactly.
2. You edit the named range they match.

You will know when 1-2-3 treats a range reference as a named range, because it replaces the cell addresses with the range name when it displays your command or formula in the Control Panel.

If you see a range name suddenly appear in place of a cell range in a formula, and you do not wish to use the named range, try correcting the situation either by editing the named range (with the *Create* option of the /Range Name command), or by including a blank (dummy) cell in the range you are specifying in your command or formula. Neither solution will work, however, if your worksheet contains formulas or functions (such as @AVG) that count blank cells in calculating their results and use that range. If you are faced with the unavoidable, you may need to delete the range name with the *Delete* option of the /Range Name command. Doing this eliminates the problem in those few instances when it occurs.

■ **Comments**

The following commands are used to create and manipulate ranges:

Command:	Used to:
/Range Erase 299★	Erase cell contents in a range.
/Range Format 300★	Control the appearance of numeric values in a range; in Release 2, also control date and time formats and prevent display of range contents.
/Range Input 304★	Limit pointer movement only to unprotected cells in the range.
/Range Justify 306★	Adjust labels in a text "paragraph" (range) for display or printing in a specified "line length."
/Range Label 308★	Control label alignment (left, center, or right) in a range.
/Range Name Create 310♦	Name or redefine a range.
/Range Name Delete 311♦	Eliminate a range name.
/Range Name Labels 312♦	Assign an existing label as a range name to the cell adjacent to the label.
/Range Name Reset 313♦	Eliminate all range names from a worksheet.
/Range Name Table 313♦	Display a list of named ranges and corresponding addresses (Release 2 only).

Command:	Used to:
/Range Protect 314★	Keep cell contents in a range from being altered.
/Range Transpose 316★	Rotate a range so rows become columns and vice versa (Release 2 only).
/Range Unprotect 317★	Enable cell contents in a range to be altered.
/Range Value 318★	Convert formulas to values (Release 2 only).

/Range Erase   /RE

```
Worksheet Range Copy Move File Print Graph Data System Quit
Format Label Erase Name Justify Protect Unprotect Input Value Transpose
```

■ **Description**

The /Range Erase command erases the contents of all cells in the range you specify. Unlike the /Worksheet Erase 358★ command, which removes all traces of the current worksheet, the /Range Erase command distinguishes between the cell contents and the formatting and protection status (applied with /Range Format 300★ and /Worksheet Global Protection Enable 369♦) of the erased cells. Thus, even though you remove cell contents with /Range Erase, you do not remove current formats. Nor can you erase the contents of protected cells (if you try to do so, 1-2-3 beeps and refuses to carry out the command).

Note: Be careful when you use the /Range Erase command on cells that are referenced in formulas elsewhere in your worksheet. The cells you blank out take on a value of 0, and your formulas will use 0 in calculating their results. 1-2-3 does not warn you of inaccurate results by displaying *ERR* in formula cells, unless 0 itself is an unacceptable value.

To avoid the possibility of such errors occurring, you should either document your formula references or check them with the *Text* option of either the /Worksheet Global Format 366★ or the /Range Format command before issuing the /Range Erase command.

/Range Erase · /Range Format

If you do need to blank out a range of cells that are referenced in formulas, you can save their values by copying the range to another part of the worksheet, by saving the range in a new file with the /File Xtract 133★ command, or by pressing the F2 (Edit) 144◆ and then the F9 (Calc) 144◆ keys with the cell pointer on the formula cell.

If, on the other hand, you simply need a blank area where the range currently exists, try rearranging the worksheet with the /Copy 31★ and /Move 250★ commands. Also, Release 2 of 1-2-3 provides a means of hiding portions of worksheets. You can use /Range Format Hidden 303◆ to suppress the display of values in a range of cells. You can use /Worksheet Column Hide 356◆ to hide an entire column.

Bear in mind, when using the /Range Erase command to increase available memory, that you must use the /File Save 130★ and then the /File Retrieve 128★ commands to regain full use of the memory used to store the erased portion of your worksheet.

- **Procedure**

When you choose the /Range Erase command, 1-2-3 prompts: *Enter range to erase:* and moves you into POINT mode 249◆. You can type the addresses of two diagonally opposite corners, type a range name or choose one from a menu by pressing the F3 (Name) 144◆ key, or highlight the range by expanding the pointer. When the range is specified, press Return to carry out the command.

/Range Format /RF

```
Worksheet Range Copy Move File Print Graph Data System Quit
Format Label Erase Name Justify Protect Unprotect Input Value Transpose
Fixed Scientific Currency , General +/- Percent Date Text Hidden Reset
```

- **Description**

The /Range Format command lets you control the appearance of the numeric values in a range of cells on your worksheet. Using this command, you can specify number of decimal places (from 0 to 15), and whether numbers should be displayed as currency or as percentages, in scientific format or as dates, and even whether formulas, rather than their calculated values, should be displayed. In addition, Release 2 of 1-2-3 enables you to specify time formats, and to hide the contents of specified ranges.

/Range Format

Regardless of the option you select, 1-2-3 remembers and uses the exact values of all numbers, to about 15 decimals. Thus, even though you display the value 1⅓ as 1.33, 1-2-3 uses the value 1.333333333333334. In this respect, as well as in the choice of formats, the /Range Format command is very similar to the /Worksheet Global Format command.

- **Procedure**

When you select the /Range Format command, 1-2-3 presents you with the options shown at the beginning of this entry. Here is a description of each of those options:

Fixed displays the number of decimal places you specify. 1-2-3 prompts you with 2, but you can choose any number from none (0) to 15. Example:

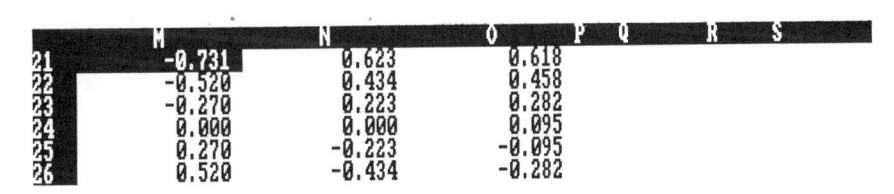

	M	N	O
21	-0.731	0.623	0.618
22	-0.520	0.434	0.458
23	-0.270	0.223	0.282
24	0.000	0.000	0.095
25	0.270	-0.223	-0.095
26	0.520	-0.434	-0.282

Scientific displays numbers in scientific (exponential) format. The number being multiplied can have up to 15 decimal places (again, 1-2-3 prompts with 2). The exponent can be any number from −99 to +99. Example:

	M	N	O
21	-7.31E-01	6.23E-01	6.18E-01
22	-5.20E-01	4.34E-01	4.58E-01
23	-2.70E-01	2.23E-01	2.82E-01
24	-1.36E-18	2.04E-18	9.51E-02
25	2.70E-01	-2.23E-01	-9.51E-02
26	5.20E-01	-4.34E-01	-2.82E-01

Currency displays a currency symbol and a separator, such as a comma, between thousands. As for fixed and scientific formats, 1-2-3 prompts 2 decimal places, but allows up to 15. Negative amounts are displayed in parentheses. Example:

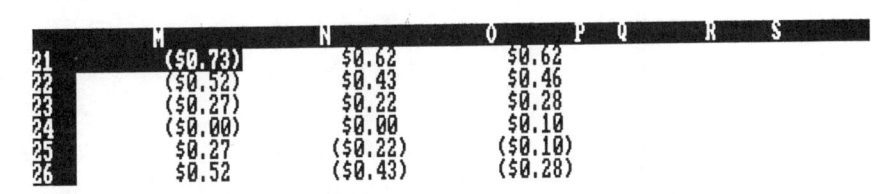

	M	N	O
21	($0.73)	$0.62	$0.62
22	($0.52)	$0.43	$0.46
23	($0.27)	$0.22	$0.28
24	($0.00)	$0.00	$0.10
25	$0.27	($0.22)	($0.10)
26	$0.52	($0.43)	($0.28)

/Range Format

Comma (,) displays numbers just as *Currency* does, but without the currency sign.

General displays numbers in 1-2-3's default format:

☐ Zeros at the ends of decimal numbers are not displayed. (For example, 123.45000 is displayed as 123.45.)

☐ Whole numbers containing more than 15 digits and/or numbers wider than the column width minus one character, are shown in scientific notation. (For example, 1234567890123456 is converted to 1.2E+15. But if the column is, say 9 characters wide, any whole number that takes more than 8 spaces is converted to scientific notation—123456789 becomes 1.2E+08. These rules apply only to whole numbers, however: The decimal number 1.2345678901234567 is displayed as 1.234567 in a column 9 characters wide.)

Note: 1-2-3 eliminates decimal places, if necessary, in converting numbers to scientific notation for display in narrow columns. This results in a loss of precision in the displayed format. 1-2-3 still stores the actual value, however, so you need not worry about precision in your calculations. As with all other numeric formats, numbers too wide to be displayed, even in scientific notation, in the existing column width are replaced with asterisks on the screen.

Plus/minus (+/−) converts a number to the equivalent number of symbols, if allowed by the current column width. The symbol is a plus sign if the number is positive, a minus sign if the number is negative. Thus, 5 becomes +++++ and −5 becomes −−−−−. If the number is 0, or between −1 and 1, the symbol is a period.

Percent displays numbers as percentages with up to 15 decimal places. It is important to remember that, when numbers are to be shown as percentages, 1-2-3 automatically multiplies the value of the number by 100 before displaying it as a percent. Thus, the number 4 will be displayed as *400%*. To have 1-2-3 display *4%*, you would have to enter or calculate the value as *0.04*.

Date ♦ displays the date in one of five formats:

D1	DD-MMM-YY	Day-Month-Year	21-Feb-87
D2	DD-MMM	Day-Month	21-Feb
D3	MMM-YY	Month-Year	Feb-87
D4	Long International	Month/Day/Year	02/21/87
D5	Short International	Month/Day	02/21

Formats D4 and D5 are in Release 2 only.

/Range Format

The Date format works with the @DATE, @NOW, and @TODAY functions by converting a serial number generated by these functions into the date represented by the number. 1-2-3 always aligns dates with the right edge of a cell. If the cell width is too narrow for the date, 1-2-3 displays asterisks (****) in the cell. For example, the serial number 32136 (Christmas 1987) formatted in the D1 format appears as asterisks in a standard column. After the column is widened to 10 characters, it appears as 25-Dec-87.

The international date formats (D4 and D5) each have four possible alternative formats. They are chosen with the /Worksheet Global Default Other 364♦ option, and appear as follows:

A	MM/DD/YY	02/21/87
B	DD/MM/YY	21/02/87
C	DD.MM.YY	21.02.87
D	YY-MM-DD	87-02-21

Time♦ displays the time (Release 2) in one of four formats. Time formats are an extension of date formats and their codes: D6-D9:

D6	HH:MM:SS AM/PM	05:21:00 PM
D7	HH:MM	05:21 PM
D8	Long International	21:10:00
D9	Short International	21:10

Each of the international time formats (D8 and D9) has four possible alternate formats. The formats are chosen with the /Worksheet Global Default Other option:

A	HH:MM:SS	21:10:00
B	HH.MM.SS	21.10.00
C	HH,MM,SS	21,10,00
D	HHhMMmSSs	21h10m00s

Text displays formulas, rather than the values calculated by them. When you choose the *Text* option, the numbers in your worksheet are displayed in *General* format.

Hidden♦, in Release 2, suppresses the cell display within a range. A good precaution is to protect hidden data with /Range Protect 314★ so that it isn't accidentally overwritten.

/Range Format · /Range Input

Reset cancels special formatting for the range of cells specified. Format reverts to the global numeric display format currently specified by the /Worksheet Global Format command.

- **Using /Range Format**

When you use the /Range Format command, any formats you set for specific ranges override the default values that have been set with the /Worksheet Global Format **366★** command. The opposite, however, does not hold true: Formats you set with the /Worksheet Global Format command affect all cells on a worksheet *other than* those that have been formatted with the /Range Format command.

In addition, formats you set with the /Range Format command:

☐ Remain in effect, even if you erase the contents of the cells with the /Range Erase **299★** command.

☐ Stay with the range when you move it with the /Move **250★** command.

☐ Transfer to cells you copy to with the /Copy **31★** command.

If you attempt to increase available memory by erasing the contents of cells formatted with /Range Erase, remember to use the *Reset* option to remove the range formatting. Then, save and retrieve the file to maximize the amount of memory available to you.

/Range Input /RI

```
Worksheet Range  Copy  Move  File  Print  Graph  Data  System  Quit
Format  Label  Erase  Name  Justify  Protect  Unprotect  Input  Value  Transpose
```

- **Description**

The /Range Input command is used to limit movement of the cell pointer to unprotected cells within a specified range. The command is a complement of the /Worksheet Global Protection **369★** and the /Range Unprotect **317★** commands. The /Range Input command is useful in guarding against inadvertent changes to valuable cell contents and in simplifying routine data entry on form-type input worksheets.

■ **Procedure**

Before using the /Range Input command, you should finish constructing your entire worksheet and decide which cells can and cannot be changed. You can then:

1. Unprotect the cells that can be changed, with the /Range Unprotect command.
2. Select the /Range Input command. When 1-2-3 prompts: *Enter data input range:*, specify the rectangular block containing the unprotected cells in which you want to restrict pointer movement.

Note: Remember that a range must always be a rectangular block of cells. Thus, even though protected and unprotected cells are scattered around your worksheet, the *range* of cells you specify with the /Range Input command begins with the top left-hand cell to which you want the cell pointer to move, and ends with the bottom right-hand cell to which you want the cell pointer to move.

During this time, 1-2-3 allows you to press Esc to cancel an entry, and to use the backspace key to correct your typing errors, but it restricts certain other activities:

- ☐ You cannot choose commands.
- ☐ You cannot use the Pg Up and Pg Dn keys.
- ☐ You can use the Home key only to move the cell pointer to the first unprotected cell in the range.
- ☐ You can use the End key only to move the cell pointer to the last unprotected cell in the range.
- ☐ You can use only the F1 (Help) **144♦**, F2 (Edit) **144♦**, and F9 (Calc) **144♦** function keys.

1-2-3 remains in this input state until you press either Esc or Return while you are in READY **249♦** mode—in other words, when line 2 of the Control Panel **29★** is empty.

■ **Comments**

The /Range Input command with macros can be enormously useful in situations where individuals who are unfamiliar with 1-2-3 and/or with your worksheet are entering large amounts of data. 1-2-3 can be programmed to loop through the same series of data-entry cells time after time, thus eliminating the need to check the location of the cell pointer.

/Range Justify

/Range Justify /RJ

```
Worksheet Range  Copy  Move  File  Print  Graph  Data  System  Quit
Format  Label  Erase  Name  Justify  Protect  Unprotect  Input  Value  Transpose
```

■ **Description**

The /Range Justify command lets you arrange the words in a single column of labels, so that the resulting lines fit within the width and depth of a specified range, up to a maximum width of 240 characters. You can use the /Range Justify command in many situations: for example, to break labels that are too long to be displayed on the screen, or to break consecutive rows of labels in a column so that all the lines are relatively the same length. In terms of what it does for you, the /Range Justify command works something like a word processor, arranging text to fit the space you have.

■ **Procedure**

Before you select the /Range Justify command, place the cell pointer on the first label in the column you want to justify. Choose the /Range Justify command, and 1-2-3 will prompt you to *Enter justify range:*. Expand the cell pointer or type the address of the diagonally opposite corner cell. When you press Return to carry out the command, 1-2-3 will rearrange consecutive labels, down to the first non-label cell in the column, aligning each with the left edge of the column and assigning it the label prefix for left alignment ('):

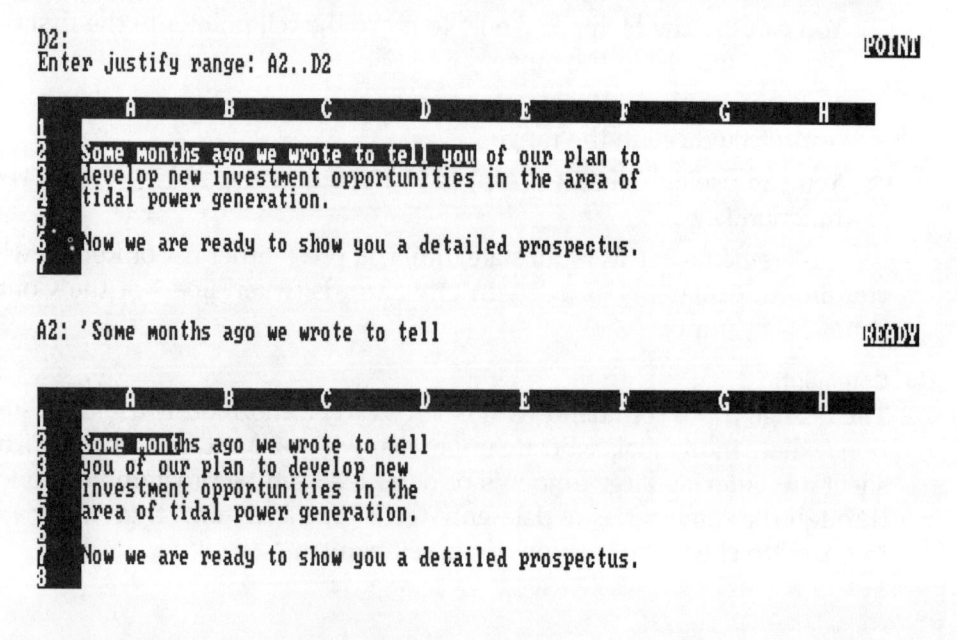

```
D2:                                                          POINT
Enter justify range: A2..D2
         A        B        C        D        E        F        G        H
1
2  Some months ago we wrote to tell you of our plan to
3  develop new investment opportunities in the area of
4  tidal power generation.
5
6  Now we are ready to show you a detailed prospectus.
7
```

```
A2: 'Some months ago we wrote to tell                        READY
         A        B        C        D        E        F        G        H
1
2  Some months ago we wrote to tell
3  you of our plan to develop new
4  investment opportunities in the
5  area of tidal power generation.
6
7  Now we are ready to show you a detailed prospectus.
8
```

/Range Justify

The results of using the /Range Justify command differ somewhat, depending on whether you are justifying one row or more than one.

When you specify one row:

- 1-2-3 includes all rows down to the bottom of the worksheet, or to the first non-label cell it encounters.
- 1-2-3 shifts non-label cell contents below the range up or down, depending on the number of rows occupied by the justified labels.

When you specify more than one row:

- 1-2-3 justifies rows of labels down to the first non-label cell or to the bottom of the range you specify, stopping when it reaches one or the other.
- 1-2-3 shifts cell contents up and down, as when you specify one row, but only within the range you specify.

When you justify more than one row, you must bear in mind that the space you are selecting must be wide enough, and deep enough, to hold all the labels you are asking 1-2-3 to justify. If the range is too small, 1-2-3 will beep and display the message *Justify range is full or line too long*. If you see this message, press Esc or Return to see how much justification 1-2-3 can do within the range you specified.

Although you can justify one row or many, you can justify only a single column at a time.

Note: Do not /Range Justify cells which have been given range names—they may be invalidated. Also, attempting to justify protected cells may produce an error message.

■ **Comment**

For large amounts of text, or substantial text editing, a word processor is easier and faster to use than /Range Justify. To prepare text for word processing, save it with the /Print File **269★** command. Conversely, to incorporate word-processed text in a worksheet, use the /File Import **126★** command.

/Range Label /RL

```
Worksheet Range Copy Move File Print Graph Data System Quit
Format Label Erase Name Justify Protect Unprotect Input Value Transpose
Left Right Center
```

- **Description**

    The /Range Label command allows you to control the alignment of existing labels in the specified range of cells in the current worksheet, by automatically assigning them the appropriate label prefix character for the display format you specify. Use this command to control the appearance of labels you have already entered into a worksheet.

- **Procedure**

    When you select the /Range Label command, 1-2-3 offers you the following choices: *Left*, *Right*, and *Center*.

    Select *Left* to left align all existing labels in the range, like this:

    ```
    C5: [W13] 'shipping                                          READY

              A                B            C           D        E      F
    1 ===========================================================================
    2 Personnel Database
    3 ---------------------------------------------------------------------------
    4 Name                    SSN        Department    Salary   Vac. Sick Days
    5 Smothers, Tom        386558833     shipping     $22,000.00  10    3
    6 Wellington, George   376524251     accounting   $27,994.00  10    2
    7 Smithfield, Sue      293832302     admin        $26,888.00   5    7
    8 Robinson, Glenda     142990957     shipping     $19,982.00   6    0
    ```

    Select *Right* to right align all existing labels in the range, like this:

    ```
    C5: [W13] "shipping                                          READY

              A                B            C           D        E      F
    1 ===========================================================================
    2 Personnel Database
    3 ---------------------------------------------------------------------------
    4 Name                    SSN        Department    Salary   Vac. Sick Days
    5 Smothers, Tom        386558833       shipping   $22,000.00  10    3
    6 Wellington, George   376524251     accounting   $27,994.00  10    2
    7 Smithfield, Sue      293832302          admin   $26,888.00   5    7
    8 Robinson, Glenda     142990957       shipping   $19,982.00   6    0
    ```

Select *Center* to center each existing label in its cell, like this:

```
C5: [W13] ^shipping                                                    READY
```

	A	B	C	D	E	F
1						
2	Personnel Database					
3						
4	Name	SSN	Department	Salary	Vac.	Sick Days
5	Smothers, Tom	386558833	shipping	$22,000.00	10	3
6	Wellington, George	376524251	accounting	$27,994.00	10	2
7	Smithfield, Sue	293832302	admin	$26,888.00	5	7
8	Robinson, Glenda	142990957	shipping	$19,982.00	6	0

Press Return, and 1-2-3 will prompt *Enter range of labels:*, followed by the current location of the cell pointer. Specify the range of labels you wish to affect, either by expanding the cell pointer with the arrow keys or by typing the addresses of two diagonally opposite corner cells of the range, then press Return to execute the command.

The /Range Label command does not affect subsequent labels you type, even though you enter them in the range specified in the /Range Label command. To align labels you have not yet typed, you must use the /Worksheet Global Label-Prefix 368★ command.

Exception: The /Range Label command works as described, except on long labels or formulas that produce string 332★ values. These always appear at the left edge of the cell, no matter which type of alignment you specify with either the /Range Label or /Worksheet Global Label-Prefix command.

- **Comment**

The /Range Label command is the same as the /Range Label-Prefix command in Release 1a, except that the /Range Label-Prefix command does not affect string values as described here, because there was no capability for producing string values in Release 1a.

/Range Name /RN

```
Worksheet Range Copy Move File Print Graph Data System Quit
Format Label Erase Name Justify Protect Unprotect Input Value Transpose
Create Delete Labels Reset Table
```

- **Description**

    Five commands related to named ranges are accessible through the /Range Name command menu. Using these commands, you can:

    □ Create or redefine a range name (with /Range Name Create).

    □ Delete an existing range name (with /Range Name Delete).

    □ Use a label as a name for the cell adjacent to the label cell (with /Range Name Labels).

    □ Eliminate all range names in a worksheet (with /Range Name Reset).

    □ See a list of all range names and their corresponding cell addresses (with /Range Name Table).

    The following sections discuss each of these commands in detail.

- **/Range Name Create◆**

    Use the /Range Name Create command to give a name to a particular range of cells, to change the range associated with the name, or to name a macro you have written.

    Procedure: When you choose the /Range Name Create command (/RNC), 1-2-3 prompts *Enter name:* and displays a list of current range names.

    □ If you wish to create a new name, type the name of your choice, up to 14 characters. You can include any combination of letters, numbers, punctuation marks, and symbols you wish, but avoid blank spaces and any letter/number combinations or special symbols that 1-2-3 will interpret as cell addresses (such as A1) or instructions for mathematical calculations (such as 123/2). When you have entered the name, press Return.

    □ If you wish to change the range to which an existing name refers, highlight the appropriate name and press Return.

/Range Name

With either of the preceding choices, 1-2-3 then prompts *Enter range:* and displays the address highlighted by the cell pointer. Highlight the range you want to name, or type the addresses of two diagonally opposite corners, press Return, and 1-2-3 will carry out the command.

Comments: With either Release 1a or Release 2, you can assign more than one name to the same range of cells. Because you can do so, however, you cannot use the /Range Name Create command to *change* the name that's assigned to a range. For example, if the name Sales refers to cells A1..D5, you cannot change the name to Sold with the /Range Name Create command—1-2-3 will simply assign both Sales and Sold to the same range. To eliminate one name and replace it with another, you must delete the old one with the /Range Name Delete command (see the following section), then create the new name as described here.

If you have Release 2 of 1-2-3 and are uncertain about whether you have already assigned a name to the same or another range, just use the /Range Name Table **313♦** command. If you have Release 1a, you can view all defined names when 1-2-3 prompts for a range by pressing the F3 (Name) **144♦** key; to see the range associated with a name, press Return, and to cancel the viewing sequence, press Esc.

To name a macro **211★**, assign a two-character (\character) name to the beginning cell of the range in which the macro appears. Then, use the name to call up and execute the macro instructions. If you are naming a subroutine called from within a macro, give it a normal (1 to 14 characters) descriptive name.

Using range names within macros is a good idea, because modifications to a worksheet (insertions, deletions) can change the location of important cells—and since macros are labels, direct cell references within a macro will not be updated to reflect the new locations. But a range name is always accurate, since 1-2-3 adjusts the range's definition whenever any change is made to it.

- **/Range Name Delete♦**

Use the /Range Name Delete command to eliminate a range name, without affecting the cell contents associated with the name. To protect your worksheet, however, 1-2-3 changes all occurrences of the name in formulas to its corresponding cell addresses before deleting the name.

/Range Name

Procedure: When you choose the /Range Name Delete (/RND) command, 1-2-3 offers only the prompt *Enter name to delete:*.

Once you enter the name or choose it from the list 1-2-3 displays in the Control Panel, and then press Return, the name is gone. Since you have no means of undoing your action, be certain you want to eliminate the name before carrying out the command—especially if you plan to rearrange or otherwise modify your worksheet. To cancel /Range Name Delete, you can press Esc to back out of the command as long as it is before you have pressed Return.

- **/Range Name Labels◆**

The /Range Name Labels command enables you to use the first 14 characters of an existing label as the name for a single cell adjacent to it. When you use this command, 1-2-3 assigns the label as a single-cell range name to the adjoining value cell. You can then use this name in creating formulas or to invoke a macro, just as you ordinarily use a range name.

The /Range Name Labels command can be used to assign field names to entries in the first record of a database. Doing this enables you to use the names as criterion ranges in database formulas (for more information, see the /Data 51★ commands). /Range Name Labels is also useful when you build worksheets that contain certain variables you want to change in evaluating different "what if" situations. For example, you might use /Range Name Labels at the top of a project cost estimate to name such variables as expenses, salaries, overhead, profit, and so on, which occur in formulas elsewhere in your worksheet.

Procedure: When you choose the /Range Name Labels (/RNL) command, 1-2-3 prompts you for the direction to extend the range name: *Right*, *Down*, *Left*, or *Up*. Make your selection, then highlight the appropriate range of label cells and press Return.

Comments: If you use this command with cells containing long labels, 1-2-3 uses only the first 14 characters as the name. Any non-label cells in the range are ignored. If a label duplicates an existing range name, the new name definition replaces the old one.

/Range Name

■ **/Range Name Reset◆**

The /Range Name Reset command is like the /Range Name Delete command, but eliminates all range names from the worksheet, while leaving cell contents unchanged. As with /Range Name Delete, the /Range Name Reset command causes 1-2-3 to change all references to range names to their corresponding cell addresses before deleting the names.

Procedure: Whenever you choose /Range Name Reset (/RNR), 1-2-3 *does not* prompt for names or ranges. Nor does it ask you to verify your intent. As soon as you press Return or type *R* for Reset, all range names in the current worksheet are eliminated. Because of this, the caution about being certain you wish to delete range names before you act holds even more true for /Range Name Reset than it does for /Range Name Delete. Remember that carrying out the command removes *all* names, not just one.

■ **/Range Name Table◆**

The /Range Name Table command exists only in Release 2 of 1-2-3. You can use this command to create a reference area in a blank part of your worksheet, to see a two-column list of range names and the cells to which they are assigned. If you are creating a large or complex worksheet with many separate or overlapping named ranges, you will want to use this command to keep track of what you have named, and where.

Procedure: When you choose /Range Name Table (/RNT), 1-2-3 prompts you to enter the range at which you want the table placed. You need not specify an entire range—as with the /Move 250★ command, you can specify a single cell address and 1-2-3 will use that as the upper left corner of the new range. When you press Return, 1-2-3 will display all range names in alphabetic order down the left-hand column, and all corresponding addresses down the right-hand column.

Comments: Be very careful to place the table range *away from* the active area of your worksheet. The /Range Name Table command is not a display-only command. The range names and cell addresses in the table will overwrite any existing information in the cells they occupy. If your computer has enough memory for you to place the table in a remote area of the worksheet, you might want to consider specifying a range you know will remain outside the farthest corner of the model you are building. To refer to

/Range Name · **/Range Protect**

the table, you can either open a second window (with the /Worksheet Window **378★** command) or you can jot down the address of the top left corner of the table range, or name the table, and use the F5 (Goto) **144◆** key whenever you wish to see it.

Since 1-2-3 does not automatically update the range-name table, you should use this command periodically to see additional names and ranges you create. You can use the same range each time, since 1-2-3 will simply overwrite the old information with the new, expanded version.

/Range Protect /RP

```
Worksheet Range Copy Move File Print Graph Data System Quit
Format Label Erase Name Justify Protect Unprotect Input Value Transpose
```

■ **Description**

The /Range Protect command lets you prevent access to cells whose contents you wish to protect from alteration. Use this command when you want to prevent other users of your worksheet from inadvertently changing information or as a reminder to yourself that certain cells should not be changed.

Although you might assume that protecting certain cells is simply a matter of choosing the /Range Protect command, that is not the case. In fact, you really need this command only when you wish to re-protect cells from which you removed protection with the /Range Unprotect **317★** command. To explain why this is so, here is a short summary of the way in which protection operates in 1-2-3:

☐ When you begin a worksheet, 1-2-3 initially considers every cell to be a protected cell. However, 1-2-3 also includes an "umbrella" protection facility that is turned off and on through the /Worksheet Global Protection **369★** command. Initially, this overall protection is turned off, and the net effect is that all cells *could* be protected, *if* the global protection were turned on.

☐ When you finish creating a worksheet, suppose you were to turn on global protection. The result would be that you could not change, enter, or delete any information. The worksheet would be frozen.

☐ Normally, however, you only want to protect certain cells. Their protection is turned on as soon as you enable global protection. Therefore, you need to remove protection (with /Range Unprotect) from those cells you want or need to change. As a further refinement, once you have unprotected the appropriate cells, you may then define an area of the worksheet (with /Range Input 304★) that will confine the cell pointer only to those unprotected cells within the range you have specified, during the time the /Range Input command is active.

Since cell protection thus becomes a matter of taking protection away, rather than adding protection to, the /Range Protect command becomes your way of telling 1-2-3, "I've changed my mind...these cells should not be unprotected, after all."

■ **Procedure**

If you have turned on global protection and have unprotected cells you now want to protect, or if you want to protect cells that are part of a range specified with the /Range Input command, you should choose the /Range Protect command. When you do, 1-2-3 prompts *Enter range to protect:* and waits for you to highlight the range or type appropriate addresses. Once you do this and press Return, the cells you specified become protected. If global protection is turned on, 1-2-3 displays *PR* in the Control Panel whenever you place the cell pointer on a protected cell.

■ **Comments**

Protecting cell contents is not the same as hiding them from view. If you have Release 2 of 1-2-3 and want to prevent display of information, you can use the options for hiding cells with the /Range Format 300★ and /Worksheet Column 355★ commands. To restrict access to an entire worksheet, you can assign it a password with the /File Save 130★ command.

Note: These options are not available in Release 1a.

/Range Transpose

/Range Transpose /RT

```
Worksheet Range Copy Move File Print Graph Data System Quit
Format Label Erase Name Justify Protect Unprotect Input Value Transpose
```

■ **Description**

The /Range Transpose command enables you to rotate a range of cells 90 degrees, so that rows become columns and columns become rows. This command does not, however, allow you to redo a worksheet—if you decide that your column headings should appear as row headings, and vice versa, the /Range Transpose command will not allow you to rearrange your worksheet and all its formulas.

Rather, this command is valuable when you want to *copy* the data segment of a worksheet to another area, but rotate the headings and values (not formulas—relative references are not adjusted) so that vertical becomes horizontal and horizontal becomes vertical.

■ **Procedure**

Whenever you choose the /Range Transpose command, 1-2-3 asks for both a FROM range—the location of the original—and a TO range—the location of the transposed copy. The FROM and TO ranges cannot be synonymous; in other words, you cannot indicate the same cell address as the top left corner of both ranges.

When you press Return to carry out the command, 1-2-3 both transposes the cells in the FROM range and copies the results to the TO range.

Note: If you specify a TO range that already contains information, be certain you know how the transposed cells will affect existing data and formulas. Like many other 1-2-3 commands, /Range Transpose overwrites the contents of receiving cells, and can thus replace values with others you may not have anticipated. Also, keep in mind that relative cell references in transposed formulas will not be adjusted to reflect their new positions. If you need such adjustments, use the /Move command **250★** instead.

■ **Comment**

The /Range Transpose command is in Release 2 of 1-2-3. There is no Release 1a equivalent.

/Range Unprotect /RU

```
Worksheet Range Copy Move File Print Graph Data System Quit
Format Label Erase Name Justify Protect Unprotect Input Value Transpose
```

- **Description**

   The /Range Unprotect command allows you to remove protection from specified cells, so their contents can be changed. If you have turned on worksheet protection with the /Worksheet Global Protection Enable 369♦ command, you must use /Range Unprotect before you can alter any cells. If you have not turned on worksheet protection, cells can be altered at will, and there is no need to unprotect them. (For a discussion of worksheet protection, see the entry /Range Protect 314★.)

- **Procedure**

   When you choose the /Range Unprotect command, 1-2-3 prompts *Enter range to unprotect:* and moves to POINT mode. You can specify the range by expanding the cell pointer, typing a range name, or typing the addresses of two diagonally opposite corner cells. Once you press Return, the specified range is unprotected. The contents of these cells are displayed at bright intensity or, if you have a color monitor, in a contrasting color. When you place the cell pointer on an unprotected cell, 1-2-3 displays *U* in the Control Panel, to indicate its status.

- **Comment**

   If you unprotect a cell and later decide that it should not be altered, use the /Range Protect command. To restrict movement of the cell pointer to unprotected cells within a specified range, use the /Range Input 304★ command with a macro. To hide cell contents, use the /Range Format Hidden 303♦ command or the /Worksheet Column Hide 356♦ command (Release 2 only).

/Range Value

/Range Value /RV

```
Worksheet Range Copy Move File Print Graph Data System Quit
Format Label Erase Name Justify Protect Unprotect Input Value Transpose
```

- **Description**

The /Range Value command enables you to convert formulas to their values, in the same or another part of the worksheet. You can use this command in converting formulas to data usable by another program that cannot accept 1-2-3 formulas (another worksheet program, perhaps, that cannot use some of 1-2-3's functions) or simply to turn calculated values to constants.

The /Range Value command can also be very useful in worksheets where you want to create an analysis, or summary, section of results, but also want to retain the formulas in a calculations-type section. When you use the /Range Value command, the original formulas remain unchanged, while their values are inserted in the range you specify. If you wish, you can use the /Range Value command each time you change a set of assumptions, and thus maintain records of several "what-if" situations on the same worksheet.

- **Procedure**

When you choose the /Range Value command, 1-2-3 prompts for both a range to convert FROM and a range to convert TO. In this respect, /Range Value is similar in operation to the /Copy 31★ and /Move 250★ commands. As with those commands, you need only specify the upper left corner of the TO range. And, like /Copy and /Move, the /Range Value command overwrites any existing contents of cells in the TO range.

The /Range Value command allows you to specify the same range for both FROM and TO. This allows you to convert all formulas in the range to their values, but bear in mind that if you do this, the values replace the formulas, and the formulas are lost.

- **Comments**

The /Range Value command is in Release 2 of 1-2-3 only. To display formula values with Release 1a of 1-2-3, use the /Copy command.

Note: With any version of 1-2-3, copying formulas with the /Copy command ensures that all values are updated whenever you recalculate the worksheet. If you want your worksheet to reflect changing values based on a series of different assumptions, use the /Copy command instead of /Range Value.

@RATE()   A Release 2 financial function

- **Format**
@RATE(future value,present value,term)

- **Description**
The @RATE function calculates the periodic, fixed interest rate at which a present-value investment will grow to a future value, given the number of compounding periods occurring at regular intervals throughout the term. The function assumes that payments are made at the end, rather than the beginning, of each period.

@RATE requires three numeric arguments: future value, present value, and term. All three can be numbers or references to cells that contain either numbers or calculated values.

- **Example**
Suppose you decide to purchase a certificate for your new child. Your bank tells you that an investment of $1000 now will return $7000 when your child is 18. The interest is compounded monthly. Using the @RATE function you can calculate the periodic interest rate being paid:

@RATE(7000,1000,18*12)

You can then multiply the monthly rate by 12 to determine the annual percentage, 10.9%.

@REPEAT()   A Release 2 string function

- **Format**
@REPEAT(string,n)

- **Description**
The @REPEAT function causes 1-2-3 to duplicate a specified string the number of times indicated by the argument n. The repeated string is treated as a long label by the worksheet display.

- **Procedure**
The string of characters repeated by the @REPEAT function can either be specified in the argument, enclosed in double quotation marks, or as a reference to a cell containing a label. The number of times the string is to be repeated must be a numeric value.

For example, suppose you are formatting a worksheet in which you have 12 columns, each 10 characters wide. You have centered the title ANNUAL BUDGET in row 2. To speed your formatting and make the worksheet easier to read, you could enter:

@REPEAT(−,120)

in rows 1 and 3, to create a dashed line above and below the worksheet title.

Note: Using @REPEAT differs from using the backslash (\) label prefix in enabling you to extend a string beyond the right edge of the current cell; the backslash fills only a single cell.

@REPLACE()   A Release 2 string function

- **Format**

@REPLACE(original string,start number,n,new string)

- **Description**

The @REPLACE function replaces a specified number of characters (n) in an existing (original) string with the characters specified as the new string. The replacement begins at the character location defined by the start number.

- **Procedure**

When you enter the @REPLACE function, the original string and the new string can be entered as character strings or as cell references or single-cell range names. If they are entered as character strings, they must be enclosed in double quotation marks. If they are cell references, the cells must contain labels, but the labels need not be enclosed in quotation marks.

The start number begins at 0, the leftmost character in the original string.

Using @REPLACE, you can append information by specifying a start number immediately beyond the end of the original string. For example:

@REPLACE("Highest Sales: ",15,8,"John Doe")

returns *Highest Sales: John Doe.*

Or, you can replace characters within a string:

@REPLACE("Project Budget: ABC Co.",16,3,"XYZ")

returns *Project Budget: XYZ Co.*

Or, you can insert characters at the beginning of a string by making the start number equal to 0 and n (the number of characters to replace) equal to 0:

@REPLACE("Birthday",0,0,"Happy ")

returns *Happy Birthday.*

Note that, in the preceding examples, blank spaces count as characters. The same is true for punctuation.

To use the @REPLACE function for deleting selected information, make the new string an empty string—enter it as a pair of double quotation marks with no intervening space, "". If you are using cell references, an empty string is equivalent to a cell with only a label prefix (') in it.

@RIGHT()   A Release 2 string function

- **Format**

@RIGHT(string,n)

- **Description**

The @RIGHT function searches a string and extracts n number of characters (a substring) from the end of the string. @RIGHT complements the function @LEFT 201★, which returns n characters from the beginning of the string, and @MID 244★, which returns n characters from a specified point within the string.

- **Procedure**

The @RIGHT function allows a string argument only; a numeric value will produce the value ERR. The value n must be either a number or a reference to a cell containing a numeric value.

The string can be specified either directly, by inclusion in the argument, or indirectly, as a cell reference. If the string is included in the argument, it must be enclosed in double quotation marks. For example:

@RIGHT("Alas, poor Yorick",6)

(This would return *Yorick* because the second part of the argument (6) specifies the last six characters of the string.)

When using the @RIGHT function, remember that blank spaces and punctuation count as characters. Thus:

@RIGHT("04/12/72",2)

would return *72*, while

@RIGHT("04/12/72",5)

would return *12/72*.

@ROUND()

- **Format**

@ROUND(x,n)

- **Description**

@ROUND is a mathematical function that returns the number x, rounded to the number of digits specified by n.

- **Procedure**

The argument n can be either a positive or a negative number between -15 and 15. If n is negative, 1-2-3 will round the integer portion of x; if n is positive, 1-2-3 will round the decimal portion of x. If n is 0, 1-2-3 will round x to an integer. For example:

@ROUND(99.46,-1)

returns *100*, whereas:

@ROUND(99.46,0)

returns *99*, and:

@ROUND(99.46,1)

returns *99.5*.

- **Comments**

    When deciding whether to use @ROUND, bear in mind that this function will affect the precision of the numbers used in your calculations. If you need full precision, but prefer to display fewer decimals, use the *Fixed* option of the /Range Format 300★ command. 1-2-3 will display only the number of decimals you specify, but will preserve and calculate the full values of all numbers. Conversely, if you need only the integer portions of numbers, the @INT 183★ function may serve you better, although it will not round decimals before returning integer values.

Row

1-2-3's worksheet is a grid of cells 13★, each of which is located at the intersection of a row and a column 26★. All rows are horizontal, all columns are vertical. The worksheet contains 8192 rows in Release 2 of 1-2-3, and 2048 rows in Release 1a.

- **Inserting rows**

    You can insert one or more blank rows in a worksheet with the /Worksheet Insert 373★ command. Whether you insert one row or many, they appear above the row in which the cell pointer is currently located. Inserted rows are given the current global formatting; special formatting can be applied with the /Range Format 300★ command.

- **Deleting rows**

    You can remove unwanted rows from the worksheet with the /Worksheet Delete 357★ command. To do this, move the pointer to the row you want to delete, then select and execute the command. To eliminate more than the current row, specify a range or highlight the appropriate rows.

- **Changes in cell references**

    When you insert or delete rows, 1-2-3 automatically adjusts cell references in formulas to reflect the change. However:

    ☐ If the deleted row takes with it the endpoint of a range, the range becomes invalid and any formulas that reference it will contain ERR.

    ☐ If the deleted row contains a cell referenced in a formula, the formula's reference to the deleted cell will be replaced with ERR.

Row · @Rows() · @S()

- **One special row**
With Release 2 of 1-2-3, there is one special row you insert with the /Worksheet Page 123★ command. This is a dummy row that tells 1-2-3 to create a page break at the location specified. It is identified by a double colon, and thus should not be used for any worksheet entries because it is non-printing and such entries will inevitably be lost.

@ROWS()   A Release 2 special function

- **Format**
@ROWS(range)

- **Description**
The @ROWS function returns the number of rows included in a range. The range 123★ can be specified either with cell references or by name, so both @ROWS(A1..M17) and @ROWS(SALES_FIGS) are valid arguments. You cannot specify a single cell as a range; if you do, the function returns ERR.

@ROWS and the related function @COLS 123★ are particularly useful in determining the sizes of named ranges. They are valuable when used within macros 123★ and enhance 1-2-3's ability to automate tasks. For example, a fully automatic print macro would take a list of range names and print them with correct margins and page breaks by first determining the size of each range with @ROWS and @COLS, then determining cell widths with @CELL or @CELLPOINTER.

@S()   A Release 2 special function

- **Format**
@S(range)

- **Description**
The @S function returns the value of a single cell, the top left-hand corner cell of a range, as a string value. If the cell contains a numeric value, the function returns an empty string (no characters).

- **Procedure**
The @S function always references a single cell, but the argument must always be entered in the form of a range reference—either two cell addresses separated by one or more periods, such as A1..A1, or a single cell address or single-cell range name preceded by an exclamation point—for example, !A1 or !Cell Name.

If you are entering or pointing to more than one cell reference, make the first reference the cell whose contents you want the function to retrieve as a string value. If you are entering a range name, either make certain it refers to a single cell, or be sure that the top left-hand corner cell of the named range is the cell whose contents you want returned.

For example:

@S(!B4)

would return nothing, a blank, 0, if cell B4 contained a number, not a string.

@S(D3..D7)

would return a blank if cell D3, the top left-hand corner of the range, were blank, because blank cells are converted to empty strings.

@SECOND()   A Release 2 time function

- **Format**
  @SECOND(time number)

- **Description**
  @SECOND is a time function that returns a value between 0 and 60, representing the second of the hour indicated by a serial number corresponding to the time of day. The serial number can be generated by the @TIME 340★, @TIMEVALUE 342★, or @NOW 258★ function.

- **Procedure**
  The argument of the @SECOND function can be any fraction or serial number, as long as it is .99999 (for 11:59:59 p.m.) or less. For example:

    @SECOND(.123456)

would return the value 47.

    @SECOND(32663.500000)

would return the value 0, representing no seconds past 12 p.m.—half of the 24 hours in a day.

    @SECOND(@NOW)

would return the current time, accurate to the last time you recalculated the worksheet (1-2-3 updates the current date and time specified by the @NOW function whenever you recalculate, either by entering new information (with recalculation set to automatic), or by pressing the F9 [Calc] 144♦ key).

325

@SIN()

@SIN()

■ **Format**

@SIN(x)

■ **Description**

@SIN is a trigonometric function that returns the sine of *x*, an angle expressed in radians. The value returned by the function is a number between −1 and 1. For example:

@SIN(@PI/2)

returns a value of 1.

@SIN(−@PI/2)

returns a value of −1.

@SIN(1.047)

returns 0.866, the sine of PI/4 radians. Likewise:

@SIN(1.047+2∗@PI)

returns 0.866, thus demonstrating the periodicity of the function.

■ **Example**

Suppose you are hiking uphill on a road that slopes upward at 15 degrees. You are planning to stop at the next vantage point, which is one mile away, and wonder how much higher you will be when you get there. Given this information, you can construct a right triangle with an acute angle of 15 degrees and a hypotenuse of 5280 feet. If you then use the formula:

+5280∗@SIN(15∗2∗@PI/360)

you find that you will gain 1367 feet in elevation by hiking one mile.

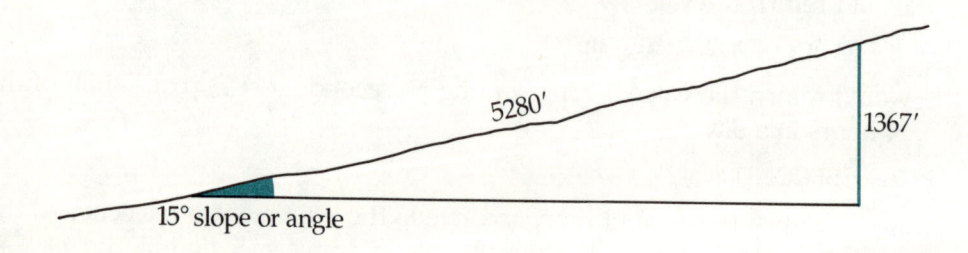

@SLN() A Release 2 financial function

- **Format**

@SLN(cost,salvage,life)

- **Description**

The @SLN function is one of three functions in Release 2 of 1-2-3 that calculates depreciation of an asset. @SLN calculates straight-line depreciation; the other functions, @DDB **101★** and @SYD **336★** calculate double-declining balance and sum-of-the-years' digits depreciation, respectively.

With the straight-line method of depreciation, depreciable cost (purchase price minus salvage value) is divided evenly over the estimated useful life of the asset. Depreciation is linear, assuming that an item with a useful life of n years will lose 1/n of its value each year, so the value returned by @SLN represents the depreciation for any period.

1-2-3 uses the following formula to calculate straight-line depreciation:

(cost−salvage value)/n

where: n is the life of the asset.

- **Procedure**

The arguments to the @SLN function are values, which can be entered either as numbers or as references to cells containing the values. The cost of the asset is its original price; the salvage value is the amount the asset will be worth at the end of its useful life; the life of the asset is the number of periods until the asset is depreciated to salvage value.

- **Example**

Suppose you want to find the total undepreciated balance (book value) of a $200,000 asset after four years. The asset has a salvage value of $40,000 and it has a useful life of 10 years.

```
B9: (C2) [W14] +B7-(@SLN(B4,B5,B6)*4)                               READY
```

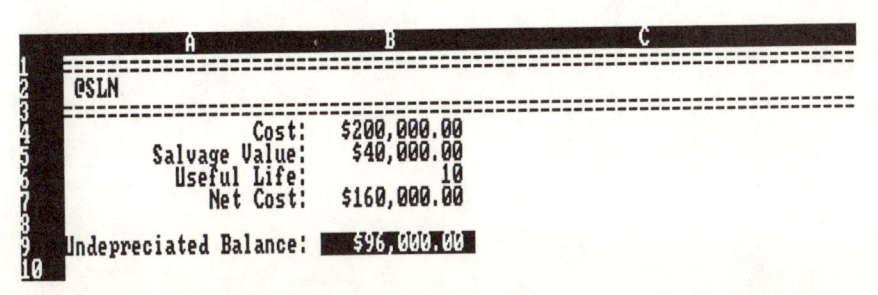

	A	B	C
1			
2	@SLN		
3			
4	Cost:	$200,000.00	
5	Salvage Value:	$40,000.00	
6	Useful Life:	10	
7	Net Cost:	$160,000.00	
8			
9	Undepreciated Balance:	$96,000.00	
10			

The value returned in cell A5 ($96,000) is the total undepreciated balance after four years: net cost minus total depreciation thus far.

@SQRT()

- **Format**

@SQRT(x)

- **Description**

The @SQRT function returns the positive square root of a numeric value, x.

- **Procedure**

The @SQRT function requires a positive number as its argument. The argument can be entered as a number, a cell address, single-cell range name, or another formula. Thus, as long as the referenced cell or cells contain positive numeric values, any of the following would be valid arguments: @SQRT(400), @SQRT(A1), @SQRT(Number), or @SQRT(A1*A2+A3).

The @SQRT function will return the value ERR if x is negative. However, you can take the square root of a negative by using the @ABS 2* function to remove the minus sign. For example:

@SQRT(@ABS(−400))

Status indicators

1-2-3 has two ways of keeping you informed about its operations. One way is represented by the mode indicators 248* it displays at the top right-hand corner of the screen. The second is represented by the status indicators it displays at various times at the bottom right-hand corner of the screen.

A status indicator tells you when you have turned on a toggle-type key, informs you of a particular condition in your worksheet, or tells you what is happening during macro execution. The following table lists the keyboard-related status indicators:

Status indicator:	Description:
CAPS	You have toggled the Caps Lock key to on. All subsequent letters you type will be capitalized.
END	You have toggled the End key to on. When a pointer-movement key is pressed, the cell pointer will be moved as described in the entry Keyboard **194★**.
NUM	You have toggled the Num Lock key to on. The numeric keypad will produce numbers, rather than pointer movements.
OVR	You have toggled the Ins key to off. Characters you type in EDIT mode will replace existing characters.
SCROLL	You have toggled the Scroll Lock key to on. Pressing the arrow keys will scroll the window (screen display) but the pointer will remain on the currently highlighted cell until bumping a border, then the cursor scrolls with the screen.

The table on the next page lists the work-related status indicators that 1-2-3 displays when appropriate.

Status indicators · @STD()

Status indicator:	Description:
CALC♦	You have set worksheet recalculation to *Manual* with the /Worksheet Global Recalculation 371★ command; the current worksheet contains new or modified entries, and to update the formulas you need to recalculate the worksheet by pressing the F9 [Calc] 144♦ key.
CIRC	You have created a circular formula reference, and recalculation order is set to *Natural* (the default). (A circular reference may or may not be intentional; see Iteration 188★ for details.) The first circular reference 1-2-3 detected can be found by checking the /Worksheet Status 374★ screen in Release 2.
CMD	You are executing a macro 211★.
STEP and SST	You have turned on single-step macro execution with the ALT-F2 [Step] keys.

@STD()

- **Format**

    @STD(list)

- **Description**

@STD is a statistical function that returns the standard deviation of the values included in a list. Standard deviation is used to determine the degree to which values for a given population deviate from the mean.

@STD()

- **Procedure**

  The @STD function requires a list of arguments separated by commas. Each argument can be a single value or a range of values, and can be a number, a cell or range reference, or the result of a formula calculation.

  @STD ignores any blank cells within a range, but treats label cells as equal to 0. The count of a population is used in calculating standard deviation, however, so your results will be inaccurate if you inadvertently specify label cells as part of a range.

- **Example**

  By way of illustration, suppose you had the following table of weights for a group of men, women, and children:

225	17	42	128	97	190
84	157	185	208	36	110
132	179	163	112	55	172
89	43	94	167	122	141
201	188	153	87	9	129

  The formula:

  @STD(weights)

  would return 58.598, the standard deviation—the degree to which the individual weights deviate from the mean, 123.833. If your table contained only the weights of men, women, or children, the standard deviation would be smaller, because the weights within any one group would fluctuate much less widely.

- **Comments**

  The @STD function calculates population, not sample, standard deviation. To calculate the sample standard deviation, use the formula:

  @SQRT(@COUNT(list)/(@COUNT(list)−1)) * @STD(list)

  Standard deviation is the square root of variance (see @VAR **350★**).

String

One of the ways in which Release 2 of 1-2-3 differs from earlier versions is in its support of strings and string functions.

A string is simply a series of characters: letters, numbers, punctuation marks, and special symbols. When a string is preceded by a label prefix and is entered in a worksheet cell, it is called a label. In other uses, a string is no different from a label, except that it is not necessarily a cell entry; it may be part of a formula, or may even be created by a formula.

- **String codes**

1-2-3 converts all of the characters you type into ASCII/LICS **203★** codes. The complete set of characters and corresponding LICS values can be found in Appendix 2 of the 1-2-3 manual (Release 2); a partial set, showing 1-2-3's international characters and codes is included in the entry LICS.

Empty strings: In addition to "normal" strings, such as *Lotus* and *the numbers 123*, there is one special string called an empty string. An empty string is equivalent to a "null" and has an ASCII/LICS value of 0. It can be created either by typing a label-prefix character into a cell or by entering it in a string function as a set of double quotation marks with no intervening characters—in other words, "".

An empty string differs from an empty cell, which contains no characters, and thus has no value but is treated like a 0 or ignored, depending on the situation.

- **String functions and formulas**

The string functions @CODE and @CHAR are used to convert characters to and from their code and string values. For example, @CODE("A") returns the number 65, which corresponds to the ASCII/LICS code for a capital A. Conversely, @CHAR(65) returns the single-character string A.

Note that, in the @CODE example, the character string A is an argument to the function. Strings are always enclosed in double quotation marks when they are being used in functions. For example:

@IF(A1>0,"We made money","We lost money")

String arguments to functions and formulas can be specified in any of four ways:

- By entering the string value directly. For example: @CHOOSE(A1,"up","down "). Note the double quotation marks.
- By referring to their locations in a worksheet. For example: @CHOOSE(A1,B1,B2) would be equivalent to the preceding example, if B1 contained the label 'up and B2 contained the label 'down.
- By referring to the range name of a string. For example: @CHOOSE(A1,Zero,One) if Zero is the range name of cell B1 and One is the range name of cell B2.
- By specifying a string-valued expression within the function. For example: @CHOOSE(A1,+"profits were "&B1,+"profits were "&B2)

The string-valued expression within the @CHOOSE function in the preceding paragraph is also known as a string formula. A string formula creates a string value when it is calculated by 1-2-3. The only string operator available for string formulas is the ampersand (&), which performs a concatenation (combine) on its operands. The @CHOOSE example in the preceding paragraph shows one use of the ampersand, in which the string *profits were* is combined with either *up* or *down*, depending upon the result of the @CHOOSE function. Here is another example:

+"You are overdrawn by "&@STRING(X20,2)

returns the unhappy phrase combined with a string representation of the amount in cell X20. The @STRING function must be used in such instances to convert a numeric value to string, or the formula will return the value ERR. 1-2-3 will not allow you to use both numeric values and strings to create combined strings in formulas.

Index numbers: Often, a string function requires a value to identify a character position within a string. The functions @LEFT, @RIGHT, and @MID all require that you specify the number and/or the location of the characters to be returned.

1-2-3 counts character positions within a string as an offset from 0. Thus, the first character in a string has the index number 0, not 1; the second character has the number 1, not 2; and so on. The last character of a string is equivalent to the length of the string minus 1.

When specifying a character position, always use a positive number. A negative number will return ERR. If you specify a fraction, 1-2-3 uses the integer portion of the number.

- **Strings and macros**

One application of string formulas is in the creation of custom macro commands. Since macros are labels, it makes sense that a string formula can be used to create a macro command. For example:

+"{BRANCH routine"&@IF(A1<10,"1","2")&"}"

will branch to routine1 or routine2, depending on the value of cell A1.

String formulas of this type can be quite convenient at times. Since most of the macro commands do not allow string formulas within the braces, the solution is to create the entire command with a string formula.

Strings in macro commands should generally be enclosed in double quotation marks. They aren't always necessary, but they don't hurt. And in some instances, such as:

'{GETLABEL "Please enter the dollar amount: ",A1}~

the double quotation marks are required. Here, for example, one of the 1-2-3 macro argument separators, the colon, is used in the prompt string. To avoid confusing the macro utility, the entire string must be enclosed in double quotation marks.

@STRING()   A Release 2 string function

- **Format**

@STRING(x,n)

- **Description**

The @STRING function converts a numeric value to a string. Because 1-2-3 does not allow you to combine numeric and string values in creating a string-valued expression, the @STRING function is a useful conversion facility and helps prevent string formulas from returning the value ERR.

- **Procedure**

@STRING requires two arguments. x is the number you wished to have returned as a string, and n is the number of decimal places (between 0 and 15) you want. The arguments can be entered as numeric values, cell references, or single-cell range names. Thus, as long as the cells contain numeric values, any of the following arguments would be allowed: @STRING(123.456,2), @STRING(A1,B1), or @STRING(value,decimals).

When converting the number to a string, @STRING uses the Fixed format (see /Range Format 300★). If you specify fewer decimal places than the number contains, the function rounds the number. For example:

@STRING(1.6789,2)

is converted to the string 1.68.

@STRING(1.9,0)

is converted to the string 2.

@SUM()

- **Format**
@SUM(list)

- **Description**
@SUM is a statistical function that returns the sum of the values included in a list of arguments.

- **Procedure**
Each argument to the @SUM function can be a single value or a range of values, and it can be a number, a cell reference, a cell range or range name, or a formula. Thus, any of the following would be allowed: @SUM(A1,B17,C17), @SUM(A1..A20,C1..C20), @SUM(Sales), or @SUM(A1∗A2/A3,B2+C2).

The function ignores any blank cells within a range; label cells equal 0. For example:

☐ If a six-cell range contains three blank cells and the values 2, 4, and 6, the @SUM function returns 12.

☐ If a six-cell range contains three label cells and the values 2, 4, and 6, the @SUM function returns 12.

☐ If a six-cell range is blank or contains only labels, the @SUM function returns 0.

@SYD() A Release 2 financial function

- **Format**

    @SYD(cost,salvage,life,period)

- **Description**

    The @SYD function is one of three functions in Release 2 of 1-2-3 that calculate depreciation of an asset. @SYD uses the sum-of-the-years' digits method; the other functions, @SLN **327★** and @DDB **101★**, calculate straight-line and double-declining balance, respectively.

    Sum-of-the-years' digits is a simple method for making the depreciation allowances large during the early years in the useful life of the asset. The depreciation for each year is calculated as a fraction of the depreciable (net) cost. The denominator of the fraction, which gives this method its name, is the sum of the digits for the years considered to be the useful life of the asset. For example, if the estimated life is four years, the denominator is 1+2+3+4, or 10. The numerator for the first year is the estimated useful life. Each year, the numerator is reduced by 1.

    1-2-3 uses the following formula to calculate depreciation by the sum-of-the-years' digits method:

    $$(\text{cost}-\text{salvage value}) * (n-p+1)/(n*(n+1)/2)$$

    where: n is the estimated useful life of the asset and p is the period for which you want to calculate depreciation.

- **Procedure**

    The arguments to the @SYD function are values, which can be entered either as numbers or as references to cells containing the values. The cost of the asset is its original price; the salvage value is the amount the asset will be worth at the end of its useful life; the life of the asset is the number of periods until the asset is depreciated to salvage value; the period is the particular period whose depreciation allowance is to be calculated.

- **Example**

    Suppose you want to calculate the sum-of-the-years' digits depreciation allowance for a machine that cost $110,000. It has an estimated useful life of 10 years, and at the end of 10 years it will be worth $25,000. Depreciation for the first year is:

    @SYD(110000,25000,10,1)

which returns $15,454.54 ($85,000 * 10/55). For the second year, the formula is:

@SYD(110000,25000,10,2)

and the function returns $13,909.09 ($85,000 * 9/55). And so on.

/System   /S

```
Worksheet  Range  Copy  Move  File  Print  Graph  Data  System  Quit
```

- **Description**

/System is a Release 2 command that enables you to temporarily suspend 1-2-3, use a DOS command, and return to the current worksheet when you have finished.

- **Procedure**

In order to use /System, you must first have copied the DOS file COMMAND.COM onto your 1-2-3 System Disk. If you use 1-2-3 from a hard disk, a copy of COMMAND.COM must be in the root directory.

To execute the command, simply choose /System and press Return. Your current worksheet will be replaced on-screen by the DOS version header and prompt, and you can carry out a DOS command. To return to 1-2-3, type *exit*. You can use any DOS command that does not load a program that stays resident in memory. Some such DOS commands to avoid include Print, Graphics, and Mode.

If you try to use the /System command and see the message *Cannot invoke DOS*, that means 1-2-3 cannot find the COMMAND.COM file. If you are using a floppy-disk system, replace the 1-2-3 System Disk with your DOS disk, press Esc, and try again. If you are using a hard disk, you will have to quit 1-2-3 in order to use DOS. Be sure to add COMMAND.COM to your root directory. In either case, refer to your 1-2-3 *Getting Started* manual for instructions on making DOS available to the /System command.

- **Comments**

The /System command can be enormously helpful when you need to format a new data disk, copy files, change the date, and so on. For checking directories or changing subdirectories, however, the /File 117★ commands in Release 2 can also help by displaying lists of files and subdirectories and by allowing you to move up and down in the hierarchy of the current directory.

Also, it is important to remember that DOS commands can be either internal or external. An internal command is one such as Dir or Copy, which is part and parcel of the COMMAND.COM file. Such commands can be used through the /System command without any problem. An external command, however, is one like CHKDSK (Check Disk) or DISKCOPY, which exists as a separate file on your DOS disk.

In any situation where you feel uncertain about the DOS command you are trying to use, err on the side of caution and save your work before choosing the /System command.

@TAN()

- **Format**

  @TAN(x)

- **Description**

@TAN is a trigonometric function that returns the tangent of *x*, an angle expressed in radians. There is no limit to the value of @TAN(x)—the range is between −infinity and +infinity. 1-2-3's approximations of these "limits" however, are:

@TAN(@PI/2)

which returns 2.9E+18, and:

@TAN(−@PI/2)

which returns −9.2E+18.

Like @SIN, @TAN is a periodic function. Thus:

@TAN(1.047)

returns 1, the tangent of PI/4, whereas:

@TAN(1.047+2*@PI)

also returns 1.

- **Example**

Say you have an antenna that you are mounting on your roof and you want to attach a support wire connecting the top of the antenna to the roof for added protection against wind damage. Your antenna is 10 feet high and its anchor is the chimney, which is 20 feet away from the base of the antenna.

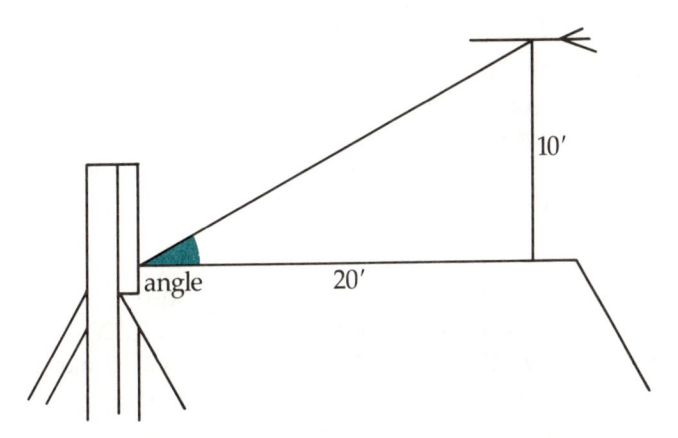

For best support you decide that the maximum allowable angle between the wire and the roof is 35 degrees. What angle will result from attaching the wire to the chimney? The tangent function:

@TAN(10/20)*180/@PI

returns the answer, 31 degrees.

@TERM()   A Release 2 financial function

- **Format**

@TERM(payment,interest,future value)

- **Description**

The @TERM function calculates the number of periods required for an ordinary annuity to earn a specified future value, given a fixed payment and a fixed periodic interest rate.

Procedure

As when entering other 1-2-3 financial functions, you can type the interest rate either as a percent, such as 10.5%, or as the decimal equivalent (.105). 1-2-3 automatically converts percentages to decimal values.

1-2-3 uses the following formula in its calculations:

ln(1+(future value*interest/payment))/ln(1+interest)

where: ln is the natural logarithm.

In using this function, you should be certain that the payment periods match the interest rate in units of time. For example, if payments are monthly and the periodic interest is based on an annual percentage, you should divide the interest rate by 12 to determine the monthly rate.

Example

Suppose you decide you can afford to set aside $100 per month toward a camera safari in East Africa. You expect that the holiday will cost $3500. If you put the money aside in an account that pays 6.75%, how long will it take to save for your vacation? The formula:

@TERM(100,.0675/12,3500)

tells you it will take 32 months to accumulate the necessary funds.

Like 1-2-3's other financial functions, @TERM assumes that payments are made at the end, not the beginning, of each period. If, in the preceding example, you decide you can just as easily put the money aside at the beginning of each month, you can calculate the number of periods with the formula:

@TERM(payment,interest,future value/(1+interest))

@TIME()   A Release 2 time function

Format
@TIME(hour,minutes,seconds)

Description

The @TIME function converts the time entered in the argument to a time serial number, the decimal fraction of a number ranging from .000 (for midnight) to .99999 (for 11:59:59). @TIME is the standard method for creating a time serial number in the worksheet.

*@*TIME()

■ **Procedure**

The @TIME function requires three numeric values, which can be entered as numbers, cell names or addresses, or formulas:

- ☐ Hour, which can be any number between 0 and 23, for midnight and 11 p.m., respectively.
- ☐ Minute, which can be any number between 0 and 59.
- ☐ Second which, like minute, can be any number between 0 and 59.

If any of these three numbers is invalid, the function returns the value ERR. Thus:

@TIME(22,13,55)

returns the serial number .9263310185 (10:13:55 p.m.). But:

@TIME(22,13,61)

returns the value ERR, because there are not 61 seconds in a minute.

Even though the time of day is returned as a serial number, it can be formatted to a more recognizable standard time appearance, such as 12:11:04, with the /Range Format Date Time **303**◆ command. Of 1-2-3's four time formats, 2 through 4 display time values within a standard 9-character column width. These formats are:

- ☐ Format 2: HH:MM AM/PM; for example, 08:14 PM.
- ☐ Format 3: HH:MM:SS (24-hour clock default configuration); for example, 20:14:30.
- ☐ Format 4: HH:MM (24-hour clock default configuration; for example, 20:14.

Formats 3 and 4 can each be configured in four ways with the /Worksheet Global Default Other International Time **365**◆ command. Format number 1, which displays the time serial number in the form HH:MM:SS AM/PM, requires a column width of 11 characters or more.

@TIMEVALUE()   A Release 2 time function

■ **Format**
@TIMEVALUE(time string)

■ **Description**
The @TIMEVALUE function translates a text string into a time serial number, which represents the time of day as a decimal fraction between .000 (midnight) and .99999 (11:59:59 p.m.).

■ **Procedure**
The time string required as the argument to the @TIMEVALUE function must be in one of 1-2-3's time formats, D6 to D9, each of which is a different way of presenting the hour, minute, and second of the day (not all are present in all formats). For example, the time 10:35:15 p.m. is represented as 10:35:15 PM in D6 format, 10:35 PM in D7 format, 22:35:15 in D8 format, and 22:35 in D9 format (complete tables can be found in the entries @CELL **18**★ and /Range Format **300**★).

The time string can be entered in the argument, enclosed in double quotation marks, or it can be a cell reference. Thus, @TIMEVALUE("35:15"), @TIMEVALUE(A1), and @TIMEVALUE(Late Night) would all be appropriate arguments providing that the cell reference contains a valid string.

Translate

Translate is the 1-2-3 utility that provides a means of exchanging data between 1-2-3 and other programs. The utility supports DIF (Data Interchange Format), as well as a number of widely used application programs.

If the file you wish to use (a document being passed to or from a word processor, for example) cannot be translated with this utility, you also have the option of saving and retrieving documents as standard ASCII text files with the /Print File **269**★ and /File Import **126**★ commands.

Note: There is no need to translate files created with Release 1a of 1-2-3 for use with Release 2. Furthermore, 1-2-3 will automatically replace occurrences of the Release 1a @TODAY function with the Release 2 @NOW equivalent.

■ **Procedure**

The Translate utility can be used either from the Lotus Access System or directly from DOS. From the Access System, you highlight *Translate* and press Return or press *T*.

```
┌─────────────────────────────────────────────────────────────────┐
│ 1-2-3  PrintGraph  Translate  Install  View  Exit              │
│ Allows files to be interchanged between 1-2-3 and other programs│
├─────────────────────────────────────────────────────────────────┤
│                     1-2-3 Access System                         │
│                  Lotus Development Corporation                  │
│                        Copyright 1985                           │
│                       All Rights Reserved                       │
│                          Release 2                              │
│                                                                 │
│  The Access System lets you choose 1-2-3, PrintGraph, the Translate utility, │
│  the Install program, and A View of 1-2-3 from the menu at the top of this   │
│  screen.  If you're using a diskette system, the Access System may prompt    │
│  you to change disks.  Follow the instructions below to start a program.     │
│                                                                 │
│    o  Use [RIGHT] or [LEFT] to move the menu pointer (the highlight bar at   │
│       the top of the screen) to the program you want to use.    │
│                                                                 │
│    o  Press [RETURN] to start the program.                      │
│                                                                 │
│  You can also start a program by typing the first letter of the menu         │
│  choice.  Press [HELP] for more information.                    │
└─────────────────────────────────────────────────────────────────┘
```

From DOS, if you have a floppy disk system, insert the 1-2-3 Utility disk in drive A and type *trans* at the A> prompt. If you have a hard disk, set the path to the 1-2-3 directory and type *trans* at the C> prompt.

Once you are in the Translate utility, you will be prompted *What do you want to translate FROM?* and you will see a list of options from which to pick the type of source file you will be translating.

Translate

```
          Lotus Translate Utility  Version 2.01
   Copyright 1985 Lotus Development Corporation  All Rights Reserved

What do you want to translate FROM?

        1-2-3, release 1A
        1-2-3, release 2
        dBase II
        dBase III
        DIF
        Jazz
        SYMPHONY, release 1.0
        SYMPHONY, release 1.1
        VISICALC




        Move the menu pointer to your selection and press [RETURN].
            Press [ESCAPE] to leave the Translate Utility.
                 Press [HELP] for more information.
```

Next, you will be prompted *What do you want to translate TO?* and will be offered another list of options from which to pick the type of file to create (the destination file).

```
          Lotus Translate Utility  Version 2.01
   Copyright 1985 Lotus Development Corporation  All Rights Reserved

Translate FROM: 1-2-3, release 1A    What do you want to translate TO?

                                     1-2-3, release 2
                                     dBase II
                                     dBase III
                                     DIF
                                     SYMPHONY, release 1.0
                                     SYMPHONY, release 1.1




        Move the menu pointer to your selection and press [RETURN].
        Press [ESCAPE] to return to the source selection menu.
                 Press [HELP] for more information.
```

Translate will then present a list of existing files of the source type you specified. Choose the file you wish to translate, then type a file name (including a path name, if you wish) for the destination file. Translate will automatically provide an extension that corresponds to the destination file type.

Note: Release 2 worksheets that are password-protected cannot be translated.

- **Common translations**

The following notes discuss specific translations.

From Release 2 to Release 1a: Release 2 of 1-2-3 uses memory differently from Release 1a, and Release 2 files may thus be too large for the earlier worksheet, and you will see a *Memory Full* error message when you load the translated file into Release 1a. If this happens, retrieve the file into the Release 2 program and rearrange the worksheet so that the data fits into as small a rectangular area as possible. Save the rearranged file and try the translation again.

If you see the message *FORMULA TRANSLATION ERROR*, it means there are formulas in the Release 2 file that cannot be translated. These formulas will be replaced with the label '*FORMULA TRANSLATION ERROR* in the destination file and will need to be translated manually.

Functions that have no equivalents in Release 1a will be translated as labels. These are:

- Date functions: @TIME, @HOUR, @MINUTE, @SECOND, @DATEVALUE, @TIMEVALUE.
- Financial functions: @CTERM, @DDB, @RATE, @SLN, @SYD, @TERM.
- Logical functions: @ISNUMBER, @ISSTRING.
- Special functions: @@, @COLS, @INDEX, @ROWS, @CELL, @CELLPOINTER.
- String functions: @CHAR, @CODE, @EXACT, @FIND, @LEFT, @LOWER, @LENGTH, @MID, @N, @PROPER, @REPLACE, @RIGHT, @REPEAT, @S, @STRING, @TRIM, @UPPER, @VALUE.

Symphony: There is no need to translate:

- Symphony 1.0 files for use with Release 2 of 1-2-3.
- Symphony 1.1 files for use with Release 2 of 1-2-3.
- Release 2 files for use with Symphony 1.1.

You do need to translate Release 2 files for use with Symphony 1.0. Because of different memory-allocation schemes, Release 2 files may not fit into a Symphony 1.0 worksheet. If you see a *Memory Full* message after loading a translated Release 2 file into Symphony, follow the steps outlined in the preceding Release 2-to-Release 1a section.

The following Release 2 functions will be changed to labels by the Translate utility: @CTERM, @DDB, @RATE, @SLN, @TERM, and @SYD.

dBASE II and III: dBASE files translated for use with Release 2 of 1-2-3 will have labels longer than 240 characters truncated. Because each record occupies a row in the 1-2-3 worksheet, no more than 8191 dBASE records can be translated.

If you are planning to translate a Release 2 file for use with dBASE II or III, you must format it along the following guidelines before translation:

- The worksheet or range must be a 1-2-3 database in which the first row contains field names and the second row is the first record.
- Each field in each record must either contain data or be formatted.
- Each record can have up to 32 fields if you are translating to dBASE II; up to 128 fields if you are translating to dBASE III.

Also, note that the formatting in the first record sets the format for the entire translation. Only data displayed on-screen is translated, so be certain the 1-2-3 column widths are wide enough to display complete entries.

Do not use scientific format in the 1-2-3 database because it is not supported by dBASE.

DIF: If you are translating a Release 2 worksheet to DIF, it must first have been put on disk with the /File Save **130★** command. Worksheets created with the /File Xtract **133★** command must be saved to disk with /File Save before translation.

If you are translating a DIF file to 1-2-3, you can transpose the rows and columns of the DIF file by choosing the *Rowwise* option. Choose *Columnwise* if you want to preserve the format of the original file.

@TRIM() A Release 2 string function

■ **Format**
@TRIM(string)

■ **Description**
The @TRIM function removes preceding, trailing, and multiple blank spaces from its argument. This function is a useful one for helping assure valid keyboard input or for standardizing the spacing of strings within a worksheet or in a database.

■ **Procedure**
@TRIM requires a string argument, which can be a reference to a cell containing a string or can be enclosed in double quotation marks and included in the function itself. For example, providing the referenced cells contain strings, any of the following arguments would be valid ones: @TRIM(A1), @TRIM(Title), or @TRIM("   BUDGET — 1986 - 1987   ").

The @TRIM function can be used with the & concatenation operator, as well as with individual strings. Thus, for example:

@TRIM(" Ronald   Reagan ")

would return *Ronald Reagan*, with the preceding and following blank spaces removed, and with the internal spaces trimmed from two to one.

@TRIM("One for all   "&"   and all for one")

would return *One for all and all for one*.

@TRUE

■ **Format**
@TRUE

■ **Description**
@TRUE is a logical function that can be used in a formula to return the numeric value 1. Although you don't ever *need* to use the @TRUE function (you can use 1 in a formula instead), this function is useful in making the purpose of a formula easier to understand.

No argument is used with @TRUE.

- **Procedure**

  The @TRUE function is usually used inside the functions @CHOOSE **23**★ and @IF **179**★. Its logical companion is the function @FALSE **117**★, which returns the value 0.

  The following two examples demonstrate the same situation. The first example uses the @TRUE and @FALSE functions; the second uses the values 1 and 0. In both instances, the formula returns 1 (true) if the value in cell A1 is less than the value in cell A4, and 0 (false) if the value in A1 is greater than or equal to the value in A4:

  @IF(A1<A4,@TRUE,@FALSE)
  @IF(A1<A4,1,0)

  Both formulas accomplish the same purpose, but to someone unfamiliar with the worksheet, the first might be much easier to interpret.

@UPPER()   A Release 2 string function

- **Format**

  @UPPER(string)

- **Description**

  The @UPPER function returns the string specified in its argument as uppercase letters only, whether or not the string contains all lowercase letters or a mixture of upper- and lowercase letters.

  The @UPPER function is an efficent means of assuring standardized input to data-entry macros. Its companion function is @LOWER.

- **Procedure**

  @UPPER allows string arguments only; numeric values produce the value ERR. The string can be specified directly, by inclusion in the argument, or indirectly, as a cell reference. If the string is included in the argument, it must be enclosed in double quotation marks. You can also use the & concatenation operator to combine two or more strings. Thus, any of the following arguments would be acceptable:

@UPPER("You are overdrawn")

would return *YOU ARE OVERDRAWN*.

@UPPER("Alice "&"in Wonderland")

would return *ALICE IN WONDERLAND*.

@UPPER(A1)

would return the label in cell A1, in all uppercase characters.

@UPPER(A1&A2)

would return the combined labels contained in cells A1 and A2, in all uppercase characters.

@VALUE()   A Release 2 string function

- **Format**

@VALUE(string)

- **Description**

The @VALUE function converts a number that has been entered as a string into a numeric value that can be used in mathematical calculations.

- **Procedure**

@VALUE allows you to specify strings either directly, by inclusion in the argument, or indirectly, as cell references. If the string is included in the argument, it must be enclosed in double quotation marks.

The string you specify must look like a number, but it can be in any of the following forms:

- An integer, such as 123.
- A decimal number, such as 123.456.
- A number in scientific notation, such as 123E4.
- A fraction, such as ¾.

If a numeric value is specified, it is returned unchanged. Leading and trailing spaces in the string disappear from the converted string, since 1-2-3 automatically aligns all numbers at the right edge of the cell. Currency symbols, separators, and other such non-numeric characters should be specified with the /Range Format 300★ command after conversion, rather than as part of the string, because some symbols can cause the function to return ERR. If a cell is blank or contains an empty string (a label prefix), the function returns 0. Thus, in the following examples:

@VALUE("1066.00")

returns the string as the value 1066.00.

@VALUE(A1)

returns 0 if cell A1 is blank or contains only a label prefix.

@SUM(@VALUE(A1),@VALUE(B1))

converts the strings in cells A1 and B1 into numeric values and returns the sum of the two numbers.

@VAR()

- **Format**
@VAR(list)

- **Description**
@VAR is a statistical function that returns the variance of the values included in a list—the degree to which individual values deviate from the mean for all of the values.

- **Procedure**
The @VAR function requires a list of arguments separated by commas. Each argument can be a single value or a range of values, and can be a number, a cell or range reference, or the result of a formula calculation.

@VAR ignores any blank cells within a range, but treats label cells as equal to 0. The count of a population is used in calculating variance, however, so your results will be inaccurate if you inadvertently specify label cells as part of a range. If all cells in a range are empty, @VAR returns ERR.

■ **Example**
By way of illustration, suppose you had the following table of weights for a group of men, women, and children:

225	17	42	128	97	190
84	157	185	208	36	110
132	179	163	112	55	172
89	43	94	167	122	141
201	188	153	87	9	129

The formula:

@VAR(weights)

would return 3433.739, the variance—the degree to which individual weights deviate from the mean, 123.833. If your table contained the weights of only men, only women, or only children, the variance would be smaller, because the weights within any one group would fluctuate much less widely.

■ **Comments**
The @VAR function calculates population, not sample, variance. To calculate the sample variance, use the formula:

@COUNT(list)/(@COUNT(list)−1) * @VAR(list)

Variance and standard deviation (see @STD **330★**) are related statistical devices; standard deviation returns the square root of variance.

@VLOOKUP()

■ **Format**
@VLOOKUP(x,range,column number)

■ **Description**
@VLOOKUP is a special function that searches for, and returns, a value that is located within a table. Like the companion function @HLOOKUP **176★**, @VLOOKUP is useful when you have a number of alternative choices, such as tax rates, discounts, or commissions, from which you want to select different elements in different situations.

@VLOOKUP()

The function name is a reference to *vertical* table lookup, and describes the order in which 1-2-3 searches the table range: First, 1-2-3 searches vertically, comparing the value x, which you provide in the argument, to the comparison values that you have already entered in the leftmost, or index, column of the table.

If 1-2-3 finds a value equal to x, it stops on that row and goes across to the column specified by the argument's column number, and retrieves the value in the cell at the intersection of the column and row. If 1-2-3 does not find a value equal to x, it stops at the first value greater than x, *moves up* one cell to the row headed by the preceding comparison value, then moves across it to retrieve the value in the cell specified by the argument's column number.

Note: Horizontal and vertical lookup sequences are diagramed in the entry Lookup Tables 207★.

- **Procedure**

@VLOOKUP requires three arguments: x, range, and column number:

- ☐ x must be a numeric value or a reference to a cell containing a numeric value. If x is less than the smallest value in the index column, the function returns ERR. If x is greater than the largest value in the index column, 1-2-3 stops at the largest value. For example, if the index column contains the numbers 2, 4, 6, and 8, the function would return ERR if x=1, and would stop at 8 if x=9.

- ☐ The range is a reference to all of the cells in the lookup table, including the index column. The range can be specified by name or by cell addresses. The index column must contain numeric values arranged in ascending order.

- ☐ The column number designates the column from which the lookup value is to be retrieved. The column number can be 0 or a positive number. If it is 0, 1-2-3 returns a value from the index column. If the column number is 1 or greater, 1-2-3 moves across the table to the column specified, and retrieves the value in that cell.

@VLOOKUP() · /Worksheet

■ **Example**

The following example illustrates the use of a vertical lookup table.

```
C19: @VLOOKUP(C17,TABLE,C18)                                        READY
```

```
      A      B      C      D      E      F      G      H      I      J
 1  ================================================================
 2  Compound Interest -- Compounded Annually
 3  ================================================================
 4  Principal:    $100
 5                                         Period (Yrs)
 6           1     2     3     4     5     6     7     8     9
 7    9%  9.00  18.81  29.50  41.16  53.86  67.71  82.80  99.26 117.19
 8   10% 10.00  21.00  33.10  46.41  61.05  77.16  94.87 114.36 135.79
 9   12% 12.00  25.44  40.49  57.35  76.23  97.38 121.07 147.60 177.31
10   14% 14.00  29.96  48.15  68.90  92.54 119.50 150.23 185.26 225.19
11   16% 16.00  34.56  56.09  81.06 110.03 143.64 182.62 227.84 280.30
12
13
14
15
16
17  Interest:      10%
18  Years:          5
19  Function:      61.05
20
```

Note: The lookup table illustrated here could be organized as a horizontal lookup table, in which 1-2-3 would search across the first (index) row, then down to the designated row number. This format is illustrated in the entry @HLOOKUP.

With Release 2 of 1-2-3, rows and columns in a lookup table can be transposed with the /Range Transpose 316★ command.

/Worksheet

1-2-3's /Worksheet commands give you control over entire worksheets—the way they look, the parts you want to see, how you want to recalculate, even whether a worksheet continues to exist at all.

The /Worksheet commands let you assign default formats to numbers and labels (text), set column widths, insert or delete whole rows or columns, tell 1-2-3 when and how many times to recalculate formulas, assign your worksheet *global* settings, and so on. The commands are as follows; each is discussed in its own entry:

Command:	What it does:
/Worksheet Column 355★	Sets the width of a single column to a new value or to the global (default) value; in Release 2, also hides or redisplays columns.
/Worksheet Delete 357★	Deletes whole rows or columns.
/Worksheet Erase 358★	Erases the current worksheet.
/Worksheet Insert 373★	Inserts whole rows or columns.
/Worksheet Global Column-Width 359★	Sets default column widths throughout the worksheet.
/Worksheet Global Default 360★	Tells 1-2-3 about your particular system and printer; it also obtains the current worksheet default settings; in Release 2, specifies the defaults for punctuating numbers and displaying currency, date, and time; sets 1-2-3's method of using the Help file; specifies how (and whether) to display the date and time.
/Worksheet Global Format 366★	Sets the default format of numbers and calculated values.
/Worksheet Global Label-Prefix 368★	Sets the default alignment (left, center, or right) of worksheet labels.
/Worksheet Global Protection 369★	Sets the entire worksheet to protected (on) or unprotected (off) status.
/Worksheet Global Recalculation 371★	Sets the order, method, and number of times a worksheet is recalculated.
/Worksheet Global Zero 372★	Specifies whether 0 values are displayed on screen (Release 2 only).

Command:	What it does:
/Worksheet Page 374★	Specifies a page break (Release 2 only).
/Worksheet Status 374★	Displays the current global settings and the amount of available memory.
/Worksheet Titles 377★	Keeps row and/or column headings on screen while the remainder of the worksheet scrolls.
/Worksheet Window 378★	Splits the screen into two and displays parts of a worksheet in each window.

/Worksheet Column /WC

```
Worksheet Range Copy  Move File Print Graph Data System Quit
Global  Insert Delete Column Erase Titles Window Status Page
Set-Width Reset-Width Hide Display
```

■ **Description**

Note: In Release 1a of 1-2-3, the /Worksheet Column command is called /Worksheet Column-Width, and it offers two options, *Set* and *Reset*, which are equivalent to the *Set-Width* and *Reset-Width* options in Release 2.

The /Worksheet Column command lets you set the width of a single column of the current worksheet, or reset the column width to the global default setting. (To set column widths throughout the worksheet, use the /Worksheet Global Column-Width 359★ command.) Additionally, in Release 2, the /Worksheet Column command enables you to hide and redisplay the contents of one or more columns.

■ **Procedure**

When you select the /Worksheet Column command, 1-2-3, offers two column-width options, *Set-Width* and *Reset-Width*, and two column-display options, *Hide* and *Display*.

Set-Width: If you choose *Set-Width*, you can enter a value either by typing the new width in number of characters (1-2-3 allows values from 1 to 240 in Release 2 and 1 to 72 in Release 1a), or you can adjust the width of the column visually by pointing with the arrow keys.

/Worksheet Column

When a column is given a new width, 1-2-3 displays the width in brackets in the first line of the Control Panel. If you are using split windows (/Worksheet Window 378★), each window can be given its own column widths.

Reset-Width: If you choose *Reset-Width*, 1-2-3 returns the width of the column to the global column-width setting (nine characters, if you have not changed the default, or whatever value you most recently entered with the /Worksheet Global Column-Width command).

Notes on column widths: Whichever option you choose, if you make a column too narrow to display a complete value, 1-2-3 will display a row of asterisks (*) in the cell or cells affected. To eliminate the asterisks, widen the column. The values will then be displayed.

Note: This situation is not comparable to entering labels or formulas that are longer than a cell is wide. If you print a worksheet containing cells filled with asterisks, 1-2-3 prints the asterisks. In contrast, you could, if you wished, enter a 240-character label in a column one character wide, and 1-2-3 would print the entire label (if the page were wide enough and the entire label could be displayed). Or, you can print long formulas with the /Print Printer Options Other Cell Formulas 286♦ command.

To make effective use of the fairly limited display width of your computer screen, it's advisable to keep column widths as narrow as possible, though still wide enough to show the contents of each cell. Using the default setting of nine characters, your screen can display eight columns (A through H). If several columns are only a few characters wide, you can gain display space by adjusting their widths to match their contents.

In addition, varied column widths can make your printed documents more attractive and easy to read. The 1-2-3 manual, for example, recommends placing narrow blank columns between columns of data, and also suggests outlining with 1-2-3 by creating a series of narrow columns and indenting subordinate entries the required number of column widths.

Hide: You can use the *Hide*♦ option when you do not wish to print certain columns of information or, simply, when you want to hide data. When you choose *Hide*, enter the range of columns you want to hide by typing a range name or cell addresses, or by pointing with the arrow keys. The columns will be hidden without affecting the data they contain.

Once a column is hidden with this option, the cell pointer cannot be moved to the column while you are in READY 249♦ mode, and the column heading no longer appears in the reverse-video worksheet border.

Note: In POINT 249♦ mode, hidden columns are temporarily displayed. Those that have been selected for hiding are identified by an asterisk that appears next to the column letter in the worksheet border.

If you wish to hide selected cells, rather than entire columns, you can do so with the /Range Format Hidden 303♦ command, which suppresses the display of cell contents in a specified range.

Display: When you choose the *Display* option, 1-2-3 redisplays hidden columns and places an asterisk to the left of the letter of each hidden column. To make the display permanent (to "unhide" one or more columns), highlight a cell in the column or specify a range, and press Return.

/Worksheet Delete /WD

```
Worksheet  Range   Copy    Move   File   Print   Graph   Data   System   Quit
Global     Insert  Delete  Column Erase  Titles  Window  Status Page
Column     Row
```

■ **Description**

The /Worksheet Delete command removes entire columns or rows from the current worksheet. (For less comprehensive deletions, use the /Range Erase 299★ command to delete portions of columns and rows from a worksheet. To rearrange scattered parts of a worksheet, use the /Move 250★ command.)

Note: The /Worksheet Delete command must be used with care, because any information in the columns or rows being deleted will be lost, whether or not it is currently visible on screen.

■ **Procedure**

Once you select the /Worksheet Delete command, 1-2-3 presents two options: *Column* and *Row*♦. Select the option you wish to use, then either highlight a range with the cell pointer or type the addresses of the range (for example, C1..E1) to be deleted, and press Return.

/Worksheet Delete · **/Worksheet Erase**

When using the /Worksheet Delete command, bear the following points in mind:

☐ When you delete columns, all remaining columns to the right are moved left, to fill the gap; when you delete rows, all following rows are moved up.

☐ Formulas and cell ranges are adjusted to maintain their original cell references. 1-2-3 does this automatically.

☐ Formulas in other parts of the worksheet that depend on values or formulas in the cells being deleted will become invalid. References to the deleted cells will be given the value ERR.

☐ Portions of cell ranges can be deleted, as long as the top left and bottom right corners of the range are not affected. If either of these endpoints is deleted, formulas referring to the range will be given the value ERR.

/Worksheet Erase   /WE

Worksheet Range Copy Move File Print Graph Data System Quit
Global Insert Delete Column **Erase** Titles Window Status Page

■ **Description**

The /Worksheet Erase command erases the current worksheet, restores all settings to their global default (/Worksheet Global Default 360★) values, and frees the memory used to hold the deleted worksheet. There is no need to use /Worksheet Erase if all you wish to do is erase the current worksheet and load another from disk: The /File Retrieve 128★ command automatically replaces the current worksheet with the one you specify.

Note: Both the /Worksheet Erase and /File Retrieve commands cause you to lose all unsaved entries in the current worksheet. If you are updating a previously saved worksheet, you will not affect the version that exists on disk; you will, however, lose all changes and new information entered during the current session. Be certain the version you are erasing contains nothing you wish to keep.

To erase part of a worksheet, use the /Range Erase 299★ command.

- **Procedure**

Once you have selected the /Worksheet Erase command, 1-2-3 prompts for confirmation by requesting that you choose *Yes* or *No*. To cancel the command, choose *No* or press Esc. If you are certain you wish to erase the worksheet, choose *Yes*.

/Worksheet Global Column-Width   /WGC

```
Worksheet  Range  Copy    Move    File   Print    Graph    Data    System  Quit
Global     Insert Delete  Column  Erase  Titles   Window   Status  Page
Format     Label-Prefix   Column-Width   Recalculation  Protection  Default  Zero
```

- **Description**

The /Worksheet Global Column-Width command sets the widths of all columns in the current window to a new value, which can be any number of characters between 1 and 240 (72 in Release 1a). The command affects all except those columns whose widths have already been set with the *Set-Width* option of the /Worksheet Column 355★ command.

- **Procedure**

When you select /Worksheet Global Column-Width, 1-2-3 shows you the present setting and prompts you to enter a new value.

To enter a new setting, you can either type the number you wish or you can use the left and right arrow keys to vary the width. If you use the arrow keys, all columns to be affected will change as you adjust the highlighted cell. 1-2-3 also displays the current width in the Control Panel 29★.

Whether you type a new column-width setting or use the arrow keys, press Return to store the new value.

- **Comments**

If you use the /Worksheet Global Column-Width command to narrow columns that already contain information, you may see a row of asterisks (*) in a cell or cells that contain values too long to be displayed in the new, narrower width. Depending on where and how many of these cells you see, either widen individual columns with the /Worksheet Column-Width command, or set the global column width to a larger value.

To check on the global column width currently in effect, use the /Worksheet Status 374★ command.

/Worksheet Global Default /WGD

```
Worksheet Range Copy Move File Print Graph Data System Quit
Global Insert Delete Column Erase Titles Window Status Page
Format Label-Prefix Column-Width Recalculation Protection Default Zero
Printer Directory Status Update Other Quit
```

■ **Description**

The /Worksheet Global Default command is a hardware- and display-related command that tells 1-2-3 about your system and how you want to use it. It works in conjunction with a special file 117★ called 123.CNF, located on your program disk. Although you need not understand your hardware in detail to use 1-2-3, some understanding of how 1-2-3 interacts with your system (including your printer) will make life much easier for you in the event you want or need to make any changes.

The 123.CNF file: Whenever you start up 1-2-3, it reads the 123.CNF file to find out about:

☐ Your printer and interface.

☐ The margins and other settings you normally use for printed output.

☐ The directory you usually use for data files.

☐ The default settings for currency display, punctuation of numbers, use of the Help facility, and date and time displays (Release 2 only).

Because 1-2-3 can look in the 123.CNF file for this information, you do not have to repeat the same things each time you start a new session.

Computer systems and printers have many things in common, but they also differ in certain ways, too. Sometimes the difference stems from the parts of the system and the way they have been combined; at other times, a piece of equipment has certain special requirements. One immediately obvious area of difference is whether or not your system has a hard disk drive. Another is whether your printer uses a serial or a parallel interface to connect with your computer, or whether you have more than one printer connected.

Because most systems using the same software are likely to be put together (configured) very similarly, 1-2-3 comes to you with a built-in, or default, set of standard guesses about your system. These guesses are stored in 123.CNF, and they initially tell 1-2-3 to assume:

☐ Your data files are on the current drive and directory.

/Worksheet Global Default

- ☐ You have a parallel printer.
- ☐ Your printer does not issue a special character (called a line-feed) each time it encounters a carriage-return character in your document, nor does it need to receive a special sequence of characters (called a setup string) from your computer in order to print your documents.
- ☐ You use standard 8½- by 11-inch tractor-feed paper.
- ☐ Your printed documents should start and stop two lines from the top and bottom edges, and your left and right margins should each be four characters wide.

■ **The /Worksheet Global Default command**
If your system or printer is not quite as 1-2-3 assumes, or if you want your printed documents to have different margins or wider lines, you can use the /Worksheet Global Default command to tell 1-2-3 to change its assumptions. Although the /Worksheet Global Default command has less to do with your data than most 1-2-3 commands, it works just like any other. The only difference is that you may have to refer to your printer manual or another outside source for some of the printer specifications 1-2-3 will ask you for.

■ **Procedure**
When you select the /Worksheet Global Default command, as illustrated at the beginning of this entry, 1-2-3 displays its list of options (*Printer, Directory, Status, Update, Other,* and *Quit*). The following sections describe the choices for each option.

Printer: When you select *Printer♦*, you see the following choices:

Interface Auto-LF Left Right Top Bottom Pg-Length Wait Setup Name Quit

Interface: The default setting is: *(1) Parallel 1.* This is the setting you use if you have an IBM Monochrome Display Adapter or parallel printer adapter. You can change the setting to:

- ☐ *(2) Serial 1* if you have a serial printer and an RS-232C interface, such as the IBM Asynchronous Communications Adapter.
- ☐ *(3) Parallel 2* if you have more than one parallel printer attached to your system.

☐ *(4) Serial 2* if you have more than one serial printer attached to your system.

☐ *(5)* through *(8)* in Release 2 to designate the DOS devices LPT1 through LPT4. These choices apply if your computer is part of a local area network; check with your network manager for instructions.

Auto-LF: The default setting is *No.* If your printer does issue a line feed to advance the paper to the next line, change the setting to *Yes.*

You can easily tell whether or not your *Auto-LF* setting is correct. Print a short line ending in a carriage return. If the paper does not advance when your printer reaches a carriage return, or if it advances an extra line, you need to change the *Auto-LF* setting to its opposite.

Margins: The default settings, as mentioned earlier, are: *Left,* 4 characters; *Right,* 76 characters (from the left edge of the paper); *Top,* 2 lines (from the top of the paper); *Bottom,* 2 lines (from the bottom of the paper). Possible settings are: 0 to 240 for left and right margins; 0 to 32 for top and bottom margins.

The *Left* and *Right* margin settings assume normal-sized printing on paper 8½ inches wide. If you are using wide paper or condensed print, make the right margin larger.

The *Top* and *Bottom* margin settings assume your printer does not automatically avoid printing on the perforations between sheets of continuous-feed paper. If it does, set these margins to 0.

You can change the margin settings permanently by storing the new values in 123.CNF with the *Update* option described later in this entry. If you wish to change margin settings temporarily, use the /Print Printer Options 281★ command instead of /Worksheet Global Default.

Page-Length: The default value is 66 lines per printed page, but can be any number between 10 (20 in Release 1a) and 100. The default value assumes a printer that does not automatically avoid printing on the perforations in continuous-feed paper. If your printer skips over the perforations, shorten the page length to about 60 lines per page.

Wait: The default value is *No.* Change to *Yes* if you feed paper into your printer one sheet at a time.

Setup: The default here is a blank string—no setup information. This means your printer does not require special "initializing" information. Setup strings are used for another purpose, too: To turn on special printing modes, such as condensed type.

1-2-3 does not provide choices here, because setup instructions (control codes) vary from printer to printer. To find out what instructions you need to transmit, you must refer to your printer manual. 1-2-3 does, however, require that you enter setup strings in a certain format—three digits preceded by a backslash, such as \044. The entries /Print Printer Options and LICS 203★ provide some information, as does your 1-2-3 manual.

Name: This Release 2 option allows you to specify the printer you wish to use, if you have more than one. If you use this option, be certain to specify the correct interface. The default is the first printer you installed.

Directory♦: 1-2-3 initially assumes that the current directory is the default directory for data files. Use this option if you wish to change to a different data drive or you want to change the current directory (DOS versions 2 and above only).

Status: The *Status* option shows you the default configuration settings that are currently in effect. If you choose this option, press any key to return to the Default menu.

Update: The *Update♦* option tells 1-2-3 to store new settings you have entered with the *Printer, Directory,* and *Other* options in the 123.CNF file. When you choose *Update,* you change the default settings until the next time you update the 123.CNF file.

If you use *Update*, remember that 1-2-3 must store your changes on the program disk if you have a system with two floppy disk drives. If you have covered the write-protect notch, uncover it temporarily so that 1-2-3 can modify the 123.CNF file for you.

Other International: In Release 2, the *Other International* option enables you to specify the way in which numbers are punctuated and currency, date, and time are displayed. This option offers four choices, *Punctuation, Currency, Date,* and *Time,* and a *Quit* option that allows you to leave the menu.

Punctuation: This option lets you choose the type of separators to be used in decimal fractions and numbers over 1000. The choices you make here also determine which character you will use in separating arguments

/Worksheet Global Default

within functions and macro commands. The choices are shown in the following table:

Choice:	Point separator:	Argument separator:	Thousands separator:
(A)	Period	Comma	Comma
(B)	Comma	Period	Period
(C)	Period	Semicolon	Comma
(D)	Comma	Semicolon	Period
(E)	Period	Comma	Blank space
(F)	Comma	Period	Blank space
(G)	Period	Semicolon	Blank space
(H)	Comma	Semicolon	Blank space

Currency: This option lets you choose the currency symbol you wish to use, and to specify whether the symbol should precede or follow currency amounts. The default setting is a dollar sign ($), preceding the amount, but any monetary symbol in the Lotus International Character Set can be used. Those available are shown in the entry LICS and in your 1-2-3 manual.

Date♦: This option enables you to display the date in international format. There are two such formats, D4 and D5, and they are the same, except that D4 displays month, day, and year, while D5 displays month and day only. The choices are as follows (D4 is shown):

Choice:	Format:	Example:
(A)	MM/DD/YY	12/11/80
(B)	DD/MM/YY	11/12/80
(C)	DD.MM.YY	11.12.80
(D)	YY-MM-DD	80-12-11

Note: The default setting is *(A)*. The format you choose here is the one you must use if you use an international format with the @DATEVALUE 96★ function. This is also the format in which the date is displayed if you specify *International* with the /Worksheet Global Default Other Clock command that is described on the next page.

/Worksheet Global Default

Time♦: This option is similar to *Date*, and allows you to display the time in international format. There are two international time formats, D8 and D9. Both use a 24-hour clock; D8 displays seconds, whereas D9 does not. The forms are as follows (D8 is shown):

Choice:	Format:	Example:
(A)	HH:MM:SS	08:14:30
(B)	HH.MM.SS	08.14.30
(C)	HH,MM,SS	08,14,30
(D)	HHhMMmSSs	08h14m30s

Note: The default setting is *(A)*. The format you choose here is the one you must use if you use an international format with the @TIMEVALUE 342★ function. This is also the format in which the time is displayed if you specify *International* with the /Worksheet Global Default Other Clock command described below.

Other Help: The *Other Help♦* option, in Release 2 only, lets you determine how 1-2-3 will access the Help facility. The choices are *Instant* and *Removable*.

Instant means that 1-2-3 will open the Help file when you press the F1 [Help] 144♦ key, and keep the file open for immediate access throughout your work session. If you choose this option, the disk containing the Help file must remain in the program drive.

Removable means that 1-2-3 closes the Help file each time you finish using the Help facility. If you choose this option, the disk containing the Help file need not remain in the program drive, but access to the Help facility will be slower.

Other Clock: The *Other Clock* option, also in Release 2 only, lets you specify whether or not, and in what format, the time and date are to be displayed in the lower left-hand corner of the screen. You have three choices: *Standard*, *International*, and *None*.

Choose *Standard*, which is the default, to display the date and time in the form DD-MMM-YY (for example, 25-Dec-86) and HH:MM AM/PM.

Choose *International* to display the date in long international format (month, day, and year) and the time in short international format (hours and minutes), based on a 24-hour clock.

Choose *None* to suppress display of the date and time.

/Worksheet Global Default · **/Worksheet Global Format**

Quit: *Quit* is your exit command from the Default menu. Use it when you are through making changes to your configuration settings or to avoid making permanent changes to 123.CNF after selecting the *Update* option.

/Worksheet Global Format /WGF

```
Worksheet Range    Copy    Move     File    Print     Graph    Data    System    Quit
Global    Insert   Delete  Column   Erase   Titles    Window   Status  Page
Format    Label-Prefix  Column-Width  Recalculation  Protection  Default  Zero
Fixed     Scientific  Currency  ,  General  +/-  Percent  Date  Text  Hidden
```

- **Description**

The /Worksheet Global Format command determines the standard on-screen appearance of all numbers and calculated values displayed in a single window, *other than* those you have already formatted with the /Range Format 300★ command. You can think of the /Worksheet Global Format command as something of an overlay that "tells" numbers what to look like, but does not affect their actual values in any way.

Release 2 of 1-2-3 offers two options not available in Release 1a: *Date*, which enables you to format the appearance of the date and time, and *Hidden*, which suppresses the display of cell contents.

You can use the /Worksheet Global Format command either to format numeric values for whatever appearance you use most often (decimals, dollars, and so on) or to temporarily set the display to whatever format you want for a particular worksheet (scientific notation, perhaps).

Regardless of when or how you use the /Worksheet Global Format command, bear the following two points in mind:

☐ 1-2-3 remembers and stores actual values to about 15 decimal places. Thus, even if you were to display the value 1⅓ as 1.33, 1-2-3 would save and use the value as 1.333333333333334.

☐ Whether you use the /Worksheet Global Format command to format the appearance of numbers before or after entering formulas, the results of the formula calculations will be displayed in the current format, unless you have specified another appearance with /Range Format.

/Worksheet Global Format

■ **Procedure**

When you select the /Worksheet Global Format command, 1-2-3 presents you with the options shown at the beginning of this entry. The options and the manner in which you use them are the same as those in the /Range Format command. A complete list, including illustrations, is given in that entry; the following is an abbreviated discussion:

Fixed: Displays the number of decimal places you specify, from 0 to 15.

Scientific: Displays numbers in scientific (exponential) format. The number being multiplied can have up to 15 decimal places; the exponent can be any number from −99 to +99.

Currency: Displays numbers as monetary values.

Comma (,): Displays numbers just as *Currency* does, but without the currency symbol.

General: Displays numbers in 1-2-3's default format:

☐ Zeros at the ends of decimal numbers are not displayed.

☐ Whole numbers containing more than 15 digits and/or numbers wider than the column width minus one character are shown in scientific notation.

Note: 1-2-3 eliminates decimal places, if necessary, in converting numbers to scientific notation for display in narrow columns. This results in a loss of precision in the displayed format. 1-2-3 still stores the actual value, however, so you need not worry about precision in your calculations. As with all other numeric formats, any numbers too wide to be displayed, even in scientific notation, in the existing column width are replaced by asterisks on screen.

Plus/minus (+/−): Converts each unit in a number into a symbol: a plus sign if the number is positive, a minus sign if the number is negative, or a period (.) if the number is 0 or between −1 and 1.

Percent: Displays numbers as percentages with up to 15 decimal places.

Date: Displays the date and time in the specified format (see the /Range Format command).

Text: Displays formulas, rather than formula values. When you choose *Text*, the numbers in your worksheet are displayed in *General* format.

Hidden: Hides cell contents so they are not displayed.

- **Comments**

  The /Worksheet Global Format command affects numeric values only. If you wish to format text, use the /Worksheet Global Label-Prefix command. To tailor the appearance of individual values or ranges of values, use /Range Format—for example, to format a single column for percentages in a worksheet that displays all numbers as dollar values.

/Worksheet Global Label-Prefix   /WGL

```
Worksheet Range Copy Move File Print Graph Data System Quit
Global  Insert Delete Column Erase Titles Window Status Page
Format  Label-Prefix Column-Width Recalculation Protection Default Zero
Left Right Center
```

- **Description**

  The /Worksheet Global Label-Prefix command sets the standard alignment (left, center, or right) of all labels entered after the command has been carried out. In other words, if the /Worksheet Global Label-Prefix command is used to change label alignment from left to right, all labels entered prior to the change will remain left-aligned, but all labels entered after the change will be right-aligned.

  Using the /Worksheet Global Label-Prefix command tells 1-2-3 to automatically assign the new label prefix character to any labels you type. The prefix characters are:

Character:	Meaning:
'(apostrophe)	Left-aligned (the default)
"(double quotation mark)	Right-aligned
^ (caret mark)	Centered

  The global prefix character is visible in the Control Panel 29★ whenever you highlight the cell containing a label, but you do not see the prefix character in the cell itself in the worksheet display.

1-2-3 offers one additional prefix character, a backslash (\), that you can use to repeat a label across a cell (to create dashed lines, for example, that visually set off portions of a worksheet). The backslash is not an option with the /Worksheet Global Label-Prefix command: It's doubtful that you would ever need to repeat every label you type across every cell on your worksheet.

To override the global setting, precede any label you type with the appropriate prefix character.

To change the alignment of an existing label, use the /Range Label 308★ command, which affects only labels already typed.

- **Comments**

The /Worksheet Global Label-Prefix command controls the alignment of text only, not numbers. To format numbers, you use the /Worksheet Global Format command. 1-2-3 does not, however, offer you a way to align numbers at the left, right, or center of the cells they are in unless you enter those numbers as labels by preceding them with a label-prefix character or by converting them to labels—for example with the Release 2 @STRING 334★ function or the {CONTENTS} 229♦ macro command. If you do this, bear in mind that such numbers are not treated as numeric values and thus cannot be used in your calculations.

/Worksheet Global Protection   /WGP

```
Worksheet Range Copy Move File Print Graph Data System Quit
Global Insert Delete Column Erase Titles Window Status Page
Format Label-Prefix Column-Width Recalculation Protection Default Zero
Enable Disable
```

- **Description**

The /Worksheet Global Protection command implements cell protection so that cell contents are protected from being changed (unless they have been explicitly unprotected with the /Range Unprotect 317★ command).

- **Procedure**

When you choose the /Worksheet Global Protection command, 1-2-3 displays two options: *Enable* and *Disable*.

Enable♦ protects all cells in the worksheet except those from which you have removed protection with the /Range Unprotect command.

Disable turns off the cell-protection feature.

/Worksheet Global Protection

When you begin work on a new worksheet, the /Worksheet Global Protection status is disabled, but each cell is protected by default. The net effect is that you protect every cell in the worksheet by choosing the *Enable* option of the /Worksheet Global Protection command. In order to protect only the cells you want to keep from being changed, do the following:

1. Choose the /Worksheet Global Protection command and select the *Enable* option.
2. Choose the /Range Unprotect command and remove protection from those cells that can be changed.
3. Later, if you decide that you need to remove protection from some cells, or apply protection to others, you can do so by using the /Range Unprotect or /Range Protect 314★ commands.

Once you have protected a worksheet, the information is saved as part of the file and remains in effect each time you load the worksheet (with the /File Retrieve 128★ command).

To check on the current protection status, as well as all other global worksheet settings, use the /Worksheet Status 374★ command. The first line of the Control Panel 29★ shows the status of the current cell by preceding the cell contents with a capital U if it is unprotected.

If you apply protection to a worksheet, bear the following points in mind:

☐ You cannot delete columns or rows that contain protected cells.

☐ Enabling protection with /Worksheet Global Protection does not change the status of cells that have been unprotected with the /Range Unprotect command.

☐ To further secure protected cells in a worksheet, you can use the /Range Input 304★ command to permit access to a range of unprotected cells only. The /Range Input command prevents the cell pointer from being moved outside the specified range or to protected cells.

If you use Release 2 of 1-2-3, you can protect an entire worksheet file by assigning it a password with the /File Save 130★ command.

/Worksheet Global Recalculation /WGR

```
Worksheet  Range  Copy  Move  File  Print  Graph  Data  System  Quit
Global  Insert  Delete  Column  Erase  Titles  Window  Status  Page
Format  Label-Prefix  Column-Width  Recalculation  Protection  Default  Zero
Natural  Columnwise  Rowwise  Automatic  Manual  Iteration
```

- **Description**

  The /Worksheet Global Recalculation command gives you control over when, how, and how many times 1-2-3 recalculates the formulas in a worksheet. By using the /Worksheet Global Recalculation command, you can restrict recalculation only to those times you want the worksheet updated, or you can tell 1-2-3 to calculate row by row or column by column, or you can specify the number of times you want recalculation to occur (this is useful for worksheets built with circular references).

- **Procedure**

  When you choose the /Worksheet Global Recalculation command, 1-2-3 offers the six options shown at the beginning of this entry. *Natural*, *Columnwise*, and *Rowwise* let you control the order in which formulas are recalculated. *Automatic* and *Manual* let you control when formulas are recalculated. *Iteration* lets you control the number of times 1-2-3 loops through the formulas in one recalculation session.

  Recalculation order: When you create a worksheet, more often than not you create formulas that are dependent on values calculated by other formulas. In complex worksheets, this dependency can "echo" through one or more series of related formulas.

  When 1-2-3 recalculates formulas, it observes the *Natural* order and calculates needed values before moving on to the formulas that depend on those values. If you have inadvertently created a circular reference, 1-2-3 notifies you of your mistake by displaying the word CIRC in the bottom right corner of the screen. (For details on circular references, see the entry Iteration 188★.)

  Sometimes, however, you will want 1-2-3 to recalculate a worksheet in other than natural order. When this happens, you can use the *Columnwise* or *Rowwise* options to tell 1-2-3 to recalculate down columns or across rows, beginning at cell A1 (see the entry Macro Commands 225★ for information on two macro keywords, {RECALC} and {RECALCCOL}, that provide macro control over recalculating portions of a worksheet).

/Worksheet Global Recalculation · /Worksheet Global Zero

Recalculation method: 1-2-3 normally recalculates a worksheet whenever you enter or change a value. With large or complex worksheets, however, this continuous updating can become time-consuming and may be unnecessary (for example, when you are simply entering data). To control when recalculation occurs, change the /Worksheet Global Recalculation setting from *Automatic* to *Manual*. When you want the worksheet recalculated, press the F9 [Calc] **144◆** function key. With recalculation set to *Manual*, you will see the word CALC **330◆** appear in the lower right corner of the screen when you change a value but do not recalculate the worksheet. 1-2-3 displays this message as a reminder that the worksheet has been changed, but not updated.

Iteration: Iteration is covered in an entry of its own. Briefly, however, iteration becomes necessary when you deliberately build circular references into a worksheet. (Circular references are formulas that depend on values they, themselves, calculate.) In order to gain the result you want, you must tell 1-2-3 to recalculate the formulas more than once. Each time the formulas are recalculated, their values become more and more precise.

The *Iteration* option lets you tell 1-2-3 how many times to recalculate such formulas. You can specify any number of iterations from 1 to 50.

/Worksheet Global Zero /WGZ

```
Worksheet Range Copy Move File Print Graph Data System Quit
Global Insert Delete Column Erase Titles Window Status Page
Format Label-Prefix Column-Width Recalculation Protection Default Zero
No Yes
```

- **Description**

The /Worksheet Global Zero command is available in Release 2 of 1-2-3 only. You use this command to specify whether or not values equal to 0 are displayed on screen.

- **Procedure**

When you select the /Worksheet Global Zero command, 1-2-3 offers the two choices *Yes* and *No*. Choose *Yes* to keep zero values from being displayed; choose *No* (the default) to have those values displayed.

■ **Comments**

The /Worksheet Global Zero command can be very helpful in keeping a screen from becoming cluttered with zeros. It is, however, potentially dangerous in that a cell that looks empty may, in fact, contain the value 0, and that value may inadvertently be replaced by another entry you make. To protect non-displayed zeros from being overwritten, protect their contents with the /Worksheet Global Protection 369★ and /Range Protect 314★ commands. (/Range Protect reverses the effect of the /Range Unprotect 317★ command.) Alternatively, you may want to suppress the display of those cells with the /Worksheet Column Hide 356◆ or /Range Format Hidden 303◆ commands.

/Worksheet Insert /WI

```
Worksheet  Range   Copy    Move   Print  Graph   Data  System  Quit
Global     Insert  Delete  Column Erase  Titles  Window Status Page
Column     Row
```

■ **Description**

The /Worksheet Insert command inserts new (blank) rows or columns into the current worksheet, either above (rows) or to the left (columns) of the cell pointer. Rows and columns inserted into a worksheet have the global settings specified with the /Worksheet Global Default 360★ command, so you must apply any other formatting or cell widths you require.

The /Worksheet Insert command is useful in finalizing the appearance of a worksheet prior to printing, or (as often happens) in inserting rows or columns of information you had previously overlooked or entered elsewhere.

The command itself is quite simple to use, because 1-2-3 automatically adjusts any existing cell or range references to accommodate the inserted rows or columns.

■ **Procedure**

When you choose the /Worksheet Insert command, 1-2-3 offers two options: *Column* and *Row*. Select the appropriate choice and press Return.

Note: Because you must apply new formatting to inserted rows and columns, you may sometimes find it easier and faster to move or copy already formatted rows or columns to a new location. The /Move 250★ and /Copy 31★ commands carry with them all current formatting, and if your worksheet is still at a fairly empty, preliminary stage, you may find it faster to copy or move a row or column.

/Worksheet Page /WP

```
Worksheet Range Copy Move File Print Graph Data System Quit
Global Insert Delete Column Erase Titles Window Status Page
```

- **Description**

    The /Worksheet Page command is available in Release 2 of 1-2-3 only. You can use it to place a page break in a worksheet at the location of the cell pointer.

- **Procedure**

    Before you select the /Worksheet Page command, move the cell pointer to the row at which you want to begin a new page. Once you select the command, all you need do is press Return. 1-2-3 will insert a dummy row into the worksheet and mark the page break by displaying two colons (::). This page break will override the /Print Printer Options Page-Length 285♦ setting.

    You can use this command to advantage when printing lengthy worksheets or those that are separated into distinct sections. By inserting page breaks where you want them, you can ensure that segments of a worksheet are printed in coherent units.

    When you use this command, the row indicating the page break is simply there to hold the page break. You should not use the row for any data, because none will be printed.

    If you inadvertently insert a page break, or decide you do not need one you have inserted, erase the marker with the /Range Erase 299★ command, overwrite it with another entry, or use the /Worksheet Delete Row 357♦ command to remove the dummy row.

/Worksheet Status /WS

```
Worksheet Range Copy Move File Print Graph Data System Quit
Global Insert Delete Column Erase Titles Window Status Page
```

- **Description**

    The /Worksheet Status command displays a full-screen status report that tells you how much memory is currently available for use, and what your current global worksheet settings are. In addition, in Release 2, the report tells you whether 1-2-3 has detected a circular reference in the worksheet and, if so, where the first occurrence is. Unlike other commands, the /Worksheet Status command is display-only: It doesn't *do* anything to your current worksheet.

▪ Procedure

When you choose the /Worksheet Status command, 1-2-3 displays a status report like this one:

STAT

```
Available Memory:
  Conventional..... 409088 of 409088 Bytes (100%)
  Expanded......... (None)

Math Co-processor: (None)

Recalculation:
  Method.......... Automatic
  Order........... Natural
  Iterations...... 1

Circular Reference: (None)

Cell Display:
  Format.......... (G)
  Label-Prefix.... '
  Column-Width.... 9
  Zero Suppression. Off

Global Protection: Off
```

Here, *Recalculation* is set to *Automatic* and the *Natural* order of recalculation. These are the initial settings for the /Worksheet Global Recalculation **371★** command.

Format refers to the on-screen appearance of numbers; the *(G)* in this example stands for the initial *General* setting of the /Worksheet Global Format **366★** command.

Label-Prefix refers to the standard alignment (left, right, or center) given to labels unless you specify otherwise. The alignment is indicated by a label prefix; the prefix (') shown in the example is the initial setting of the /Worksheet Global Label-Prefix **368★** command.

Column-Width tells you the standard column width, in characters, for the current worksheet. *9* is the initial setting of the /Worksheet Global Column-Width **359★** command.

Zero Suppression (Release 2 only) tells whether 1-2-3 displays zeros on screen. The default is suppression off—zeros are displayed (Release 2 only).

Available Memory tells you how much memory remains free for your use. This number varies, depending on the total amount of memory your computer has and on the amount of memory being used by the current worksheet. If your system contains expanded memory, that is reported as well.

Global Protection tells you whether or not you have enabled 1-2-3's protection facility. *Off* is the initial setting of the /Worksheet Global Protection 369★ command.

- **Comments**

Other than for checking on the settings currently in effect, the /Worksheet Status command is particularly helpful in two areas:

- ☐ Tracking down circular references. This feature is in Release 2, and 1-2-3's display of the cell address in which it has detected a circular reference considerably eases the task of finding and correcting an inadvertent circular reference.

- ☐ Determining whether your computer has enough memory available for you to enlarge a worksheet or, perhaps, combine another one with it (with the /File Combine 121★ command). You may want to use the /Worksheet Status command if you are using a fairly limited amount of RAM, such as 256K, along with a very large or complicated worksheet.

  When you are nearing the limit of available memory, you will notice 1-2-3 slows down and takes longer to recalculate. If this happens, try to make the worksheet more compact by: rearranging the worksheet to eliminate or minimize large blocks of unused space; deleting unnecessary cell ranges and (if they are formatted), eliminating the formatting; then saving and retrieving the altered worksheet.

  The point of making a worksheet more compact is simple: The closer the bottom right corner of the active area is to cell A1, the less memory your worksheet requires.

/Worksheet Titles /WT

```
Worksheet  Range  Copy  Move  File  Print  Graph  Data  System  Quit
Global  Insert  Delete  Column  Erase  Titles  Window  Status  Page
Both  Horizontal  Vertical  Clear
```

- **Description**

   The /Worksheet Titles command enables you to keep designated columns, rows, or both on screen at all times. Use /Worksheet Titles when you want to keep category headings or labels on the screen as you scroll through data. If you are using a split screen (/Worksheet Window 378★), titles can be set separately for each window.

- **Procedure**

   Before you select the /Worksheet Titles command, move the cell pointer to a location immediately below or to the right of the rows or columns you want to freeze on screen. Then choose the /Worksheet Titles command, and 1-2-3 will present four options: *Both*, *Horizontal*, *Vertical*, and *Clear*. Select:

   □ *Both* to freeze both the rows above the cell pointer and the columns to the left of it. When you choose this option, the current cell will become the top left-hand corner cell to which the Home key jumps.

   □ *Horizontal* to freeze the rows above the current location of the cell pointer.

   □ *Vertical* to freeze the columns to the left of the current location of the cell pointer.

   □ *Clear* to unfreeze previously specified rows or columns.

   When you freeze rows, columns, or both, the pointer-movement keys will not move the pointer into the titles area when you are in READY 249♦ mode. To highlight a cell in this area, use the F5 [Goto] 144♦ key instead.

   When you are in POINT mode, however—indicating a range during a command or entering a formula—the pointer-movement keys *will* move the cell pointer into the titles area. This may temporarily cause extra copies of your titles to appear. To eliminate them, scroll away from the area when you return to READY mode, and then scroll back again.

/Worksheet Window

/Worksheet Window /WW

Worksheet Range Copy Move File Print Graph Data System Quit
Global Insert Delete Column Erase Titles **Window** Status Page
Horizontal Vertical Sync Unsync Clear

■ **Description**

The /Worksheet Window command enables you to split the display screen into two, either horizontally or vertically, so you can view different parts of a single worksheet. You can switch between the two windows by pressing the F6 [Window] **144◆** key.

You can give different global formats or column widths to each window, so /Worksheet Window makes it easy to compare two sets of data or to display values in one window and the formulas that work on them in the other (use the *Text* option of the /Worksheet Global Format command **366★** to display the formulas).

In addition, the /Worksheet Window command allows you to scroll each window independently or in tandem. You can also make the windows different sizes.

■ **Procedure**

When you choose the /Worksheet Window command, 1-2-3 offers the following choices: *Horizontal* and *Vertical* to split the screen; *Sync* and *Unsync* to scroll the windows; and *Clear* to close the second window.

Initially, both windows have the same column widths and global formats. You can change the settings in either or both windows, but bear in mind that when you *Clear* the extra window from the screen, the titles, column widths, global formats, and global label prefixes will return to those specified for the original (top or left-hand) window.

Here are the details on each /Worksheet Window command option:

☐ *Horizontal* splits the screen from side to side, above the location of the cell pointer. The two resulting windows display a total of 19 rows of data, rather than the 20 you see in a single window, because one row is needed to display the border of the second window.

- You can split the screen at any point, as long as the smaller window can display at least one row. When 1-2-3 splits the screen horizontally, it automatically moves the cell pointer to the bottom of the first (top) window. To move the pointer back and forth, use the F6 function key.

- *Vertical* splits the window from top to bottom, along the column just left of the cell pointer. You can split the screen at any point, as long as the smaller window can display at least one column. When you split the screen vertically, the left border of the second window takes up an extra four spaces. Unlike splitting the window horizontally, however, you do not lose any display space, because 1-2-3 shifts the second window four spaces farther toward the right edge of the screen. When you split the window vertically, 1-2-3 automatically moves the cell pointer to the right edge of the first (left-hand) window. To move the pointer back and forth, use the F6 function key.

- *Sync*, the default setting, synchronizes scrolling in both windows. If the screen is split horizontally, *Sync* keeps the same columns in both windows, but it allows you to scroll up and down to view different rows. If the screen is split vertically, *Sync* keeps the same rows in both windows, but it allows you to scroll from side to side to view different columns.

- *Unsync* unsynchronizes the scrolling in the two windows so that each scrolls independently of the other. With unsynchronized windows, you can use one to wander wherever you wish in a worksheet, while the information in the other window remains stationary.

- *Clear* closes the second window and returns column widths and text and numeric formats to the settings specified for the original (upper or left-hand) window.

/X

/X

■ **Description**

/X represents a number of special commands used in constructing macros **211★**. The /X commands are present in both Release 1a and Release 2. In Release 2, however, they are supplemented by (and can be used interchangeably with) macro commands **225★** you enter as keywords enclosed in braces. For example, /XR is equivalent to the Release 2 macro command {RETURN}, and either can be used to return from a subroutine to the main macro.

Release 1a is restricted to the use of the /X commands only.

■ **List of commands**

The following paragraphs briefly describe each of the /X commands and command formats, and give their equivalents in Release 2.

/XI♦: /XI is equivalent to the {IF} **234♦** macro command. It is entered in the form /XIcondition~ ... and represents a logical if-then-else statement in which the condition is evaluated and returns a true or a false value. If the condition is true, 1-2-3 executes the macro instructions immediately following the /XI statement; if the condition is false, 1-2-3 executes the macro instructions in the cell immediately below the /XI statement.

/XG♦: /XG is equivalent to the {BRANCH} **228♦** command. It is entered in the form /XGlocation~ and tells 1-2-3 to branch to, and execute, the macro instructions at another location in the worksheet. Like {BRANCH}, the /XG command does not return to the main macro unless you end the routine instructions with another /XG command.

/XQ♦: /XQ is equivalent to the {QUIT} **237♦** command. It is entered in the form /XQ. When 1-2-3 encounters a /XQ command in a macro, it terminates macro execution and returns control to the keyboard.

/XC♦: /XC is equivalent to the {SUBROUTINE_NAME} **241♦** command. It is entered in the form /XClocation~ and causes 1-2-3 to execute the subroutine instructions at the location you specify. 1-2-3 returns to the main macro when it encounters either /XR or the end of the subroutine.

/XR♦: /XR is equivalent to the {RETURN} **240♦** command. It is entered in the form /XR and causes 1-2-3 to return from a subroutine to the instructions in the cell immediately below the /XC statement in the main macro.

/XL♦: /XL is equivalent to the {GETLABEL} 233♦ command. It is entered in the form */XLmessage~location~*. One of three /X commands that enable you to construct interactive macros (macros that pause for user entry), /XL displays your message in the Control Panel and waits for input from the keyboard. When the input is received, it places the typed characters as a left-aligned label in the cell specified as the location; if no location is specified, the keystrokes are entered in the currently highlighted cell.

Note: /XL allows you to display a message that's up to 39 characters long; {GETLABEL} allows a message up to 80 characters long.

/XN♦: /XN is equivalent to the {GETNUMBER} 233♦ command. It is entered in the form */XNmessage~location~*. /XN operates like /XL, but accepts numeric values, rather than text. With /XN, a macro user can enter numbers, formulas, and functions; range names are also accepted. /XN has the additional feature of validating input. If something other than a valid numeric value is entered, /XN will refuse to accept it. This is different from the {GETNUMBER} approach—{GETNUMBER} will put the ERR value in the location when input is invalid.

Note: Like /XL, /XN allows a message up to 39 characters long, whereas the command {GETNUMBER} allows up to 80 characters.

/XM♦: /XM is equivalent to the {MENUBRANCH} 235♦ command. It is entered in the form */XMlocation~*. This command enables you to create customized menus of up to eight items from which users can choose. When 1-2-3 encounters a /XM command, it goes to the location specified, displays the menu entered there, pauses for the user to make a choice, then executes the macro instructions appropriate to the menu selection. The menu itself is entered as a range of rows and columns, as follows:

- Each cell in the top row contains a menu choice.
- Each cell in the second row contains a description of the menu choice immediately above it.
- Each cell in the third and subsequent rows contains either the macro instructions appropriate for the menu choice above, or a branch to supporting macro code.

(More details and an illustration of a customized menu can be found in the entry Macro Commands.)

/X · @YEAR()

■ **Examples**

The following examples illustrate the same interactive macro written in two ways. The first uses the /X commands; the second uses the equivalent Release 2 macro commands.

```
P20:                                                          READY

         P    Q    R    S    T    U    V    W
1
2        \i        /xlDate: ~a1~
3                  /xnInvoice Number: ~a2~
4                  /xnPurchase Order #: ~a3~
5                  /xlDepartment: ~a4~
6                  /xnAmount: ~a5~
7                  /xlDescription: ~a6~
8                  /xgRecord_Routine~
9
10       \i        {GETLABEL "Date: ",a1}
11                 {GETNUMBER "Invoice Number: ",a3}
12                 {GETNUMBER "Purchase Order #: ",a4}
13                 {GETLABEL "Department: ",a4}
14                 {GETNUMBER "Amount: ",a5}
15                 {GETLABEL "Description: ",a6}
16                 {BRANCH Record_Routine}
17
```

@YEAR()

■ **Format**

@YEAR(date number)

■ **Description**

@YEAR is a date function that returns the number of the year (0 to 199) represented by a specific date serial number.

■ **Procedure**

The argument of the @YEAR function must be a five-digit date serial number representing the number of days elapsed since December 31, 1899. The lowest number is 00001, for January 1, 1900, and the highest is 73050, for December 31, 2099. As with 1-2-3's other date functions, it is not necessary to try and determine the serial number of the date you wish to specify. The @DATE 92★, @DATEVALUE 96★, and @NOW 258★ functions generate the number for you.

The argument must be numeric, but can be entered as a number, a cell reference, or a value calculated by another formula or function. For example:

   @YEAR(29675)

returns 81, because 29675 is the serial number of March 30, 1981.

382

Index

A

@@() function, 1–2
@ABS() function, 2
Absolute values, 2
Access System, 3–4, 62, 119
  converting other program files into, 119
  File-Manager, 119
  PrintGraph program, 271–78
  Translate utility, 342–46
@ACOS() function, 4–5
Alt-F1 [Compose], 144, 198
Alt-F2 [Step], 198
Arguments
  logical, 185–86
  string, 114–15
Arrow keys, 267
ASCII, 5–6
  characters into numbers, 25
  Compose characters, 25
  files, formatting, 61–65
  non-printing characters, 22
  numbers into characters, 22
  uppercase and lowercase characters, 22
@ASIN() function, 6–7
@ATAN() function, 7–8
@ATAN2() function, 8–9
@AVG() function, 9–10

B

Backspace key, 15, 110, 196
Backtab, 197, 267

Bar graphs, 149, 152, 173
  data ranges, 153
  label ranges, 174
  symbols used in, 155
Baud rate, 276
{BEEP} command, 227
Bin, 12
{BLANK} command, 228
Boldfacing, 284
Borders, 270
{BRANCH} command, 228
{BREAKOFF} command, 228
{BREAKON} command, 228

C

Caps Lock key, 329
@CELL() function, 18–21
  attribute keywords, 18
@CELLPOINTER() function, 21
  and macros, 21
Cells, 249, 262, 265–67
  anchor, 17, 268–69, 293–94
  assigning names, 16
  copying, 16, 31–33
  current, 14, 17, 30
  destination, 31–33
  editing, 15, 15, 110–11
  entries, 14
  formatting, displaying, 18–21
  free, 293–94
  hiding, 16, 315
  inserting characters into, 15
  jumping past blocks of, 268
  labels, 10
  moving, 16

385

Index

Cells *(continued)*
  moving pointer to, 144
  named, moving cells from, 253–55
  overwriting, 32
  pointer, 14
  printing contents of, 286
  protecting, 16
  ranges, 16–17
  references, 17–18
    absolute, 17, 37–38
    mixed, 18, 38–40
    relative, 17, 37, 39
  referring to, 14
  replacing contents, 15
  source, 31–33
  unprotecting, 16
  width, 13–14
    default, 13
Characters, initial capitalization of, 288
@CHAR() function, 22
CheckDisk command (DOS), 119
@CHOOSE() function, 23–24
Circular references, 188–94
{CLOSE} command, 228
@CODE() function, 25
@COLS() function, 26
Columns, 26–28
  deleting, 28, 354
  hidden, 28
    displaying, 28
    printing, 28
  inserting, 27, 354
    blank, 373
  transposing in ranges, 28
  width, 354–57
    changing, 26–27
    default settings, 354
Compressed print, 284
Configuration file, 29
{CONTENTS} command, 229
Control Panel, 14, 27, 29–31, 129
/Copy command, 31–40
Copy command (DOS), 119
Copying
  cells, 31–33

Copying *(continued)*
  formulas, 37–40
  ranges, 33–36
@COS() function, 40–41
@COUNT() function, 10, 42
@CTERM() function, 43
Ctrl-break key combination, 15
Ctrl-right arrow key combination, 111, 197

D

Databases, 44–51
  counting records in, 99–101
  criterion ranges, 47–49
    arranging, 49
    types of, 47–48
  functions, 146
  input ranges, 46
  maximum values in single field, 102–3
  mean values, 97–98
  minimum values in, 104–5
  output ranges, 50
  population standard deviation in, 105–6
  population variance in, 108–9
  sum of values in single field, 107–8
  using, 46
/Data commands, 51
/Data Distribution command, 12, 52–55
  bin range, 53–55
/Data Fill command, 56–58
/Data Matrix command, 59–61
/Data Parse command, 61–65
/Data Query commands, 65–74
  criterion ranges, 66–69
  /Data Query Delete, 65, 73–74
  /Data Query Extract, 65, 71–72
  /Data Query Find, 65, 70–71
  /Data Query Unique, 65, 73
  input ranges, 66
  output ranges, 70
  quitting, 74
/Data Regression command, 74–76

Index

/Data Sort command, 76–79
/Data Table 1, 80–83, 87–89,
/Data Table 2, 83–86, 89–92
Data tables, 79–86
@DATE() function, 92–93
Date-related analyses, 93–95
Dates
  adding, 93
  converting into serial numbers, 93–95
  converting text strings into serial numbers; 96, 99
  creating daily calendars, 95
  formatting, 92–93
  in formulas, 96
  functions, 94
  sorting, 92, 93
  strings, 96
  subtracting, 93
@DATEVALUE() function, 96
@DAVG() function, 97–98
  criterion range, 97
  input range, 97
  offset, 97
@DAY() function, 98–99
dBASE II and III files, converting, 126, 346
@DCOUNT() function, 99–101
  criterion range, 100–101
  input range, 100
  offset, 100
@DDB() function, 101–2
{DEFINE} command, 230
Del (Delete) key, 110, 197
DIF (Data Interchange Format) files, 342, 346
Directories, 125
  changing, 123–24
Disks
  comparing, 119
  copying, 119
  Disk-Manager, 119
  formatting, 119
{DISPATCH} command, 230
@DMAX() function, 102–3
  criterion range, 103

@DMAX() function *(continued)*
  input range, 102
  offset, 103
@DMIN() function, 104–5
  criterion range, 104–5
  input range, 104
  offset, 104
Documents
  translating, 342–46
DOS commands, 11, 119–20, 337–38
Down arrow key, 111, 195, 196, 197, 219
@DSTD() function, 105–6
  criterion range, 106
  input range, 106
  offset, 106
@DSUM() function, 107–8
  criterion range, 107
  input range, 107
@DVAR() function, 108–9

E

Editing
  cell entries, 110–11
  formulas, 15
Editing keys, 110–11
EDIT mode, 15, 141, 144, 197–99, 249
End-Down arrow key combination, 195
End-Home key combination, 195
End key, 110, 129, 195, 197, 329
End-Left arrow key combination, 196
End-Right arrow key combination, 196
End-Up arrow key combination, 195
Epson printers, setup strings, 284–85
@ERR function, 111–13, 250–55
Error messages, 113–14
ERROR mode, 249
Esc (Escape) key, 15, 110, 196
@EXACT() function, 114–15
@EXP() function, 116

F

F1 [Help] key, 113, 144, 176, 197
F2 [Edit] key, 95, 110, 144, 196, 197

387

Index

F3 [Name] key, 144, 198
F4 [Absolute] key, 144, 198, 293
F5 [Goto] key, 144, 198
F6 [Window] key, 144, 198
F7 [Query] key, 144, 198
F8 [Table] key, 144, 198
F9 [Calc] key, 18, 95, 144, 197–98
F10 [Graph] key, 144, 198
@FALSE function, 117
/File Combine command, 121–23
/File Directory command, 123–24
/File Erase command, 124–25
/File Import command, 126–27
/File List command, 128
File Manager, 11
/File Retrieve command, 128–30
Files, 117–35
   ASCII, 61–62, 120
   backing up, 11
   checking, 119
   creating new, 130
   directories, 120
      copying, 119
      erasing, 119
      renaming, 119
   erasing, 119, 120, 125
   extensions, 121
   listing, 120
   managing, 11
   merging, 120
   naming, 118
   overwriting, 130–31
   retrieving, 128–30
   saving, 130–32
/File Save command, 120, 129, 315
{FILESIZE} command, 231
FILES mode, 249
/File Xtract command, 61, 120, 133–35
@FIND() function, 135–36
Fonts, 283–84
Footers, 270, 282
{FORBREAK} command, 232–33
{FOR} command, 231–32
Formulas, 136–43
   calculating, 142
   cell references in, 139–41

Formulas *(continued)*
   circular references in, 142
   converting to values, 318
   copying, 37–40
   creating, 137–39
   dates in, 96
   displaying, 16
   editing, 15, 141
   entering, 17
   error messages in, 28, 111–13, 141
   numbers in, 138
   operators, 138–39
   parentheses in, 139
   printing, 270, 286
   range names in, 141
   sorting records with, 78
   strings in, 333
   with values of zero, 117
Frequency distribution table, 52–55, 142
Function keys, 143
Functions, 145–47
   arguments, 145
   creating, 249
   database statistical, 146–47
      @DAVG, 97–98
      @DCOUNT(), 99–101
      @DMAX(), 102–3
      @DMIN(), 104–5
      @DSTD(), 105–6
      @DSUM(), 107–8
      @DVAR(), 108–9
   date
      @DATE(), 92–93
      @DATEVALUE(), 96
      @DAY(), 98–99
      @MONTH(), 250
      @NOW(), 258–59
      @YEAR(), 382
   error messages, 253
   financial
      @CTERM(), 43
      @DDB(), 101–2
      @FV(), 147–48
      @IRR(), 184–85
      @NPV(), 259–60

Index

Functions *(continued)*
  @PMT(), 265–67
  @PV(), 289
  @RATE(), 319
  @SLN(), 327–28
  @SYD(), 336–37
  @TERM(), 339–40
  format, 145
  logical
    @FALSE, 117
    @IF(), 179–80
    @ISERR(), 185–86
    @ISNA(), 186–87
    @ISNUMBER(), 186–87
    @ISSTRING(), 187–88
    @TRUE, 347–48
  lookup, 208–10
  mathematical
    @ABS(), 2
    @EXP(), 116
    @INT(), 183–84
    @LN(), 205–6
    @LOG(), 206–7
    @MOD(), 247–48
    @PI, 265
    @RAND, 290–91
    @ROUND(), 322–23
    @SQRT(), 328
  special
    @@(), 1–2
    @CELL(), 18–21
    @CELLPOINTER(), 21
    @CHOOSE(), 23–24
    @COLS(), 26
    @ERR, 111–13
    @HLOOKUP(), 176–78
    @INDEX(), 181–82
    @NA, 257–58
    @ROWS(), 324
    @VLOOKUP(), 351–53
  statistical
    @AVG(), 9–10
    @COUNT(), 42
    @MAX(), 243–44
    @MIN(), 246
    @STD(), 330–31

Functions *(continued)*
    @SUM(), 335
    @VAR(), 350–51
  string, 332–33
    @CHAR(), 22
    @CODE(), 25
    @EXACT(), 114–15
    @FIND(), 135–36
    @LEFT(), 201–2
    @LENGTH(), 202–3
    @LOWER(), 210
    @MID(), 244–45
    @N(), 255–56
    @PROPER(), 288
    @REPEAT(), 319–20
    @REPLACE(), 320–21
    @RIGHT(), 321–22
    @S(), 324–25
    @STRING(), 334–35
    @TRIM(), 347
    @UPPER(), 348–49
    @VALUE(), 349–50
  time
    @HOUR(), 178–79
    @MINUTE(), 247
    @NOW(), 258–59
    @SECOND(), 325
    @TIME(), 340–41
    @TIMEVALUE(), 342
  trigonometric
    @ACOS(), 4–5
    @ASIN(), 6–7
    @ATAN(), 7–8
    @ATAN2(), 8–9
    @COS(), 40–41
    @SIN(), 326
    @TAN(), 338–39

G

{GET} command, 232
{GETLABEL} command, 233
{GETNUMBER} command, 233
{GETPOS} command, 233
Global default settings, 29
/Graph A...F commands, 158–60

Index

/Graph commands, 148–58
/Graph Name command, 160–62
   /Graph Name Create, 161, 171
/Graph Options command, 162–70
/Graph Quit command, 171
/Graph Reset command, 171–72
Graphs, 148–58, 199
   colors used in, 155
   data ranges, 153–54
      assigning colors to, 274
      formatting, 164
      symbols, 165
   deleting, 162
   erasing, 125, 171–72
   font sizes in, 274
   formatting, 156–57
   grid lines, 156, 166–67
   labels, 156
   legends, 163–64
   naming, 160–62
   printing, 271–78
      canceling, 272
      height, 273
      margins, 273
      more than one, 272
      rotation, 273
      sizes, 273
      width, 273
   range settings, canceling, 171–72
   scales, 157, 167–69
   shading, 155
   titles, 156, 165–66
   types of, 173
   viewing, 157, 174
   x-scale formatting, 169
/Graph Save command, 172–73
/Graph Type command, 173
/Graph View command, 174
/Graph X command, 174–75

H

Headers, 281–82
Help, 144, 176
   key, 198
   options, 365

HELP mode, 196–97, 249
@HLOOKUP() function, 176–78
Home key, 195–97, 218, 268
@HOUR() function, 178–79

I

IBM Monochrome Display Adapter, 361
IBM printers, setup strings, 284–85
{IF} command, 234
@IF() function, 179–80
@INDEX() function, 181–82
{INDICATE} command, 234
Insert key, 110, 197
Install program, 182–83
@INT() function, 183–84
@IRR() function, 184–85
@ISERR() function, 185–86
@ISNA() function, 186
@ISNUMBER() function, 186–87
@ISSTRING function, 187–88
Italic type, 284
Iteration, 188–94

K

Keyboard, 194–99
   editing keys, 196–98
   pointer-movement keys, 195–96
   special keys, 198–99

L

LABEL mode, 137, 249
Labels, 199–201
   aligning, 16
   printing, 286
Left arrow key, 111, 129, 195, 197
@LEFT() function, 201–2
@LENGTH() function, 202–3
{LET} command, 235
Line graphs, 149
   creating, 149
   data ranges, 174–75
   ranges, 152–54

Line graphs *(continued)*
   shading, 155
   types of, 173
@LN() function, 205–6
@LOG() function, 206–7
Logical operator, 263
{LOOK} command, 235
Lookup tables, 207–10
Lotus 1-2-3
   quitting, 290
   Translate Utility, 62
   using DOS commands in, 337–38
   utility programs, 3–4
   worksheet program, 3–4
@LOWER function, 210

M

Macros, 22, 25, 211–24
   auto-execute, 215–16
   column widths, adjusting with macros, 211
   commands, 221, 225–43
      arguments, 225
      customized, 223
      format, 225
      syntax, 225
   creating, 208, 213–15
   debugging, 217
   executing, 216–17
   formatting with macros, 222
   label arithmetic in, 223–24
   lookup tables, 207–10
   menus, 223–24, 226–27
   naming, 215
   non-character keys in, 217–18
   numeric arguments in, 219
   special-key statements, 212
   subroutines, 226
   using, 220–24
   /X commands, 380–82
Margins, 270, 282–83
Matrices, 59–61
   adding, 61
   inverting, 59–60
   multiplying, 59–60

Matrices *(continued)*
   subtracting, 61
@MAX() function, 243–44
{MENUBRANCH} command, 235
{MENUCALL} command, 236
MENU mode, 196–97, 249
Merging, 121–23
@MID() function, 244–45
@MIN() function, 246
@MINUTE() function, 247
Mode indicators, 30, 248–49
   EDIT, 15, 141, 144, 197–99, 249
   ERROR, 249
   FILES, 249
   FIND, 70, 249
   HELP, 196–97, 249
   LABEL, 137, 249
   MENU, 196–97, 249
   POINT, 30, 141, 144, 195–96, 198, 249
   READY, 15, 30, 92, 160, 171, 195–96, 199, 220, 248–49
   VALUE, 137, 144, 199, 246, 249
   WAIT, 249
@MOD() function, 247–48
@MONTH() function, 250
/Move command, 250–55

N

@N() function, 255–56
@NA function, 257–58
@NOW function, 258–59
@NPV() function, 259–60
Numbers, 261–62
Num Lock key, 329

O

{ONERROR} command, 236
{OPEN} command, 236–37
Operators, 263–64
   arithmetic, 263
   concatenation, 263
   logical, 263
   order of precedence, 263–64

P

Page layout, 270
{PANELOFF} command, 237
{PANELON} command, 237
Parallel printers, 361
Passwords, 131–32
Pg Dn (Page Down) key, 111, 195, 197–98, 267
Pg Up (Page Up) key, 111, 197
Pie charts, 149, 152, 173
   data ranges, 153
   label ranges, 174
@PI function, 265
@PMT() function, 265–67
Pointing, 267–69
POINT mode, 30, 141, 144, 195–96, 198, 249
/Print commands, 269–70
Printers
   baud rate, 276
   default configuration settings, 363
   interface, setting number, 275, 360
   line-feed setting, 362
   manual paper feed, 362
   parallel, 361
   serial, 361–62
PrintGraph program, 3, 271–78
   Align command, 272, 277
   commands, 272.
   configuration file, saving, 277
   Exit command, 272, 278
   Go command, 272, 277
   graphs directory, 275
   Image-Select command, 156, 272
   Page command, 272, 277
   printer interfacing, 275
   quitting, 278
   Settings command, 272, 273–77
   starting, 271
Printing
   adjusting page line count, 278
   advancing
      to bottom of page, 270, 286–87
      by line, 270, 280

Printing *(continued)*
   blank lines, 270
   boldfacing, 284
   borders, 283
   compressed print, 284
   to disk, 280
   as displayed on screen, 285
   font sizes, 283–84
   footers, 270, 282, 286–87
   formatting
      currency, 364
      date, 364, 365
      punctuation, 363–64
      time, 365
   graphs, 271–78
      advancing the page, 277
      canceling, 272
      default paper size, 276
      more than one, 272
      pausing between, 276
      setting margins, 273
   headers, 281
      alignment, 281–82
      ignoring, 286
   italic type, 284
   line spacing, 283–84
   lines per page, 285
   margins, 282–83, 362
   page breaks, 324, 374
   page length, 362
   print options, clearing, 278–79
   print range, 287–88, 279–80
   quitting, 270
   resetting internal line counter, 270
   setting, clearing, 270
   specified range, 270
   worksheets, 271–78
/Print Printer Align command, 270, 278
/Print Printer (File) Clear command, 270, 278–79
/Print Printer (File) Go command, 270, 279–80
/Print Printer (File) Line command, 270, 280

Index

/Print Printer (File) Options command, 270, 281–86
/Print Printer (File) Page command, 270, 286–87
/Print Printer (File) Quit command, 270
/Print Printer (File) Range command, 270, 287–88
@PROPER() function, 288
{PUT} command, 237
@PV() function, 289

Q

/Quit command, 290
{QUIT} command, 237

R

@RAND function, 290–91
Random Access Memory (RAM), 117
/Range Erase command, 299–300
/Range Format command, 300–304, 315
/Range Input command, 304–5
/Range Justify command, 306–7
/Range Label command, 308–9
/Range Name command, 310–14
   /Range Name Create, 310–11
   /Range Name Delete, 311–12
   /Range Name Labels, 312
   /Range Name Reset, 313
   /Range Name Table, 313–14
/Range Protect command, 314–15
Ranges, 158–60, 247–48, 291–99
   addresses, 292–93
   adjusting, 297–99
   copying, 33–36
   defining, 17
   deleting endpoints of, 28
   erasing cell contents in, 298, 299–300
   filling with number sequences, 56–58
   formatting
      canceling, 304
      commas, 302

Ranges *(continued)*
   currency symbols, 301
   dates, 302–3
   decimal places, 301
   formulas, 303
   hidden cells, 303
   numeric values, 298
   percentages, 302
   scientific notation, 302
   text, 306–7
   time, 303
   formulas, converting to values, 299
   highlighting, 293–95
   labels
      adjusting, 298
      alignment, 298, 308–9
      formatting, 306–7
   mixed references, 293
   named, 295–96, 298
      assigning labels as, 298, 312
      creating, 310–11
      deleting, 311–13
      editing, 298
      eliminating, 298
      listing of, 298, 313–14
      menu, 296
   naming, 17
   protecting cells in, 29, 314–15
   redefining, 298
   referring to, 292–93
   rotating, 299, 316
   specifying, 267–69
   unprotecting cells in, 299, 317
/Range Transpose command, 316
/Range Unprotect command, 317
/Range Value command, 318
@RATE() function, 319
{READ} command, 238
{READLN} command, 238
READY mode, 15, 30, 92, 160, 171, 195–96, 199, 220, 248–49
READY prompt, 176
{RECALCCOL} command, 240
{RECALC} command, 238
Records
   copying, 65

393

Records *(continued)*
  deleting, 65
  locating, 65
  sorting, 76–79
  unsorting, 77
@REPEAT() function, 319–20
@REPLACE() function, 320–21
{RESTART} command, 240
{RETURN} command, 240
Return key, 111
Right arrow key, 129, 195, 196, 197
@RIGHT() function, 321–22
@ROUND() function, 322–23
Rows, 323–24
  creating page breaks, 324
  deleting, 323, 354
  inserting, 323, 354
  inserting blank, 373
@ROWS() function, 324

S

@S() function, 324–25
Saving
  files, 117, 130–32
  graphs, 157–58, 172–73
  worksheets, partial, 133–35
Scrolling, 263, 267
Scroll Lock key, 329
@SECOND() function, 325
Serial printers, 361–62
{SETPOS} command, 241
@SIN() function, 326
@SLN() function, 327–28
@SQRT() function, 328
Stacked-bar graphs, 149, 173
  data ranges, 153
  shading, 155
Status indicators, 328–30
  CALC, 330
  CAPS, 329
  CIRC, 330
  CMD, 330
  END, 329
  NUM, 329

Status indicators *(continued)*
  OVR, 329
  SCROLL, 329
  SST, 330
  STEP, 330
@STD() function, 330–31
@STRING() function, 334–35
Strings, 332–34
  codes, 332
  empty, 332
  error messages, 135
  formulas, 333
  functions, 332–33
  index numbering of, 333
  and macros, 334
  statistical functions, 146
{SUBROUTINE_NAME} command, 241
@SUM() function, 2, 335
@SYD() function, 336–37
Symphony 1.0, using 1-2-3 files with, 346
/System command, 337–38

T

Tab key, 111, 196, 197, 267
Tables, 176–78
  alignment, 200
  frequency distribution, 12
@TAN() function, 338–39
@TERM() function, 339–40
@TIME() function, 340–41
@TIMEVALUE() function, 342
Translate Utility, 119, 342–46
  memory difficulties, 345
@TRIM() function, 347
@TRUE function, 347–48

U

Up arrow key, 111, 129, 197
@UPPER() function, 348–49
Utility disk
  Install program, 3–4
  Translate program, 3–4, 119, 342–46

Index

V

@VALUE() function, 349–50
VALUE mode, 137, 144, 199, 246, 249
@VAR() function, 350–51
VisiCalc files, transferring to 1-2-3, 126
@VLOOKUP() function, 251–53

W

{WAIT} command, 241
WAIT mode, 249
Wildcard characters, 125
Windows
  closing, 379
    scrolling through more than one
      synchronized, 379
      unsynchronized, 379
  splitting, 378–79
{WINDOWSOFF} command, 242
{WINDOWSON} command, 242
/Worksheet Column command, 315, 355–57
/Worksheet commands, 353–55
/Worksheet Delete command, 354, 357–58
/Worksheet Erase command, 354, 358–59
/Worksheet Global Column-Width command, 354, 359
/Worksheet Global Default command, 354, 360–66
/Worksheet Global Format command, 354, 366–68
/Worksheet Global Label-Prefix command, 368–69
/Worksheet Global Protection command, 304, 354, 369–70
/Worksheet Global Recalculation command, 14, 354, 371–72
/Worksheet Global Zero command, 354, 372–73
/Worksheet Insert command, 354, 373
/Worksheet Page command, 355, 374
/Worksheet Status command, 355, 374–76
/Worksheet Titles command, 355, 377
/Worksheet Window command, 355, 378–79
{WRITE} command, 242
{WRITELN} command, 242

X

/XC command, 380
/XG command, 380
/XI command, 380
/XL command, 381
/XM command, 381
/XN command, 381
/XQ command, 380
/XR command, 380
XY graphs, 173
  data ranges, 153–54
  formatting, 168
  label ranges, 174
  symbols used in, 155

Y

@YEAR() function, 382

Eddie Adamis

Eddie Adamis earned his Bachelor of Arts degree in Languages at Beirut's American University, and worked as a reporter for the newspaper, *Le Jour L'Orient*, until the end of World War II. After moving to Paris in 1945, he began a very successful career as a music composer and arranger, and in 1964 was selected to become the managing director of United Artists Records and Publishing in France. Eddie Adamis now devotes his time to writing about computers. Since 1979, he has contributed articles to *Temps Réel* and *Microsystèms* magazines, and has written more than 20 books, including *Command Performance: Multiplan for the Apple Macintosh*, published by Microsoft Press in December 1985. He currently makes his home in Paris, France.

Eddie Adamis's other titles include:
- BASIC Formules et Programmes Usuels
- BASIC for the TRS 80, Model 100
- BASIC Keywords: A User's Reference
- BASIC Keywords for the Apple III
- BASIC Keywords for the IBM PC
- BASIC Subroutines for Commodore Computers
- Business BASIC for the Apple III
- Business BASIC for the IBM PC
- Diccionario BASIC
- Diccionario BASIC del IBM PC
- Formulas y Programas Usuales en BASIC
- Iniciación al BASIC del IBM PC
- Initiation BASIC IBM
- Initiation Business BASIC
- Les Mots Clés du BASIC
- Lexique BASIC
- Lexique BASIC IBM
- Lexique Business BASIC
- Lotus 1-2-3 Volume 1—Le Tableur
- Lotus 1-2-3 Volume 2—La Base de Données
- Lotus 1-2-3 Volume 3—Les Graphiques
- Lotus 1-2-3 Volume 4—Les Macro-Instructions
- Macintosh: Multiplan MacPaint
- Macintosh aplicaciones de Multiplan y MacPaint

The manuscript for this book was prepared and submitted
to Microsoft Press in electronic form. Text files were processed
and formatted using Microsoft Word.

Cover design by Steve Renick.
Cover airbrushed by Stephen Peringer.
Interior text design by Craig A. Bergquist & Associates.
The high-resolution screen displays were created on the
IBM PC and printed on the Hewlett-Packard LaserJet.

Text composition by Microsoft Press in Palatino with Times
Roman Italic and Helvetica Bold, using the CCI composition
system and the Mergenthaler Linotron 202 digital
phototypesetter.

OTHER TITLES FROM MICROSOFT PRESS

Running MS-DOS, 2nd Edition
The Microsoft guide to getting the most out of its standard operating system
Van Wolverton $21.95

The Peter Norton Programmer's Guide to the IBM PC
The ultimate reference guide to the entire family of IBM personal computers.
Peter Norton $19.95

Command Performance: dBASE III
The Microsoft desktop dictionary and cross-reference guide
Douglas Hergert $22.95

Variations in C
Programming techniques for developing efficient professional applications
Steve Schustack $19.95

Word Processing Power with Microsoft Word
Professional writing on your IBM PC
Peter Rinearson $16.95

Presentation Graphics on the IBM PC
How to use Microsoft Chart to create dazzling graphics for corporate and professional applications
Steve Lambert $19.95

Getting Started with Microsoft Word
A step-by-step guide to word processing
Janet Rampa $16.95

Managing Your Business with Multiplan
How to use Microsoft's award-winning electronic spreadsheet on your IBM PC
Ruth K. Witkin $17.95

Online
A guide to America's leading information services
Steve Lambert $19.95

Silicon Valley Guide to Financial Success in Software
Daniel Remer, Paul Remer, and Robert Dunaway $19.95

Out of the Inner Circle
A hacker's guide to computer security
"The Cracker" (Bill Landreth) $9.95 softcover $19.95 hardcover

A Much, Much Better World
Eldon Dedini $6.95

Available wherever fine books are sold.